THE BOOK OF PONTIFFS OF THE CHURCH OF RAVENNA

MEDIEVAL TEXTS IN TRANSLATION

EDITORIAL DIRECTOR

Thomas F. X. Noble
University of Notre Dame

EDITORIAL BOARD

Paul Dutton
Simon Fraser University

Geoffrey Koziol
University of California, Berkeley

Carol Lansing
University of California at Santa Barbara

Barbara H. Rosenwein
Loyola University of Chicago

Agnellus of Ravenna

THE BOOK OF PONTIFFS OF THE CHURCH OF RAVENNA

Translated with an introduction and notes by
Deborah Mauskopf Deliyannis

The Catholic University of America Press
Washington, D.C.

To my father

Copyright © 2004
The Catholic University of America Press
All rights reserved
Printed in the United States of America

The paper used in this publication meets the minimum requirements of American National Standards for Information Science—Permanence of Paper for Printed Library materials, ANSI Z39.48-1984.
∞

Library of Congress Cataloging-in-Publication Data
Agnellus, of Ravenna, Abbot, 9th cent.
 [Liber pontificalis ecclesiae Ravennatis. English]
 The book of pontiffs of the church of Ravenna / Agnellus of Ravenna ; translated with an introduction and notes by Deborah Mauskopf Deliyannis.— 1st ed.
  p. cm. — (Medieval texts in translation)
 Includes bibliographical references and indexes.
 ISBN 978-0-8132-1358-4 (pbk. : alk. paper)
 1. Bishops—Italy—Ravenna—Biography. 2. Catholic Church. Archdiocese of Ravenna (Italy)—Biography. I. Deliyannis, Deborah Mauskopf, 1966– II. Title. III. Series.
BX4684.A3413 2004
274.5′4702′0922—dc21

2003011985

CONTENTS

Preface / vii
Acknowledgments / ix
List of Abbreviations / xi
Maps / xii

Introduction / 1
   Background / 3
   Structure and Genre / 20
   Written Sources / 46
   Oral Sources and Orality / 57
   Art and Architecture in the *LPR* / 66
   Note on Editions and This Translation / 91

The Book of Pontiffs of the Church of Ravenna / 93
   Prefatory Verses / 95 ~ Prologue / 99 ~ Apollinaris / 101 ~
   Aderitus / 104 ~ Eleucadius / 105 ~ Marcian / 106 ~
   Calocerus / 106 ~ Proculus / 107 ~ Probus I / 107 ~
   Datus / 108 ~ Liberius I / 108 ~ Agapitus / 108 ~
   Marcellinus / 109 ~ Severus / 109 ~ Liberius II / 114 ~
   Probus II / 116 ~ Florentius / 117 ~ Liberius III / 117 ~
   Ursus / 118 ~ Peter I / 120 ~ Neon / 125 ~
   Exuperantius / 134 ~ John I / 136 ~ Peter II / 157 ~
   Aurelian / 165 ~ Ecclesius / 171 ~ Ursicinus / 178 ~
   Victor / 181 ~ Maximian / 184 ~ Agnellus / 198 ~
   Peter III the Elder / 204 ~ John II the Roman / 213 ~

Marinian / 215 ❧ John III / 218 ❧ John IV / 221 ❧
Bonus / 225 ❧ Maurus / 227 ❧ Reparatus / 233 ❧
Theodore / 236 ❧ Damian / 247 ❧ Felix / 258 ❧
John V / 275 ❧ Sergius / 278 ❧ Leo / 285 ❧ John VI / 286 ❧
Gratiosus / 290 ❧ Martin / 295 ❧ George / 298 ❧

Table of the Bishops of Ravenna / 307
Glossary of Artistic and Architectural Terminology / 309
Bibliography / 349
General Index / 361
Topographical Index of Ravenna and Classe / 367

PREFACE

Since the sixteenth century, Agnellus of Ravenna's *Book of Pontiffs of the Church of Ravenna* (*Liber pontificalis ecclesiae Ravennatis*, or *LPR*) has been mined by historians and art historians for facts. Though Agnellus is alternately praised for his openness and criticized for his inaccuracy, what he says has generally been taken at face value, after cross-checking against other historical texts and surviving monuments. His reliance on hearsay and his use of invented dialogue have been seen as interfering with the facts, yet these practices were rooted in the literary traditions of his models and sources. He employs a variety of narrative and descriptive styles derived from several different literary genres, and thus only when the origin and context of each passage has been identified can his "information" be understood.

Agnellus's text was written in the 830s and 840s to demonstrate two strongly held opinions. One of these was the apostolicity and independence of the Ravennate archbishopric; the other was the moral decline of recent bishops, and their erosion of clerical rights. These views affected Agnellus's presentation of individual bishops, which often depend solely on the bishop's treatment of the clergy or his stance toward Rome: the lives of good bishops are filled with miracles, while bad bishops are unrelievedly bad. Agnellus's vehemence stemmed from his experiences as a member of the clergy in Ravenna at a time when the city had lost much of its former political importance.

Agnellus's motives for writing also strongly influenced the structure of the work. He modeled the *LPR* on the *Liber pontificalis* (*LP*) of Rome to emphasize the equal importance of Ravenna to

Rome; categories of information from the Roman *LP* are routinely provided by Agnellus, and descriptive language also imitates that of the Roman prototype. However, the *LPR* also contains two other types of text: hagiography and exegesis. In using, and in some cases borrowing, material belonging to these three genres, Agnellus also uses the language, style, and literary conventions proper to each.

Agnellus is often criticized for his seemingly haphazard use of information from his sources; many of these can be identified and range from other literary texts to documents to inscriptions and images from Ravenna. His text is at times personal, at times annalistic, erudite and colloquial, factual and miraculous, well documented and full of uncredited borrowing. Although the *LPR* seems to be a random hodgepodge of information, this is actually the result of Agnellus's difficulty in knowing how to assign information to the life of a particular bishop.

The *LPR* has always been particularly important to art historians because of the wealth of information it contains about the art and architecture of Ravenna. And yet descriptions of monuments are themselves literary conventions, and are often found within one or other of the generic types of narrative already mentioned. The functions performed by monuments in each context affect the way they are described; even the words used to refer to and describe these monuments are affected by these conventions, and yet they are also influenced by Agnellus's firsthand experiences.

Perhaps the most remarkable thing about the *LPR* is its successful integration of features taken from widely different literary genres and sources. The formulaic entries of information characteristic of *gesta episcoporum*, the narrative unit of the scene, used for miracles as well as for historical events, and the rhetorical questions and direct exhortations taken from exegetical and sermonic forms are all intermingled to produce some type of text for every bishop of Ravenna. It is a work unlike any other known from the early Middle Ages.

ACKNOWLEDGMENTS

I was first introduced to Agnellus in Cecil L. Striker's Ravenna seminar at the University of Pennsylvania. Lee encouraged me to work on the text for my doctoral dissertation, and both he and James O'Donnell have been extremely generous with their time and advice, both while I was writing the dissertation and especially after my graduation while I was preparing this volume for publication.

During the time that I have been working on the *LPR*, there has been a surge of scholarly interest in Agnellus, and the "Agnellus group" has been extraordinarily collegial. I am deeply indebted to Ruggiero Benericetti, Thomas Brown, Ann Moffatt, Claudia Nauerth, and Joaquin Martínez Pizarro, who have all been most generous with their advice, their comments on my work, and their own publications and materials.

Thomas Noble has gone well beyond his duties as series editor for Catholic University of America Press in answering many questions, and I am very grateful for his enthusiasm for this project. David McGonagle and Susan Needham of the press have been helpful throughout the process of publication, and John Osborne's comments as reader were much appreciated.

I would like to thank several others who have offered various types of assistance, advice, and support during the past several years. These include Raffaella Farioli Campanati, Florin Curta, William Diebold, Diana Greenway, Thomas Head, Renata Holod, Rand Johnson, Michael Lapidge, Traugott Lawler, Eric Owen, Franca Pierpaoli, Leah Shopkow, Paul E. Szarmach, Susan Tegtmeyer, Giordana Trovabene, and Augusto Vasina.

I am most grateful for funding I received from the University of Pennsylvania, from the Kolb Foundation at the University Museum of the University of Pennsylvania, and from Western Michigan University, without which I could not have completed the research for this volume.

Finally, none of my work would have been possible without the help of my family. My husband Constantine's support of my career has been continuous and unstinting. My sons Alex and Harry are learning to love mosaics. My parents, in-laws, and siblings have been unfailingly enthusiastic. My father, Seymour Mauskopf, was going to be a medievalist until he turned to the history of science, and his abiding interest in things medieval has been a constant influence throughout my life. He is my model of what a historian, an academic, and a teacher should be, and I dedicate this book to him.

ABBREVIATIONS

BHG   *Bibliotheca hagiographica Graeca.* 3 vols. Brussels, 1957, with suppl. 1969.

BHL   *Bibliotheca hagiographica Latina.* 2 vols. Brussels, 1899–1901, with suppl. 1911 and 1986.

CARB   *Corso di cultura sull'arte Ravennate e Bizantina.*

CCCM   *Corpus Christianorum, Continuatio Mediaevalis.*

CCSL   *Corpus Christianorum, Series Latina.*

CIL   *Corpus inscriptionum Latinarum.*

LP   *Le Liber Pontificalis: Texte, introduction et commentaire.* Ed. L. Duchesne. 3 vols. Paris, 1955.

LPR   Andreas Agnellus, *Liber pontificalis ecclesiae Ravennatis.*

MGH   *Monumenta Germaniae Historica.*

    AA   *Auctores Antiquissimi.*

    SS rer. Lang. et. Ital.   *Scriptores rerum Langobardicarum et Italicarum saec. VI–IX.* Hanover, 1878.

    SS rer. Merov.   *Scriptores rerum Merovingicarum.*

    SS   *Scriptores.*

PL   *Patrologia Latina.* Ed. J.-P. Migne. 221 vols. Paris, 1844–64.

RIS   *Rerum Italicarum Scriptores ab anno aere christianae 500–1500.* Ed. L. A. Muratori. Milan, 1723–51.

RIS, n.s.   *Rerum Italicarum Scriptores,* n.s. Ed. G. Carducci and V. Fiorini. Bologna, 1900–75.

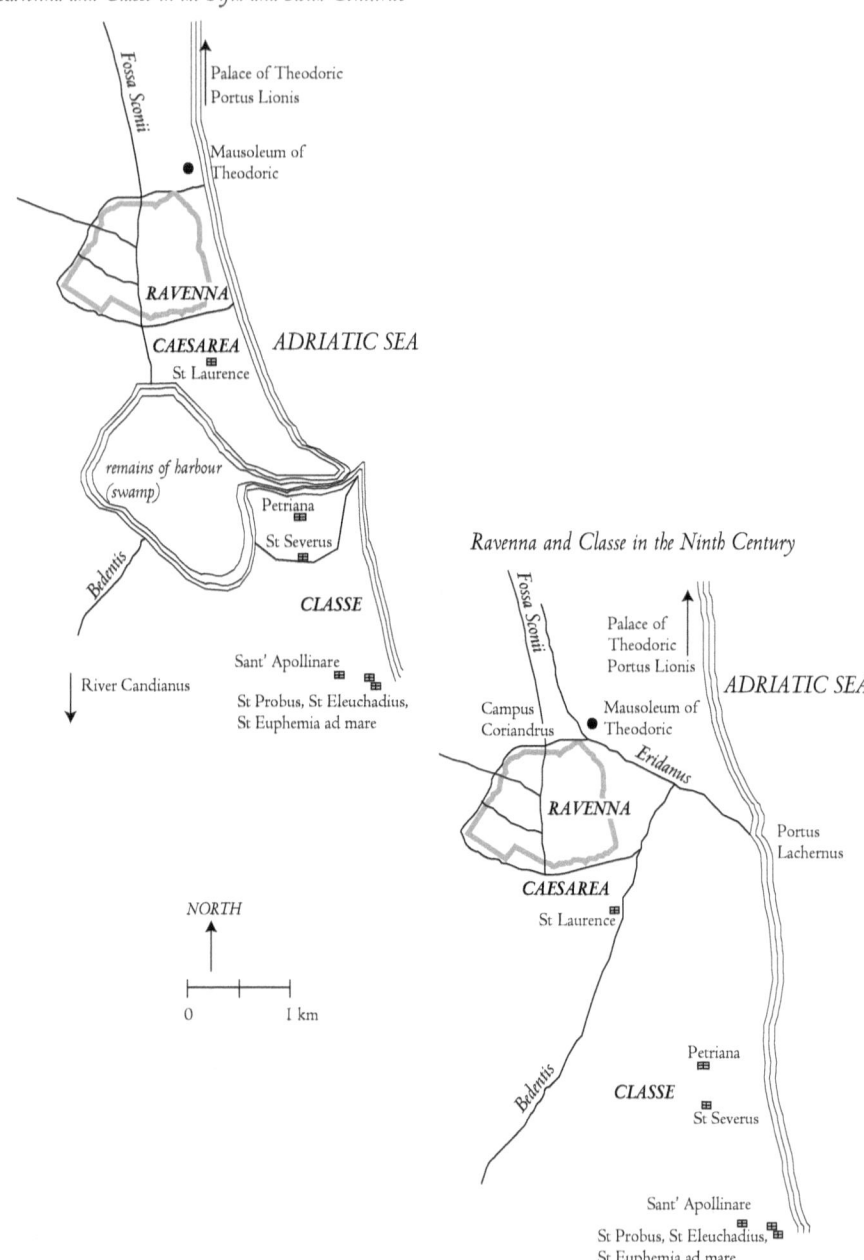

Ravenna at the time of Agnellus

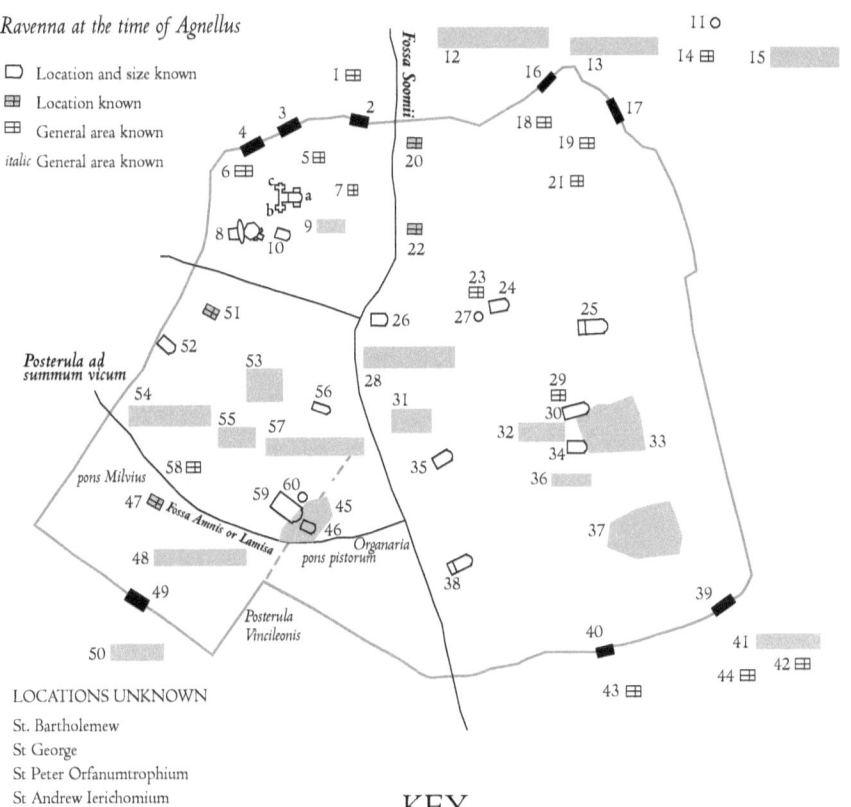

☐ Location and size known
⊞ Location known
⊞ General area known
italic General area known

LOCATIONS UNKNOWN
St. Bartholemew
St George
St Peter Orfanumtrophium
St Andrew Ierichomium

KEY

upper left
1. St Eusebius
2. Porta S. Victoris
3. Posterula Ovilionsi
4. Porta Teguriensis
5. Sts John and Barbatian
6. St Stephen Major
7. St Apollinaris
   a. Holy Cross
   b. 'mausoleum of Galla Placidia'
   c. St Zacharias
8. San Vitale, St Nazarius
9. *moneia*
10. St Mary Major

upper right
11. Mausoleum of Theodoric
12. *Campus Coriandrus*
13. *stadium tabulae*
14. St. Mary
15. *ad Farum*
16. Porta Novis
17. Porta Artemetoris

right
18. St Pullio
19. Eccl. Gothorum
20. St Victor
21. St Andrew
22. St John the Baptist
23. St Apollinaris
24. St Theodore
25. San Giovanni Evangelista
26. St Michael
27. St Mary in Cosmedin (Arian Baptistry)
28. *regio ad Frigiselo*
29. St Theodore the deacon
30. St Martin
31. *macerie Ovilionis*
32. *Chalchi*
33. Palace of Theodoric
34. St Saviour
35. Holy Apostles, St Petronilla
36. *sicrestium*
37. Palace of Valenunan? *ad Laureta*
38. St. Agatha
39. Porta Wandalaria
40. Porta S. Laurentii/ Caesarea
41. *Wandalaria*
42. St Paul
43. St Donatus in Monterione
44. St Mary ad Blachernas

lower middle
45. Episcoium
46. St Andrew

lower left
47. St. Andrew Major
48. *regio Herculana*
49. Porta Aurea
50. *amphitheatre*

middle left
51. St Euphemia ad Arietem
52. Sts John & Paul
53. *numerus bandus primus*
54. *regio Latronum*
55. *milarium aureum*
56. St Agnes
57. *regio ad Nimpheos*
58. St Severinus
59. Ursiana
60. Neonian Bapt.

INTRODUCTION

BACKGROUND

Brief overview of the history of Ravenna

Political history

Ravenna was founded during the reign of Augustus (31 B.C.–A.D. 14), immediately to the north of the port Classe, which took its name from the Roman fleet *(classis)* that was stationed there. Ravenna and Classe were surrounded by marshes, which provided a defensive barrier that greatly increased their strategic importance, and when, around 401, the emperor Honorius was faced with the threat of a Visigothic invasion, he moved the capital of the western Roman Empire from Milan to Ravenna. Ravenna remained untouched by the Visigoths and the Huns, who invaded Italy in 408 and 450, respectively, and whose attention was drawn to Rome. Possibly because Rome was in a state of decline following these attacks, Odoacer established himself in Ravenna after deposing Romulus Augustulus in 476. After the Ostrogoths conquered Italy in 493, Theodoric also made Ravenna his capital and the seat of his court. Soon after Theodoric's death in 526, Justinian I sent an army to reconquer Italy; again Ravenna, unlike Rome, seems to have been largely spared during the destructive war, which lasted from 535 to 554. Although the Lombards conquered much of Italy after 568, Ravenna remained under imperial control and was the seat of the Byzantine exarch, or governor, of Italy.

The eighth century was a time of great confusion and upheaval in Italy. The empire was unstable, with five emperors between 711 and 717 alone. Then, in the 720s, the emperor Leo III imposed heavy taxes on the Italians, and he promulgated Iconoclasm, which alienated much of the western Church, including Ravenna and Rome. In 727 the Italian churches and nobility united in rebellion against Leo III and his representative, the exarch of Ravenna. The Lombards took advantage of the chaos to attack the exarchate, in 717–18, 726–27, 732–33, 738–40, and 743–44. In 751 Ravenna was captured by the Lombards and Byzantine rule in northern Italy ceased. The struggle for control of the former exarchate involved the papacy, the archbishops of Ravenna, the Lombards, the Byzantines, and the Franks, in various shifting combinations. The Carolingian rulers of the Frankish kingdom had become involved with the Italian situation in the 750s; with the conquest of the Lombard kingdom by Charlemagne in 774, previous power relationships were disrupted. Ravenna was caught between Charlemagne's kingdom in Italy and the emerging political entity that would later be known as the Papal States. Noble identifies the political situation of Ravenna at this time as a "double-dyarchy": "on the one hand pope and king shared rule, and on the other hand pope and archbishop divided authority."[1] This was the situation in Ravenna when Agnellus was writing the *LPR*.

The Church in Ravenna

According to legend, Christianity was introduced into Ravenna by Apollinaris, a disciple of St. Peter, in the late first century A.D. However, the first archaeological traces of Christianity in the area of Ravenna are found in the cemeteries of Classe, from the late second century. The first externally documented bishop of Ravenna is Severus, who was listed as a participant at the Council of Sardica in 343. When Ravenna became the capital of the western empire, the bishop also rose in importance. Sometime in the early fifth century a bishop of Ravenna was given the pallium, with metropolitan rights over an area of northern Italy;[2] it seems clear that by the middle of the fifth century the bishop of Ravenna was ordaining bishops for large areas of northern Italy.

1. Noble, *Republic of St. Peter*, 171–72.
2. There is a controversy over who the first metropolitan bishop was; see Deliyannis, *CCCM* edition of the *LPR*, introduction.

After the reconquest of Italy from the Ostrogoths by the Byzantine empire, the bishops of Ravenna increased even more in power and prestige. Maximian, appointed to the see by Justinian himself, was made an archbishop by the pope at the order of the emperor; this elevation was part of a larger policy of raising church leaders in rank to match the secular status of their cities.[3] The popes started coming into conflict with Ravenna's archbishops over the latter's ecclesiastical status in the late sixth century. In 666, the emperor Constans II granted a privilege or *typus* of autocephaly, or independence from Rome, to Archbishop Maurus of Ravenna. Autocephaly meant that the archbishop of Ravenna would be consecrated by three of his suffragan bishops rather than by the pope, and that he would not be subject to orders from the pope. Ravenna's autocephaly did not last long; Archbishop Theodore, although consecrated in Ravenna, resubmitted Ravenna's church to Pope Agatho in 680, and returned the *typus* of autocephaly to Pope Leo II. By 682 the emperor had issued a decree formally revoking it.

Several of the archbishops of the eighth century, notably Felix and Sergius, continued the struggle for autonomy, with limited success; the shifting political situation in Italy meant that some of the time the archbishops were necessarily allied with the popes, as over Iconoclasm. After the death of Archbishop Sergius in 769, there was a contested election, which involved, besides the clergy, the Duke of Rimini, the Lombards, the pope, and the Carolingians.[4] Leo, the successful candidate, was from the pro-papal party; nevertheless, when Charlemagne conquered Italy, Leo wrote to Charlemagne, reminding him of their earlier contacts and requesting autonomy from Rome. His successors never seem to have given up hope of being granted absolute control over the old exarchate and continued to make personal appeals to the Carolingian emperors until the middle of the ninth century.

3. Brown, "The Church of Ravenna," 7. See also Markus, "Carthage—Prima Justiniana—Ravenna."
4. Agnellus's Life of Leo is missing from the manuscripts; what we know of these events comes from the Roman *Liber pontificalis.*

Ravenna in the late eighth and early ninth centuries was a city riven by factions and conflicting interests; the different civic, ecclesiastical, theological, and political concerns were inextricably linked. Various groups campaigned at various times for Lombard, Byzantine, papal, and archiepiscopal control of the territory. Ecclesiastically also there were pro- and antipapal groups, and there also seem to have been tensions between the Greek and Latin clergy within the city. Ravenna's pivotal position at the center of these various struggles maintained the strategic importance of the city up to the ninth century, but by Agnellus's day the archbishops were finding it increasingly difficult to keep up with the ruinously expensive bribes and gifts that were necessary to maintain their prominence. It was in this complicated environment that Agnellus was raised, and it is symptomatic of the complexity of the city's politics that even his sympathies for the various factions are not always clear: in some cases the exarch is a hero, in others he is a traitor. The same is true for popes, archbishops, emperors, Carolingians, Lombards, and even Ravenna's citizenry.

Agnellus's life

Everything that we know about Agnellus comes from the eighteen passages of the *LPR* in which he tells us something about himself; there is no external evidence of his existence.[5] Some of these pieces of information are included to fulfill rhetorical functions within the text, and some details may have become corrupted in transmission. It should be noted in particular that specific dates

---

5. *LPR* prologue, cc. 26, 39, 54, 64, 77, 83, 110, 113, 119, 136, 146, 149, 158, 159, 162, 163, 167. Further personal information about Agnellus appears in the *versiculi* at the beginning of the *LPR*, written by the anonymous author who calls himself *minimus scolasticorum*, often referred to by scholars as the *scholasticus*. Because the *scholasticus* says that Agnellus wrote the Lives of the bishops up through Petronax (1.66), he must have been a contemporary of Agnellus, and moreover must have written the poem before the *LPR* was concluded with the Life of Petronax's successor, George. Given the eulogistic nature of the poem and the derivative nature of the information given, we cannot rely confidently on these statements about Agnellus.

and numbers in the *LPR* are often of questionable accuracy or originality and in many cases cannot be fixed with precision. Nonetheless, the basic outline of Agnellus's life can be discovered from the text, as follows.

Agnellus tells us in c. 54 that at the time of composition he was thirty-two years and ten months old; given a date of composition for this part of the *LPR* around the year 827–36, he would have been born sometime between 794 and 804.[6] He came from distinguished families; most of what we know about Agnellus's descent comes from passages in cc. 146 and 163 that mention his relatives. However, inconsistencies within these two passages make a reconstruction of Agnellus's family tree rather difficult. Two statements in c. 146 contradict each other: "Basilius who sired Andreas [Agnellus] was the son of Andreas son of Basilius," and "Andreas . . . my grandfather, the father of my mother," which result in the two versions of the family tree found in Fig. 1.[7] One of these two sentences must be corrupt, but it is impossible to say which one. Complicating the matter is the question of what is meant by the term *cognatus*, in c. 146; in the early Middle Ages the term had vari-

---

6. The date of Agnellus's birth is thus dependent on the date of composition of c. 54, about which see below. Attempts to fix more precisely upon a specific year rely on unproven assumptions. Lanzoni, "Il 'Liber Pontificalis,'" 364, basing his chronology on an inaccurate date for the reign of Valerius and assuming that the phrase *nostra tempora* (c. 70) refers to Agnellus's lifetime, concludes that Agnellus must have been born before 802. Lanzoni also states that because the canonical age for the priesthood in the ninth century was twenty-five, Agnellus must have been born no later than 805. Testi-Rasponi, "Note marginali," 102, dates c. 54 to 830–31 and says that Agnellus was born in 799 or 800, and thus was in his teens when he was given his first *monasterium*. It seems preferable to accept an approximation, rather than to try to determine a specific year.

7. *Ex Andrea Basilii natus est Basilius qui genuit Andream* and *Andream . . . auus meus, pater matris meae*. Holder-Egger (*LPER*, 270 and 373, n. 7, accepted by Testi-Rasponi, "Note marginali," 213–14), proposed that the phrase *pater matris meae* contains a scribal error and should read *pater patris mei*. This interpretation has found its way into the many family trees that make Johannicis the ancestor of Agnellus's father, as in version (b); see Lanzoni, "Il 'Liber Pontificalis,'" 572; Gonin, *Excerpta*, 16; Brill, "Der Liber Pontificalis," 3; Fasoli, "Rileggendo," 464, n. 17, and, most recently and thoroughly, Brown, *Gentlemen and Officers*, 170–72 and n. 13.

8   INTRODUCTION

Agnellus' family tree: possible reconstructions

(a)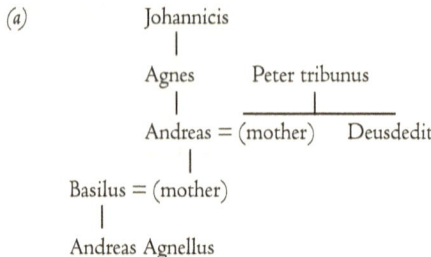

(b)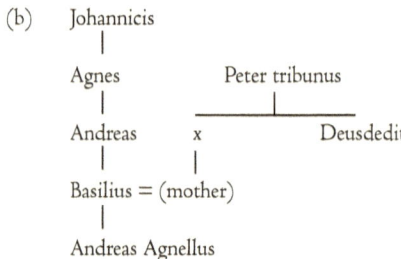

ous meanings, from "blood relative" to "in-law." In the two occurrences of the word elsewhere in the *LPR*, it has the latter meaning.⁸ If Andreas was the brother-in-law of Deusdedit, then version (a) of the family tree must be correct; if (b) is correct, then *cognatus* must mean simply "relative," or perhaps "relative by marriage."⁹ In

---

8. See Bullough, "Early Medieval Social Groupings," 11. Testi-Rasponi, "Note marginali," 231–33, claimed that the word *cognatus* in c. 163 meant that Andreas was a "relative" of Deusdedit because his son had married Deusdedit's sister's daughter (Agnellus's mother), as is found in version (b) of the family tree. However, in the *LPR, cognatus* is found in c. 128, *fratres et cognatos,* and in c. 138, *Iohanicis ad fratrem suum . . . cognata tua, uxor mea;* in the latter example, it definitely means sister-in-law.

9. It does not necessarily follow, as most scholars seem implicitly to have assumed, that Agnellus must have been named Andreas after his *paternal* grandfather. In fact, given the evidence of the passage in Paul the Deacon, just below, where the *elder* son, rather than the younger, clerical son, was named after the paternal grandfather, it would seem more likely that Agnellus was also a younger son, named Andreas after

addition to these family members, Agnellus tells us that the grandfather of his father was one of the noble Ravennate judges who were lured to Rome and died in prison there (c. 159), and his paternal cousin was the deacon Sergius, who bequeathed him a monastery (c. 110).

Agnellus's emphasis on his relatives does not simply indicate vanity or self-aggrandizement, as is often claimed; it is a topos of early medieval historiography. As Fasoli points out,[10] the passage describing Agnellus's descent is very similar to Paul the Deacon's story of the deeds of his own great-grandfather and his descent:[11]

> He [Leupchis] sired my grandfather Arichis, Arichis sired my father Warnefrit, Warnefrit by his wife Thedelinda sired me, Paul, and my brother Arichis, which bears the name of our grandfather.

Agnellus imitates Paul both in phrasing and in placing the genealogy after a legendary story about a famous ancestor, Johannicis, on whose life, career, and fate he provides extensive information. In this he imitates not only Paul the Deacon but also Gregory of Tours, who frequently refers to, and provides information about, his own ancestor, St. Gregory of Langres.[12] That Agnellus was very aware of this literary tradition is shown by another borrowing. Gregory of Tours reports that his great-grandfather used to pray secretly at night in a baptistry near his residence, until discovered by a deacon who followed him stealthily one night and saw the doors open by themselves.[13] Agnellus relates exactly the same story about Johannicis in c. 147. The borrowing of hagiographical leg-

---

his *maternal* grandfather and dedicated to the church at an early age. That he does not mention any living family members does not mean that they did not exist.

10. Fasoli, "Rileggendo," 463.

11. Paul the Deacon, *Historia Langobardorum* 4:37: "Hic [Leupchis] etenim genuit avum meum Arichis, Arichis vero patrem meum Warnefrit, Warnefrit autem ex Theudelinda coniuge genuit me Paulum meumque germanum Arichis, qui nostrum avum cognomine retulit."

12. Paul was not unique in this respect; other historians, including Jordanes and Gregory of Tours, mention their descent from people who figure in their histories. Jordanes, *Getica*, c. 266, and Gregory of Tours, *Historia Francorum* 5.5, respectively.

13. In the *Liber vitae patrum* vii. 2, a work that Agnellus knew.

ends occurs frequently in the *LPR*; in this case, Agnellus seems to be deliberately comparing himself and his descent to Gregory of Tours'. Like Gregory and Paul, Agnellus is descended from a remarkable actor in his history and therefore like them is uniquely qualified to have charge of writing it.

Agnellus was placed in the Church at an early age and was "raised in the bosom of the holy Ursiana church" (c. 25). It is sometimes suggested that he knew Greek, since in the *LPR* he provides several derivations from Greek words. As knowledge of Greek was a sign of an outstanding scholar (like his ancestor Johannicis), Agnellus probably used Greek words and etymologies to make his own work seem erudite, although he did not necessarily know the language.[14] While still a boy he was "given" the *monasterium* of St. Mary *ad Blachernas*[15] by Bishop Martin in exchange for two hundred gold *solidi*, an indication of the wealth and connections of his family.[16] Sometime later he was also given, as an inheritance from his cousin Sergius, the *monasterium* of St. Bartholemew. He mentions his two *monasteria* several times, noting that previous abbots had held high offices in Ravenna's church.[17] Agnellus states

14. Holder-Egger, *LPER*, 270. Lazard, "De l'origine," has studied the incidence of words of Greek origin in the *LPR*; she concludes that most come either from literary sources or were in common use in Ravenna at the time. The remaining few Grecisms indicate only that Agnellus may have picked up a passive understanding of Greek, not an extensive knowledge. Given that most, if not all, of Agnellus's textual sources were in Latin, it seems likely that he did not know Greek.

15. In the commentary and translation, names of churches will be anglicized, with the exception of the following, whose Italian names are more widely used in the scholarly literature: San Vitale, Sant' Apollinare Nuovo, Sant' Apollinare in Classe, San Giovanni Evangelista, and the capella arcivescovile.

16. *LPR*, cc. 25 and 167, respectively. Since Martin reigned from 810 to 818, Agnellus would have been between six and twenty-four years old at the time. Testi-Rasponi, "Note marginali," 102, who thought that Agnellus was born in 799–800, for other reasons said that the transaction must have taken place at the end of Martin's life, when Agnellus was around seventeen, which he says is more fitting; but then Agnellus would probably not have referred to himself as *adhuc puer.*

17. Archbishops Maurus and Felix had been abbots of St. Bartholemew, and, respectively, *yconomos* and *vicedominus*, before they became bishops (cc. 110 and 136); Sergius had been *yconomos* (c. 149), and Uviliaris had been archdeacon (c. 158). The

that in 833 he was the "tenth priest in order of the see" (c. 83), presumably quite high-ranking.

Other information that Agnellus gives us about his activities indicates that he was actively involved in construction and maintenance in Ravenna, perhaps to the point of being an official "master of the works."[18] He tells us of several instances of his personal involvement with antiquities and monuments. When the body of Maximian is being translated from its grave to a location inside the church, Archbishop Petronax tells Agnellus, "who was at that time filled with the skills of all the arts," to supervise the workmen so that they don't break the sarcophagus. Agnellus is then the one who removes and counts the bones before they are placed in the reliquary (c. 83). Also in the time of Petronax, when a porphyry slab is removed by the emperor Lothar and sent north, Agnellus is asked by the bishop to supervise the workmen in removing and packing it in wool, lest they break it (c. 113). He knows the details of the removal to Bologna of the sarcophagus of Rufus, which had happened five years earlier (c. 1). And finally, he tells how he went to the Petriana Church in Classe to find the bones of Bishop Peter I, and removed the lid of the sarcophagus to view the body (c. 26).

Personally, Agnellus was also a patron. Twice he describes the location of his house near the church of St. Agnes; he himself built this house on property of his mother's, using materials his servants had brought from the palace *in Lauro*, demolished by his order (cc. 39 and 77). He also completed the decoration of the altar of St. Bartholemew, which his cousin Sergius had begun (c. 149).

Although he was not widely traveled, Agnellus made at least one long trip. He tells us that he accompanied Archbishop George to assist in the baptism of the daughter of the emperor Lothar at

---

great exarch and patron Theodore, who gave many gifts to the *monasterium* of St. Mary *ad Blachernas*, was buried there with his wife (c. 119). Since Agnellus never tells us that he is *vicedominus* or *yconomus* or archdeacon, perhaps his mention of the former abbots is his subtle way of campaigning for one of these positions. Or perhaps he thought he should be archbishop; cf. Vasina, "Clero e chiese," 549.

18. "Superintendent of monuments" in Fasoli, "Rileggendo," 466.

Pavia (c. 171), and he mentions that he himself saw the palace built by Theodoric in that city (c. 94). Since the passage in c. 94 was written in 839–40 (see below), Agnellus must have made this trip between 837 and 839. In one other passage Agnellus mentions having himself seen the church at Argentea (c. 89), a town that is about twenty-two miles from Ravenna on the way to Ferrara. If he ever went to Rome he does not say so, although since George was consecrated in Rome it would be odd if Agnellus had not been one of the ecclesiastical party.

Agnellus's quarrel with Archbishop George enters the work in several places. In c. 136, Agnellus says about George that "before he ascended to such a height, we were like brothers to each other."[19] Agnellus seems to have been sufficiently friendly or highly ranked at the beginning of George's reign to have been included in the party that accompanied George to Pavia (c. 171). However, Agnellus says that later George turned against the clergy, and in particular deprived Agnellus of his *monasterium* of St. Bartholemew "without cause" for a short period of time (c. 136). He gives no further details, but we assume from the text that the *monasterium* had been restored to him by the time he wrote c. 110, in which he states emphatically that he is abbot of this structure; when Agnellus refers to St. Bartholemew in the latter part of the *LPR*, it is always with the phrase "where, God willing, I am abbot" or the equivalent. Testi-Rasponi suggested that Agnellus's insistence on his possession of this *monasterium* was a result of the legal case that nearly deprived him of it.[20]

We know nothing about Agnellus after the death of George in 846; Holder-Egger cites a papyrus charter of donation for the year 854 (or 869) that contains the name of a certain Andreas priest of the church of Ravenna,[21] but there is no evidence to connect him with our Andreas Agnellus. We do know that he never became archbishop of Ravenna.

19. There is no reason to think that the elderly Abbot George in c. 26 was the same person as the man who became bishop.
20. Testi-Rasponi, "Note marginali," 250–51.
21. Holder-Egger, *LPER*, 272, n. 2.

Agnellus presents us with a picture of himself, a nobly born, wealthy young priest, educated within the Church, abbot of two *monasteria*, and owner of a luxurious house in the center of town. At the time of writing, particularly in the latter parts of the *LPR*, he had become bitter toward the Church hierarchy; possibly he had been passed over for high office. These autobiographical facts relate directly to information about the Lives of bishops or other prominent figures and thus validate the truth of his accounts. Some of them emphasize his high social status, and may serve to express his grievances against the Church hierarchy of Ravenna. Finally, all such statements also identify the credentials of the author as a member of the community about which he is writing.[22]

Date of composition of the *LPR*

The date or dates of composition of the *LPR* have been debated by several scholars.[23] There are two main sources of evidence for the dating: Agnellus's own statements in the *LPR* referring to chronology, and the evidence of the poem that introduces the text, which was supposedly not written by Agnellus. Every date or reference is open to interpretation; not least from the fact that some numbers given in the manuscripts are clearly wrong, which leaves open the possibility that any given number has been miscopied from the original. Nonetheless, certain chronological trends can be seen.

Several times in the text, Agnellus provides information about when the passage was written.[24] For example, in c. 94 he says: "And now almost thirty-eight years ago, when Charles king of the Franks had conquered all the kingdoms and had received the empire of the Romans from Pope Leo III." Charlemagne was crowned

---

22. See Austin, "Autobiography and History," 64.
23. For a detailed discussion, see Deliyannis, *CCCM* edition of the *LPR*, introduction; see also Testi-Rasponi, "Note marginali," 86–101 and 226–57; *CPER*, passim; Lanzoni, "Il 'Liber Pontificalis,'" 358–70; Benericetti, *Il Pontificale*, esp. 65–94.
24. *LPR*, cc. 1, 70, 80, 83, 94, 113, 118, 136, 144, 149, 167, and 175.

CHART 1. *Calculated Dates of Composition in the* LPR

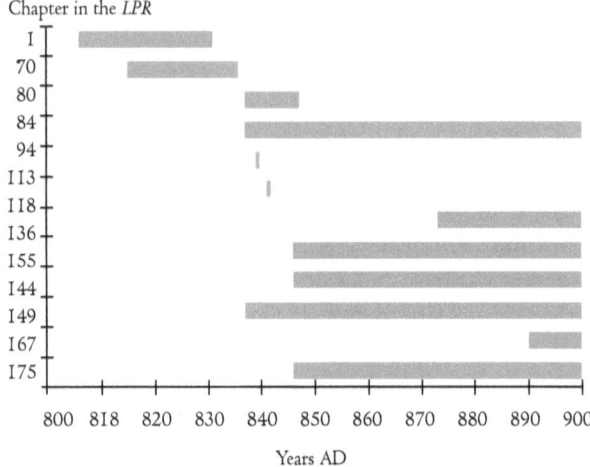

emperor in 800, so this passage must have been written in 838 or 839; this is the most precise date given in the entire text. In addition, it seems that Agnellus never identifies the present in terms of its bishop; a mention of a bishop by his name indicates that the passage was written after his death.[25] Thus some passages can be dated to after the deaths of the contemporary bishops Petronax (c. 818–37) and George (c. 837–46). It seems that the *LPR* was written

---

25. *LPR*, cc. 80, 83, 136, 144, 149, and 175. Agnellus never mentions Deusdedit, who reigned after George, anywhere in the text. Both Lanzoni, "Il 'Liber Pontificalis,'" 136, and Testi-Rasponi, "Note marginali," 101, agree that Agnellus only refers to George by name after his death. The present is described as "up to today" or by the use of the present tense, neither of which is ever used in conjunction with the name of a bishop. The past, on the other hand, is often referred to with the phrase *in ipsius temporibus*, which I have translated as "in his reign." Events that happened in the recent past, i.e., in Agnellus's lifetime, are often *nostris temporibus* (cc. 16, 31, 39, 70, 82, 102, 143), sometimes with a bishop's name attached. It is worth noting that in c. 80 he contrasts one altar cloth that had disappeared *in temporibus Petronacis* with another, which *permanet in praesenti*, clearly distinguishing between the "times of Petronax" and the present. In fact, the only units of time that Agnellus considers are the reigns of Ravenna's bishops; as such, reference to the name of a bishop must indicate that the reign was already finished, i.e., had already become a unit for dating.

over a period of at least fifteen years, from sometime during the reign of Petronax to sometime after the death of George. Using the dates from the text, we can produce the schema found in Chart 1. Leaving out the dates from cc. 118 and 167, which are based on numbers that were probably not accurate,[26] the *termini post quem* become progressively later as the text progresses. While this does not prove that the *LPR* was written in chronological order, it strongly implies it. While some precise breaks in composition can be seen, particularly between cc. 70 and 80 and between cc. 113 and 136, there is unfortunately relatively little that can be said about the date at which Agnellus began the work or the progression of the early chapters.[27]

By looking at some of the sources Agnellus used and when and how he used them, and at some of the conventions that occur only in parts of the text, we can see stylistic changes correlated with some of the dates Agnellus provides, and can identify significant breaks in composition.[28] It seems likely that cc. 1–79 were written during the years 831–36, at which point the work was probably interrupted in the middle of the Life of Maximian by the death of Archbishop Petronax and the activity of the next few years. Agnellus completed the Life of Maximian and continued through the Life of John IV or Bonus (cc. 80–107 or 109) during 837–39, after which he was again interrupted, this time by the lawsuit concern-

---

26. In c. 118 Agnellus says that Archbishop Theodore died "perhaps 180 years ago"; Theodore died in 691, thus only 148 to 160 years before Agnellus was writing. Perhaps the number in the next was miscopied, or perhaps Agnellus was only giving a round number. In c. 167 Archbishop Martin (r. c. 810–18) is said to have "obtained his see almost eighty years ago." We know that this passage was written after 846, hence the phrase "eighty years ago" refers to some time after the year 766; the passage must refer to either Martin's arrival in Ravenna or his consecration as a priest, or perhaps is again Agnellus's way of fudging a number he isn't sure about.

27. The prefatory poem contains some dating information also; it says that Agnellus began his work during the reigns of Pope Gregory III (827–44), Emperor Louis the Pious (814–40), King Lothar (823–55), and Archbishop Petronax (818–37). Taken together, these dates refer to the years between 827 and 837.

28. For a detailed discussion of these, see Deliyannis, *CCCM* edition of the *LPR*, introduction.

ing his possession of the *monasterium* of St. Bartholemew.[29] In 841–42, after a two-year hiatus, he took up again with the Life of Maurus, and wrote the succeeding chapters relatively continuously, up to or after the death of George in 846 (cc. 110–35); the Lives from that of Felix to the end (cc. 136–75) were certainly written after 846.

The *LPR* contains several passages in which Agnellus tells his audience that he is stopping for the day but will tell them more tomorrow. They do not occur throughout the text but only in cc. 17–92.[30] These statements are intended to create the effect that Agnellus is reading his work aloud to an audience, and they have always been accepted at face value; indeed, Agnellus is often noted for the fact that he read his work aloud to an audience. Rather than necessarily indicating a week of intense lecturing, however, these passages may simply reflect a style that was influencing Agnellus at the time in which he wrote, derived from written sermon collections.[31] I suggest that Agnellus inserted these passages to *mask* long breaks in the time in which he composed these parts. We know that cc. 1–113+ were written over the course of about ten years, from around 831 to 841; it is likely that Agnellus was constrained to stop and start several times during these years. Perhaps in order to give his work a sense of continuity that he felt was lacking, he included statements that imply that the work was being read out to an audience during the course of a week. This explanation would help to reconcile the disparities between the statements of closure and the dates of composition we have described above.

---

29. The anti-episcopal passages, which are sometimes assumed to have been written after Archbishop George aroused Agnellus's hatred, are found in cc. 13, 58, 68, 82, 100, 104, 105, and 116. Since cc. 13, 58, and 68 must have been written before 836, that is, during the reign of Petronax, they cannot refer to Agnellus's quarrel with George, and thus are only marginally useful for dating purposes.

30. *LPR*, cc. 17, 38, 39, 45, 46, 54, 58, 62, 79, 92.

31. See below, "Oral Sources and Orality."

Why Agnellus wrote the *LPR*

In his preface and elsewhere, Agnellus refers to a group of people who asked him to write the *LPR*. He mentions no one by name, which is rather odd, as it might be thought that he would dedicate the work, perhaps to Archbishop Petronax if not to some other patron. The vagueness of the references to the people who asked Agnellus to compose the work probably indicates that there were no such patrons, that Agnellus was writing under his own volition.[32] But what could have spurred him to write this particular work at this particular time? Two themes recur throughout the *LPR*: an anxiety for the rights of the clergy in the face of oppression by bishops, and a firm preference for the autocephaly of Ravenna, with a particular dislike of control of Ravenna by the Roman pope. That the *LPR* was directly modeled on the Roman *LP* suggests that anti-Roman feeling was probably the direct stimulus that caused Agnellus to write this text, but he undoubtedly had the rights of the clergy in mind during the entire time he was writing.

Agnellus inveighs strongly against the abuse of the clergy by bishops in part because of the quarrel between himself and Archbishop George. However, there are a few references in the early part of the text, written before George became bishop, that lead us to think that some (or one) of the bishops preceding George must also have had disagreements with their clergy. In c. 58, Agnellus quotes in full a letter of Pope Felix IV, which details the property rights of the clergy and was in force until the time of Bishop Theodore (679–93), as Agnellus later states. This is the only document Agnellus quotes in full, and it shows that the rights of the clergy were indeed very much on his mind. Unfortunately, the Life of Petronax is missing from the manuscripts of the *LPR*, and there

---

32. Whether or not his work can be seen as a manifestation of the "collective psychology" of the Ravennate clergy in the early ninth century seems to me a different question from the more direct issue of patronage and stimulus, much less from any questions of literary form. See Capitani, "Agnello Ravennate," 194–95, who cites Guillou, *Régionalisme et indépendance*.

is very little other information about the history of Ravenna at this period. It may have been a reign during which tensions ran high (perhaps this is even why the Life is missing from the *LPR*).[33]

Anti-Roman sentiment at Ravenna had been developing since the 660s and was a live issue after the Carolingian conquest of Italy and the subsequent struggle for control of the old exarchate. By the 830s Ravenna had effectively lost this struggle and was being ruled from Rome; the struggle was not over, however, at least as far as some of the bishops of Ravenna were concerned.[34] The absorption of Ravenna into the lands controlled by the pope must have been intolerable to Ravenna's clergy, or at least to one faction of it; Agnellus wistfully describes Bishop Sergius, who "administered everything just like the exarch, as now the Romans are accustomed to do" (c. 159). Again and again Agnellus makes anti-Roman statements: "if the body of the blessed Andrew . . . were buried here, the Roman bishops could not thus subjugate us" (c. 76); "As a true shepherd he lived piously with his sheep. He did not subjugate himself to the Roman see" (c. 116).[35] Stories of bishops of Ravenna defying the popes are told with approval; bishops who worked with the popes are vilified. Maurus has "many difficulties with the Roman pontiff . . . many struggles, many tempests, many disputes," and is hailed as the liberator of the church of Ravenna from Rome (c. 110–14); Sergius, who was arrested and tried in Rome, was miraculously released because he bribed the pope (c. 157–58); Martin, who was summoned to Rome and shepherded there by the bishop of Arles, feigned illness, bribed his keeper, and ended up not going (c. 169). By contrast, Theodore's main crime was that he restored the church of Ravenna to the pope's dominion, which Agnellus depicts as the result of a diabolical plot against Ravenna's clergy (c. 124).

The evidence for Ravenna's relationship with Rome during the

---

33. See Fasoli, "Rileggendo," 470–71.

34. For a comprehensive account of Ravenna's relationship with Rome and the Frankish kings in the early ninth century, see Brown, "Louis the Pious and the Papacy."

35. Cited by Brown, ibid., 304, n. 48.

time at which Agnellus was writing the *LPR* is less clear. Bishop George bought himself the sponsorship of Lothar's daughter at her baptism and went to Francia with a large part of Ravenna's treasure, apparently in order to gain influence with the emperor.[36] Agnellus might even have approved of these actions, had he not hated George for personal reasons.[37] But George's predecessor, Petronax, whose Life is missing from the manuscript of the *LPR*, seems to have pursued a pro-papal policy. Agnellus refers several times to treasure that disappeared under Petronax, possibly in bribes to the emperor or his agents, but equally possibly sent instead to the pope. Petronax received a privilege from Pope Paschal I in 819 and later attended a council held in Rome in 826 by Pope Eugene II.[38] It is likely that Agnellus, as a member of an antipapal faction to which George also belonged, was seriously alarmed by the direction in which Petronax's policies were going in the late 820s and early 830s, and that it was this rapprochement with Rome that caused him to begin the *LPR*.

But the most persuasive evidence that Agnellus was writing a work to elevate the claims of the church of Ravenna against those of Rome comes from the nature of the text itself. As we will see in detail below, the *LPR* is based in concept and format on the Roman *Liber pontificalis*. Of all the historical and literary genres available to him, Agnellus chose this one; it cannot be doubted that Rome was very much on his mind from the very conception of the *LPR*, and that the work was primarily intended to demonstrate Ravenna's ancient history of independence from Rome.

36. George lost the treasure at the Battle of Fontenoy; *LPR*, cc. 171–75.
37. Brown, "Louis the Pious and the Papacy," 305.
38. Cited by Brown, ibid., 304.

STRUCTURE AND GENRE

The *LPR* contains a Life of each bishop of Ravenna from the founding of the episcopate by St. Apollinaris to Agnellus's time. Agnellus attempts to include, at a minimum, the date and place of burial and the length of the reign of the bishop. In many of the Lives, the following information is provided when known: national or civic origin; a physical and/or spiritual portrait; information about the election and/or ordination; artistic or architectural patronage done by the bishop or during his reign; historical events and natural phenomena; exegetical and exhortatory passages, miracle stories, and other narratives. Within a Life, information is generally provided in the following order: origin, portrait, ordination, historical events, patronage, miracles, sermonettes, date and place of burial, length of reign. However, this sequence is not very precisely fixed, and there are great disparities in the amount of information included in the Lives.

Three literary genres—serial biography, hagiography, and sermon—contribute almost equally to the composition of the *LPR*. All three types of literature had close and specific connections with bishops: while the two former were often written *about* bishops, the latter was often written *by* bishops. Agnellus's combination of these three genres displays his inventiveness with respect to his subject matter.

The Roman *Liber pontificalis* and the genre *gesta episcoporum*

The *LPR* is generally classed with a group of histories of episcopal sees or monasteries that has been defined as the genre *gesta episcoporum et abbatum* (deeds of bishops and abbots).[1] This genre became popular in the Carolingian period and consists of works of serial biography, that is, institutional biographies of each bishop or abbot of a particular locality, in order of their tenure. Lists of church leaders were provided as part of historical works from as early as the fourth century and continued to exist throughout the early Middle Ages.[2] What distinguishes all of the works grouped in the genre *gesta episcoporum* is that they are modeled on the Roman *Liber pontificalis*.[3]

The first codification of papal Lives occurred in the early sixth century.[4] Around 640 the series was brought up to date and continued thereafter after the death of each pope. The papal Lives contain a variety of different types of information, depending on how soon after the reign of a given pope they were written and how much information the author(s) had. From even the earliest Lives, information in certain categories is provided for every pope: national origin and parentage, length of reign, emperor(s) or king(s) in whose reign they lived, death or martyrdom, church regulations promulgated, number of ordinations, burial place and date, and length of time that elapsed before the next pope. From the Life of Silvester on, detailed information about patronage is

---

1. See esp. Sot, *Gesta episcoporum, gesta abbatum*, for a detailed analysis of the genre.

2. In Eusebius's *Ecclesiastical History*, for example, lists are given for Rome, Antioch, Jerusalem, and Alexandria.

3. The fundamental analysis of the Roman *LP* was published by Louis Duchesne, along with his authoritative edition of the text. Excellent recent discussions of the *LP* are found in Berschin, *Biographie und Epochenstil* 1:270–77 and 2:115–38; Davis, *Book of Pontiffs* and *Ninth-Century Popes*, and Noble, "A New Look at the *Liber Pontificalis*."

4. The following notes on the early history of the *LP* are derived from Davis, *Book of Pontiffs*, ii–xv, and Berschin, *Biographie und Epochenstil* 1:270–71. For an excellent and comprehensive study of episcopal lists and their significance in early medieval Italy, see Picard, *Souvenir*. It is interesting to note that it was in the early sixth century that an interest in episcopal lists began to manifest itself in other cities in Italy, such as Milan, Ravenna, and Aquileia. This was possibly due to the influence of the early *LP*, but it is also the case that at this time these cities were all claiming to be metropolitan or patriarchal sees, and, on the model of Jerome's *Chronica*, they knew that patriarchal sees all possessed episcopal lists; see Picard, *Souvenir*, 560. It is therefore also possible that the *LP* was first produced in order to emphasize Rome's preeminent status.

given. Lives that were written soon after the reign of their subjects often contain, in addition, historical narrative, personal information about the pope, and descriptions of natural phenomena. In order to have had access to these various types of information, it is assumed that the authors of the Lives worked in some branch of the papal bureaucracy.

In the mid-eighth century, histories of the bishops of other cities began to be written, modeled on the *LP*.[5] While the first three imitations of the *LP* were written by Italian authors (the *LPR* was the third), most of them were written for institutions north of the Alps, where they formed a well-defined genre.[6] Agnellus himself may or may not have been aware of these other texts. He refers to the *LPR* as a *pontifical* several times, as though this were a generic term for the type of work he was writing.[7] It has been suggested that the Roman *Liber pontificalis* was only known by this name from the twelfth century;[8] did Agnellus make up this term for his own work, or was he writing in a genre that had already developed, of

---

5. Information in the *LP*'s format could be transmitted quite rapidly throughout Europe. Bede, in his *De temporum ratione*, written in 725, cites events that took place in 715–17; these events are found in the *LP* in the Life of Gregory II, who died only in 731. See Berschin, *Biographie und Epochenstil* 2:122–28. Capitani, "Agnello Ravennate," 193, has pointed out that in the mid-ninth century many churches were undergoing redefinitions of their relationships with the papacy following the Carolingian expansion and the rise of the papal state, and that this state of affairs may have led to the proliferation of the genre.

6. While the *LPR* is an early member of the genre, it differs in several respects from the other members of the genre, specifically because most of the others seem to have been official institutional documents, whereas the *LPR* was not commissioned by the bishop and does not seem to have had an official purpose. It thus should not necessarily be interpreted in the context of the other texts. See Pizarro, *Writing Ravenna*, 34–35, and Picard, *Souvenir*, 543–44 and 565–66, for the differences between Italian and northern *gesta*.

7. *LPR* versiculi, preface, cc. 25, 32, 54, 146.

8. Bertolini, "Il 'Liber pontificalis,'" 403–25, states that in the late eighth and ninth centuries the work was known as *Liber episcopalis* and/or *gesta pontificum*, but that the combination *Liber pontificalis* does not appear in any manuscripts until the twelfth century. In the published discussion of Bertolini's paper, Girolamo Arnaldi commented, "I have the impression that the title came from Ravenna," but Bertolini did not address this comment in his response.

which his work is one of the few surviving examples? Whether or not he was aware of other imitations of the *LP,* Agnellus was very well acquainted with the Roman work, up through the Lives of the early ninth-century popes, and he specifically imitated those aspects of it that fit his intentions and resources.

In the *LP,* almost every Life begins with the name of the pope, followed by "born in [place], son of [name]," occasionally followed by the father's rank or occupation, or by a city, province, or region. Agnellus begins the *LPR* with "St. Apollinaris, Antiochene by birth," a direct imitation of the *LP*'s Life of St. Peter. No further information is given until the Life of Peter I, "From the time of blessed Apollinaris up to this man, all his predecessors were from Syria" (c. 24). After this, however, only five bishops have their national origin specifically provided, and all are foreigners; that three of these are among Ravenna's greatest bishops is unfortunate for Agnellus, since he must explain how each became bishop in Ravenna.[9] Otherwise, most of Ravenna's bishops were of local origin.

After the name of the father of the pope, each Life in the *LP* gives the length of the pope's reign, in the formula "sedit annos [number], menses [number], dies [number]." In the surviving manuscripts of the *LPR,* the length of reign is provided for only some of the bishops of Ravenna, those for whom Agnellus knew the information.[10] The same formula is used, but the information is given at the end of each Life. A curious feature of both surviving manuscripts of the *LPR* is that for all those Lives for which the length of reign is not known, the same formula—"sedit annos menses dies"—is included at the end of each Life, with blank

---

9. Peter II, whom Agnellus erroneously claims was Chrysologus, Maximian, Damian, John II the Roman, and Marinian. One other bishop, Leo, is called *ex isto ouile,* but as his Life is mostly lost we cannot know if he was also born elsewhere.

10. Apollinaris (from the *Passio*), Ursus (years only), John I, Ecclesius, Ursicinus, Victor (possibly from epitaphs; see Holder-Egger, *LPER,* 280, n. 2; 310, n. 1 and 308, n. 1; and 322, n. 1, respectively), and all the bishops after Bishop Agnellus except Marinian, Bonus, and John V. The ends of the Lives of Sergius, Leo, Martin, and George are missing.

spaces left where the numbers should have been. This feature must have appeared in the exemplar of these two manuscripts; however, it is impossible to say whether it goes back to Agnellus.

For many of the papal Lives, the information immediately following the length of reign is the phrase "fuit autem temporibus [emperor] usque/et [emperor]," giving the consuls, emperors, or kings under whom the pope reigned. Agnellus uses a formula similar to the *LP* in only two places: c. 26, "Fuit enim in Valentiniani temporibus," about Peter I, and c. 134, "Fuit enim temporibus Constantini imperatoris," about Damian (which is incorrect).[11]

The first mention of a pope's career comes in the Life of Agapitus; he was one of the first popes whose Life was written almost contemporaneously, and thus for whom such facts might be known. This sort of information is reported only sporadically until the Life of Gregory II, after which the careers are given in some detail, with names of churches and papal sponsors. In the *LPR*, the first clerical career is that of the late-sixth-century Bishop Agnellus (c. 84). Ecclesiastical careers resume only with Maurus in the mid-seventh century, and continue with Reparatus, Felix, Gratiosus, and Martin. Agnellus may have used the *LP*, especially after Pope Gregory II, as a model for categories of information relating to the bishops' backgrounds, but the details and manner of presentation differ from the *LP*.

Encomiastic phrases and passages appear in the *LP* after Severinus (d. 638), when the *LP* began to be written regularly after the death of each pope.[12] At first the encomia are short, consisting of only a few formulaic phrases, but gradually they become much longer.[13] There is only one description of the physical appearance of a pope, in the Life of the elderly and saintly Conon.[14] Agnellus

11. In fact, most other examples of *gesta episcoporum* do not include imperial information either; Picard, *Souvenir*, 559.

12. Berschin, *Biographie und Epochenstil* 2.116, remarks on this.

13. Davis, *Lives*, 19, notes that the encomia of Leo II and Gregory III are almost identical.

14. *LP*, Life of Conon. This passage, however, comes not at the beginning of the Life but in the course of the narrative, explaining why he was elected pope.

introduces most of his Lives with an encomiastic passage, borrowing the concept and many of the same words from the *LP.* The encomia in the *LPR* also include other elements, such as etymologies of names and frequently a short physical description.[15] Agnellus tells us in two places that he has learned about the appearance of the bishops from their pictures, and he even cites St. Ambrose as an authority for doing this.[16] Agnellus's physical descriptions actually do match what he saw in the pictures, at least as far as we can tell from what survives.[17] As Paulo Squatriti notes, in both the *LP* and the *LPR,* "before the narrative truly began, a physical-moral sketch fixed in the reader's (or author's) mind the essentials of the pope's personality, preparing thus to launch into the events of his pontificate."[18] This, no doubt, is the essential aspect of the *LP* that was copied and expanded by Agnellus.

Descriptions of patronage form an integral part of the *LP.*[19]

15. There is only one instance of an etymological derivation in the *LP,* for Benedict II, of whom it is said, "he showed himself as befitted a man worthy of his name: in him grace and benediction from above truly overflowed." (*LP,* Life of Benedict II, trans. Davis.) For a discussion of etymology in history, see Guenée, *Histoire et culture historique,* 184–91, and Haubrichs, *"Veriloquium nominis."*

16. *LPR,* cc. 32, 108. These statements are actually veiled references to the iconoclastic controversy and the role of the bishops of Ravenna as staunch opponents of iconoclasm; they emphasize Agnellus's iconodule belief that pictures perform important functions. See Deliyannis, "Agnellus of Ravenna and Iconoclasm."

17. See Nauerth, *Agnellus von Ravenna, Untersuchungen.* Agnellus mentions pictures of fourteen bishops, of which seven survive—of Severus, Ursus, Ecclesius (two), Ursicinus, Maximian, and Reparatus. Physical descriptions are provided for twenty-two bishops. There are two bishops for whom pictures are mentioned but physical descriptions are absent (Peter II and Aurelian). A comparison between the phrases used in the descriptions and those of bishops with known pictures shows an identical use of terminology. For example, Agnellus describes Ecclesius, Peter III, Bonus, and John II as having grey hair *(canities),* yet only mentions pictures of Ecclesius and Peter III. Squatriti, "Personal Appearance and Physiognomies," examined the influence of physiognomic theory on Italian episcopal biography, including the *LPR;* for more on such physical descriptions and their relation to icons in Byzantine hagiography, see Dagron, "Holy Images and Likeness," 25–28.

18. Squatriti, "Personal Appearance and Physiognomies," 197.

19. Croquison, "L'iconographie chrétienne à Rome," discusses patronage in the *LP* but concentrates more on what is said rather than how it is said.

Monumental patronage represented a pope's lasting contribution to the religious life of Rome, and the lists emphasize the sanctity and piety of each donor. As with the other categories, the accounts of patronage found in the *LP* change in style and extent based on both the availability of sources to the authors and the importance of patronage to those authors.[20] By the late eighth century, the style of the accounts had become highly developed and formulaic.[21] Subjective assessments of workmanship become common: objects are *mirae pulchritudinis,* churches are *mirae magnitudinis,* marbles are *pulcherrima,* and technical work is done *mirifice.*[22] Agnellus uses terminology very similar to that in the early-ninth-century *LP* to describe decorative elements in a church, liturgical furnishings and the materials from which they were made.[23] He tells of the same sorts of patronage as the *LP,* namely church foundations, decorations, restorations, donations of property,[24] liturgical vessels of precious materials and altar cloths, all sponsored by bishops, rulers, and other wealthy patrons. Since Agnellus was attempting to outdo Rome and claim equal status for Ravenna, it is natural that he should emphasize the preeminence of the city's monuments.

But Agnellus's mention of patronage also performs a function different from that of the *LP.* In the *LP* the popes are presented, almost without exception, as good; patronage is presented as simply another category demonstrating the power and piety of the papacy. For Agnellus, by contrast, some bishops are good and others

---

20. As noted by Geertman, *More veterum,* 184. For a lengthy but somewhat outdated discussion of this evidence, see Piper, *Einleitung in die Monumentale Theologie,* 315–49.

21. In part this trend can be explained by the desire to emphasize images at the time of Byzantine Iconoclasm, which the popes condemned; see Andaloro, "Il *Liber pontificalis* e la questione delle immagini."

22. These phrases refer to the quality of the materials, and hence their value, rather than their intangible merits; see ibid., 73–74, who notes that the situation changes somewhat in the Lives of Hadrian and Leo III, when images were being attacked in the *Libri Carolini,* that is, that there are stronger hints of aesthetic appreciation in the adjectives used to describe them in the *LP.*

23. See entries in the Glossary.

24. There are two mentions of donations of property, in cc. 53 and 89.

are not. The bad bishops are not said to have founded anything and indeed are depicted as despoilers of church property, while the good bishops are responsible for construction, donations, and the receipt of gifts to the church of Ravenna.[25]

The place and date of burial is given for almost every pope at the end of each Life.[26] In the late seventh century, the manner of death begins to be reported also, and by the mid-eighth century, the death of the pope begins to be reported in quasi-hagiographical terms. Many of the bishops of Ravenna die in the odor of sanctity, especially the very early bishops—literally, in the case of Marcellinus: "And when the course of many years was run, he lost the pontificate and his life; his body emitted such fragrant odours that the noses of those burying him thought they smelled incense of most precious myrrh" (c. 12).[27] Agnellus attempts to provide the anniversary date and place of burial for each of the bishops of Ravenna. Perhaps more honest than the redactors of the *LP*, he admits when he does not know where a particular bishop had been buried, or when he is making a guess; this is true especially for the early bishops.[28] As in the *LP*, the dates of death and places of burial in the *LPR* are usually found at the end of each Life.

25. Cf. Sot, "Historiographie épiscopale et modèle familiale," 444.

26. As Picard, *Souvenir*, 131 has shown, at Rome the place of burial of the early popes had not been known, but the redactor(s) of the *LP* assumed that they had all been buried at the Vatican.

27. This is one of the most elaborate. For others, see cc. 5, 7, 8, 9, 11, 19, 20, 23, 26, 33, 44, 52, 65, 68, 97, 113.

28. Agnellus didn't know the place of burial for Proculus or Liberius II, and he says he is guessing the place of burial for Aderitus, Marcian, Calocerus, Datus, Liberius I, Agapitus, Marcellinus, Probus II, John III, and John IV. For the early bishops, dates of death are given only for Apollinaris, Aderitus, Eleuchadius, Calocerus, Probus I, and Severus; as Picard, *Souvenir*, 490, points out, each of these bishops was the object of a cult. From Ursus on, dates are given for all the bishops through Marinian, with the exception of Ecclesius and Ursicinus; the next date given is for Bonus, and then from Reparatus to George all are known (of the Lives that are complete) except for John VI. Despite the gap in the early seventh century, Picard, *Souvenir*, 553–54, proposes that Agnellus had access to a necrology, or list of the anniversaries of death, for the bishops of Ravenna, separate from the regular episcopal list, since more death dates are given than lengths of reigns.

At the end of every papal Life, the number of priests, deacons, and bishops ordained by the pope and the number of different ordination ceremonies are given. Then the length of time in which the see was vacant is given in years, months, and days. This information is completely omitted from the *LPR*, with one exception: Marcian "increased the clergy who were learned in holy doctrine and consecrated many deacons and priests." This is no doubt an echo of the *LP*, even if a very faint one, but it was not repeated.[29]

From all of this we can see that, in addition to the most basic structure, that is, the sequence of bishops' Lives as serial biography, Agnellus borrowed several specific categories of information from the *LP*. More significantly, he not only borrowed them in concept but also imported the terminology and rhetorical devices of the *LP*, particularly with regard to encomium and patronage. He also omits some categories, either because he did not have access to the information or because it was relevant only to popes.

How much of the *LP* could Agnellus have known? Redactions of the *LP* seem to have been disseminated after 715, 757, and 795. Agnellus, living in a city so closely connected to Rome, must have acquired a recent version of the *LP*. Some of the elements he includes in his Lives, such as encomia and meteorological information, first begin to be recorded in the *LP* in the early eighth century. Certain rhetorical features, particularly those related to patronage, are closely related to those in the late-eighth- and ninth-century Lives in the *LP*. Agnellus also used the Roman *LP* as a historical source, as will be discussed below. His confusion of the mid-eighth-century popes has led most scholars to believe that his copy of the *LP* ended with the Life of Constantine; however, as we shall see, the *LPR*'s close connections to the historical content of the *LP* also indicate that Agnellus had a copy of the *LP* that covered the period at least through the 770s.

It should be remembered that Ravenna, and perhaps Agnellus personally, had a connection with Pope Leo III and certain mem-

29. Testi-Rasponi, *CPER*, 33, n. 5.

bers of his administration. In c. 168 of the *LPR* Agnellus writes that Leo sent his *cubicularius* Chrisafus to oversee repairs to Sant' Apollinare in Classe; the *LP* also mentions this event, without naming Chrisafus.[30] The details of the restoration, namely, the replacement of old roof beams, agree so precisely in the two passages that it is tempting to state that Agnellus must have seen the text of the Life of Leo III. A *cubicularius* was a member of the papal household, and such a man, especially one charged with architectural responsibilities, might have had a close connection with the lists of papal donations that found their way into the *LP*.[31] Chrisafus may have brought an updated copy of the *LP* to Ravenna, or perhaps he even showed Agnellus the style in which items were recorded in the *LP*. In any event, when Agnellus wrote his own *liber pontificalis*, he drew upon the format and style of the entire *LP* in order to write about the archbishops of Ravenna.

The *LPR* and hagiography

Bishops, especially founding bishops, who were also saints were particularly honored in every Christian city, both because of civic pride and because of the later bishops' interest in maintaining ven-

30. *LP*, Life of Leo III, c. 106.
31. Noble, *Republic of St. Peter*, 212–55, provides an excellent description of the papal administration in the late eighth century. The chancery or *scrinium*, under the control of the *primicerius notariorum*, contained the papal archive, and it is here that Noble places the composition of the *LP* ("A New Look at the *Liber Pontificalis*," 354–56). On the other hand, control over the churches and their wealth was exercised by the office of the *vestiarius*, a part of the papal household, while financial matters were supervised by the *arcarius* and the *sacellarius*. For this reason, Duchesne had proposed that the *LP* was composed in the *vestiarium*. It is not clear where lists of donations would have been composed, nor whether they would have been transferred directly into the *LP* or further embellished by the addition of their characteristic adjectives and superlatives. Geertman, *More veterum*, esp. 34, places the composition of the lists in the *vestiarium*, and sees the terminology in the *LP* as directly reflecting the styles of the *vestiarii* who wrote the registers. Thus, even if the registers of donations were contained in the archives and copied by various *scrinarii* into the *LP*, the compositional style probably reflects that of the *vestiarium* in the household, to which the *cubicularius* Crisafus probably belonged.

eration for their office.³² Many early medieval saints, particularly from the fourth through the sixth centuries, were bishops. Biographies of saintly bishops, as for all saints, are intended to provide examples of virtue for its own sake, but when such hagiographical Lives are included in a work of serial biography, they also glorify the institution. Sot points out that the *gesta episcoporum* are by nature a mixture of historiography and hagiography, due in part to the sacramental or liturgical role played by these works.³³

Hagiography is almost entirely missing from the Roman *LP*. Lives of a very few of the martyred early popes retain traces of passion stories (Cornelius, Sixtus II, Marcellinus, and Marcellus), but many of the early popes are simply identified as having died as martyrs, with no elaboration. Gregory I has only a very short Life in the *LP*, although he was the subject of other biographies in which his divine exploits are recorded. Only one real miracle is documented in the whole *LP*: Bishop George of Praeneste, who consecrated the schismatic pope Constantine in 768, had his right hand shrivel up while celebrating mass, and subsequently died.³⁴ Correspondingly, very few popes are presented as bad, except for those who were schismatic; and of course, since the papacy had an interest in protecting its legitimacy as an institution, the losers in the various schisms are necessarily depicted as bad.

By contrast, in the *LPR* miracle stories make up almost a fifth of

---

32. Sot, "Historiographie épiscopale et modèle familiale," 436, notes that in northern Europe, the pretension of an apostolic foundation received new emphasis in the ninth century; however, at Ravenna this claim goes back at least to the composition of the *passio* of St. Apollinaris, sometime between the early sixth and the late seventh century, if not to the construction of Sant' Apollinare in Classe in the mid-sixth century. For a discussion of apostolicity in northern Italian churches, see Picard, *Souvenir*, 689–99.

33. Sot, "Arguments hagiographiques et historiographiques," identifies three types of argument used the authors of *gesta* to substantiate their claims to property or tradition: claiming that something was founded by a saintly bishop; providing a dated precedent or document, as old as possible; or an argument between the two, a recourse to the origins, preferably apostolic, of the entity. He identifies each of these arguments in the *LPR*.

34. *LP*, Life of Stephen III, c. 6.

the entire text. Miracles relating to the Ravenna's monuments and/or historical personalities demonstrate God's active interest in the affairs of the city, while the presence of saintly bishops in Ravenna's history increases the prestige and glory of the episcopal see. In effect, Agnellus compiled, within the framework of the *gesta episcoporum*, a collection of Lives of saintly bishops, in which he particularly emphasized episcopal functions as avenues for divine grace. Whether Agnellus borrowed stories himself or found them in "popular tradition," his inclusion of them marks a sharp distinction between the *LPR* and the Roman *LP*.

Miracles in the LPR

There are thirty-two miracle stories in the *LPR*, not counting the ones in the Life of Apollinaris that were taken directly from the *Passio* of Apollinaris. Most of these miracles are clustered in four Lives, those of Severus, John I, Damian, and Felix, which contain five each; the remainder are scattered throughout the text.[35] The miracles can be divided into two groups: those that involve the bishop and those that do not. These correspond to what Bános Vallejo has termed "hagiographic" and "literary" miracles.[36] Almost half of the miracles in the *LPR* belong in the latter category.

Two-thirds of the miracle stories in the *LPR* have analogues in earlier hagiography.[37] Borrowing from other saints' Lives was an extremely common practice among hagiographers, and such borrowings and references, rather than being regarded as theft, were often intended to add layers of meaning to a Life.[38] In c. 32 Agnel-

---

35. *LPR*, cc. 14, 15 (two), 16, 17 (Severus); 35, 36, 37, 41, 44 (John I); 125, 129, 130, 131, 133 (Damian); and 138, 142, 144, 147 (Felix). The other twelve occur in *LPR*, cc. 25, 30, 49, 87, 153, 162, 163, 175.

36. Baños Vallejo, *La hagiografía como género literario*, 130–34, explores the difference between the "hagiographic" miracle, a miracle found in the Life of a saint with that saint as the agent of divine grace, and the "literary" miracle, which is independent of hagiography and whose protagonist is the person or collectivity benefited.

37. Miracles with parallels in hagiographical literature are found in cc. 1 (3), 14, 15 (2), 16, 17, 25, 26, 30, 37, 49, 52, 125, 129, 131, 133, 144, 147, 162, 163. Miracles without parallels are those found in cc. 35, 36, 41, 44, 87, 130, 138, 142, 153, 175.

38. Heffernan, *Sacred Biography*, esp. 72–122.

lus says, "And when I did not discover any history, or what their life had been like . . . in order that there would be no gap in the holy bishops . . . I have composed their lives; and I believe that I have not lied, since they were encouraging and pure and charitable orators and acquirers of the souls of men for God." As has often been pointed out, Agnellus's justification for making up certain Lives reflects the introduction to Gregory of Tours's *Vita patrum*, in which the use of the singular *vita* is used, "since there is a diversity of merits and virtues among them, but the one life of the body sustains them all in this world."[39]

The hagiographical analogues to the miracles in the *LPR* are identified, in this translation, in the notes. Agnellus never says that he has borrowed a legend, but he does introduce some borrowed miracle stories with phrases that indicate that he has "heard it from the elders" or from a named witness.[40] By examining the miracles and exploring their meanings in the context of the *LPR*, we can see that Agnellus does seem to have included many of them for deliberate reasons related to the overall themes of his work.

A large number of Agnellus's miracles in some way emphasize the sanctity of the episcopal office and the functions of the bishop; they include the bishop saving the city from an enemy (c. 37), visions of or by the bishop while he is conducting mass (cc. 14, 44, 130, and 133), miraculous elections to the episcopate (cc. 17, 49), the restoration of a dead baby so it can be baptized (c. 125), and the restoration of civic peace through the organization of penitential processions (c. 129). In each case the bishop is seen carrying out one of his functions. The connection between this sort of miracle and pictures of bishops in works of art, depicted as carrying out

---

39. Gregory of Tours, *Liber vitae patrum*, prol., trans. James, 2; see James, *Life of the Fathers*, xiv.
40. *LPR*, cc. 15, 17, 25, 30, 35, 36, 87, 125, 153. Several passages introduced by such phrases are known to have been taken directly from other written sources. Heffernan, *Sacred Biography*, cc. 1 and 3 respectively, notes that on the one hand, all saints' Lives originate as oral tradition that is eventually written down, but that on the other hand such Lives often contained elaborate and learned references made by borrowings, especially of phraseology and metaphor, that point to a literary tradition.

their episcopal duties, deserves further study; in Ravenna, for example, Bishop John I's vision of the angel during mass may reflect a picture of him celebrating mass with an angel, found in the apse of the church of St. Agatha.[41] Most of Agnellus's episcopal miracles have analogues in other hagiographical works about bishops. By including these in the *LPR*, Agnellus glorifies the episcopate itself, and creates an image of the office as a channel through which divine grace is manifested.

Several other miracles in the *LPR* illustrate the sanctity of particular bishops in ways not directly connected to their office. Again, most of these miracles have analogues in other hagiographical works. They include bishops who foresee their own deaths, miraculous preservation of a body, healing at the tomb, and other evidence that certain bishops were aided by divine powers.[42] In addition, three stories could be called anti-miracles, in that they indicate the wickedness, rather than the sanctity, of Bishops John VI and George.[43]

Many of the miracle stories in the *LPR* are not directly related to the bishops but are rather of the "literary" type. Some are intended to explain natural phenomena, strange occurrences with no other explanation, or particularities of art or topography in Ravenna.[44] Some explain the appearance of certain objects; in these cases Agnellus usually explains that this is how it appears "up to

---

41. *LPR*, c. 44; Agnellus describes a picture of exactly this type, representing Peter I, in c. 27: "Whose image is made thus: having a full beard, with hands extended as if singing the mass, and as when the host is placed on the altar, and behold an angel of the Lord is depicted opposite that altar, bearing up his prayers." See Testi-Rasponi, *CPER*, 75, n. 7, and 132, n. 9 (who sees in the miracle in c. 130 another example of a depiction of an angel with a bishop performing mass), contradicted, however, by Nauerth, *Agnellus von Ravenna, Untersuchungen*, 31. Cf. Lucchesi, "Giovanni I Angelopte." Another example would be the vision of Honorius seeing St. Laurence with his hand on the shoulder of Lauricius (c. 35), which, as Pizarro, *A Rhetoric of the Scene*, 112 and 233, n. 3, points out, was a pose typical of a dedication mosaic, such as the one that survives in the apse of San Vitale.

42. Respectively, cc. 15 and 52, 26, 16, 15, 138, and 144.

43. *LPR*, cc. 162, 163, and 175.

44. As noted by Lanzoni, "Il 'Liber Pontificalis,'" 428–29.

today."[45] Others are used to justify unusual historical events by having them caused by divine intervention; for example, the victory of the Ravennese over a Byzantine army, inspired by a vision of a bull (c. 153). A few do not fit into any of these categories. In most of these explanatory miracles, the bishop is not an actor at all; moreover, these are precisely the legends that do not have direct literary analogues, although certain details of the stories are very similar structurally to other hagiographical legends. However, the stories in the *LPR* that contain this sort of motif are otherwise unique.

Hagiographical structure in the lives of saintly bishops

What sort of saints was Agnellus claiming for Ravenna? The Lives of six bishops are essentially hagiographic; they are Apollinaris, Severus, John I, Peter Chrysologus, Damian, and Felix. The biography of Agnellus's ancestor Johannicis, which appears across the span of several Lives, is also hagiographic in structure.

We have external evidence for the veneration of three of these saintly bishops. Apollinaris and Severus had basilicas over their graves in Classe, which were built in the mid- to late sixth century, and both bishops are mentioned in the late-sixth-century Hieronymian martyrology. Peter Chrysologus, by the seventh century, was famous for his sermons. Apollinaris's *passio*, which Agnellus knew, was written in the mid-seventh century, but apparently no written Life of either Severus or Chrysologus existed in Agnellus's day, and it is his Lives that were later copied into collections of saints' Lives.

Agnellus's other three saintly bishops are more problematic, since what we know about them is almost entirely dependent on Agnellus's text. Agnellus considered a bishop named John the first to exercise metropolitan powers; he tells us that a candle was kept burning in front of a portrait of this Bishop John, which indicates some sort of veneration in the ninth century. The last two saintly bishops were not characters out of the distant past but from the

---

45. Cc. 30, 35, 36, 41, 87, 130, and 157.

early eighth century. Bishop Damian, about whom almost nothing is known other than what Agnellus tells us, is shown working several miracles. It is entirely unclear why this bishop should have been considered so saintly. Damian's successor, Felix, was an anti-Roman activist, and as such is vilified in the Roman *LP.* Agnellus therefore takes the basic outline of his life provided there and endows it with sanctity. It is interesting that Agnellus calls John I, Damian, and Felix *papa,* a word he usually reserves for popes.[46]

Each of these saints is notable for a different reason, and the Lives are structured in different ways. Agnellus essentially offers us three models of sanctity: the martyr (Apollinaris, Felix, and Johannicis), the confessor (Severus and Damian),[47] and the sanctified version of the *gesta episcoporum*-model bishop (John I and Peter Chrysologus). The first two types are purely hagiographic and had many literary analogues; the third type, a combination of hagiography and *gesta episcoporum*–style information, Agnellus seems to have created.

Agnellus was probably the first person to write Ravenna's history after the sixth century; he may also have been the first to ask questions about events and objects which needed explaining. Although Agnellus's colloquial style has lent credibility to the idea that his stories were really oral legends, there is no reason why he could not have made up these stories to suit his own purposes. The inclusion of miracles in the *LPR* demonstrates God's interest in the bishops of Ravenna and provides the city with local saints equal in stature to those of Rome.

---

46. *LPR*, cc. 35, 37, 44 (John I), 132 (Damian), and 144 (Felix). It is not clear whether he used this word to connote sanctity or whether he thought they were saintly because they were called *papa* in Ravenna's episcopal list. Two inscriptions quoted by Agnellus also use the word *papa* to refer to Bishops Victor (c. 44) and Agnellus (c. 67).

47. Heinzelmann, "Neue Aspekte," esp. 35–37, has shown that bishops' biographies imitated the encomia of officials of the Roman empire far more than did the earlier Lives of ascetics and martyrs, because the bishops took over many of the duties of the former officials.

The *LPR* and sermons

Almost one-sixth of the *LPR* is made up of scattered passages that are homiletic, exhortatory, exegetical, or panegyrical in nature.[48] Because each of these formats is found in sermons, and because many of the passages seem to be fragments of longer sermons, I have called these passages "sermonettes." Sermonettes are found in fourteen chapters in the *LPR*; in some cases a sermonette consists of two quite distinct parts, resulting in twenty-one different subjects.[49] Their inclusion in a historical text is unprecedented.[50] Because of their anomalous nature, and because they offer little insight into Ravenna's history and culture, the sermonettes have been ignored by most historians who have studied the *LPR*. As an integral part of the *LPR*, the sermonettes deserve consideration in the overall context of Agnellus's thought. Why should he have put this type of text into a work of serial biography? Why the choice of these particular subjects? Did Agnellus write the sermonettes, and if not, where did they come from? What is the relationship between the sermonettes and the other ostensibly oral forms in the *LPR*?

Stylistic features of the sermonettes in the LPR

Two main features, other than subject matter, are found in the sermonettes that help to define them as a class.[51] All of the sermonettes address an audience. This is true of other parts of the *LPR* also, but the distinguishing feature of the sermonettes is that all but one contain questions, rhetorically addressed to the audi-

---

48. Lanzoni, "Il 'Liber Pontificalis,'" 359.

49. When two subjects are found in the same sermonette, I have identified them as parts (a) and (b). The sermonettes are found in cc. 18a, 18b, 45a, 45b, 54, 55a, 55b, 64, 68, 88, 97, 100a, 100b, 104, 105a, 105b, 109, 116a, 116b, 166a, 166b.

50. Perhaps the closest parallel would be the introductions to each of the Lives in Gregory of Tours's *Liber vitae patrum*.

51. Some features characteristic of sermons are found not only in the sermonettes but also in other parts of the *LPR*; for the very important question of the influence of sermons on Agnellus's presentation of his work as an oral performance, see below, "Oral Sources and Orality."

ence by the author and answered by the text.[52] This type of question is almost entirely absent from the rest of the *LPR*. Quotation or paraphrasing of biblical passages is the other defining feature of the sermonettes, being found in all but four of them. The number and use of the citations vary among the sermonettes. The form of the biblical citations also varies from sermonette to sermonette. Occasionally the exact words of the Vulgate are repeated,[53] while in some sermonettes the citations come from the *Vetus Latina* translation.[54] In some, the words of the Bible are quoted precisely as they are written, while in others the word order is changed, or several different passages are combined to form one pseudo-quotation.[55] Elsewhere in the *LPR* biblical quotes provided by Agnellus almost always follow the Vulgate, in a variety of different contexts, including quotes from documents and inscriptions, references within narrative, and identification of parts of the liturgy.[56] This discrepancy can be explained if Agnellus sometimes copied sermons written before the sixth century, when the Vulgate replaced the *Vetus Latina* in common use.

Content of the sermonettes in the LPR

In content, too, the sermonettes by and large do not fit into easily definable categories; indeed, their brevity and their choppiness suggest rather that they are fragments of longer sermons or other exegetical or exhortatory works. Some of them seem to be made up of two different concepts, linked together by a specific biblical phrase. Some of the passages are exegetical in tone, that is, they interpret a specific scriptural passage with references to other pas-

---

52. 166b, which is styled as prophecy, and should probably be considered as really belonging with 166a; see below.

53. In particular, sermonettes 18, 64, 109, 166.

54. In sermonettes 55, 104, 105, 116, and 166 some of the biblical passages quoted are identical to those in the Vulgate, while others are closer to the *Vetus Latina*.

55. Especially in cc. 45, 54, 68, 104.

56. *LPR*, cc. 17, 19, 25, 27, 29, 30, 37, 52, 60, 120, 131, and 136. Of these quotations, only the one in c. 25 corresponds to the *Vetus Latina* instead of the Vulgate; this passage (Isa. 58:9) is also quoted in the same form in sermonette 105.

sages; others explain a specific moral or eschatological point, including several that excoriate bad bishops and praise good ones, and some that warn about evil and the end of days.

Several of the sermonettes are made up partly or wholly of exegesis of biblical passages.[57] While the interpretations often contain ideas that can be found in the works of earlier authors, Agnellus's method of presentation, including his use of biblical quotations, often varies significantly from the known examples. Furthermore, the methods of exegesis differ between these sermonettes, or even within the same sermonette. As an example, let us examine the two sermonettes found in c. 18. Sermonette 18a begins by explaining the metaphor of the mustard seed, from Luke 17:6. The metaphor of virtue appearing when saints are martyred is followed by an explanation of the two types of martyrdom, literally, death for the faith, and metaphorically, suffering in spirit for the faith. These concepts are found in works by Augustine, Caesarius of Arles, Peter Chrysologus, Gregory the Great, and Isidore of Seville.[58] However, the ideas are greatly elaborated in the *LPR*, and the use of a series of words to describe both the carnal and the spiritual martyrial acts is not found in any of the earlier examples.

To conclude 18a, Agnellus quotes Paul's instruction to the Romans: "be wise in good, and simple in evil" (Rom. 16:19). This reminds Agnellus of a similar phrase in Christ's instructions to his apostles, "Be ye therefore wise as serpents and simple as doves" (Matt. 10:16).[59] Sermonette 18b is devoted to explaining the contradiction between the latter phrase and various other passages that define the serpent as evil. In structure it is quite different from the first part. In 18a, the passage from Luke is explained by providing a rhetorically elaborate interpretation of its meaning. In 18b, the pas-

---

57. Those in *LPR*, cc. 18a, 18b, 45a, 45b, 55a, 55b, 88, 105a, 116b.

58. Peter Chrysologus, *Sermon* 98.5, as is the word *teratur* describing the crushing of the seed. Identified by Holder-Egger, *LPER*, 286, n. 3. See also Gregory the Great, *Moralia in Iob*, pref. 2.6, Caesarius of Arles, *Sermon* 214.1; Gregory the Great, *Homiliae in Evangelia* 2.35.7; Gregory the Great, *Dialogi* 3.26.7; and Isidore of Seville, *Etymologiarum* 7.11.4. Holder-Egger, *LPER*, 286, n. 4, cites the works by Gregory and Isidore.

59. Cf. Augustine, *Sermonum classes quatuor* 64.2–3.

sage from Matthew is explained with references to other passages relating to serpents, from both the Old and New Testaments. Phrases in the passage from Matthew are repeated so that they may be explained individually. Again, similar interpretations can also be found in exegetical works by Jerome and Augustine.[60]

Two distinct styles of exegesis are found. One style consists of presenting several biblical passages that contradict each other on some specific point and reconciling them using a variety of additional passages (cc. 18b, 45b, 105a with 116b, and 109). The other style is made up of the presentation of a variety of interpretations of one passage or concept, sometimes using biblical examples but not quoting other passages directly as support (cc. 18a, 45a, 55a, 55b, and 88). While perfectly self-contained as exegesis, the sermonettes of this type generally have no apparent connections with the history of the bishops of Ravenna, although Agnellus sometimes makes awkward attempts to relate them to the bishop in whose Life they appear.[61] Other sermonettes, by contrast, do correspond better to the main preoccupations of the *LPR*.

If any subject is appropriate to a sermonette in the *LPR*, it is the qualities of good and bad bishops. We have already seen that Agnellus's antagonism toward particular bishops, including George, was one of his motivations for writing, and he is often taken to account for the several sermonettes that excoriate bad bishops in a very personal way. These are found in cc. 100a, 100b, 104, 105b, 109, and 116a, in addition to various statements in a similar vein from cc. 13, 23, 58, 82, and 118. The contrast between the saintly bishops of the past with the corrupt ones of Agnellus's time, a general theme of the *LPR*, is made explicit in the sermonettes; this theme is also a stylized literary form with comparable examples from other works. At least two biblical passages describe the ideal conduct of bishops, Christ's description of the Good Shepherd in John 10:11–16, and Paul's rules for a bishop in 1 Timothy 3:1–7;

---

60. Jerome, *Commentaria in Evangelium Matthei*, on Matt. 10:16 (suggested by Holder-Egger, *LPER*, 287, n. 10); Augustine, *Sermonum classes quatuor*, 64.3.

61. *LPR*, cc. 17, 45, 54, 105, and 116.

analysis of these passages formed the subject of many sermons and exegeses about bishops. Thus, although of all the sermonettes these are the ones most likely to have been composed by Agnellus, it is possible that he found them elsewhere.

All of the sermonettes lay similar crimes at the feet of the bishops: they devour and waste the wealth of the Church, and they do not associate with their clergy. Other literary works treat the same subjects. In two sermons Gregory the Great admonishes bishops for their various crimes, in one case specifically when he is commenting on John 10:11–16. Gregory is more concerned with the crime of remaining silent in the face of sin among the flock, however, than with outright financial corruption.[62] Peter Chrysologus, too, discusses the concept of the Good Shepherd and the Mercenary twice, but he is likewise concerned mainly with the pastor's task of keeping the wolf (sin) from his flock.[63] The metaphors of pastor, wolf, and sheep appear repeatedly in these Patristic sermons. While Agnellus's sermonettes also sometimes use the metaphors of pastor and sheep, especially in cc. 82 and 118, in them the wolf is equated with the bad bishop rather than with sin.

Two sermonettes, in cc. 68 and 166, take as their subject the "end and destruction of the world" (c. 68). This theme follows from the previous one; bad bishops are one sign that the end of the world is at hand. Sermonette 166, after an introduction about the nature of prophecy, consists essentially of a list of all the evils that will foretell the end of the world, described in great detail: civil strife, external invasion, the natural disasters of Matthew 24, the rise to ecclesiastical power of foolish and evil men, the decline of Ravenna and the Roman Empire, the overthrow of the Church, the sterility of the earth, youth mocking their elders and servants marrying their masters' daughters, and so on. Certain statements might seem to have specific applications to Agnellus's situation, or to the political situation of the time, were it not for the fact that the list of evils is so comprehensive that not all of them could

---

62. Gregory the Great, *Homiliae in Evangelia* 1.14.1–3 and 1.17.14.
63. Peter Chrysologus, *Sermons* 40.3–4 and 173.1–2.

specifically apply.[64] The conclusion, that the audience should not give in to sin, includes an extended metaphor of the human body. The entire chapter forms a complete sermon, with a rhetorical introduction, body, and conclusion, perhaps the only such complete work in the *LPR*.

Lists of disasters at the end of the world are found in several known sermons,[65] but the longest and most detailed are those by Gregory the Great.[66] The decline of the Roman senate, the emptiness of the cities, the slaughter of peoples, and other disasters are all mentioned as signs of the weariness of the world.[67]

A few sermonettes remain whose subjects cannot be categorized. The one in c. 64 is an exuberant invitation to the eucharistic banquet, full of metaphors and biblical quotes about bread and wine. In c. 97, following the story of Rosamunda's murder of her husband, the Lombard king Alboin, there is a vehement warning against women. Generally taken to be a sign of Agnellus's misogyny, it warns men not to give in to their wives, and provides examples of wicked women from the Bible.

Finally, there is Agnellus's appeal to his audience in c. 54, which is usually understood literally as evidence that Agnellus composed the *LPR* under time constraints and hence very quickly. As has been suggested above, it is possible that this sermonette was inserted, along with other passages in a similar vein, in order to mask long periods of idleness; whatever the reason, Agnellus might have borrowed the text from another work. The entire text is addressed to *dilectissimi* in the second person plural, itself a typical device of sermons. Furthermore, several biblical passages are introduced to

---

64. As Testi-Rasponi suggests ("I documenti," 8), with regard to the damage inflicted on Sant' Apollinare in Classe by the Saracens. Lanzoni, "Il 'Liber Pontificalis,'" 366, suggests that these comments refer to the battles between the sons and grandsons of Charlemagne.

65. E.g., pseudo-Ambrose, *Sermon* 24; Caesarius of Arles, *Sermon* 71; Peter Chrysologus, *Sermon* 83.3.

66. E.g., Gregory the Great, *Homiliae in Hiezechihelem* 2.6.22–4.

67. Gregory the Great, *Homiliae in Evangelia* 1.1.1, commenting on Luke 21, the equivalent passage to Matt. 24.

illustrate Agnellus's points, and the lists of tortures seem almost to have been taken from a *Passio*. On the other hand, specific references to the pontifical (twice), to Agnellus's age, and to the Lives of Aurelian and John, indicate that even if Agnellus did borrow structure and phrases, he tailored the text to fit his own circumstances. Even where other sermonettes are linked at the beginning or end to the historical narrative, or where their subject matter is appropriate to the history just related, internally they are entirely independent of the narrative and the composition of the *LPR*. I have considered c. 54 as a sermonette because of its many specific stylistic features, but it differs from the others in that it contains so many personal elements. Personal references, however, are not unknown in early medieval sermons. In some of Gregory the Great's homilies, the desire of his audience to hear his words is frequently expressed as the reason for his preaching, the external concerns that keep him from preaching are provided in detail, and health problems are also mentioned.[68]

The differences between the sermonettes are so striking that only two conclusions are possible: either Agnellus was imitating a large variety of works while composing his own sermonettes, or he was importing sections of other texts that have not survived. It is quite possible that he had either a collection of homilies or a book of exegetical fragments, from which he took various pieces that he then recombined and rewrote. That the sources were sermons would explain the instances of address to the audience found in the sermonettes, which Agnellus would then have simply copied along with the content.[69]

The subject matter and the interpretations found in the sermonettes are similar to those of the sermons of various Patristic authors, most notably Peter Chrysologus and Gregory the Great. Both of these preachers had specific ties to Ravenna, acknowledged by Agnellus; it is surely worth noting that Gregory's homi-

---

68. E.g., Gregory the Great, *Homiliae in Hiezechihelem* 1, pref.; ibid., 2.10.24; ibid., 1.11.5–6 and 29; *Homiliae in Evangelia* 2.21 and 2.22.1; cf. also *Moralia in Iob, ad Leandrum* 5.

69. Testi-Rasponi, *CPER*, identifies this practice in certain places, e.g., 159, n. 13 (55a); 160, n. 22 (55b); 178, n. 7 (64); 221, n. 6 (88).

lies on Ezechiel are dedicated to a Bishop Marianus, who is none other than Marinian of Ravenna, appointed by Gregory. However, no sermonette exactly parallels any known sermon by these or other authors.

Some of the sermonettes that are distributed in different parts of the *LPR* can be combined to produce longer sermons; for example, the end of sermonette 104, in which the bishops are exhorted to behave themselves for fear of the Day of Judgment, leads directly to the sermonette in 105b, which begins, "and the overseers [*inspectores*] of the church are not only examined for themselves, but for their sheep." The use of the term *inspectores,* found toward the end of 104, the address to the *inspectores* in the second person, and the continuation of subject matter of judgment, imply that 104 and 105b make up a single, larger whole. There are a few other indications of this. Sermonette 45b is broken in the middle by a statement that it will be continued "tomorrow" because of the weariness of the author; the passage may taken directly from Agnellus's source, indicating that it was a set of sermons given on consecutive days.[70] This set of sermons probably also contained 55a, since at the end of 45b the text reads, "In the future sermons I will explain as necessary the manifold things about the latter, . . . who dried up the river Etham," while immediately preceding 55a Agnellus says, "where in the life of blessed John I said that I was your debtor . . . over this question of the river Etham." These examples are evidence that at least some of Agnellus's sermonettes existed as longer works.

One work can be specifically identified. Agnellus states in c. 136: "He [Bishop Felix] gave us the *expositum* on the day of judgment, where it says in the gospel, 'When ye therefore shall see the abomination' [Matt. 24:15], which we have up to now. And this alone was saved by the priests, for he burned in the fire all the other volumes with his own hands." The sermonettes in cc. 68 and 166 both make specific references to Matthew 24, and indeed sermonette 166

---

70. This is a feature of Agnellus's text that was probably copied from collections of sermons; see below, "Oral Sources and Orality."

seems to be a complete and self-sufficient sermon. It is possible that Agnellus copied this sermon, by one of Ravenna's distinguished bishops, into the *LPR* as an appropriate example of a work by such a bishop. If this is true, it is strange that Agnellus placed the sermon in the Life of Gratiosus rather than Felix, unless this was because he needed to fill out the Life of Gratiosus.

The sermonettes have varying degrees of relevance to the main text of the *LPR*, and Agnellus integrates them with varying degrees of smoothness. Some of them are specifically connected to whatever the preceding subject was, as for example the interpretation of the Magi in Sant' Apollinare Nuovo (88), which has just been mentioned, or the diatribe against women (97) immediately following the story of the treacherous Rosamunda.[71] Those sermonettes about good and bad qualities of bishops (100a, 100b, 104, 105b, and 116a) occur either in the Lives of the good bishops of the past, as a contrast, or in the Lives of the bad bishops, as a warning: "Oh, how he was, and how [different] they are now!" (c. 104). The sermonettes about the end of the world (68, 109, 166a, and 166b) sometimes also are related to the evils of bad bishops, as a sign of the times: "but now it is destroyed by evil men. . . . Why? Because the end of the world is near, the finish and destruction of the world is near" (c. 68). Finally, as Agnellus specifically says in c. 54, some of the sermonettes are inserted simply to fill space, "lest this history appear too brief"; this is probably also true of cc. 55, 104, 109, and 116.

Agnellus himself does not particularly distinguish the sermonettes from the rest of the text, other than by the change of style described above. While he uses the word *sermo* many times to mean "word," he uses it to refer to the sermonettes only twice.[72] Some references to future discussions, such as in c. 84 ("but let us return to the sequence and discuss women later," which is generally taken

---

71. Perhaps also 45a, comparing the saintly Bishop John I with various biblical characters.

72. In c. 46, at the end of sermonette 45b: "in the following sermon," probably a statement taken directly from the source sermon; and in c. 105, "O beloved friends, this sermon . . ."

to refer to sermonette 97),[73] indicate that Agnellus knew that he had such a work available and planned to include it.[74] Thus his inclusion of the sermonettes seems to be deliberate rather than random, even if it is not entirely clear why he included particular subjects.

Most of the sermonettes are located at the end of a Life, often preceding only the account of the death and burial of the bishop. Testi-Rasponi suggests that the sermons mark the end of the lectures given by Agnellus as he read his work aloud.[75] While several characteristics of sermons do seem to have been adopted by Agnellus throughout his text to produce the effect of oral performance, the sermonettes themselves do not necessarily mark any particular divisions of the text. And yet, the sermonettes are distributed rather evenly throughout the text, with a large gap occurring only between cc. 116 and 166. Perhaps Agnellus simply felt that his work should contain moral as well as historical points, and he scattered sermonettes at regular intervals to conclude the Lives of some of the most notable, and provide texts for the least notable, bishops of Ravenna. As a type of work closely associated with bishops, and perhaps specifically connected to certain bishops of Ravenna, the sermonettes provide yet another way for Agnellus to express episcopal greatness.

73. Testi-Rasponi, *CPER*, 215, n. 5.
74. Other examples, already mentioned, in cc. 45, 46, and 54.
75. Testi-Rasponi, "Note marginali," 86–101.

WRITTEN SOURCES

Agnellus's historical methodology

In two passages, Agnellus describes how he has researched his work:

Prologue: . . . that I might reveal to your ears not only what I have seen of their deeds, but indeed what I have heard, those things which our elders have reported to me.

c. 32: I, Agnellus, also known as Andreas . . . have composed this abovementioned pontifical book from the time of blessed Apollinaris and after his death lasting almost 800 years and more. And when I found out what they certainly did, these deeds were brought to your attention, and what I heard from elders and old men I have not stolen from your eyes. And when I did not discover any history, or what their life had been like, neither from aged and old men, nor from buildings, nor from any authority, in order that there would be no gap in the holy bishops, in the order in which each obtained this see, one after the other, with God aiding me by your prayers, I have composed their lives; and I believe that I have not lied, since they were encouraging and pure and charitable orators and acquirers of the souls of men for God.

In these passages Agnellus names the sources he uses in his work, which fall into three main categories: oral tradition, written texts and documents, and his own personal experience (including inspection of monuments with their inscriptions and pictures). In the case of information derived from the third category, it is usually obvious what the source was. Agnellus is particularly specific about inscriptions on buildings and objects, which he often quotes, and whose precise locations he sometimes identifies. He is equally informative about the things he knows because he personally saw or participated in them, telling us the circumstances and locations.[1] Agnellus is not so explicit, however, about his use of the other two categories, written records and oral legends, and apparent references to such sources are sometimes misleading.[2] An examination of the way in which Agnellus used the written sources that we can identify will help us to understand the origins of other, less easily traceable pieces of information.

The *LPR*'s basic unit of time is the reign of a bishop. Some bishops with very long reigns—for example, John II (sixteen years)—have extremely short Lives, while others who reigned for only a short time—such as Ursicinus (three and a half years)—have relatively long Lives; the length of a Life is based on the amount of information that Agnellus was able to find about that bishop. Agnellus does not provide any external dates for the reigns of the bishops; all that is given is the length of reign. In fact, Agnellus provides very few dates at all, and those that appear usually come directly from a quoted source. Rather than rely on a numerical chronological system, he assigned information to a Life when he found the name of a bishop in his source.[3] Because bishops with the same name were generally not identified by numbers in this period, it was easy for Agnellus to put information into the wrong Life. This methodology has significant implications; Agnellus's seemingly arbitrary use of sources becomes more understandable, and some of his chronological errors can be explained.

---

1. *LPR*, cc. 26, 39, 70, 77, 83, 167–75.

2. Agnellus mentions only two written sources by name: the *passio* of St. Apollinaris and the *Chronicon* of Bishop Maximian. The latter is cited twice, but it is clear that Agnellus used it far more extensively than for these two passages. Perhaps only these two works are identified because they are products of Ravenna, directly by or about the city's bishops.

3. See Deliyannis, "Year-Dates," for a discussion of the ways historians, and Agnellus in particular, understood dating systems.

Episcopal lists[4]

Agnellus must have compiled a list of bishops before he began to write the *LPR*; he tells us occasionally that "for such and such a bishop I could find no information," indicating that he knew from a list that the bishop had existed, but could find no records, buildings, or inscriptions relating to him (cc. 19, 31, 53). It is probable that some type of record or records of the sequence of bishops of Ravenna already existed in Agnellus's day, on which he relied for information; indeed, some such lists are mentioned in the text. Agnellus tells us that in the mid-sixth century, Bishop Maximian "made another altar-cloth from gold, on which are all his predecessors; he ordered the images to be woven in gold" (c. 80).[5] Maximian must have had, or created, a list of bishops, possibly the first such list compiled for Ravenna, but it seems to have been somewhat different from the list made by Agnellus.[6] Perhaps the official list of the Ravennate church was altered after Maximian, resulting in the list known to Agnellus.

In the poem at the beginning of the *LPR*, the poet states that Agnellus "included their dates and names and sequence, since these were depicted on a wall"; this statement is usually interpreted as indicating a list of bishops, with the lengths of their reigns, painted on a wall in some church in Ravenna, probably the cathedral. Such a publicly displayed list would doubtless be the official list of Ravenna's church. We have no way of knowing when such a

---

4. For an excellent and comprehensive study of episcopal lists and their significance in early medieval Italy, see Picard, *Souvenir*.

5. Maximian's altar cloth, which has not survived to our day, may have been similar to the so-called *velo di Classe*, an eighth-century altar cloth whose border, surviving in the Museo Nazionale in Ravenna in fragmentary condition, contains portraits in medallions of the bishops of Verona with their names written above them. It has been pointed out that the chronology of the Veronese bishops on the *Velo* contains several errors (Picard, *Souvenir*, 515–19), which should caution us against accepting Maximian's altar cloth as necessarily accurate.

6. Picard, *Souvenir*, 124 and 483–84, suggests that Maximian padded the number of early bishops in order to make Apollinaris seem older, proposing in particular that Maximian had added an extra Probus (II) and an extra Liberius (II).

list would have been placed on a wall, but because this list must have originated with, or postdated, Maximian, we cannot assume that Agnellus had access to two independent early sources for the early bishops of Ravenna.

Historical and literary texts

Agnellus quotes several times from an annalistic source that spanned the fifth and sixth centuries; the exact nature of this source or sources has been under debate for more than a century.[7] Because the original annals used by Agnellus are now lost, it is difficult to say whether he always quoted directly from the work or whether he changed words and word order. Testi-Rasponi argued that Agnellus must have had a set of volumes containing historical writings that, by the ninth century, were all attributed to the sixth-century archbishop Maximian, as Agnellus says several times that he is using a chronicle written by Maximian.[8] Testi-Rasponi suggests that some of the writings were actually by Maximian, including the description of his voyages to Alexandria, but that the annalistic chronicle was a separate work, continued until 573, when Agnellus stops quoting it.[9] That such works would be bound together, and that Maximian may have even had a hand in the process, is perfectly likely; Agnellus, writing 250 years later, would have assumed that all of the writings in the volumes were attributable to Maximian.

Because his copy of the annals does not survive, we cannot defi-

---

7. The passages are found in *LPR*, cc. 22, 31, 37, 39, 42, 62, 76, 78, 79, 90, 93, 94, 95, 96; the notices refer to years from around 423 to 573. The first passage, in c. 22, is extremely obscure and does not correspond to any information known in any other chronicle; Agnellus or his source must have misread or conflated several different entries. See Holder-Egger, "Die Ravennater Annalen," 312–13, n. 5.

8. Testi-Rasponi, *CPER*, 202–6, n. 3.

9. Testi-Rasponi bases his distinction on the fact that Agnellus refers to *chronica* in c. 42, to *volumina* in c. 78 before the quotation, and then to *chronica* again before the annalistic passages. Testi-Rasponi suggests that Maximian's own work, the *volumina* quoted by Agnellus, was about the theological and political struggles that preceded the Three Chapters' Controversy in which Maximian was a major player (*CPER*, 201, n. 7).

nitely say how many, if any, other notices it contained that Agnellus did not copy. The subjects of Agnellus's quotations can be divided into six main topics: imperial events in Ravenna; Galla Placidia's life and related events; Theodoric's struggle with Odoacer; Theodoric's reign and death; the Gothic Wars; and the arrival of the Lombards. The first four topics are intimately connected with Ravenna and its monuments.

Direct paraphrases of several passages, all from Book IV of Paul the Deacon's *Historia Langobardorum (HL)*, are found in the Lives of John II, Marinian, and John IV.[10] These pieces of information relate either to events in Ravenna or to Byzantine and imperial history; they do not, however, include every event of this type in the *HL*. There are also several entire narrative passages in the *LPR* that are derived from the *HL*.[11] We have seen that Agnellus copied Paul's format for presentation of a distinguished ancestor (c. 146). The Life of Peter III contains the story of the Lombard queen Rosamunda, which is derived directly from the *HL*, although with many additions and changes.[12] Finally, in the Life of Sergius, Agnellus transfers a rather dramatic story found in the *HL*, about the origins of one Lamissio, to the Lombard King Aistulf. Again Agnellus alters the details of the story: in the *HL*, the mother is a prostitute, in the *LPR* she is the wife of the king; in the *HL* the mother throws her septuplets in a lake, in the *LPR* the king orders the quintuplets placed in a basket; in the *HL* the king is moved by admiration to save the one child that has grasped the spear, in the *LPR* the king announces that the child who grasps the spear will be saved. An ironic consequence is that in the *HL* the story really provides the source for the child's name, while Agnellus, who states

---

10. *LPR*, cc. 98, 101, 102, 106, and 107. Agnellus's citations are not direct quotations by any means; sometimes he replaces almost all of the words with synonyms, and sometimes he changes the word order around. For a detailed discussion, see Deliyannis, *CCCM* edition of *LPR*, Introduction, and Deliyannis, "Year-Dates."

11. The relevant passages are *LPR*, cc. 137 and 151, corresponding to Paul the Deacon, *Historia Langobardorum* 6.31. 49.

12. Paul the Deacon, *Historia Langobardorum* 2.28–30. For a detailed discussion of this borrowing, see Pizarro, *Writing Ravenna*, 119–41.

that his story explains the name Aistulf, offers no etymological connection.

We have seen that Agnellus was well acquainted with a late-eighth- or early-ninth-century version of the Roman *Liber pontificalis*. It is not surprising that he used the *LP* as a historical source, but because one of the main purposes of the *LPR* was to justify Ravenna's independence from Rome, Agnellus used this vehemently pro-Roman text subtly, never quoting from it directly but always responding to its information.[13] Every mention of an archbishop of Ravenna in the *LP*, up to the year 731, has a corresponding passage in the *LPR*.[14] Not only do the passages correspond, but Agnellus takes pains to present each event according to his Ravennate, anti-Roman bias, which means that his text often contradicts information in the *LP*.[15] Where he could not contradict the evidence of the *LP* regarding the control of the papacy over the old exarchate in the eighth century, he ignored it, and at the same time portrayed the popes in question as vindictive, corrupt, greedy, and unjust.[16]

---

13. He may have disguised his use of the *LP* for "facts" because quoting the work openly would give it a historical validity that he denied.

14. In the Life of Gregory III (731–41), Archbishop John [V] of Ravenna is listed among the participants in a council at Rome; in the Life of Stephen III, the events surrounding the death of Sergius and the election of Archbishop Leo, including the involvement of the pope, are narrated; in the Life of Hadrian I, Archbishop Leo is deeply involved in the affair of Paul Afiarta. These are the only three mentions of archbishops of Ravenna up to the time of Agnellus for which we have no corresponding information in the *LPR*, but this is mainly because the end of the Life of Sergius and the Life of Leo in the *LPR* no longer survive in the manuscript. For the reasons why the presence of John V at Rome is not mentioned, see Deliyannis, "Agnellus of Ravenna and Iconoclasm," 563–66.

15. *LPR*, cc. 112, 116, 124, 125, 137–43, 151, 155–59, 168. For a detailed discussion of these correspondences, see Deliyannis, *CCCM* edition of the *LPR*, introduction.

16. For example, he ignores several passages in the *LP* that assert the right of the papacy to control the former exarchate (*LP*, Life of Zacharias, cc. 9, 12–17, Life of Stephen II, cc. 26, 37, 47). It should also be pointed out that the inclusion of such passages in the *LP* is itself a political statement by the authors in the papal administration, who were as much concerned with asserting Rome's control over Ravenna as Agnellus was with refuting it.

The *passio* of St. Apollinaris was Agnellus's primary source for the Lives of Apollinaris, Aderitus, Eleuchadius, Marcian, and Calocerus. Certain details in the Life of Apollinaris are very similar to those in the *passio*, and in the Lives of Eleuchadius and Marcian, Agnellus mentions the *passio* by name (cc. 4, 5).[17] Although today its date of composition is somewhat controversial,[18] Agnellus apparently accepted the *passio* as an ancient and accurate piece of historical writing; he may also have known of monuments within the church of Sant' Apollinare in Classe that repeated the information in the *passio*.[19]

Peter Chrysologus was bishop of Ravenna in the early fifth century, by far the most famous of Ravenna's bishops, and best known today, as he was to Agnellus, for his 176 sermons.[20] Agnellus used sermon 165 as a historical source: it was delivered on the

17. The *passio* is published in *RIS* 1.2:529–33; the relevant sentence is: "And thus in twelve years he made two priests, Aderitus and Calocerus, and made Marcian the most noble man and Eleucadius the philosopher deacons."

18. The debate over the date of the *passio* can be followed in Zattoni, "La data della 'Passio'"; Zattoni, "Il valore storico"; Lanzoni, "Le fonti," 111–76; Mazzotti, "Per una nuova datazione"; and Orioli, "I vescovi di Ravenna," 67–75. The arguments consist primarily of comparative linguistic analysis of the terminology used in the *passio* to establish a *terminus post quem*, correlated with historical events. Zattoni put the date of the *passio* in the 660s, at the time of Maurus and the *typus* of autocephaly; Lanzoni agreed with this date, but said that the legend must have developed over a longer period of time (134–42); Mazzotti pushed the date back to the 530s, to the time of the construction of Sant' Apollinare in Classe; and Orioli suggested the work was composed in the very late fifth century as anti-Arian propaganda. Some legends must have existed at the time of the construction of Sant' Apollinare in Classe, and we know that veneration of Apollinaris as a saint goes back at least to the time of Peter Chrysologus, since the latter's *Sermon* 128 was delivered in Apollinaris's honor. We will see, below, that the early bishops of Ravenna listed in the *passio* are different from those known to Maximian; therefore the *passio* must have been written at least after the mid-sixth century. Thus the most likely explanation is that it was composed in the 660s.

19. Agnellus also mentions silver plates inscribed with Apollinaris's story ("he set in silver letters the history of that martyr") and placed in his tomb by Bishop Maurus (c. 114). For a detailed comparison between Agnellus and the *passio*, see Testi-Rasponi, "Note marginali," 257–59, and Lanzoni, "Le fonti," 158–65.

20. Agnellus incorrectly identifies the second bishop Peter, rather than the first, as Chrysologus.

consecration of Projectus as bishop of Imola, and in it Chrysologus says that both he and Projectus came from Imola and were taught by Cornelius. Agnellus also names and partially quotes a letter written by Chrysologus to the heretic Eutyches and read aloud at the Council of Ephesus.[21]

Manuscripts and documents

Two literary dedications are alluded to by Agnellus, both relating to bishops of Ravenna. In c. 99 he says that Gregory the Great dedicated his "Liber pastoralis" to Bishop Marinian. Gregory the Great actually dedicated the *Liber pastoralis* to a Bishop John of an unknown see.[22] Agnellus seems to be referring to a personal dedication in a copy of his book that Gregory gave to Marinian, his friend and nominee to the see of Ravenna.[23] The second passage occurs in the deathbed scene of Bishop Felix: "'You have the books of Peter Chrysologus, which you see; he wrote ingeniously and most brilliantly'" (c. 150). Archbishop Felix collected and "published" the sermons of Peter Chrysologus in the form in which we now have them.[24] Agnellus does not mention Felix's compilation directly but seems to refer obliquely to this work in Felix's statement.[25]

Besides the sermons of Chrysologus and the *Chronicon* of Maximian, Agnellus mentions several other works written or commissioned by various bishops of Ravenna, and for some he says that they survived to his day. These include Eleuchadius, who was said

---

21. *LPR*, c. 48. No record of any such letter exists in the records of the Council of Ephesus; however, there does survive a letter written by Chrysologus to Eutyches before, rather than during, the Council. For a full discussion of the authenticity of this letter, see Olivar, *Sermones*, 89–94, and Testi-Rasponi, *CPER*, 141, nn. 1, 4, 7; 142, nn. 2, 3, 12; 143, nn. 2, 3, 6.

22. Paul the Deacon, in his *Life of Gregory the Great*, said that the *Liber pastoralis* was dedicated to Bishop John of Ravenna, but it is unlikely that Agnellus knew this, because then he would have put the information in the Life of John II.

23. Testi-Rasponi, *CPER*, 250, n. 4.

24. For a full discussion of the *Collectio Feliciana*, see Olivar, *Sermones*, 227–77.

25. Ibid., 46–47, 51.

to have written several works (*libri* and *volumina*) on the Old and New Testaments, the Incarnation, and the Passion (c. 4); Maximian's revision of the Septuagint, the Gospels and the Epistles after Jerome, and a book of masses (*missales*) for the liturgical year (c. 81); one surviving work (*expositum*) about the Day of Judgment in Matthew, by Felix (c. 136);[26] and a book of antiphons in Greek and Latin produced by Agnellus's ancestor Johannicis at the request of Felix (c. 146).

Agnellus had access to the archives of Ravenna, which, despite the fire of around 700, probably contained many documents pertaining to the legal rights and property of the Ravennate church. The following is a list of documents that Agnellus certainly or possibly saw while doing his research:[27]

Documents used or possibly used by Agnellus

c.	Document
32	*Acta* of the Council of Rome of 769
40	the (false) diploma of Valentinian III granting metropolitan rights
52	a description of gifts from Peter Chrysologus to the church of Imola
53	a charter of property acquisition under Aurelian
60	a *constitutio* of Pope Felix IV about the clergy and Ecclesius
74	a diploma of Justinian to Maximian confirming ownership of a forest
84	the will and testament of Bishop Agnellus

---

26. This *expositum* was probably paraphrased by Agnellus as the sermonette in c. 166.

27. Lanzoni, "Il 'Liber Pontificalis,'" 429–30, compiles a similar list, but includes as documentary evidence some items that Agnellus probably learned from sources other than documents: the money spent on San Vitale by Julianus Argentarius (c. 59), which was probably found on the epitaph on his tomb; information about the joint excommunications of Maurus and Pope Vitalian (c. 112), which was probably taken from the Roman *LP*; a letter from Pope Agatho to Bishop Theodore (c. 124), when Agnellus probably invented the letter; and the story of Sergius's trial at Rome (cc. 157–59), which was derived from the *LP* and other sources.

85   a diploma of Justinian to Bishop Agnellus granting him the Arian churches
110 a diploma of autocephaly from Constans to Maurus
115 a diploma of Constantine IV Pogonatus to Reparatus about church rights
124 an agreement between Theodore and Pope Leo II
143 a description of the gifts from Philippicus to Felix
158 a list of the money and objects given to/taken by pope Stephen

Perhaps he also saw:
111 a letter of Maurus or a tax list about the Sicilian patrimony[28]
123 some sort of document relating to the struggle between the clergy and Bishop Theodore
134 documents from the fire in the archive
144 a set of privileges from Philippicus to Felix
152 a document relating to the court case against the exilers of John V
154 a decree of Sergius in favor of the Ravennate deacons

The likelihood that Agnellus saw each document is based on what he says about it. Some are quoted directly (cc. 32, 60, 85, 143), while the one from c. 53 must refer to a document, for Agnellus says, "of this man I could not find any facts, except this one thing," implying that he had found one charter of property donation with the bishop's name on it. Several others are inferred from the specificity with which Agnellus mentions their contents; these citations are of two types. Certain documents are named (cc. 74 *praeceptum,* 115 *praeceptum,* and 124 *capitula*) whose contents, pertaining to the rights of the Ravennate church, are related in specific and legalistic terms. Agnellus probably also saw the two diplomas mentioned in cc. 40

---

28. While Agnellus claims to be quoting a letter from Maurus to the governor of the Sicilian patrimony, it is possible that he made the letter up for dramatic purposes; although the specificity of the items listed as tribute seem to indicate a fiscal document, in fact this list may have been made up also.

and 110, versions of which survive today.[29] Unlike those just mentioned, Agnellus does not name the diplomas as documents, but their contents are described as actions of the emperors and bishops involved. The second type of document can be inferred from the specific items or lists of items provided, which Agnellus must have found on relevant documents (cc. 84, 158). Finally, certain events in the *LPR* have no easily identifiable source, and documents have been proposed to account for Agnellus's knowledge of some of them.[30] The most remarkable thing about Agnellus's use of documents is that he took dry pieces of information and wove elaborate stories around them.

---

29. Both are contained in the *Codex Estensis*, the former on fol. 44r and the latter on fols. 43v–44r. The diploma of Valentinian is published in Marini, 94, n. 57, while the diploma of autocephaly is published in *RIS* ii.1:146.

30. Three of these involve disputes between the clergy and the bishop. In two (cc. 123 and 154), Agnellus says that each resulted in a *foedus* made between the parties as a conclusion; another such event in c. 152 may also have been known from a document, in this case one of judgment against those who exiled Bishop John V.

ORAL SOURCES AND ORALITY

While Agnellus often speaks of "putting pen to parchment," indicating that he thought of the work as a written composition,[1] he includes many phrases and passages that imply that he is reading the *LPR* aloud to a group of Ravennate clergy and citizens, and that he is writing the work at their request.[2] Furthermore, Agnellus refers many times to the "elders" who have provided him with information; these statements are generally taken to mean that oral tradition was one of his sources. The references to orality are somewhat unusual in form, and are moreover somewhat ambiguous. For example, much of the information attributed to "elders" can be traced to written texts used by Agnellus. When we examine all of the references carefully, it appears that in most cases an oral reference indicates ambiguity or uncertainty, but probably *not* an actual oral source or oral performance.

Oral sources

Agnellus introduces many passages with phrases such as "some say" *(quidam dicunt)*, "I have heard it told" *(audivi a narrantibus)*, or "our elders report."[3] All of the words in these phrases have to do

---

1. *LPR*, prologue, cc. 17, 38, 110, 141.
2. *LPR*, cc. 38–39, 58, 62, 79, 92, 154.
3. *Quidam* or *alii dicunt* or *aiunt* or variations—cc. 3, 6, 9, 10, 15, 17, 23, 24, 26, 27, 36, 41, 47, 62, 66, 73, 77, 94, 95, 97, 105, 112, 172, 174, 175. *Audivi narrantibus* or variations—cc. 15, 25, 35, 39, 70, 87, 125, 153. *Seniores retulerunt* or variations—cc. 17, 30, 31, 116, 117, 125, 127.

with verbal communication: telling, saying, narrating, recounting, and, on Agnellus's part, hearing. At first glance, a good half of the *LPR* can be attributed to "verbal" information.[4] In his prologue Agnellus gives an elaborate justification for using material taken from the tales of elders, citing as authorities Moses, Job, Mark, Luke, Gregory of Tours, and Gregory the Great. Moreover, Agnellus mentions by name only two of the written sources at his disposal, despite their importance to his work.

The *topos* of evidence from the elders is found in the works of many early medieval historians, as Agnellus notes.[5] Gregory the Great, for example, names his witnesses many times, and offers a justification in which he cites the same examples of oral testimony in Luke's and Mark's Gospels as are used in Agnellus's justification.[6] Bede, paraphrasing Gregory the Great in the prologue to his *Ecclesiastical History*, also justifies using oral evidence and names his own sources.[7] However, there is a significant difference between these authors and Agnellus. Whereas Bede and the Gregories identify specific witnesses by name and attest to their personal trust-

---

4. Lanzoni, "Il 'Liber Pontificalis,'" 427.

5. Agnellus says, "as it is read in the Lives of the Fathers: 'A certain old man told me . . .' [etc.]" This statement is generally taken to refer to Gregory of Tours's *Liber vitae patrum*, which Agnellus knew. It is equally possible that he is simply referring to saints' Lives in general, since he does not refer to Gregory by name. *Liber vitae patrum* 17. prol., contains Gregory's defense of using oral sources: "I fear that I shall be criticised by some, who will say 'You are a young man, so how can you know about the deeds of those in the past? How has what they have done come to your knowledge? Surely the things that you have written can only be regarded as fictions made up by you.' This is why it is necessary to make known the narrator of what I have learnt" (trans. James, 104).

6. Pizarro, *Writing Ravenna*, 72–73, n. 6. *LPR*, prol.: "Did not Gregory, bishop of the see of the Roman church, in several places in his *Books of Dialogues* recount thus: 'Such and such a man told me,' and other things like this?" In the *Liber dialogorum* 1.prol.10, Gregory says, "Those things which are known to me from the narration of venerable men, I tell unhesitatingly, on the example of sacred authority . . . since the evangelists Mark and Luke taught what they wrote, not from seeing, but from hearing." Agnellus's prologue also contains similarities to the dedication to Leander at the beginning of Gregory's *Moralia in Iob*.

7. Bede, *Historia ecclesiastica gentis Anglorum*, pref.

worthiness, Agnellus almost never does this, but refers only in a general way to "elders" or even just to "others."[8] Agnellus knew that the other authors had named their witnesses; that he himself does not may indicate that he could not, or that he had some other reason for being vague. And in fact, in one of the few cases in which Agnellus does name an eyewitness (c. 147), the story that he tells is borrowed directly from Gregory of Tours's *Vita Patrum*; thus this eyewitness seems to be an invention.

It has been shown that some of the oral-type phrases introduce direct quotations from written sources, in particular from a consular annal.[9] Many other passages introduced by these phrases are miracles that have been borrowed from other written hagiographies. In the latter cases it is not clear whether Agnellus himself has done the borrowing and has attributed it to "elders," or whether the legend had already been appropriated and was told to Agnellus in the context he gives it.[10]

It is interesting to note that in introducing a quotation from Maximian's *Chronicon*, Agnellus also uses an oral phrase: "as he says [*loquitur, dicens*] in his volumes" (c. 78). Furthermore, quoting from a supposed letter of St. Ambrose, Agnellus says, "Ambrose sang, saying [*cecinit, dicens*]" (c. 32). These phrases may provide the key to interpreting Agnellus's emphasis on "what the elders have told." If Maximian and Ambrose are "speaking" through their written works, then other authors of the past, or "elders," may also "speak" through their writings. In that case, Agnellus's "narrations

---

8. Pizarro, *Writing Ravenna*, 73. Agnellus names witnesses in only two other cases: George of Classe, who could validate the truth of his claim to have found the tomb of Petrus (c. 26), and the deacon Maurus, who saw the tomb of Johannicis in Constantinople (c. 148).

9. E.g., *LPR*, cc. 39 and 95. See Holder-Egger, "Die Ravennater Annalen," 312, who says that "the *seniores* are always cited when an old source was used." This is not quite the case; in c. 39 the word is *grandaeui* and in c. 95 *ut aiunt quidam*, while the word *seniores* is usually used in connection with borrowed miracles or legends. Giani, "Alcune osservazioni," 476–78, suggests that the facts so identified may have been derived from written sources, but it was the elders who helped Agnellus attribute historical facts from these sources to the correct bishop.

10. *LPR*, cc. 15, 17, 24, 25, 30, 35, 36, 87, 125, 153.

by the elders" could refer to any piece of information that Agnellus did not experience directly but learned from an older source, whether oral or written.

Moreover, much of the information that Agnellus attributes to "elders" is dubious in one way or another. Legends may perhaps have been borrowed or invented by Agnellus and applied to certain bishops. Some information, especially from the annal and chronicle, does not fit well in his chronological framework, which was based on the sequence of bishops. Agnellus thus uses the elders to authenticate the validity of these pieces of information, or perhaps to justify himself when he is not quite sure about something. It is significant that phrases of orality are almost never used for information from inscriptions or documents; these would not be considered testimony from authors of the past, and moreover they usually contain the name of a bishop, so that Agnellus knew exactly where to put them in his history.[11] Thus, just because Agnellus says that he has heard something from the "elders" or from "certain people" does not necessarily mean that his source was oral legend, even if he might have wished his audience to think that it was.[12]

Oral performance

Agnellus wrote the *LPR* over a period of at least sixteen years, yet he implies that he read at least parts of it aloud over the course of a few weeks. There are twelve places in the text in which Agnellus addresses an audience who is listening to him and mentions stopping or starting for the day.[13] He does this using phrases such as "now let these things suffice for today," "it is time for ending this *lectio*; we will see what follows tomorrow," "yesterday I was slightly ill and couldn't tell you about this man, but today I'm bet-

---

11. There is one case, in c. 66, in which Agnellus uses "some say," and cites information taken from an inscription, which he then quotes in its entirety.

12. Cf. Clanchy, *From Memory to Written Record*, 216.

13. *LPR*, cc. 17, 38–39, 45–46, 54, 58, 62, 79, 92, 100, 133, 148, and 154.

ter," and so on. These statements are usually interpreted as evidence that Agnellus read his text aloud to an audience as he was writing it.

Even assuming that the *LPR* was written to be read aloud, why should Agnellus have included statements of this sort in his written script or *post facto* transcript? There are other examples of this type of statement in early medieval literature, but they are not found in any type of historical writing. Rather, they occur at the beginning and end of sermons that were delivered in a series, often about the same subject. Agnellus knew at least three series of sermons, one by Peter Chrysologus and two by Gregory the Great, although he did not copy any of these directly into his own work. One other work possibly known to Agnellus, which is framed as a discourse although probably an artificial construct, is Gregory the Great's *Dialogues*.

Sermons, although they are oral compositions, are known to posterity only through their written forms.[14] For many of the Church Fathers it is not known whether their sermons were written down before or after they were pronounced, whether they were transcribed by someone in the audience, or even whether they were merely commentaries written in sermon style but never intended to be given orally.[15] Gregory the Great, however, in his prefaces to the Homilies on Ezekiel and the Homilies on the Gospels, explains how his oral works have been written down and collected together for publication after the fact.[16] To Gregory, the act of publication is an opportunity for correcting and polishing works he had writ-

---

14. McLaughlin, "The Word Eclipsed?" 98, notes that written sermons are actually oratorical, rather than oral in nature.

15. Longère, *La prédication médiévale*, 155–60.

16. Gregory the Great, *Homiliae in Hiezechihelem* 1. pref.: "The homilies on the blessed prophet Ezechiel, which are collected just as I spoke them to the people, I had abandoned because of many inrushing cares. But after eight years, at the request of my brothers, I have striven to look for the pages of the notaries, and, running across them by the will of God, I have emended them in as much as was permitted within the limitations of my tribulations." Similar examples are found in Gregory the Great, *Homiliae in Evangelia*, pref., and in Gregory's dedication to the *Moralia in Iob, Ad Leandrum* 2.

ten for oral delivery, although the only evidence of such an intervention by the author is found in the prefaces themselves. The text may have changed as a result of its transformation from oral to written form, yet the conventions of orality, such as references to the audience, are not removed but are perhaps also polished and made uniform.

The sermons of Peter Chrysologus existed in some written form up to the early eighth century, at which time they were compiled and ordered by Bishop Felix of Ravenna, whose collection was known to Agnellus. While Agnellus alludes only tangentially to this compilation, his story about why the blind Bishop Felix burned his own sermons illuminates the importance of the transfer from an oral to a written, published text (c. 150):

> When his death approached, he made the priests and clergy promise that whoever might have homilies or any other words spoken by him, they should bring them before him. When all of these had been brought before him, at once he ordered a pyre to be prepared, and burned them all in the fire. When he was asked by the priests why he had done this, he said, "I, deprived of my eyes, can see nothing or retract what I wrote in those books. Perhaps I might have overlooked something, or a scribe might have made a mistake; may no one come after me and find evil in my words."

Although the story may be apocryphal, the premise that homilies or other orally delivered works would be corrected before they were published is stated clearly.

Agnellus would have known oral texts such as sermons primarily through their written versions. Indeed, the stylistic devices that distinguish a published series of sermons from a written work of exegesis are the continual reference to an audience, through the use of the first person or the second person plural, and the phrases marking divisions between sermons. These are the very *topoi* used by Agnellus in the examples cited above. Let us now compare Agnellus's passages to examples from the sermons of Gregory and Chrysologus.

Several sermons of Peter Chrysologus end with the promise of continuation in the next sermon, or begin with mention of the previous sermon.[17] Chrysologus occasionally uses a phrase such as "let these things suffice for today" at the end of a sermon, and he sometimes says that he will continue on the same topic "in the following sermon" or that he is continuing yesterday's topic.[18] In each case the individual sermon is part of a series about the same biblical passage, or about continuous biblical readings read over the course of several continuous days. Gregory the Great, who arranged his own sermons for publication so that they would be in the order either of the liturgical readings or of the biblical texts, uses similar phrases, especially the most common "let these things suffice for today," and sometimes even quite lengthy statements referring to his personal affairs and illnesses.[19] It seems, then, that this type of phrase was an important rhetorical device in written versions of sermons; it emphasized the continuous nature of the collection, enabled the reader to visualize the setting and circumstances of the original delivery, and differentiated a collection of sermons from a purely exegetical work.

Many of the phrases of closure in the *LPR* are found in connection with Agnellus's sermonettes, which, as parts of real sermons, incorporate their rhetorical devices.[20] Most of these sermonettes also contain words and phrases indicating oral performance, in particular reference to the audience as "beloved" (*dilectissimi, carissimi*) or "brothers" (*fratres*).[21] However, some of the phrases of clo-

17. Testi-Rasponi, "Note marginali," 86–101.
18. Peter Chrysologus, *Sermones* 1, 15, 22, 75, 76, 78, 97, 98, 148. For example, he ends *Sermon* 1 with, "And since the series of reading compels us to speak more fully about this long parable ... let us inquire with common intentions in the following sermon," and *Sermon* 78, "We will treat the remaining part of the reading, God aiding us, in the following sermon."
19. For example, *Homiliae in Hiezechihelem* 2.3.23; *Homiliae in Evangelia* 2.21.1.
20. Those from cc. 17, 45–46, 54, 58, 100, and 166.
21. The particular phrases referring to the audience are extremely common in patristic sermons, but they originate not in oral discourse but in the Epistles in the Bible, another ostensibly written format. E.g., "my brothers" in the Epistles of Paul; "my dearest brethren" in James 1:19 and 1:16; and "dearly beloved" in 1 Pet. 4:12, 2 Pet. 3:1, 1 John 4:1, and Jude 3:20. But references to an audience by themselves are also

sure are not related to the sermonettes but are found in the "historical" parts of the text.

These passages referring to starting and stopping are usually interpreted literally by scholars, as indicating breaks in the reading of the text as a series of lectures. There have been two careful examinations of these passages, by Alessandro Testi-Rasponi and Francesco Lanzoni, each of whom divided the text into the individual *lectiones* or public readings and even assigned them dates.[22] The idea that the *LPR* was delivered orally has subsequently found its way into most of the literature on the subject. Rather than necessarily indicating a week of intense lecture giving, these passages may simply reflect the influence of the written sermon collections on Agnellus's style. And he had other reasons for including the statements.

Most of the statements about starting and stopping are found in the first half of his text. Yet it is impossible that these texts were written and delivered orally in the course of a few weeks. I have suggested above that Agnellus's borrowing of phrases and elements of style from sermons was intended to compensate for long breaks over the course of the time in which he composed these sections, particularly those in cc. 1–113. Agnellus was attempting to create the impression that his historical work had been delivered orally in a series of lectures by imitating such expressions of closure found in published volumes of sermons.

Finally, Agnellus may have been using the *topos* of a lecture with an audience as a way of showing that he was not writing completely on his own but had supporters and backers. In the prologue he states that he has been asked to write this history by the other clergy, and in another long passage he bewails the demands of the other clergy in compelling him to write this history, and how they are

---

found in works of other historians whose works were primarily intended as written texts, and indeed some of which Agnellus himself knew and quoted, such as the *History of the Lombards* of Paul the Deacon.

22. Lanzoni, "Il 'Liber Pontificalis,'" 360–68 and Testi-Rasponi, "Note marginali," 86–101 and passim.

afflicting him (c. 54). All of these passages create the illusion of a group of followers who have asked him, as one best suited to do it, to write this history and are listening to him eagerly. While many historical works are dedicated to people who have asked the authors to write them, these patrons are usually named. With Agnellus, we cannot in fact even tell whether anyone asked him to write the work, much less whether it was ever read aloud.

Agnellus's "false orality" goes beyond the use of general phrases; even a witness named and identified in the approved early medieval historical fashion was a smokescreen, devised to hide the fact that a story was borrowed from another author. The deliberate blurring of the distinction between oral and written is also seen in the lengths to which Agnellus goes to present his written history as a series of oral lectures.

Perhaps statements of orality, rather than providing definite information, imply the opposite. Following historiographical convention, oral testimony is used to validate the reliability of information, but Agnellus actually mentions it when he is uncertain as to attribution, in doubt as to accuracy, or fabricating a story outright; oral sources are contrasted with the certainty of inscriptions and named written sources. Indications of oral performance, used to refer to a specific literary genre closely associated with Ravenna's bishops, also serves to disguise lack of continuity in composition. There is thus a deliberate tension between oral and written in the *LPR*, created by Agnellus for reasons specific to the subject of the text, the way in which he wrote it, and the sources on which he relied for information.

ART AND ARCHITECTURE IN THE *LPR*

Agnellus is somewhat unusual among medieval authors in that he seems to have had a genuine, perhaps even professional, interest in art and architecture. This personal angle has captured the attention of modern art historians. Agnellus is looked upon as an unusually reliable recorder of such things, and the passages in the *LPR* about Ravenna's monuments, objects, and topography have been extensively cited and analyzed. As with other information, the way Agnellus describes or mentions art and architecture depends on the reasons that they are included in the text and what his sources were. The terms he uses to describe these things are derived from a variety of sources and should not necessarily be interpreted literally. Moreover, because Agnellus wrote at least three centuries after the construction of most of these monuments, his accounts of the magnificent structures that were built in the fifth and sixth centuries are based on his experience of them, not necessarily on original sources. Let us examine the implications of these issues.

What Agnellus describes

Agnellus names fifty-seven churches, chapels, monasteries, baptistries, or other religious structures in Ravenna, Classe, and their immediate surroundings. Most of these were built between 400 and 600, although some construction and decoration activity went on until Agnellus's time. A map with structures and topographical indications mentioned by Agnellus can be found on p. xv. The structural, textual, and archaeological evidence for all of Agnellus's churches are fully discussed by F. W. Deichmann in his four-volume compendium, *Ravenna, Hauptstadt des spätantiken Abendlandes*, and many have been the subject of separate studies.

Agnellus mentions more than just religious structures; he also includes the names of palaces, *episcopia*, private houses, public buildings, watercourses, bridges, and regions within the city. The topography of Ravenna and Classe has been extensively analyzed, beginning with Testi-Rasponi, who produced a map of early medieval Ravenna that is still widely consulted.[1] Testi-Rasponi identified locations for most of Agnellus's churches within Ravenna; later studies have focused on urban development, especially the locations of walls, gates, and waterways within the city, the identification of which has been refined by new archaeological evidence.[2] Agnellus gives topographical information for most of the structures he mentions, except, as Cortesi pointed out, for the few that are themselves landmarks.[3]

Agnellus often describes the decoration of religious structures, although in many cases his descriptions are made up of formulaic phrases, as will be discussed below. On several occasions he describes decoration more precisely, either using very specific terms for decorative materials or mentioning pictures.[4] In no case does he

1. Testi-Rasponi, *CPER*, between 116 and 117. See especially Bovini, "Le origini di Ravenna"; Mazzotti, "Note di antica topografia Ravennate"; Felletti Maj, "Una carta di Ravenna romana e bizantina"; Deichmann, *Ravenna* 2.3:11–75; Farioli Campanati, "La Topografia Imperiale di Ravenna"; and Farioli Campanati, "Ravenna, Constantinopoli."

2. For example, Testi-Rasponi identified five phases in the city's development, but it has been shown that there were only two such phases, the Roman *oppidum* and one expansion under Valentinian in the mid-fifth century (Christie, "The City Walls of Ravenna").

3. Cortesi, "Andrea Agnello," 60. These landmarks are generally the structures that survive today, such as San Vitale, the Ursiana cathedral, Sant' Apollinare in Classe, etc.

4. Nauerth, *Agnellus von Ravenna, Untersuchungen*, has analyzed all the descriptions of pictures in the *LPR*, comparing them to surviving examples and minutely examining the structure and language of the descriptions. Although she does not compare Agnellus's descriptions to descriptions of pictures, bishops, and patronage found in

tell everything about a structure's decoration, nor does he consistently mention any particular material whenever it occurs. For example, in the Neonian baptistry he mentions only "the images of the apostles and their names in mosaic and gold tesserae," and not the scene of the baptism of Christ (c. 28); he mentions the portraits of Maximian, Justinian, and Theodora in San Vitale, but not any other part of the decoration (c. 77). If these two examples and others in which the pictures survive can be taken as a guide, Agnellus is accurate in his accounts of pictures, as far as what he does tell. As Nauerth points out, however, Agnellus's accounts can not be assumed to mean anything more or less than exactly what they say, as the description of the imperial images in San Vitale makes clear: a similar account of pictures of Bishop Agnellus and Justinian in Sant' Apollinare Nuovo could refer to the same type of scene as in San Vitale, or to a very different representation.[5]

When Agnellus mentions a picture or an inscription, he usually tells where in the building it is located. This can tell us both about the layout of buildings that no longer survive and also about how such spaces were thought of and used in Ravenna in the ninth century. Within a church, Agnellus has words for the apse, the narthex, the wall surfaces, the north and south sides, various doors and side-chambers. However, the nave and aisles are not defined as spaces with particular names. Agnellus's terminology for these spaces and surfaces can be compared to surviving structures, and applied to monuments that do not survive (see Glossary for individual terms).

Finally many liturgical objects and vestments are mentioned and described, usually in the context of their donation to the church of Ravenna. These include altar cloths, vessels for the mass, *ciboria*, processional crosses, gospel-book covers, and other items of value. Many seem to have been known to Agnellus, especially when he provides an inscription, describes a picture, or tells that it still ex-

---

other texts, particularly the Roman *LP,* her evaluation of Agnellus's monumental sources for these descriptions is invaluable.

5. Ibid., 22–23.

ists. Agnellus occasionally tells of the use of these objects in his own day; while this is important evidence of ninth-century liturgical practice, it must be remembered that these practices cannot be inferred farther back in time.

Ravenna in the ninth century

Several times Agnellus mentions that a certain building has been destroyed or is in decay; sometimes he says that a building "is seen today." Other things, such as pictures and objects, are also described in this way. Agnellus's description tells us not only what physically existed in the 830s but also what was known about them. Although this aspect of the *LPR* is frequently overlooked, the state of knowledge that Agnellus reports is extremely useful, as it reveals how Ravenna would have been described to Charlemagne and other visitors, over whom the city still exercised a powerful fascination.[6]

Of the churches mentioned by Agnellus, most were still standing and presumably in use in the early ninth century. Only four are definitely described as destroyed: St. Euphemia *ad mare* in Classe, which had been flooded and had fallen down;[7] the Basilica Petriana in Classe, which "fell in an earthquake" in the mid-eighth century (c. 151); and the Arian *episcopia* of St. Eusebius and St. George, which Agnellus says "were demolished almost twenty-six years ago" (c. 70) There is evidence of other damage also, perhaps much of it the result of the same earthquake; Agnellus says that the disaster destroyed the apse of Sant' Apollinare Nuovo, although it had been restored (c. 89). The roof of Sant' Apollinare in Classe,

---

6. See, for example, Deliyannis, "Charlemagne's Silver Tables."
7. St. Euphemia *ad mare* is twice described as "demolished" (cc. 8, 97); St. Euphemia *ad arietem* is described as "which was formerly covered by water" (c. 168). These two appellations have been taken to refer to the same church; see Lanzoni, "Le fonti," 167 and "L''ad arietem.'" But Deichmann, *Ravenna* 2.2:358–59, notes that Agnellus says twice that St. Euphemia *ad mare* is destroyed, but says that Bishop Martin restored St. Euphemia *ad arietem*. See also Cortesi, *Classe paleocristiana e paleobizantina*, 120–25, who quotes twelfth-century documents that name two separate churches.

perhaps also damaged by the earthquake, had to be rebuilt by Pope Leo III around 814; if it had taken more than fifty years and outside funding to rebuild the church of Ravenna's founding bishop, many other churches must have remained in a similarly decrepit state. According to Agnellus, the Lombard king Aistulf, presumably after his conquest of Ravenna in 751, had wanted to rebuild the Petriana and had begun the work, but it was never completed; the columns he had set up remained as testimony to his attempt (c. 155). After years of sieges by the Lombards, many of the churches outside the city walls must have been somewhat neglected. In addition, with the end of the exarchate, the palaces and administrative buildings built by centuries of rulers must have also fallen into disuse.

And yet, in spite of a certain amount of decay, the past glory of Ravenna was still very evident in the ninth century. Much of the mosaic and painted decoration survived in the churches and palaces, and is mentioned by Agnellus. In particular, he tells us of many pictures and mosaics of various rulers in the city's history, and of their foundations and donated objects. Honorius sponsored the construction of St. Laurence (c. 36); Valentinian III is remembered for having built the city walls (c. 40). The latter's mother, Galla Placidia, founded several of the most prominent churches and endowed them with rich objects. In one of her larger foundations, San Giovanni Evangelista, there was a mosaic in the apse depicting Galla Placidia and various other "emperors and empresses," probably her daughter Justa Grata Honoria and her son Valentinian, who are mentioned in the dedicatory inscription (c. 42). Her portrait was also found on a gold candelabrum used by the church of Ravenna (c. 27), and Agnellus even reports a rumor that she was buried in the chapel of St. Nazarius in San Vitale, which is a chronological impossibility (c. 42).[8]

Nor were these the only imperial figures to be seen in Ravenna. Agnellus describes the still-extant mosaics in the apse of San Vitale

---

8. It is probably a later misinterpretation of Agnellus's own passage that led to the small cruciform chapel next to Holy Cross becoming known as the mausoleum of Galla Placidia; see Deliyannis, "Bury Me in Ravenna?"

that depict Justinian and Theodora and their court, radiating imperial splendor (c. 77). Another mosaic, depicting at least Justinian and Bishop Agnellus, was found in Sant' Apollinare Nuovo, on the interior of the entrance wall (c. 86). Agnellus also mentions the mosaic panel in Sant' Apollinare in Classe, which still survives, showing the Emperor Constans II and his sons Heraclius and Tiberius giving privileges to Bishop Reparatus, an event of the later seventh century (c. 115). Given that several other churches were also founded by or associated with imperial patrons, there may have been other depictions of this type, which were customary in such structures.[9] And, finally, there were the works and images of Theodoric, including at least one mosaic depiction of the Ostrogothic ruler on horseback, somewhere in the palace (c. 94), an equestrian statue bearing his name (c. 94; see below), and his mausoleum just outside the city (c. 39).

Agnellus provides us with much of our information about the palaces in Ravenna, and the results of archaeological excavation are often interpreted in light of his statements.[10] While Galla Placidia and Odoacer may have built palaces, their existence is based more on speculation than on any direct evidence from the *LPR*, and in any case they may not have existed separately from the other palaces by the ninth century.[11] Agnellus says explicitly that Valentinian III "ordered a royal hall built in the place which is called At the Laurel," which was apparently still visible in the ninth century.[12] Theodoric built several palaces in the Ravenna area, including

---

9. For example, pictures of Honorius and Lauricius in the church of St. Laurence, identified by name and associated with St. Laurence, may have given rise to Agnellus's legend of the founding of that church in cc. 34–35.

10. For recent discussions of all of the archaeological and textual evidence for the palaces referred to here, see Deichmann, *Ravenna* 2.3:49–58 and Porta, "Il centro del potere."

11. The thirteenth-century *Aedificatio civitatis Ravennae* says that Odoacer "made a palace on the River Padenna; and there he remained," but this statement may be based on a misreading of *LPR*, c. 39. Testi-Rasponi's theory, *CPER*, 119–22, that the area around the church of the Holy Cross contained a palace built by Galla Placidia, is also untenable; see Deliyannis, "Bury Me in Ravenna?"

12. *LPR*, c. 40; also mentioned in *Anonymus Valesianus* 55; cf. Deichmann, *Ravenna* 2.3:50. In c. 132, Agnellus mentions a *palatium Laurenti* as part of a topographical refer-

72 INTRODUCTION

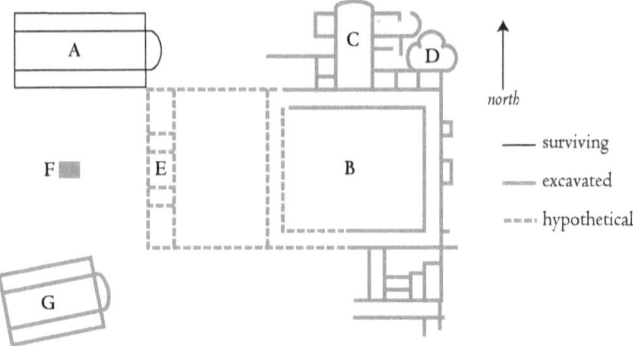

The excavated "palace of Theodoric," with a hypothetical reconstruction of the western area.

the one in the city that was the largest and most prominent by Agnellus's day, as it had subsequently been used by the exarchs.[13] Both Valentinian's and Theodoric's palaces were located in the southeast section of the city and probably made up one large imperial and administrative complex; the palace of Valentinian seems to have been to the south of Theodoric's later constructions, based on Agnellus's topographical references.[14]

The church of Sant' Apollinare Nuovo, originally dedicated to Christ, was probably Theodoric's "palace chapel," as Agnellus records that it was built by Theodoric (c. 86); excavations have revealed part of a large building complex, dating to the early sixth century, directly to the east of this church, which is accepted as be-

---

ence in the midst of a story, which may be the same as the palace *ad Laureta*, or may rather refer to an imperial palace in Caesarea. One of these may be the same as the palace *in Lauro* in which Agnellus says that Odoacer was killed (c. 40).

13. See Deichmann, *Ravenna* 2.3:51–52. In addition to this palace, Theodoric built at least one other habitation outside Ravenna, six miles north along the coast (*LPR*, c. 39). Agnellus, who calls this a *palatium modicum*, says that it was built within a bath and that the site had become a *monasterium*; it is from this palace that Agnellus himself has removed building materials.

14. *LPR*, c. 132: "having traversed Caesarea, and from the Wandalarian gate, which is near the Caesarean gate, having passed the Laurentian palace, he entered the [palace of] Theodoric, and he asked to be presented to the exarch." Cf. this description with the maps, pp. xiv–xv.

ing part of Theodoric's palace.[15] The remains consist of a large peristyle courtyard (**B**) flanked by rooms to the north and south.[16] Among the rooms to the north, and thus directly to the east of the apse of Sant' Apollinare Nuovo (**A**), two are particularly noteworthy: one, apparently on the central north-south axis, was a large apsed hall (**C**), with flanking spaces to the east and west near the apse; and the other, to the east of this space, was an apsed trichonch room, with its eastern apse projecting beyond the line of the eastern wall of the courtyard (**D**).

These remains have been compared to Agnellus's accounts of the palace of Theodoric and the exarchs.[17] In c. 94 Agnellus describes the location of a picture of Theodoric that was once found in Theodoric's palace in Ravenna:

There was a similar image of him in the palace which he built in this city, in the apse of the dining hall which is called By the Sea, above the gate and at the front of the main door which is called Ad Calchi, where the main gate of the palace was, in the place which is called Sicrestum, where the church of the Saviour is seen to be. In the pinnacle of this place was an image of Theodoric, wonderfully executed in mosaic . . .

"In the apse of the dining hall [*triclinium*]" seems to refer to one of the apsed niches or *accubitae* in a dining room, and it has been proposed that the triconch room found in the excavations was this space, since it was located in the eastern part of the palace, thus facing the sea.[18] However, the passage clearly states that the *regia*, or main gate to the palace, was located near the church of the Saviour; part of the latter still survives to the west of the palace, not near the excavated *triclinium*. If the whole passage is read together, it seems rather that Agnellus was referring to a mosaic in the dome

---

15. See Porta, "Il centro del potere," and Deichmann, *Ravenna* 2.3:58–70.

16. Porta, "Il centro del potere," 273, notes that the eastern wall found in the excavations of 1908–14 marked the eastern limit of the palace; exploratory excavations farther east reveal no traces of contemporary construction. The western part of the complex could not be excavated.

17. See esp. Porta, "Il centro del potere," and Duval, "Que savons-nous."

18. See Deichmann, *Ravenna* 2.3:53.

(*pinnaculum*) of an apse, in a *triclinium* which was located above the main gate (*supra portam*), and thus overlooking the sea (*ad Mare*), within the entrance building at the west known as the *regia*. Major palaces and villas often had more than one dining room, often for different seasons; it should not be surprising that Theodoric's palace may also have had more than one. Since the *regia* was at the western limit of the palace, only if the *triclinium* was in an upper story could the sea be seen from such a room, entitling it to the name *ad Mare*.[19]

Our understanding of the relationship between the palace and church is hampered by the limitations of the archaeological evidence. The northern edge of the excavated courtyard, if extended to the west, would run exactly adjacent to the south wall of Sant' Apollinare Nuovo, providing direct access between palace and church. The resulting courtyard, however, would be gigantic, an unusual arrangement for an interior courtyard of a palace. It seems more likely that the excavated courtyard (**D**) was much smaller, perhaps symmetrically arranged around the apsed hall on the north side. Since the palace was probably connected somehow to the church, there must have been other structures and perhaps even another courtyard to the west of the excavated courtyard, terminating at the west in the Chalke gate (**E**), which, as Agnellus tells us, was flanked by the churches of Sant' Apollinare Nuovo (**A**) and the Saviour (**G**).[20]

Finally, the palace in Ravenna seems to have had at its gates, until the ninth century, an equestrian statue of Theodoric (c. 94).[21]

19. Dining halls in upper storys are known to have existed in early medieval palaces. The *triclinium* of Leo III in the Lateran, according to later representations of it, was located in an upper story and included a balcony overlooking the plaza below (Krautheimer, "Die Decanneacubita"). A *triclinium* in an upper story may also have been found in the *episcopium* of Ravenna (c. 29, possibly the same as the dining hall in c. 162; see Rizzardi, "Note sull'antico episcopio," 719).

20. Agnellus mentions "the main door which is called Ad Calchi, where the main gate of the palace was ... where the church of the Savior is seen to be" (c. 94), and "the place which is called *ad Chalchi*, next to the church of St. Martin the confessor which is called the Golden Heaven" (Sant' Apollinare Nuovo, c. 119).

21. It should also be remembered that Agnellus, who was born around the year

Agnellus identifies the location of the statue in Ravenna as *in aspectu ipsorum* (in their sight); the passage is problematic because of an apparent gap in the text just before these words. He has just described the mosaic of Theodoric in the palace; if only a few words are missing, he would be saying that the statue was located close to the mosaic in the palace. But the sentence that is broken off is an impassioned statement about Ravenna's decline, and her citizens' quarrels; *ipsorum* could refer to the citizens generally, and could indicate simply a public place.

Since, as has been suggested, the mosaic seems to have been located near the western gate of the palace, it seems most likely that the statue was located in a courtyard in front of this gate (F).[22] Two important early medieval palaces are known to have had equestrian statues as part of their decoration:[23] at the Lateran palace in Rome the statue of Marcus Aurelius, thought to depict Constantine, stood close to the palace, possibly in a courtyard between the palace and the cathedral,[24] while in Constantinople, an equestrian statue of Justinian stood on the plaza called the *Augusteion*, between the Chalke gate of the palace and the church of Hagia Sophia.[25] It is likely that, as at Constantinople and Rome,

---

800, probably never saw the statue, at least not to remember it, since it was removed in 801 and taken to Aachen; Schmidt notes this in "Das Reiterstandbild," 5. Agnellus may have seen the base on which the statue had stood, since he mentions its construction and height.

22. A later tradition, which fixes the location of the statue on the "pons Austri" or "pons Augusti" in Ravenna, is clearly a fabrication. This tradition, based at least partially on the *LPR*, equates the Ravenna statue with the so-called *Regisole* statue in Pavia, claiming that the statue of Theodoric was never taken to Aachen but was diverted to Pavia. (For a more detailed discussion, see Deliyannis, *CCCM* edition of the *LPR*, Introduction).

23. Hoffmann, "Die aachener Theodorichstatue," 319.

24. Falkenstein, *Der "Lateran,"* 61, points out that the earliest evidence for the location of the statue between palace and cathedral comes from the tenth century, and that it is not certain that this is where the statue was in earlier times.

25. As described by Procopius, *De aedificiis* 1.2 and many later writers; for bibliography, see Lehmann, "Theodosius or Justinian?" 39–42. It is possible that Justinian himself appropriated an earlier statue of Theodosius; see Mango's letter in response to Lehmann. For a comparison of the Lateran palace of the ninth century to

there was a large public plaza between the palace and the church of Sant' Apollinare Nuovo, and that the statue was located there.[26]

Ravenna in the ninth century undoubtedly appeared to westerners as a highly Byzantinized city.[27] Despite the fifty years since the end of the exarchate, the glamor of Ravenna's status as a Byzantine capital lingered, and was especially apparent in the number of churches with particularly eastern dedications, such as St. Mary *ad Blachernas*.[28] The centrally planned church of San Vitale, with its similarity to churches in Constantinople, undoubtedly evoked the Byzantine capital also. The decorative materials of several churches had been imported from Constantinople, and this fact was also remembered in the ninth century; Agnellus describes some marble as coming from the island of Proconnesus, in the Sea of Marmara.[29]

Furthermore, certain topographical designations had probably been deliberately bestowed in order to evoke locations in Constantinople, especially those connected with the palace complex. The naming of the area near the main entrance to the palace "Ad Chalchi" was probably done in imitation of the Chalke gate in Constantinople,[30] while the name "palace at the Laurel" may be a translation of the Greek name of the palace of *Daphne* (laurel) which was the first imperial palace in Constantinople.[31] Indeed, in the exarchal period and later, the palace was commonly referred to as the *sacrum palatium*, which was a deliberate imitation of the designation of the Byzantine center.[32] It is not clear how far back these

---

the Great Palace in Constantinople, see Verzone, "La distruzione dei palazzi imperiali."

26. Lusuardi-Siena, "Sulle tracce della presenza Gota," 526. See also Farioli Campanati, "Ravenna, Constantinopoli," 149. The date of the establishment of the Marcus Aurelius statue at the Lateran is not known; Theodoric lived before the statue of Justinian was placed on the *Augusteion*. It is thus not clear who was imitating whom.

27. See esp. Farioli Campanati, "La Topografia Imperiale di Ravenna" and "Ravenna, Constantinopoli."

28. Deichmann, *Ravenna* 2.3:183–87.

29. See Glossary, s.v. *proconnisus*.

30. *LPR*, cc. 94 and 119; see Testi-Rasponi, *CPER*, 228, n. 4.

31. Farioli Campanati, "La Topografia Imperiale di Ravenna," 142, who gives other examples of connections between Ravenna and Constantinople.

32. Porta, "Il centro del potere," 277. Interestingly, the Lombard king Liutprand's

names go, given that Agnellus is in most cases the first to mention them. The western emperors, Theodoric, and the exarchs all had close connections with Constantinople, and any or all of them might have wished to imitate the Byzantine imperial palace in any way they could. At any rate, by the ninth century the associations were part of local tradition.

Spoliation in the Carolingian period. If memories of Ravenna's imperial past were apparent on all sides, by the ninth century they seem to have inspired the desire to remove pieces in order to appropriate some of that glory. One consequence of the decaying state of the city's fabric is that older buildings were often destroyed, or at least mined, for building and decorative materials. The best-known example of such spoliation is that done by Charlemagne, but Agnellus mentions several other instances of destruction or removal. He tells us that he himself dismantled a palace built outside the city by Theodoric, in order to use the building materials for his own house (c. 39). Bishop Valerius apparently did the same thing to two *episcopia* built by the Arian Ostrogoths; according to Agnellus the destruction took place around the year 816 (c. 70). A bishop of Bologna "carried off" a sarcophagus supposedly dating to the time of Apollinaris, and took it to his own church at Bologna around 834 (c. 1).

It is documented in two places other than the *LPR* that Charlemagne took *spolia*, that is, used building materials, from Ravenna. In his *Vita Karoli Magni*, as part of the description of the Aachen Palatine Chapel, Einhard notes that, "since he could not get columns and marble from elsewhere, he took the trouble of having them brought from Rome and Ravenna."[33] This is confirmed by a letter from Pope Hadrian I to Charlemagne, dating to 787, authorizing him to take "mosaic and marble and other materials both from the floors and the walls" of an unnamed palace in Ravenna.[34]

---

palace at Pavia is also once referred to as the *sacrum palatium*, with the same connotation; see Bandmann, "Die Vorbilder der Aachener Pfalzkapelle," 435–36.

33. Einhard, *Vita Karoli Magni*, c. 26.
34. *Codex Carolinus* 81.

Since Ravenna was no longer the residence of a high-level ruler, it is often assumed that Charlemagne dismantled the main Ostrogothic/exarchal palace, but we know from Agnellus that there were several other palaces inside and near Ravenna that may have been meant. In the Aachen chapel, the so-called "throne of Charlemagne" is made of antique spolia, as are most of the columns, including some of green porphyry and red Egyptian granite. None of these pieces can be definitely linked to Ravenna, but the rarity and high quality of the stones would justify bringing them all the way from Italy.

Agnellus does not mention the removal of these building materials by Charlemagne, but he does tell us of an event that took place some fourteen years later, just after Charlemagne's imperial coronation.[35] Agnellus tells of an equestrian statue whose rider was accepted as being Theodoric, although Agnellus relates that some thought it had actually been made as a statue of the emperor Zeno: Charlemagne took this statue back to Francia and set it up in his palace at Aachen (c. 94).[36] The presence of the statue in Aachen is confirmed by a poem written in 829 by Walahfrid Strabo, entitled *De imagine Tetricis*.[37] Strabo describes such a figure in the palace complex at Aachen and interprets it allegorically as a sym-

35. As Löwe pointed out, "Von Theoderich dem Großen," 67. Löwe remarks that this statue was probably not the only equestrian monument available to Charlemagne, and sees his choice of a statue of Theodoric as significant; see below. However, there are few recorded equestrian statues from this time, so it is not so obvious that others were available to Charlemagne.

36. This statement by Agnellus seems to have resulted from his confusing a passage in Jordanes's *Getica*, which tells that Zeno did erect a statue of Theodoric, to honor him, before the gate of the palace in Constantinople (see Testi-Rasponi, *CPER*, 231, n. 1; also Hoffmann, "Die aachener Theodorichstatue," 321). But Agnellus probably did not know Jordanes's work directly.

37. Strabo, *Versus in Aquisgrani Palatio*. Although Grimm, *Das Reiterstandbild*, and others have suggested that the statue had never really been taken to Aachen and that Strabo's poem was based on a statue somewhere else, these ideas are not generally accepted; see especially Schmidt, "Das Reiterstandbild," for a clear summary of the various arguments. Testi-Rasponi, *CPER*, 230–31, n. 4, suggests that Agnellus knew the poem of Strabo, written almost ten years earlier, and that he was introduced to it during his trip to Pavia (cf. c. 171).

bol of pride and greed. Some physical details that correspond to the statue described by Agnellus can be picked out, with difficulty, from Strabo's allegorical language: it was gilded, the rider held a shield in his left hand and a spear in his right and was identified as Theodoric. In addition, according to Strabo, the horse was depicted in a running position and was part of a figural group that included smaller, ungilded figures beneath it. It stood atop a column or on a pedestal with columns, in a park in the palace.[38] The exact identity of the statue, and its fate after the reign of Charlemagne, are a mystery; the significance of this statue in the context of the Carolingian Renaissance has been debated for a century and a half.[39]

Charlemagne was not the last emperor to take *spolia* from Ravenna. Agnellus describes a large piece of polished porphyry in the church of St. Severus, which was taken to Francia on the order of Emperor Lothar and used as a table in the church of St. Sebastian; Agnellus knows this because he himself was the one who supervised its packing, "but with my heart full of grief" (c. 113).[40]

Agnellus disapproved of the removal of Ravenna's material heritage by outsiders, and he injects a strong moral commentary into accounts of such appropriation.[41] The theft of the sarcophagus of Rufus by the bishop of Bologna was apparently a failure: "But

---

38. See Hoffmann, "Die aachener Theodorichstatue."

39. Ably summarized by Hoffmann, ibid., 11, n. 21, and Thürlemann, "Die Bedeutung der Aachener Theoderich-Statue," 26–28. In addition to these two articles and the bibliographies cited in them, see also Bovini, "Le vicende," and Beutler, *Statua*, 96–101.

40. One other later source mentions marble columns from Ravenna being used at Ingelheim; in his eulogy of Charlemagne, the poet Saxo states, "To which he ordered marble columns from Rome, he gave noble ones from beautiful Ravenna." Saxo Poeta, *Annalium de gestis Caroli Magni* 5:439–40.

41. Agnellus does not seem to object to spoliation by citizens of Ravenna, such as himself and Valerius, if the objects remain in the city, but only condemns removal of material from Ravenna. This includes his condemnation of certain bishops in whose reigns certain church treasures were "lost" (often directly stating that they were given as bribes or sold for cash): Petronax (cc. 80, 149), Sergius (c. 158), Martin (c. 169), and George (cc. 173, 174).

what did it benefit him, that he cast out others from it? He was not placed in it, for he acted too slowly to establish it" (c. 1). Significantly, he relates two legends about spoliation that is foiled by miraculous intervention.[42] In one case, the splendid sarcophagus of the *cubicularius* Lauricius is going to be removed by an unknown emperor for his own use. A vision of Lauricius tells the night watchmen to smear the surface with ash and water, after which its beauty vanishes and it is not removed (c. 36). In the other case, "a certain king of the Vandals" plans to remove the pavements from Sant' Apollinare Nuovo. The night before the lifting of the stone is to take place, a wind races through the church and all the marbles are smashed, and thus are not removed (c. 87). The Vandals no longer existed in the time of Bishop Agnellus, but it is possible that Agnellus was using the word as it is used today, to refer to destroyers. In one sense, these stories are obviously meant to explain the decrepit appearance of specific objects that were once magnificent. In another sense, the oblique references to the kings who planned to remove these objects from Ravenna, and the preference shown for the objects' remaining in Ravenna in a spoiled condition rather than being taken away, is a clear comment by Agnellus on the practice of the Carolingian emperors of removing such materials.

A Carolingian emperor appears in one other story related by Agnellus, and this one also is related to the treasures of Ravenna. In recounting a list of liturgical objects given to Bishop Felix by the Byzantine emperor Philippicus, Agnellus mentions:

one crown of ordinary gold, but having such precious gems, that in our day, when a Jewish merchant was asked by the emperor Charles how much he could sell it for, he stated that if all the wealth of this church and all the ornaments and houses were sold, he could not make up the price. (c. 143)

The emperor must be Charlemagne,[43] who obviously did not take this object, as Agnellus adds that "It disappeared at the time of

---

42. As noted by Pizarro, *Writing Ravenna*, 21.
43. Although Charles the Bald enters Agnellus's narrative in cc. 173–74 (in the sto-

George," that is, in 843. The story may simply be meant to provide reputable testimony to the value of the crown, but it also hints at the excessively rapacious interest that Charlemagne, in Agnellus's opinion, had displayed toward Ravenna's treasures.

Structures, church decoration, liturgical furnishings, and other examples of art and architecture appear throughout the text of the *LPR*. Why are these things mentioned, and what do terms used to describe them mean? What can we learn about the objects they refer to, what can they tell us about Agnellus's technical vocabulary, and about the role played by art and architecture in historical texts? These questions are interrelated: the contexts in which monuments are mentioned affect the words used to describe them, as do the sources that Agnellus used for information about them. Terms may carry specific connotations relating to other texts. Separating Agnellus's literary aims from his own technical vocabulary is not always easy; it cannot be said that just because he uses a word, it must have been current in the ninth century. And separating the rhetorical use of words from the reality they reflect poses other problems. At the back of this volume a glossary of the terms used by Agnellus is provided.

Art and architecture appear primarily in three different contexts in the *LPR*. Monuments are the objects of patronage, displaying the piety and power of their donors; they are sources of information about Ravenna's history, through their inscriptions and pictures; and they appear in narrative scenes as the settings or objects of the stories. In each of these contexts the language is determined by, and serves to identify, the type of discourse and the function of these objects within the *LPR*. It is therefore important that the contexts and sources of these descriptions first be identified; only then may the terms be compared to objects and structures that still survive.

---

ry in which the loss of this and other objects is told), he is always called *rex*, never *imperator*.

Patronage. Monuments are objects of patronage, displaying the piety and power of their donors, a *topos* derived from the Roman *LP*. The importance of the Roman *LP* to the *LPR*, in the matter of patronage, cannot be overemphasized. There has been a tendency to downplay the influence of the Roman work on Agnellus, and one result of this is that the passages relating to art and architecture have not been compared. Sometimes more has been read into Agnellus's descriptions than is necessarily there, in that he often uses stock phrases derived from the Roman *LP* and elsewhere to glorify a monument. As has been shown above, Agnellus uses terminology very similar to that of the *LP* to describe decorative elements in a church, liturgical furnishings, and the materials from which they were made; in other words, in descriptions relating to patronage. In these contexts, therefore, it should be remembered that phrases such as "most precious marbles," "various figures," "gold tesserae," and the like probably reflect the language appropriate for such an account of donation and construction, rather than any specific decorative materials.

The Roman *LP* was based on archival records of donations to the Church of Rome.[44] Although the fire in the archive no doubt destroyed many of Ravenna's records of this type, the specificity of terms in the *LPR* related to liturgical objects donated to or removed from the church indicates that some lists survived the fire. Lists of gifts given to the church, and possibly gifts given to outsiders by the Ravennate bishops are found in cc. 52, 143–44, 158, 170, and 173–74. The gifts mentioned in c. 52, given by Peter Chrysologus to the church of Imola, are described using very general terms, and Agnellus may have made them up. In the latter passages, however, he provides specific names and descriptions of objects, and in c. 143 he says that the information is from the "list made of them," an apparent reference to a list of some sort. A list of these objects, including some additional gifts mentioned in c. 144, would have looked like this:

---

44. See esp. Geertman, *More veterum*.

one crystalline bowl, large and decorated with gold and gems
two other bowls made of onyx, and decorated with gold and gems
one great container on which were images of men and various birds, of clear glass, like crystal
wine ewers, one of them beautifully carved
a water pitcher shaped like a hand
and a hand-washing basin with such a covering of silver on top as can no longer be seen by the sight of man in this time
two wine ladles of crystal
one crown of ordinary gold, but having such precious gems

In both cc. 158 and 169, Agnellus identifies the objects as bribes; in the former passage, they are "stolen" by a pope to whom they have been promised as the price of Bishop Sergius's release from custody, while in the latter passage they are in thanks for the aid given to Bishop Martin by Bishop John of Arles. In c. 170 the gifts are to the church of Ravenna from Charlemagne and include the silver table mentioned in Einhard's *Life of Charlemagne*.[45] In all of these cases, specific items are mentioned by name and description, and thus it is possible that they were taken from some sort of register. Finally, it should be noted that several items are said to have "disappeared in the time of Petronax," whose Life is missing; it is possible that these too were listed as gifts from the bishop to someone on such a register (cc. 80, 113, and 149). It must be remembered that the events from cc. 169, 170, and the Life of Petronax took place in Agnellus's lifetime, and he may have known the items directly.

Otherwise, Agnellus relies on his own experience of buildings and objects, particularly those with dedicatory inscriptions, to tell him about patronage. Some of his descriptions, therefore, are more personal than those of the *LP*. Although topographical references are a feature of descriptions of patronage found in the Roman *LP* and may be included in the *LPR* in imitation of this practice, the topographical references given are specific to Ravenna and must also be considered accurate for the ninth century; some of these

---

45. Einhard, *Vita Karoli Magni*, c. 33.

are also verifiable through surviving or archaeological evidence. Churches appear in these topographical references in two ways: either as the subject for which the reference is provided, or within a reference to another structure.

Agnellus always tells how he knows when something was built: from an inscription, because it was named after its founder; from the pictures of the founder(s) or donor(s); or, if he is less sure, from stories and legends. He quotes many inscriptions directly, and these are generally dedicatory in nature; he quotes the inscriptions of eighteen of the religious structures he mentions. He also uses words because he found them in dedicatory inscriptions; for example, he describes the *chrismataria* made by Bishop Maximian; in the subsequently quoted inscription, this is what the object is called (c. 80). Galla Placidia is said to have donated a lamp *(lucerna)*; the inscription on this object contains the biblical quote, "I will prepare a lamp *(lucerna)* for my Christ."[46] Other similar items that are only mentioned once may have had such inscriptions on them also.

Information. Not all of the monuments are described as objects of patronage. Sometimes Agnellus tells about them because they provide information about Ravenna or its bishops; indeed, when he describes his research methodology, he emphasizes his reliance on buildings and pictures.[47] The most notable examples are the portraits of bishops, which tell Agnellus what the bishops looked like. The tombs of bishops, too, are described sometimes in some detail, and many epitaphs are quoted, from which Agnellus took information. Agnellus describes such buildings and objects as he himself has seen them, using the *topos* of the eyewitness as verification of his information.

Agnellus frequently uses the phrases "and so we see it today" and "if you look there you will see." The phrase "up to today" is a *topos* in early medieval historiography, used by almost every historian as a way of verifying himself as an eyewitness or at least a secondhand witness.[48] Agnellus uses these phrases in the same way, as

---

46. Ps. 132:17; c. 27.   47. *LPR* prologue, cc. 32 and 108.
48. Even in the Roman *LP*, the phrase occasionally appears (Life of Vigilius, Life

verification of the truth of his statements, but not every mention of this phrase reflects his personal experience.[49] For example, in c. 1 he tells of a *monasterium* presumably near Rome, in which the imprint of St. Peter has lasted "up to this day"; where he learned this information is not clear, but it is very unlikely that he had seen it himself. Thus, although he says that some fifteen churches and various precious objects exist "up to today," we cannot rely completely upon the accuracy of these statements.

While we must understand that the very practice of offering firsthand testimony is itself a *topos,* fortunately Agnellus tells of his own experience in more convincing ways, in his quotation of inscriptions, for example. Often he gives less rhetorical, more realistic descriptions, especially of pictures; since some of the buildings, pictures, and objects still survive and correspond fairly well in both appearance and date, the reliability of his descriptions can be gauged.[50] Even as we take all of these passages as examples of Agnellus's personal experience, we must remember that his inclusion of them in his text serves the purpose of verifying and supporting his statements about the patrons of the buildings and objects.

Narrative. Finally, monuments form the settings of and are used in narrative scenes; in these passages Agnellus employs a variety of sometimes unusual words in order to embellish the scene rhetorically. A glance through the glossary reveals that many words are used only once in the *LPR* and that in the majority of cases these words are found in hagiographical or historical narratives. By itself this might not be unusual, but Agnellus uses synonyms of these words more frequently. Certainly in some of the narratives, especially those found toward the end of the *LPR,* Agnellus seems to have been deliberately using more elaborate language. His borrow-

---

of Zacharias, c. 25), inserting an author writing at a particular time into a text in which the author is generally nonexistent.

49. Agnellus uses the phrases *usque hodie, usque nunc, usque in praesentem diem,* and others at least thirty-five times, referring not just to monuments and objects but also to toponyms, liturgical practices, ecclesiastical privileges, etc.

50. This has been done by Nauerth, *Agnellus von Ravenna, Untersuchungen.*

ing of Vergilian phrases is an indication of this, as is his use of elaborate lists or descriptions to set the scene.

This reaches its height in the account of the civic strife during the reign of Bishop Damian (cc. 127–29). Pizarro has noted that this account is made up almost entirely of lists and sequences of various types.[51] Wherever Agnellus heard this story, probably from local legend, he presents it in a style that is highly embellished; the variety of words indicating structures and objects enhances the descriptions, and the same can be said of many other sequences in the *LPR*, which include unusual words for art and architecture.[52] An example are the words used for "house"; in most cases Agnellus uses *domus*, but in three passages he chooses other words: *mansio* in c. 128, *casa* in c. 129, and *villa* in c. 163. The use of these words does not mean that Agnellus was referring to specific types of structures in these three cases or that he did not know what these words meant, only that he was using their rarity to enhance the effect of his text.

The most unusual example of this, and perhaps the most significant in a consideration of architectural terminology, are three passages in which Agnellus gives lists of construction materials: in c. 73, a legend about the rapid construction of St. Stephen; in c. 130, a legend about a man hearing "all the building materials praising God"; and in c. 168, an account of the reconstruction of the roof of Sant' Apollinare in Classe. In each of these passages we encounter an accumulation of technical terms for building materials; undoubtedly Agnellus had experience with these items and used the words advisedly, but here their specific meanings are subordinated to their function as embellishment. Furthermore, many of the words can be found in other written texts from which Agnellus may have taken his vocabulary.

Agnellus did not necessarily take these words directly from his

---

51. Pizarro, *Writing Ravenna*, 156–58.

52. Especially *LPR*, cc. 26, 37, 83, 112, and 163. A few particular types of descriptions may be singled out. The language describing processions and civic celebrations is very similar in cc. 37, 39, 71, and 153; lists of gems, which are always the same and which reflect the symbolic lists of gems in the Vulgate version of the Bible (Exod. 28:8 and Apoc. 21:19–21), are found in cc. 80, 171, and 174.

written sources, or from other written accounts of similar scenes. Agnellus always reworked his written sources, and frequently substituted synonyms for the original words. A specific example of this in the context of church furniture is found in c. 14: Agnellus has taken the story from Gregory of Tours's *De virtutibus Martini*, but where Gregory's lector, reading an Epistle of Paul, stands "before the altar," in Agnellus's version the deacon reads the Epistle from the *pulpitum*.[53] Thus, while a few words can be traced precisely to known written sources used by Agnellus, in most cases even the borrowing of legends can be identified only by unusual words that Agnellus may have introduced precisely to distinguish his own work from his source.

As we have seen above, Agnellus was familiar with a wide variety of written texts, and his architectural vocabulary would have been enhanced by all of them. Two works in particular may have furnished him with many of the terms he uses, even if he assigns different meanings to them. One is the Bible, which provided terms and rhetorical forms used in the *LPR;* the other, as we have seen, was the Roman *LP,* Agnellus's model for accounts of patronage.[54] Some terms found in Agnellus's narrative passages are also found in the Vulgate, which may indicate they are being used for embellishment rather than to refer to specific items. For example, the *trabes* and *laqueares* (beams and panels) made of *ligna abiegna* (fir wood), in c. 168, are frequently mentioned as materials used in the construction of Solomon's temple. Other words and phrases that have particularly biblical connotations also appear frequently. The words *vectes* and *serrae* (bars and bolts), for example, which Agnellus uses singly or in combination several times, are commonly found in biblical accounts of city gates.[55] In a few passages, lists of gems are given as appearing on certain objects; the names of these gems are

---

53. *De virtutibus sancti Martini episcopi*, 1.5.

54. I have suggested elsewhere (Deliyannis, "A Biblical Model") that the models for the first redaction of the *LP* were the biblical Books of Kings and Chronicles; for art and architecture, there are many similarities between the language in the *LP* and the descriptions of Solomon's temple.

55. *LPR*, cc. 37, 92, 127, and 147. Cf. 2 Chron. 8:5, and Neh. 3.

always the same, and in fact go back to symbolic lists of gems found in the Vulgate.[56] The influence of the Vulgate on artistic and architectural terms in the Middle Ages, and indeed the influence of late antique terms for these things on the translators of the Bible, is a complex question that deserves further study.

Another influence is Isidore of Seville's *Libri Etymologiarum*. Isidore's influence has been identified in several passages of the *LPR*,[57] and it seems likely that Agnellus did know some version of the work. Oswald Holder-Egger noted that a few unusual words used by Agnellus are also found in the *Libri Etymologiarum*; significantly, two of these words are used in the highly embellished narrative sequence of cc. 127–29 mentioned above.[58] Furthermore, Isidore includes several long sections on architectural forms and decorative materials, especially in books 15, 16, and 19. A very large number of the terms used by Agnellus are identified by Isidore, including several that are found only once in the *LPR*, in the type of narrative we have been discussing. Isidore notes, for example, that "A building consists of a foundation, stones, plaster, sand, and wood."[59]

Isidore undoubtedly used as sources many of the works Agnellus consulted, beginning with the Bible, and a study of Isidore's artistic and architectural terminology would be invaluable. Here I would simply observe that such terms were readily available to Agnellus from literary texts, and thus their use in the *LPR* may have literary, rather than descriptive, aims. It cannot be said that Agnellus did not know the meaning of some of the words he used; but it is entirely likely that he used them deliberately for particular rhetorical effects rather than purely descriptive reasons.

If a word is used as embellishment, determining its exact meaning in the context is not only impossible but irrelevant. Informa-

---

56. *LPR*, c. 80, 171, and 174; cf. the twelve gems on the breastplate of the high priest (Exod. 28:8), repeated with slight variations (in brackets) as the foundations of the heavenly Jerusalem of the Apocalypse (Apoc. 21:19–21).

57. *LPR*, cc. 18, 40, 55, 64, and 98.

58. *LPR*, cc. 128 (18.6.7—*chelidoniacus gladius*) and 129 (19.31.19—*perscelidas*); the other word identified by Holder-Egger, *casula*, appears in c. 111; see below.

59. Isidore, *Etymologiarum* 19.10.2.

tion about liturgical or architectural practice cannot be derived from the presence of such words in the text; all that can be said is that their presence indicates Agnellus's knowledge of them and the possibility of his transmitting them to later readers. In the glossary, such terms are identified by a phrase such as "in a narrative that was derived in its plot and/or its descriptive framework from some other source." References to Isidore and to the Vulgate are provided, especially when Agnellus's meaning is different from the one found in those texts.

In sum, there is a sharp distinction between architectural and artistic terminology used in historical and hagiographical narratives and the terms used in descriptions of patronage and decoration. These differences depend in part on the sources used by Agnellus and in part on the different styles of language and effects in the different types of writing. In description of patronage and decoration, there are three influences: the formalized patronage descriptions of the Roman *LP,* which provided Agnellus with a great deal of rhetorical language; documents and lists of donations that he used or even copied; and his own experience of monuments, which he recounts as evidence for his information. In narrative passages, even those that deal with patronage, decoration, or Agnellus's own experiences, he also relied on various other written sources, including other histories and hagiographies. In many of these narratives, words are found that occur nowhere else in the *LPR,* sometimes even synonyms for other words that Agnellus uses more frequently. Clearly, Agnellus was creating a different effect by using these unusual and often idiosyncratic words; many times they are found in sequences of words designed to give a cumulative effect.

That all factors must be considered in looking at Agnellus's descriptions can be seen in the following example. In c. III Agnellus gives an account of the tribute paid to the church of Ravenna from its lands in Sicily. That he quotes a letter, and that he lists various gifts that seem quite specific in quality and amount, make it appear that he has based his story on specific documents that he has seen in the archive. The following are the items listed as gifts:

honored [the *manipularius*] with various presents and gifts: gold and silver, desirable vases [*vasis concupiscibilibus*], and many other things. And when the two men had been brought down to the boat, they kissed each other and said farewell, and [Benedict] gave [the *manipularius*] three hundred gold pieces. . . . He loaded the longships with fifty thousand *modia* of wheat, not counting many other grains and vegetables, reddened hides of rams [*pelles arietum rubricatas*] and purple robes [*pluuiales syrias*] and decorated silk episcopal vestments [*iacintinas casulas*], wool [*laenas*] and other garments, vases [*vasa*] of brass and silver, and thirty-one thousand gold *solidi*.

It is possible that the monetary figures were indeed taken from a document, but the associated objects are probably rhetorical embellishments. Both *vasa concupiscibilia* and *pelles arietum rubricatae* are phrases straight out of the Vulgate.[60] The remaining highlighted words, all referring to clothing or vestments, are mentioned in various places by Isidore, particularly in his section on clothing and fabric.[61] As we saw above, an apparently straightforward account of patronage in c. 168 also contains several words that have more to do with rhetoric than with reality. Even when description seems to be based on very specific and identifiable sources, it may be nothing more than borrowing of terms for effect.

It is difficult, in the case of the *LPR*, to talk of the "vocabulary of ninth-century Ravenna," when so many of the words can be traced to other sources. The terminology Agnellus uses reflects not only the vocabulary of a ninth-century Ravennate, but also the vocabularies of other writers of previous centuries. Certain words may have been already archaic by Agnellus's time, or confined to literate or highly technical audiences.[62] Agnellus's knowledge of artistic and architectural terminology was certainly highly sophisticated, and his use of terms reflects both the reality he was describing and the literary effects he was attempting to create.

60. Respectively 1 Macc. 1:23 and Exod. 25:5.
61. Isidore, *Etymologiarum* 19.21–29.
62. While Lazard, in "De l'origine" and "Les byzantinismes," takes these factors into account in her analyses of Greek-derived words in the *LPR*, she does not distinguish between Agnellus's contexts and written sources, and thus underestimates the influence of several key texts and documents known to Agnellus.

NOTE ON EDITIONS AND THIS TRANSLATION

The *LPR* is known to us from two manuscripts. One, in the Bibliotheca Estense in Modena (Cod. Lat. 371 X.P.4.9), dates to shortly after 1413 and contains the entire text that we know. The other, in the Vatican Library (Vat. Lat. 5834), dates to the mid-sixteenth century and breaks off in the middle of the Life of Peter II (c. 48). In addition, starting in the tenth century Agnellus's Lives of two saintly bishops of Ravenna, Severus and Peter Chrysologus, were copied into lectionaries and catalogues of saints.[1] Editions of the text of the *LPR* include:

Bacchinius, Benedictus, ed. *Agnelli, qui et Andreae Abbatis S. Mariae ad Blachernas et S. Bartholomei Ravennae Liber Pontificalis sive vitae Pontificum Ravennatum* (Modena, 1708). Reprinted in *Rerum Italicarum Scriptores* 2 (Milan, 1723), with an introduction by L. A. Muratori. *RIS* edition reprinted in *PL* 106 (Paris, 1864), 477–750.

Holder-Egger, Oswald. *Agnelli qui et Andreas liber pontificalis ecclesiae Ravennatis, MGH Scriptores rerum Langobardicarum et Italicarum saec. VI–IX* (Hanover, 1878), 265–391. Reprinted, with a German translation, in *Agnellus von Ravenna: Liber pontificalis: Bischofsbuch*, trans. Claudia Nauerth (Freiburg, 1996).

Testi-Rasponi, Alessandro, ed. *Codex Pontificalis Ecclesiae Ravennatis, Rerum Italicarum Scriptores*, new series, 2.3 (Bologna, 1924). Only contains the text up to c. 104.

Deliyannis, Deborah M., ed. "*The Liber Pontificalis Ecclesiae Ravennatis:*

1. For a list of these, see Deliyannis, *CCCM* edition of the *LPR*, introduction.

Critical Edition and Commentary." Ph.D. diss., University of Pennsylvania, 1994.

Deliyannis, Deborah M., ed. *Liber pontificalis ecclesiae Ravennatis. Corpus Christianorum Continuatio Mediaevalis.* Forthcoming.

This translation is based on the most recent edition of the text, prepared by the translator for the series *Corpus Christianorum Continuatio Mediaevalis.* The text is divided into the Lives of individual bishops and is further subdivided into 175 chapters. Oswald Holder-Egger devised this system for his 1878 edition of the text for the *Monumenta Germaniae Historica,* and it has been used by all subsequent scholars.

I have attempted to translate Agnellus's often oblique Latin as literally as possible. Personal names have been translated into their English equivalents; place names to their modern versions. Names of churches are likewise almost all given in English versions, except for the following, which are more commonly referred to by their Italian names: San Vitale, Sant' Apollinare in Classe, and Sant' Apollinare Nuovo. Biblical quotations are taken from the Douai-Rheims translation.

Poems have been translated into English prose, with references to the original line numbers given in brackets. One deviation from the manuscripts, however, is that in the table of contents and the titles of the Lives, Roman numerals have been added for bishops with the same name (e.g., John I, John II, and so on).

THE BOOK OF PONTIFFS OF THE CHURCH OF RAVENNA

PREFATORY VERSES

Here begin the verses of one unworthy scholar introducing the work of the following book.[1]

In the name of the Father and the Son and the Holy Spirit!

Since many masters have been eager to write about the correct interpretation of time and of the birth of Jesus, Redeemer of men, and of kings and bishops, they have written of how long each ruler sat on the imperial throne [5], and each noble shepherd in the pontifical see, of the warlike realms of emperors, whose lofty empire at length shone forth in western parts, where the bountiful waves rise, and of the length of the holy life of the apostles [10], and of how those noted ones shone in word and deed.

Through the round of eight hundred years the lazy pens of Ravennate authors have long neglected to tell how their highest bishops regulated their kindly lives, famous throughout the world [15]. Although it is late in the day, finally the faith and hands of charming Agnellus have fortunately begun to write the pontifical book of our church, this little work about [our] patriarchs.

At the time when the vigorous Pope Gregory fitly holds the high powers of loosing and binding [20], in place of gracious Peter, and the kindly emperor Louis holds the scepter of the empire, peaceful descendant of mighty Charlemagne, and his son, fierce Lothar, war bringer, holds the Italian kingdoms and possesses Rome, chosen for the imperial throne by kings and people [25], also when the kindly Archbishop Petronax, rejoicing, leads the clergy of the Ravennate church and the people,[2] this same highest bishop, deservedly on the throne of this rich city, blessed the tenth[3] of the priests. That priest, wiser than all the others [30], shone in

   1. These verses, according to the information in them, were written by someone who knew Agnellus while he was working on the *LPR*; since Petronax is the last bishop mentioned, the poem must have been composed before 837.
   2. Lines 21–28 refer to the years 827–37.
   3. *Alter ab undecimo presbiterum*, literally "the one from eleventh of the priests," is a

95

intellect and holy nature; called by the name Agnellus from boyhood, in youth he became Andreas.

Hail, descendant and heir of very proud stock! Hail, Ravenna, which furnished him thus, second to none: beautiful of appearance, brilliant in speech, eloquent of mouth [35], meager in the limbs of his body, but large of mind; great in sense although small of body.

Just as in the springtime the tiny nightingale fills the high heavens with her cries, singing sweetly in the flowery woods, pouring out sound from her curving throat [40], a songstress sitting on a branch under a green leaf—for the musician rejoicing under the sky, and the traveler, the shepherd, the watching horseman, desiring to hear her sweet songs for free, everywhere desire and earnestly attend to the one whom they can never best in song, however long they sing [45]—such is this one, sitting under these very proud roofs, which his noble father left him by paternal inheritance, in the see and suburbs of Ravenna, and in the place which is called by the ancient name of Blacherna, built in honor of Mary the mother of the Lord God [50].[4]

Here the charming author of the pontifical book, mentioned above, sighing at the long neglect, anxiously frets, and eagerly undertakes to give himself without recompense to the mass of work; remembering the monuments of the fathers and elders, not deaf when listening to poets, but with a willing mind [55], resourcefully following the precepts of Moses, who says: "Ask your fathers, the elders will be messengers to you; you who are always seeking the deeds of your ancestors and former miracles of the Lord your God, they will inform you of what they saw and heard, teaching the truth" [60].[5]

When he had collected together the acts of the former patriarchs, he wrote this work; he gathered together their chronology, since it is depicted on a wall, and their names and order, and he collected information about their regulation of life partly by reading, but partly by his ears, although he was accustomed to gathering from books [65].

He wrote with Aderitus at the head of the series, and Petronax at its close,[6] arranging the body of the work in between the two, eleven times

---

reference to *LPR*, c. 83, where Agnellus calls himself the "tenth priest in order of the see."

4. Agnellus's *monasterium* of St. Maria *ad Blachernae*.
5. Cf. Deut. 32:7; Agnellus himself cites this passage in the Prologue.
6. The *LPR* as we know it begins with St. Apollinaris and ends with Archbishop

four patriarchs, wisely writing of the magnificent leadership of word and deed of each, regulating the things he heard and read, astutely conserving [70] those that were certain, abandoning those which he found uncertain. Acting like the greedy, earth-bearing, overflowing Po, which crosses the sand, keenly seeking the tawny strands on the curved shore, his resounding reed, pouring out black ink on parchment [75], disclosing the holy miracles of certain saints publicly, nobly put them into language. Since his ear was filled with elaborate tales of others, but he was wavering as to whether they were truthful, he preferred to inform briefly in polished speech [80].

Just as a sailor rejoices when, sitting on the thwarts and taking up goblets, loaded plates having been brought, and belching out songs, looking with a serene face at the calm sky, he eagerly gives the open sea to the mooring stakes, the sails to the favorable winds, racing over the glassy fields [85], he fears no crags nor sees land, nor does the gripping anchor sent down into the depths touch sandbanks. But he is sad when heaven is black with dense clouds, for on every side he sees the winds coursing through the air, and he fears to be close to a cliff [90], then, hastily drawing the oars in and the sails down, he timidly pins down the ship with the lead anchor, guiding the creaking ropes cast into the deep sea, and eagerly he greatly desires to reach port.

Likewise this one [Agnellus], where cognizant of the facts, wishes to place them [95] in complex language, arranging his discourse more richly everywhere, rejoicing in the reported magnificence and fame of those before him; he expresses it gloriously, with the reins of his voice loosened. But where ignorant, having heard only a few words, he has hoped, by speaking with pride laid by, to express with a restrained voice [100], and to produce it briefly for you in truthful speech.

Here begins the dactylic song, a misticon with six feet, that is, mixed, but first arranged in fours, then arranged in twos, and a monosticon, great intentions . . .

George. This has led to suggestions that there were two drafts of the text, and the poet knew only the earlier one, but it is more likely that the poet simply wrote before the work was complete.

TETRASTICON

POET: Once, by chance, the crowd of Ravennate priests came together, among whom was one called Andreas, whom his brothers, with humble voice, besought to write this pontifical book.

AGNELLUS: Then he answered humbly, but with the voice of wisdom [5]: "What sense or knowledge do I have, that I might understand, with my little sense, eight hundred cycles of years and the deeds of those gone before?"

PRIESTS: "Since you have usually been accustomed to explain to us [10], face to face, those confidential things which seem hidden from us the indiscriminate, as long as you disappoint us, we are very saddened, cruel friend."

ANDREAS: "Since I am conquered, I ask you, pray to the Thunderer, who turns the stars and controls the marine waters, that he might sharply change my life in its original course [15], and give me the sense to write a pontifical book."

DISTICON

PRIESTS: "Thus we will do very eagerly, and when we thus make a prayer, let the deed respond to our words; although strong, he works so much further."

AGNELLUS: "I will report the deeds and acts of prior bishops" [20].

MONASTICON

PRIESTS: "Formerly Agnellus, now Andreas, hail perpetually!"
ANDREAS: "Hail, priests through all the ages!"

Oh shining and faithful royal muse, provide small songs written for you [25], friends, to say praises always toward the faithful [30].

PROLOGUE

For you who request it, here is an ordered little book about the series of pontifical succession of bishops who entered the see of St. Apollinaris, just as the honesty and explanation of your Agnellus, also known as Andreas, of the orthodox see of Ravenna, has been able to discover and know it.

HERE BEGINS THE PROLOGUE

It is necessary for you to thank God the Father, and his Son, together with the Holy Spirit, triple in majesty, unique in power, for he has unclosed my polluted lips and made my dry tongue eloquent, insofar as it pleased him.

For indeed by your prayers I trust that God will give the grace of speaking to my words; so that, in that you have compelled me to speech, I might recall to memory as much as I could, whatever deeds each of the holy preceding bishop-fathers of the see of the Ravennate church had accomplished in his time, that I might reveal to your ears not only what I have seen of their deeds, but indeed what I have heard, those things which our elders have reported to me.

Indeed Moses, that most excellent man, wrote down the book of Genesis by God's inspiration, for he said: "Ask your fathers, and they will inform you, your elders, and they will tell you," and Job: "Inquire of former generations, and diligently give heed to the memory of the fathers."[1] For Moses was descended from the stock of Abraham, and before Abraham was born, it is told that the creation of all this world was made by God. Indeed Mark, the disci-

1. Deut. 32:7; Job 8:8.

ple of the apostle Peter and his son in baptism, did not physically follow the footsteps of the Lord, nor did he see any miracles done by him, but wrote the gospel as Peter narrated it. Luke, the attendant of the apostle Paul, instructed in doctrine by him, opened the fountain of his gospel.[2] Indeed many others have composed volumes based on hearsay of things, as it is read in the Lives of the Fathers:[3] "A certain old man told me ..." etc. Did not Gregory, bishop of the see of the Roman church, in several places in his *Books of Dialogues* recount thus: "Such and such a man told me," and other things like this?[4]

But I cannot say that I am at all similar to these men. For indeed I confess that just as a faint spark placed in the sight of the burning sun at noon is overshadowed, and its light does not appear, thus are my pages completely extinguished in the presence of the philosophers. Nevertheless, I am able to draw out other things like them; I use discourse, parchment, and ink.

For I am like those who are placed in woods or the wilderness, and see dense trees around them, places opaque and dark and impassable with many thorns, and do not know what part to seek or where to cut through, if there is no safe road to escape into cultivated areas.

Thus, on account of this narration of the holy bishops of this see of Ravenna, it is as if I have entered into the hazards of the sea, just as if the tempestuous gale should struggle against me, or the tumult of the whole abyss should pursue me, or the waters of the cerulean waves.[5] But I do not fear, since I am sheltered by your prayers, and the Lord is with me, who is blessed forever.

---

2. Cf. Luke 1:1.

3. It has been suggested that this refers to Gregory of Tours's *Life of the Fathers* (e.g., Holder-Egger, *LPER*, 279, n. 2) but it is more likely that it simply refers to saints' Lives in general.

4. This entire justification for the use of oral sources is very similar to Gregory's argument at the beginning of the prologue of the *Book of Dialogues*.

5. The convention of the author facing a tempest is common in medieval literature; Gregory the Great uses it in the prologue to the *Book of Dialogues*. See Sot, "Rhétorique et technique," 185, n. 15.

By your charity I will pass over to the above-mentioned study, which I have undertaken at your urgings, because long ago I hinted in your ears, that I ought to produce something from what has been told to me about the above-mentioned see. If perhaps I have deceived you, forgive me. The collector ought not be troublesome, when someone is about to pay his debt.

But in all these things let us bless God the Father and the Son and the Holy Spirit, who lives and reigns forever and ever. Amen.

HERE ENDS THE PROLOGUE

HERE BEGINS VERSE IN METER, ON THE NAME OF THE BLESSED APOLLINARIS.

Let this be read at the same time.[1]

That kind apostle and true prince of the apostles [Peter], giving the highest seat of bishops to one [Apollinaris] whom as a disciple he taught with holy admonitions, sent him to call Ravenna and her people correctly to God.

He [Apollinaris] gave sight to the blind and he raised Tecla [5], who long lay on her bed, enfeebled in her limbs. Joyfully he arrived at the high temple, he overthrew the crowds of demons in the name of the Lord. Smiting the bonds of greedy death, he restored to life the daughter of Rufus through the Lord [10]. Through the divinity of the Lord he restored the gift of speech to a citizen of Classe, whose name is Boniface.

By the executioner he was crowned with martyrdom, but first he bore many wounds from whips. Recalled by the king of heaven, his spirit then seeks the assemblies [15] of heaven and the angelic choruses.

Let him not be displeased, who, however capable, is unable to understand meter, I humbly beseech. But taking a journey of prose, let him di-

---

1. Information in both the poem and the text of cc. 1–2 is taken from the seventh-century *Passio S. Apolenaris*; Testi-Rasponi (*CPER*, 19, n. 1) dates the poem to the tenth or eleventh century on the basis of style, and says that it must have become part of the *LPR* at a later date.

rect his steps through accessible ways, and rejoicing let him enjoy it in peace with me [20].

Here end the pentameter and hexameter verses. Whoever does not understand it, let him turn to the prose.

CONCERNING ST. APOLLINARIS

1. St. Apollinaris, Antiochene by birth, educated in Greek and Latin letters, was a disciple of the apostle Peter, and arrived with him in the city of Rome.[2]

After much time Peter ordained him a bishop and bestowed upon him the Holy Spirit through the laying on of hands and gave him the kiss; and traveled together with him about thirty miles from the city of Rome, where the *monasterium* of blessed Peter which is called *ad Janiculum* is located. There the apostle of Christ prayed, and where he placed his knee, the stone appeared soft, like wax by fire, and thus the stone was hollowed out by his knee.[3]

And at another *monasterium* of this apostle, which is called "at the Elm,"[4] they slept together that night, and furrows appear in that stone where his head or back and rump and shins occupied it, up to this day. And then he sent Apollinaris to Ravenna.

And that most blessed one, before he would enter the city of Ravenna, gave light to the blind son of Hereneus—Hereneus indeed means "peaceful"[5]—and he performed many miracles within

---

2. The first archaeological evidence for Christianity in Ravenna and Classe dates to the late second century, too late for Apollinaris to have been a disciple of St. Peter, or to have died during the reign of Vespasian, as the Life says below.

3. This part of the legend is not found in the *Passio*, and thus it is not clear whether Agnellus means here the church of St. Peter *ad Ianiculum* in Rome (not thirty miles away), or whether he has garbled some other tradition. Lugari, *Il culto di S. Pietro sul Gianicolo*, suggests that the text should be interpreted to mean that Peter first prayed at the *monasterium ad Ianiculum* in Rome, then went thirty miles to the *monasterium ad Ulmum*. Lugari notes that the quarter of Rome known as *Urberauennatium* was at the foot of the Janiculum.

4. The identity of this *monasterium* is unknown, nor is it certain where Agnellus got the name, which is not found in the *Passio*.

5. From εἰρηναῖος.

this city: he overthrew the temples of the gods and smashed the idols, he ordained priests and deacons, he cured the sick, he put demons to flight, he cleansed lepers, he baptized many in the river Bedento and in the sea.

In the basilica of blessed Euphemia, which is called *ad Arietem*,[6] he first performed baptism, and where his feet stood, the rock was liquefied, and his footprints are impressed as a sign.[7]

He also revived the dead daughter of the patrician Rufus. And we see the house of that patrician as the episcopal residence of the church of Bologna up to the present day;[8] thus indeed I know that house to be whole and unharmed, as it was in antiquity. And almost five years ago now, Theodore the bishop of Bologna[9] carried off the stone sarcophagus in which the patrician Rufus was placed with his daughter, and took it away to his church at Bologna, so that, after his death, he might be buried there. But what did it benefit him, that he cast out others from it? He was not buried in it, for he acted too slowly to set it up.

2. Therefore most blessed Apollinaris was sent [shackled] with a huge weight of iron into the prison not far from the center of this city of Ravenna, in which, with the guards looking on, angels supplied him with heavenly food.

And again they forced him out and threw him out of the city not far from the sixth milestone, where the ancient church of St. Demetrius was built.[10] After this he was led as a captive to parts of

   6. Lanzoni, "L' 'ad arietem,'" suggests that the name came from the word *aries* in its meaning as a mole or levee on a river, since the church was built next to the river Bedento.

   7. Impression miracles are very common in medieval literature; this one, like the two previous ones, is not found in the *passio*. Lanzoni, "Le fonti," 165, suggests that since St. Euphemia was thought to be the first baptistry of Ravenna, it is possible that footsteps where the bishops stood had worn into the stones after several centuries of baptisms.

   8. This *episcopium* must have been the house that the bishops of Bologna maintained in Ravenna, in which they stayed when they visited Ravenna as suffragans; see Testi-Rasponi, *CPER*, 23–24, n. 7.

   9. The mention of a bishop of Bologna named Theodore indicates a date of composition between 806 and 831.

   10. It is not clear from the text whether the church was still standing in Agnellus's

Illyria, and then through Salona, also Pannonia, along the banks of the Danube and into Thrace, and there and on the shores of Corinth the Lord worked many miracles through him.

After three years he returned to Ravenna and was received with great joy by his faithful followers and clergy. After a longer interval, the savage pagans made him stand with bare feet on live coals and inflicted many other torments on him.

He demolished by his prayers the temple of Apollo, which stood before the gate which is called the Golden Gate, next to the amphitheater.[11]

His sanctity and mildness were so great that never, while he suffered, did he do any injury to anyone, or curse anyone, except, while he was being strongly tortured, he said to the governor: "O most wicked one, why do you not believe in the Son of God, so that you might escape eternal torments?"

In the exceeding fullness of days, he became stooped. In the time of the emperor Vespasian he was crowned with martyrdom. He occupied the pontifical throne twenty-eight years, one month, four days.

CONCERNING HOLY ADERITUS

3. Aderitus, the first bishop, a man holy and fearful of God, was ordained priest by most blessed Apollinaris,[1] and like a wise architect built on the foundation of his master and teacher.[2] He inces-

---

day; *antiqua* (ancient) might mean that the church was ancient, or might have the connotation of "formerly." If the excavated remains of the church known as the Ca' Bianca are indeed those of the church of St. Demetrius, then it may have been destroyed before Agnellus's day. See Deichmann 2.2:319–22.

11. Agnellus knew where the amphitheater of Ravenna had stood (see also c. 129); either it still stood in his day or the place carried its name.

❧

1. The *Passio* of Apollinaris does not say that the priests and deacons consecrated by Apollinaris became the first four bishops, but the legend of a founding bishop consecrating his next few successors is common; Agnellus here parallels the account of the early popes in the *Liber pontificalis* (see Lanzoni, "Le fonti," 151). This was noted by Peter Damian in his *Sermon* 6.1.

2. Cf. 1 Cor. 3:10.

santly prayed to God on behalf of his flocks, that they might turn away from the worship of idols and confess the living God, Father and Son and Holy Spirit. And in his days, after the storm of persecution, many accepted baptism; then he gathered many to the Lord.

He died in the city of Classe on September 27, as some say. He is buried in the basilica of blessed Probus, not far from the church of blessed Apollinaris, about one stade.[3] He reigned __ years, __ months, __ days.[4]

CONCERNING HOLY ELEUCADIUS

4. Eleuchadius, the second bishop, whose name means "white" in Latin.[1] He was gentle and wise, and holy Apollinaris consecrated him deacon. His love of wisdom was so great that he put together many books about the New and Old Testaments, and wrote volumes on the incarnation of our Lord Jesus Christ and on His passion. Wherefore in the *passio* of Apollinaris, the athlete of Christ, it is read, "he made Eleuchadius the philosopher a deacon." He indeed preached correctly to the peoples, and in his church, anointed with the oil of piety, he shone like the light of a lamp.

He died on February 14, and was buried outside the walls of Classe, where up to today a church in praise of his name is built and consecrated to God. He sat __ years, __ months, __ days.

---

3. A stade was 625 Roman feet. For an excellent description and analysis of the burial places of Ravenna's bishops in the context of episcopal burial in early medieval Italy, see Picard, *Souvenir*. The basilica of St. Probus in Classe was one of the oldest churches in Ravenna, possibly built as early as the late fourth century. The church was probably dedicated to Probus by Bishop Maximian, who translated the body of Probus and other bishops into it (c. 77). The idea that the basilica of St. Probus was the original cathedral of Ravenna, proposed by Testi-Rasponi and Lanzoni, is now generally discredited; see Farioli Campanati, "Edifici paleocristiani di Classe," 43–45, and Deichmann, *Ravenna* 2.2:357–59.

4. The lengths of many reigns is omitted from the manuscripts of the text; perhaps Agnellus could not find this information.

1. From λευκός, "bright, white," or *candidus*.

CONCERNING HOLY MARCIAN

5. Marcian, the third bishop, a distinguished prelate, was sprung from noble stock. He remained, full of the Holy Spirit, in the holy church. He increased the clergy who were learned in holy doctrine and consecrated many deacons and priests. And he was ordained deacon by blessed Apollinaris together with wise Eleuchadius, as is reported in the *passio* of the one who ordained him, where it says, "He consecrated Marcian the most noble man and Eleuchadius as deacons."

After many miracles he gave up his soul in peace to God his Creator. From which I judge that he was buried in the church of blessed Eleuchadius. He sat __ years, __ months, __ days.

CONCERNING HOLY CALOCERUS

6. Calocerus, the fourth bishop, is translated "good time"; and if by chance the "c" is turned into an "i," it says *"ieros,"* meaning "elder," or "priest," or "lord."[1] For he was a very old man in advanced age.[2] In his days the Lord performed many graces and great miracles through him for the people. His preaching was so great, and he took such care of his flock, that not only did he teach the sheep already acquired, but also cast out the dwelling place and strength of the devil from the souls of the gentiles and created them anew at the holy font of baptism for the heavenly Lord.

He died and was buried, as some say, on February 11, in the basilica of blessed Probus the confessor. He sat __ years, __ months, __ days.

---

1. From the Greek: *bonum tempus*, that is, καλός, "good time"; *ieros*, that is, ἱερός, "holy"; *senior*, that is, γέρων, "old man"; *sacerdos*, that is, ἱερεύς, "priest"; *dominus*, that is, κύριος, "lord" (Holder-Egger, *LPER*, 282).

2. The *Passio* of Apollinaris says that Apollinaris consecrated Calocerus as priest, but Agnellus omitted this information. Holder-Egger, *LPER*, 282, n. 3, proposed that this statement was an interpolation by Agnellus based on the *passio*, i.e., Calocerus must have been an old man when elected bishop because he had been consecrated by Apollinaris so long before. It seems more likely that Agnellus had seen a picture depicting Calocerus as an old man.

CONCERNING HOLY PROCULUS

7. Proculus, the fifth bishop. He was faithful, like a father to his sons, and brought many into the bosom of the church, and gave to his people the nourishment of his preaching, like honey in sweetness, and provided it like cups of milk to those who are thirsting.

When he reached old age, grey of head, filled with grace, he ended his priesthood along with his life. And I do not know where his tomb might be; it is uncertain to me whether he is placed in the basilica of blessed Probus, or in that of holy Eleuchadius the confessor.[1] He sat __ years, __ months, __ days.

CONCERNING HOLY PROBUS I

8. Probus, the sixth bishop, gentle and upright, shining in appearance, gleaming in work, wise of speech, judicious of heart, full of the grace of the Holy Spirit. Whosoever might come to him sick would return cured, by Probus's prayers, no matter to what sort of debility he had been subject. And he cast out impure spirits and made whole the wounded or broken bodies of the masses.

At the close of his life, after he saw the angelic host, suddenly his holy soul slipped from his body on November 10. Then all the people in mourning buried his body with great reverence, and his tomb is venerated by us up to the present day; and his church is located to the east.

And in no churches inside the city of Ravenna or Classe is the mass celebrated over the people except in this one alone.[1] This said

---

1. The ambiguity of Proculus's burial site may mean that he never actually existed; the same is true of some of the other early bishops.

1. The mention of the *missa super populum* suggests that an older liturgical practice was maintained only in this basilica, but it is not clear what the phrase means (cf. Lanzoni, "Reliquie della liturgia ravennate," col. 338). Testi-Rasponi, *CPER*, 36–37, n. 14, suggests that it refers to a prayer said by the bishop over the people, the *oratio super populum* known from liturgical manuscripts. Gerola, "Il valore della frase 'ante altare,'" notes that in c. 23 the bishop is said to stand during the mass *ante altare*, hence with his

basilica was built next to the narthex of blessed Euphemia by the Sea,[2] which we now see to have been demolished.

He sat __ years, __ months, __ days.

CONCERNING HOLY DATUS

9. Datus, the seventh bishop. He indeed was a religious man and very dutiful and vigilant about night prayers, and a distinguished gatherer of men's souls and frequently a preacher to the heathen; and like a mirror his face shone forth clearly over all.

For when he was called to celestial grace, his holy soul receded from his body. And, as some assert, he was buried in the church of blessed Probus. He sat __ years, __ months, __ days.

CONCERNING HOLY LIBERIUS I

10. Liberius the eighth bishop, a great man, full of charity, a refreshing fountain, distinguished in faith, kindly in mind. In his days he increased the church with all honor. By the great humility of his life he preserved his soul and held dominion over every branch of learning.

However after these things he died and was buried, as indeed some suspect, with his predecessor. He sat __ years, __ months, __ days.

CONCERNING HOLY AGAPITUS

11. Agapitus, the ninth bishop, whose name in the Latin tongue is translated "full of charity."[1] He daily performed works of chari-

---

back to the congregation (see note to c. 23, below), and explains the *missa super populum* as meaning that only in St. Probus did the bishop face the congregation.

2. The church of St. Euphemia by the Sea, destroyed in the ninth century, was different from St. Euphemia *ad Arietem*, mentioned in c. 1.

1. From ἀγάπη, "alms."

ty to strangers, he eagerly bestowed gifts upon paupers, and daily offered up goodness in the temple of his body, daily offered up his soul, like the host, at the altar of his heart, in the presence of the almighty Lord.

Later the divine command came to him, and his holy soul was released from the flesh. He was buried, as [some] suspect, with the others named above. He sat __ years, __ months, __ days.

CONCERNING HOLY MARCELLINUS

12. Marcellinus, the tenth bishop, just and God-fearing, he destroyed the camps of demons by his prayers and diligently guarded the sheep that had been bestowed upon him by the Lord, so that that monstrous wolf, which daily rants and raves against them, should not be able to tear them to pieces outside his church and carry off prey from among his sheep; so that it might not devour in its bestial maw the souls of Christians which the holy man had acquired for Almighty God, nor deliver them to the power of hell with its infernal chains binding them.

And when the course of many years was run, he let slip the pontificate and his life; his body emitted such fragrant odors that the noses of those burying him seemed to smell incense of precious myrrh.[1] He was buried, as some allow, in the basilica of blessed Probus. He sat __ years, __ months, __ days.

CONCERNING HOLY SEVERUS, C. 340'S

13. Severus, the eleventh bishop,[1] whose name in its formation means "true fierce." This does not pertain to savagery, but to

---

1. The miraculous preservation and odor of saintly bodies is a common topos in hagiography; compare, for example, Gregory of Tours, *Liber vitae patrum* 7.4 and *Gloria martyrum* 62, and *LPR*, c. 26, below.

1. "Severus ab Italia de Ravennensi" is listed as having been present at the Council of Sardica of 343 (Mansi, *Sacrorum conciliorum* 3, col. 39); Severus is thus the first

strength: "fierce," that is, "strong," "true" high priest. His priesthood was so predestined by Almighty God, that in his election the holy spirit was sent in the form of a dove, which the whole people saw corporeally with their eyes, and it rested on his head. From this event a proverb concerning him is said up to today by some people, "Blessed be that land, where in the election of a bishop the holy spirit descended in the likeness of a dove, and the one on whose head it rested was ordained."[2] But woe unto you,[3] unhappy Ravenna, neighbor of destroyed Classe, since now a bishop is ordained in your city with great strife and controversy.

14. While this blessed above-named Severus was celebrating mass, when his deacon had ascended into the pulpit and was reading the letters of the blessed apostle Paul, so that the assembly of the people might be refreshed with spiritual words, suddenly the holy man went into a trance, as if held in sleep, neither fully sleeping nor awake. His attendants, thinking that he had fallen asleep, began to strike his sides. He, however, rose up as if from deepest sleep and said to them with sad spirit, "Oh, what have you done? Why did you disturb me? Although I seemed to you to be here, I was in another place." But they persisted in asking him, saying, "Tell us, where were you, father?" He said to them, "May the Lord pardon you, most esteemed sons, for having woken me up; for I was in the holy church of Modena and there I committed the soul of my brother and fellow bishop Geminianus, bishop of that church, to almighty God, and there I stood, until his holy body was placed in the tomb."

On account of this, so that the truth might be discovered, the citizens of Ravenna and Classe sent riders to the above-mentioned city of Modena, in order that the words of the holy man might be

---

bishop of Ravenna for whom an independent date is known. For more on Severus, see Lanzoni, "S. Severo vescovo."

2. In the eleventh and twelfth centuries, this statement about the proverb led to the assumption that all of the first twelve bishops of Ravenna were elected by manifestations of doves; see Laqua, *Traditionen und Leitbilder*, 319–35, and Lucchesi, *Note agiografiche*, 93–95.

3. Cf. Eccles. 10:16.

confirmed. The Modenese, when they had been asked the day and hour in which the holy soul of blessed Geminianus had passed to the Lord, said, "Did not lord Severus your bishop commit his soul to heaven and stand here a long time, until his body had been closed in the tomb? When it was closed, he suddenly vanished from our eyes." The riders, having returned, told their citizens the story as it had been told to them. From that day they began to venerate his sanctity even more.

15. The life of this blessed man is not told to us in written history;[4] but some say that the Lord performed many miracles and prodigies for the people through him, about which my pen did not have the power to reveal. It is said that his sanctity was so great that his wife, though dead for a long time, rolled over on her side.

When the daughter of this most blessed confessor of Christ Severus, by the name of Innocentia, had died, everyone came to place her small body in the tomb of her mother Vicentia. They saw that the tomb was small and said, "Two bodies cannot rest here, since the container is too small."

With tears the lord Severus said, "O wife, why are you troublesome to me? Why do you not make a place for your daughter? Take what you bore, do not hesitate to receive what was taken from your flesh. Behold I give to you what you have given to me; do not delay. She has returned to whence she came. Give her a place for burial, do not sadden me." At his voice the bones of his wife moved by themselves to the side with great speed, so fast that living bodies of men could hardly move more swiftly, and she allowed her daughter a space for burial.

4. Despite Agnellus's statement, it has been proposed that Agnellus did not write the Life of Severus himself. Lanzoni, "S. Severo vescovo," part 2, 394–96, noted that all of the miracles in the Life of Severus have parallels in other hagiographic works, and postulated the existence of a written Life older than that of Agnellus, perhaps lost, but whose contents remained in communal memory. That Severus had been revered as a saint in Ravenna for some time before the ninth century is seen by the mention of him in the late-sixth-century Hieronymian Martyrology (326–27), and in the fact that a basilica was built next to his tomb in Classe at the end of the sixth century. Nevertheless, it seems more likely that Agnellus was the one who borrowed the legends and composed this Life.

It happened after this that his holy soul, which men loved on earth, by divine command was to be lifted up by holy angels to the pleasant realm. I shall confide to your ears, just as I have heard people tell about the passing of the blessed man. One day when he had celebrated mass and had received the holy flesh and blood of the Lord, wrapped in the pontifical stole, he ordered his tomb to be opened, he entered alive, and lying himself down between his wife and daughter he ordered it to be closed. There while praying he rendered up his precious soul to God. He died in such peace and tranquillity on the first of February. And the Lord displays many miracles at his tomb in his church, which is located in the former city of Classe, not far from the region which is called Salutaris, up to the present day.[5]

16. And again I will tell you that we have seen these deeds in our time; I call it to memory, that you might remember it. One man, who is still alive, when he was young, because of an illness of his body, when his mother had prostrated herself at the tomb of Severus the blessed confessor of Christ, and everyone had fallen asleep, that sick boy, alone, grew frightened of the dead of night and sent out a cry, waking everyone. And they saw the candles, which had been previously extinguished, shining with their usual light. And when everyone saw the great light, terrified in mind they gave glory to God and to Severus his confessor.

When the boy was led into their midst, his mother began to ask him, "What has happened to you, my son?" He said in the presence of everyone, "I saw coming forth from this tomb a man in the habit of a bishop, adorned with a grey-haired head, with an angelic face; he touched me, and I was frightened." And suddenly the sickness of the boy left him, and he was feverish no longer.

These things happened in our time, not only these, but many other things.

---

5. A different legend (*BHL* 7681–82) tells that the body of St. Severus was stolen from Classe and taken to Mainz in 837; Agnellus does not mention this event because this part of the *LPR* was written before 836. It is also possible that the tale of the theft is not true; see Geary, *Furta Sacra.*

17. Let me tell of the election of this holy man, as I began above, and which was told to me by many elders.

One day when he was wearied by the work of wool-making—he with his spouse, as I said, worked at the task of spinning wool—he said to his wife, "I will go and see a miraculous vision, of how a dove will come from high heaven and will settle on the head of the chosen one." His wife began to mock and rebuke him, saying, "Sit here and work, do not be idle. Whether you go or not, the people will not ordain you as bishop; return to work!" But he said to her, "Let me go." And she said, "Go, since in the hour that you go you will be ordained as bishop immediately."

He then, rising, proceeded to where the assembly of the people was with the priests, and because of the unsightliness of his clothes, since he was wearing squalid garments, he hid himself behind the door of that place where all the congregation were gathered praying. After the prayer was completed there suddenly came from the heavens a dove whiter than snow, and it rested on the head of blessed Severus the confessor of Christ, who was concealed behind the doors. Although he drove it away from him, flying through the air it rested on him again, a second and a third time.

All the authorities who were standing around giving greatest thanks to God were amazed; he was ordained bishop. When she heard this, his wife, who had recently derided him, afterward gave thanks for his sake.

Then the word of the gospel was fulfilled, as it is written, "Among men this is impossible, but to God all things are possible," and in the voice of Paul, "But God hath chosen the weak of the world to confound the mighty."[6]

And, as some say, blessed Heraclian, bishop of the city of Pensauris, was a disciple of this confessor Severus and held the episcopal see, having been taught sacred doctrine by him.

Let what you have heard about the life of the blessed man Severus suffice you for now, I beseech. But let me explain somewhat

---

6. Matt. 19:26; 1 Cor. 1:27.

of why he was elected to the pontifical see in the life of blessed Liberius, his successor, because I have found almost nothing about the life of the said Liberius. It is therefore necessary that we add to his pages a small part about the life of Severus the confessor of Christ, so that the reading about Liberius might appear not small but great, and so that you might read it with desire rather than with boredom, and give great thanks to God, who is blessed forever. Amen.

He sat __ years, __ months, __ days.

CONCERNING HOLY LIBERIUS II

19. Liberius, the twelfth bishop, a distinguished man, father to orphans, generous with alms, he ruled the pontificate in peace. He truly guarded the evangelical preaching, as it is written, "In your patience you shall possess your souls."[1] He did not steal or seize anything from anyone else; he honored God with his just labors.

After the end of his life he was most dutifully buried and possesses eternal rest. I have told you as much as I have learned about the life of the above-mentioned Liberius.

18.[2] But I ask, O most beloved, that you direct your attention with greater care to the many virtues which the all-powerful God gives to his faithful; not only those alive in the flesh, but even the bones of the dead would obey him. Thus the truth states, "If you had faith like to a grain of mustard seed, you might say to this mulberry tree, Be thou rooted up, and be thou transplanted into the sea; and it would obey you."[3]

Why among the other plants is only the mustard seed mentioned? Because unless the mustard seed is ground, its power is not

---

1. Luke 21:19.

2. In this translation the chapter numbering developed by Holder-Egger for his *MGH* edition has been retained. Holder-Egger placed the sermonette about the mustard seed in the Life of Severus and called it c. 18. In the edition of the text on which this translation is based (ed. Deliyannis), this sermonette is restored to the Life of Liberius; however, it is still numbered as c. 18.

3. Luke 17:6.

known; when it has been ground, at once strength and sweetness proceed from it. And thus when the saints arrive at martyrdom, their prudence and humility appear when they sustain harsh torments, and do not fear the blows or attacks of the executioners, and remain silent.

In his kindness, he would call his sons all those whom he has brought to the Lord from the worship of idols, since there does not seem to be only one type of martyrdom. One type is performed openly before all, another in secret. It is martyrdom in public when someone is led before the judge, is dragged, beaten, wounded, mocked, derided, bound in chains, thrust through the entrance of prison, and after all these things is decapitated, and as a martyr does not deny the name of Christ. The secret martyrdom of man is to abstain by himself, to fast, to keep vigils, to pray, to beware of evil habits, to renounce carnal desires, not to do to another what he does not want to happen to him, to keep no worldly desire, to give alms to the crowds of paupers from his own property, to preach urgently to the unbeliever and to the infidel and to snatch them from blind error and to show them the road of truth and light, as it is written: "be wise in good, and simple in evil."[4]

Again it is written, "Be ye therefore wise as serpents and simple as doves."[5] And if a serpent is wise, why does that truth of Solomon say, "There is no head worse than the head of a serpent"?[6] And if it is wise, why therefore is it written, "The serpent was more subtle than all the beasts of the earth"?[7] And if wise, why was it cursed by God among all the other animals of the world, as it is written, "And the Lord God said to the serpent, 'Thou art cursed among all beasts of the earth; upon thy breast and belly shalt thou go, and earth shalt thou eat all the days of thy life'"?[8]

Why is this? Because it tempted man, it made him eat from the forbidden fruit, the devil entered into the poisonous throat of the

4. Rom. 16:19.
6. Ecclus. 25:22.
8. Gen. 3:14.

5. Matt. 10:16.
7. Gen. 3:1.

serpent and expelled the first man from paradise. Why does it not move on its tail or on some other part, but on its breast and belly? "And earth shalt thou eat all the days of thy life," that is, you will not rise to the heavens, but you will wallow in earthly, filthy pollutions.

But for this reason the Lord teaches the saints to be wise like serpents, since the serpent, when it is struck by someone, gives its body to the beating, but hides its head; and thus the bodies of the saints are beaten, but they hide the head of us all, which is Christ, under the veil of their hearts and prayers. "And simple as doves": although other birds have gall, this is absent from the dove, which is a sweet animal, lacking bitterness, a gentle bird.

And the dove takes its name from the clapping of its wings, whence the beating of wings is said in Greek: "peristera," this means "dove" in Latin.

(19.) This most blessed man sat __ years, __ months, __ days.

CONCERNING HOLY PROBUS II

20. Probus, the thirteenth bishop, rich in divine grace and beautiful of form, decrepit with age, heavy of body, cheerful of face,[1] infused with heavenly grace, he always stoutly sought God. He did not cease to admonish his sheep, but stood out as a great preacher. Such great excellence of divinity was in him, that he excelled those who had been instructed in spiritual wisdom and he refreshed with the grace of the Holy Spirit those who had not.

Placed in the vicinity of death, contemplating the hosts of angels, joyful and exulting, stretching his hands to the stars, he closed his flaming eyes and rendered up his spirit. And this most blessed man was buried, as I suspected, with his predecessor. He sat __ years, __ months, __ days.

1. Agnellus gives a portrait of the bishop at the beginning of many of the Lives; see Introduction. Nauerth, *Agnellus von Ravenna, Untersuchungen,* 15, n. 30, notes that *hilaris* can mean cheerful, friendly, or obliging. In the Roman *LP* Popes Agatho, Zacharias, and Leo III are described as *hilaris,* which probably reflects the same meaning (see Squatriti, "Personal Appearance and Physiognomies," 197).

CONCERNING HOLY FLORENTIUS

21. Florentius, the fourteenth bishop, a just man, father of paupers and protector of widows, a great preacher, humble and gentle and dutiful, daily exhorting his sheep to come swiftly to the harbor of salvation and the rewards of penitence.

This holy man was buried in the *monasterium* of St. Petronilla,[1] clinging to the walls of the church of the Apostles. He ruled his church __ years, __ months, __ days.

CONCERNING HOLY LIBERIUS III

22. Liberius, the fifteenth bishop, a holy man, he was beautiful in form, yet brighter in understanding; his eloquence flowed like milk. For he was a true worshipper of God, a leader of pagans toward the good, a destroyer of idols; in his reign the population of pagans began to diminish and the holy church began to swell with Christian people. His kindness was so great that he was not called "lord" by his priests, but was addressed by his name as a fellow priest; he took precedence among them only in the chair of the pontifical title. He daily exhorted the shamed, that they should approach penitence with confidence.

In his reign the emperor Valentinian I was killed outside the Artemetorian Gate, not far from the *stadium tabulae*[1] near the Coriandrian Field; and there was very great sedition among the people, and many were wounded in the place which is called the

---

1. Ravenna's church of the Apostles is next mentioned in the Life of Neon, who lived almost a century after the death of Florentius (cc. 29–30). Deichmann, *Ravenna* 2.2:354, points out that the dedication of a chapel to St. Petronilla next to St. Peter's in Rome, on which this dedication in Ravenna is surely modeled, took place only in the mid-eighth century. Thus the Ravennate dedication may only date to the eighth century, although the *monasterium* was surely built some time earlier, if not necessarily by Florentius himself.

1. Deichmann, *Ravenna* 2.3:40, suggests that the *stadium tabulae* might have been a circus.

Blessed Well. And the emperor, sent out from the walls of Ravenna, finished his life in the hands of his attackers.[2]

And Liberius was buried in the *monasterium* of St. Pulio, which was built in his time, not far from the gate which is called the Porta Nova; his tomb is known to us. The above-mentioned bishop sat __ years, __ months, __ days.

CONCERNING HOLY URSUS, C. 405–31

23. Ursus, the sixteenth bishop, most chaste in body, most holy in works, had a thin and beautiful face, and was moderately bald. He first began to construct a temple to God here, so that the Christian populace, which was scattered in separate dwellings, might be collected by that most dutiful shepherd into one flock. He never polluted his church, nor sold the Holy Spirit, nor stretched out his hand to receive any gift in return for the laying on of hands.

This most blessed leader built within this city of Ravenna that holy catholic church, where we all regularly assemble, which he named Ursiana after his own name.[1] He founded it in his time and, with the aid of God, brought it to completion. He lined the walls with most precious stones; he arranged diverse figures in multicolored mosaics over the vault of the whole temple. The whole populace, as one man, joyful and rejoicing, labored with spontaneous spirit, and greatly praised the God of the heavens, since their salvation was advanced in their hands through the intercession of His priest and confessor.

Euserius and Paul decorated one wall surface, on the north side,[2] next to the altar of St. Anastasia, which Agatho made. That is the wall where columns are placed in a row up to the wall of the

---

2. This information seems to be taken from an annalistic source; however, none of the emperors named Valentinian died in Ravenna.

1. The cathedral of Ravenna.

2. In the Latin, the north and the south sides are identified as the *pars virorum* ("men's side") and *pars mulierum* ("women's side"); this usage seems to have its origin

main door. Satius and Stephen[3] decorated the other wall on the south side, up to the above-mentioned door, and here and there they carved in stucco[4] different allegorical images of men and animals and quadrupeds, and they arranged them with greatest skill.

The said church is now located in the Herculana region—it is called Herculana because it was consecrated by Hercules—not far from the Vincileonian gate, called so because Vincilius built it.

This holiest man lived in the episcopal residence,[5] which is placed next to the Fossa Amnis, where it goes out, flowing under the Bridge of the Millers, from the place which is called Organaria, a thing wonderful in size and completely constructed of a built device, where now there seems to be a destroyed stable.[6]

After all these things had been completed and the buildings fully constructed, he sensed a slight infirmity in his body, and thus as if bursting he rendered up his spirit on April 13; in such peace and tranquillity he finished his life on the day of the holy Resurrection.

---

in the separation of men and women during the sacred service; see Glossary, s.v. *pars virorum* and *pars mulierum*.

3. Euserius, Paul, Agatho, Satius, and Stephen were probably the patrons of the decoration, whose work was commemorated by inscriptions (Testi-Rasponi, *CPER*, 67, n. 4), and not, as Holder-Egger (*LPER*, 289, n. 1) and others suggest, the artists. Cf. the mosaic of St. Reparata in Florence, in which floor inscriptions name the donors; see Toker, "Early Medieval Florence."

4. *Gipsea metalla* is some type of material that according to Agnellus is incised (c. 23), sculpted (c. 41), and embedded (c. 86), and probably refers to stucco or plaster; see Glossary, s.v. *gipsea metalla*.

5. The episcopium of Ravenna, next to the Ursiana cathedral, was added to many times over the course of its history, as Agnellus tells in cc. 29, 50, 66, 75, 145. About this complex, see esp. Rizzardi, "Note sull'antico episcopio," Deichmann, *Ravenna* 2.1:193–208, and Miller, "The Development," and Miller, *The Bishop's Palace*, 22ff.

6. The Latin here is corrupt, and its meaning is obscure. As Testi-Rasponi, *CPER*, 68, n. 3, points out, the *organaria* was probably some sort of lock or waterwheel used in regulating water levels and providing power to the mills near the Bridge of the Millers. The Organaria was under a bridge, probably blocking off the waterway with constructions; that there was now a destroyed stable on the site indicates that the waterway was no longer in use. Would it be too much to suggest that perhaps the stables had been for animals used to work the mills after the water ceased to provide power? Miller, "The Development," 159, suggests that perhaps the stable was part of the episcopal complex.

And on that same festival the church was dedicated by him and called Anastasis.

And he was buried, as some assert, in the aforementioned Ursiana church, also called Anastasis, which he built, in front of the altar under a porphyry stone, where the bishop stands when he sings the mass.[7] Because of this, after a short time his sanctity shone forth, and in mosaic on the upper wall of the apse of blessed Apollinaris his name is written "Holy Ursus," together with his image.[8] He sat twenty-six years, ___ months, ___ days.

CONCERNING HOLY PETER I, C. 431–50

24. Peter, the seventeenth bishop, a most saintly man, with a slender body, a tall stature, lean in appearance, with a long beard. From the time of blessed Apollinaris up to this man, all his predecessors were from Syria.[1]

He was the founder of the Petriana church, building the external walls all around but not completing everything. No church like it in construction was larger, either in length or in height; and it was greatly adorned with precious stones and decorated with multicolored mosaics and greatly endowed with gold and silver and

---

7. Gerola, "Il valore della frase 'ante altare,'" considers the meaning of the phrase "in front of the altar [*ante altare*] ... where the bishop stands," and compares it with similar phrases in cc. 30, 38, 42, 44, 157. Gerola concludes that *ante altare* means on the congregation's side of the altar, while *post altare* means between the altar and the apse. Thus, in the ninth century, the bishop stood with his back to the congregation when performing the mass.

8. The image of Ursus still survives in Sant' Apollinare in Classe, on the apse wall at the level of the windows.

✥

1. "From the time ... from Syria" in imitation of the Roman *LP*, in which the national or regional origin of each pope is given. This Peter is the first bishop of Ravenna with this name; he reigned in the 430s and 440s and was the famous sermon-writer and saint who is known as Chrysologus (on the life and works of Peter Chrysologus, see Olivar, *Sermones*; Olivar, *Sancti Petri Chrysologi collectio sermonum*; and Benericetti, *Il Cristo nei sermoni*). Agnellus confuses the chronology of the fifth-century bishops and identifies Peter II (cc. 47–52) as Chrysologus.

with holy vessels, which he ordered to be made. They say that there an image of the Savior was depicted over the main door, the like of which no man could see in pictures; it was so very beautiful and lifelike that the Son of God himself in the flesh would not have disliked it, when he preached to the nations.[2]

25. However I want you to know what I heard about the abovementioned holy image of our Lord from individual elders, both ordinary people and priests, just as they had it handed down from their own elders. Not only is it known to me, I who wish to write this book of bishops, but also to others of my fellow disciples and brothers, we who have been raised in the bosom of the holy Ursiana church.[3]

There was a certain spiritual father in the wilderness, and he daily besought the Lord to show him the form of His incarnation. When after much time in such prayer he grew exhausted in the weariness of his soul, there stood before him by night a man in white garments, wearing an angelic habit, who said to him, "Behold your prayer is answered and I have seen your labor. Rise, go to the city which is called Classe, and seek there the Petriana church; and when you have entered there, look above the doors of that church in the narthex; there you will see me depicted in plaster on the wall, as I was in flesh in the world."

Then the hermit, filled with great joy, happy and rejoicing at hearing the word, left the wilderness, and two lions accompanied him. And rising, after a lengthy journey over land he arrived at the city of Classe, and when he had entered the aforementioned church together with the lions, long wailing and praying he began to search for the holy image on the walls. After he had not found it, he came to the place where it had been revealed to him while

---

2. In c. 151 Agnellus tells of the destruction of the Petriana in an earthquake; this picture was therefore destroyed before Agnellus's day. For the meaning of *regia* as door, see Glossary, s.v. *regia*.

3. The following legend refers to the iconoclastic controversy, indicating Ravenna's, or at least Agnellus's, iconodule position; the legend is also known about an image in a church in Thessalonike (*BHG* 798), as noted by Lanzoni, "Leggende Orientali"; see Deliyannis, "Agnellus of Ravenna and Iconoclasm."

sleeping that the depicted image was, and seeing it, he fell flat on the ground weeping, and giving thanks he adored it, since he saw it just as it had been revealed to him in sleep.

And gazing at it for a long time, he said, "I thank you, God, who listens to everyone; you who do not scorn those seeking you nor do you desire the death of sinners, but are present to those invoking you;[4] you for whom no mediator, nor messenger, nor intermediary is necessary, in whom there is no delay for the entreating faithful, as you have promised us through the prophets, 'while you are speaking, behold here I am.'[5] Behold my desire has been fulfilled not because of my merits, but because of your pity. Now I am filled with your holy riches, now I am enriched from the heavenly treasury. Take my soul into your holy hall, and let me deserve to enter your kingdom and sit at your table, received at the banquet of the lamb."

And with these words, praying and rejoicing for a long time, between the two lions roaring around him he rendered up his spirit. Since thereupon the lions desired the people [to come], they rushed together, digging up the earth with great fear and veneration, with the lions licking his limbs and remains and pouring out tears, with great grief they buried him. Then the lions, one prostrate at his head and the other at his feet, giving great roars between them, rushing around either side of the body of the holy man, groaning with great voices and desiring to lay their necks under his tomb—the people wept most bitterly with these lions—they both perished. The people buried them in pits in the earth next to the body of the holy man, one on each side.[6] Since, howev-

---

4. Cf. Ps. 9:11 and Ezek. 33:11.

5. Isa. 58:9, *Vetus Latina* version: "adhuc loquente te, dicet: ecce adsum" (cf. Vulgate: "clamabis, et dicet: ecce adsum").

6. Lanzoni, "Il 'Liber Pontificalis,'" thought the story of the hermit and the lions (c. 25) was inspired by a sarcophagus carving showing a man between two lions; but, as shown by Testi-Rasponi, *CPER*, 73, n. 2, it is more likely that the lions were introduced into the story as a topos of a hermit. See Elliott, *Roads to Paradise*, 151–66, for examples of lions and hermits and especially where lions aid in the burial of their hermits.

er, the people were terrified by great fear, having returned home they told of the miracles which the Lord had worked through men and beasts.

26. Now this was in the time of Valentinian. When Valentinian began to rule, in the beginning of his reign this blessed Peter, robbed of life, sought the stars.[7] As some say, he was buried in the Petriana church which he founded. You may know with great certainty that I speak the truth to you, not any lie.

While I was living in my *monasterium* of the blessed and ever-virgin Mary which is called *ad Blachernas*, which is located not far from Wandalaria, when I wanted to examine the lives of all the bishops of Ravenna, I had doubts in my soul about the tomb of this holy man. While I was thinking thus, one of the boys, who daily placed himself in my sight, announced to me that George, the priest of the church of Classe, had arrived. He at that time had the care of the church of St. Severus the confessor of Christ, a very venerable man, constant in all things, firm without weakness.

When he had come before me, after he sat down, at once I began to ask him whether perhaps he knew anything from older men, from hearing or sight, about the tomb[8] of this blessed bishop.

He, with a cheerful face, said to me, "Come, I will show you what you greatly desire, where a most precious treasure rests."

When we had mounted horses, we hastened to Classe, and I ordered my men, who had accompanied us, to withdraw a distance of about half a stade; and we entered the *monasterium* of St. James, which is located within the baptistry of the above-mentioned church. We saw a tomb of precious proconnesian stone,[9] and with difficulty we raised the cover slightly. We found in this sarcophagus a chest of cypress wood, and when we had raised its cover, we both saw the holy body, lying as if it had been buried at that moment,

---

7. Valentinian III reigned 425–55; therefore Peter I (c. 431–50) did not die at the beginning of Valentinian's reign.

8. *Glosochomum*: see Glossary, s.v.

9. On Agnellus's use of the term "proconnesian," referring to marble from the island of Proconnesus near Constantinople, see Glossary, s.v. *proconnesus*.

having a tall stature and skin showing pallor, limbs whole everywhere, the chest and stomach whole, nothing was missing, except the little pillow for the head was diminished. It spread such an odor that we felt as if we were inhaling incense mixed with myrrh and balsam. A horrible and most vehement terror overcame us, and such sadness, that with sighs and groans we could scarcely even close what we had eagerly opened before. The odor finally overcame us in all things and thus it was that for more than one week the odor never receded from our nostrils. And above that sarcophagus was his image wonderfully depicted, which contained the words: "Lord Peter Archbishop."[10]

27. And in the church of blessed John the Evangelist, because of his sanctity, Galla Placidia[11] ordered that his image in mosaic should adorn the lower wall of the apse, behind the back of the bishop, over the seat where the bishop sits. This image was made thus: having a long beard, with hands extended, as if he is singing the mass, and as if the host is placed on the altar, and behold an angel of the Lord is shown facing the altar, receiving his prayers.

In his reign the empress Galla Placidia offered many gifts to the church of Ravenna and made a lamp with a candelabrum of purest gold weighing, as some say, in public weight seven pounds, made with her likeness in a medallion in the scene-painters' art, and around it reading, "I will prepare a lamp for my Christ."[12]

And most blessed Peter made covers for the Gospels from the best gold and brightest gems, and his likeness was made there, which remain up to the present day, and letters showing this are written above his head: "Lord Peter, the bishop, offered this on the day of his ordination to the holy church."

He died on July 31. He sat __ years, __ months, __ days.

10. The word *archiepiscopus* was not used in Ravenna until the mid-sixth century; therefore, this must have been the tomb of Peter III, about whose burial, c. 97, Agnellus is not entirely sure (Deichmann, *Ravenna* 1:124). Peter Chrysologus, as Agnellus tells in c. 52, was buried in Imola.

11. Galla Placidia was the daughter of Emperor Theodosius I and the mother of Emperor Valentinian III.

12. Ps. 131:17. Agnellus may have seen this object, or perhaps, because he specifies its weight, he saw it listed in an archival record.

CONCERNING HOLY NEON, C. 450–73

28. Neon, the eighteenth bishop. He had a beautiful appearance, a most holy and spiritual life.

He was the builder of the above-mentioned Petriana church, only part of which his predecessor had constructed from the foundation, whence it was necessary for the successors to complete the work for their predecessor. Thereupon, after all the buildings were built and the renovations of the temple were completed, he had it painted with different colors.

He decorated the baptistries of the Ursiana church most beautifully: he set up in mosaic and gold tesserae the images of the apostles and their names in the vault, he girded the side-walls with different types of stones.[1] His name is written in stone letters:[2]

Yield, old name, yield, age, to newness! Behold the glory of the renewed font shines more beautifully. For generous Neon, highest priest, has adorned it, arranging all things in beautiful refinement.[3]

29. Within the episcopal palace of the Ursiana church he built from the foundations and brought to completion a structure which is called the Five Couches.[4] On each side of the dining hall he built wondrous windows, and there he ordered the pavement of the dining hall to be decorated with different types of stones. The story of the psalm which we sing daily, that is, "Praise ye the Lord from the heavens,"[5] together with the Flood, he ordered to be

---

1. This decoration still survives; see Deichmann, *Ravenna* 2.1:17–47 and 2.3:370, and Nauerth, *Agnellus von Ravenna, Untersuchungen*, 50–51.

2. Testi-Rasponi, *CPER*, 77, n. 14, suggests that "letters" refers to the monogram for *Neon episcopus dei famulus* (Neon the bishop, servant of God), which still survives, but since the phrase introduces a poetic inscription, it is better to see it used in the same way as "letters" in the same context, to refer to the "words" of the inscription.

3. For similar dedicatory inscriptions in churches in Rome and Tebessa, see Deichmann, *Ravenna* 2.1:17.

4. The name *quinque accubitas*, "five couches," refers to the number of dining couches the room would hold, and possibly to its appearance; see Glossary, s.v. *triclinium*. For more on this dining hall, see de Angelis d'Ossat, "Sulla distrutta aula," and Miller, *The Bishop's Palace*, 23–27.

5. Ps. 148:1. This psalm would make a good illustration because it lists all of the various parts of creation praising God.

painted on the side wall flanking the church; and on the other side wall, which is located over the stream,[6] he had it adorned in colors with the story of our Lord Jesus Christ, when he fed so many thousands of men from five loaves and two fishes, as we read. On one side of the interior façade of the dining hall he set out the creation of the world, in which daily we read these verses written in hexameter:[7]

At the beginning of the shining world in its first origin, when the swift power of the Father and the might of his Son made the sea, the earth, the bright kingdoms of heaven, and when the new sun, moon, day, dawn shone forth, from that light the star-bearing heaven shone [5].

One man in the new world, made from the virgin earth, leapt up from the soil, innocent in sense and in body. He alone deserved to be called the image of God, for the love of the supreme Progenitor produced man as his likeness in the world, and made him its master [10].

The all-powerful Begetter, richest in things, Himself endowed him with manifold wealth for the future: at the same time he yielded him all the gifts of the forests, he ordered the earth to produce fruits for eternity. His were the snowy-white sheep, gleaming cows at grass [15], his the high-maned horses and tawny lions, his everywhere the deer with branching horns, and the winged flocks of birds, and fishes in the waves.

For God gave all things to man, whatever He had produced, and made them equally subject to his word [20]. He ordered him, however, in the first heavenly admonitions, to observe his law and vital things in time to

---

6. Rizzardi, "Note sull'antico episcopio," 719, connects this passage, where the dining hall is located between the church and the *Fossa Amnis*, with another passage in c. 163, in which Archbishop John VI is said to be sitting "at the table, behind the apse of the church above the *uiuarium*." Rizzardi shows that an area between the Ursiana and the *Fossa Amnis* would have been "behind the apse" of the church, and thus concludes that in c. 163 John was sitting in the dining hall of the Five Couches. Deichmann, however, suggests that "table" in c. 163 refers to a smaller, more private dining chamber ("Studi sulla Ravenna scomparsa," 107, and *Ravenna* 2.1:206–7).

7. According to Agnellus, two or more of the walls contained windows, while all the walls seem to have been decorated with images selected for their references to food and eating. Specific studies reconstructing the decoration and the iconography of this chamber are Wickhoff, "Das Speisezimmer," Weis, "Der römische Schöpfungszyklus," and de Angelis d'Ossat, "Sulla distrutta aula."

come; he commanded him not to eat the forbidden apple. Spurning the command, thus man lost himself and everything else.

And on the other façade was depicted the story of the apostle Peter, and underneath are written metrical verses:

Receive gladly, O saint, and do not despise this small song, we must say a few words in your praise.

Hail, Simon Peter, and accept the gift sent to you, in which the great King wanted you to take from on high. Take the full linen sheets hanging from heaven [5], sent to you, Peter; they bear these diverse animals, which God ordered you to kill and eat. It is permitted to doubt no pure thing which the Almighty Creator, who has the highest power over things, created.[8]

Hail, Simon Peter, apostolic light, whom the golden mind of Christ rejoices [10] to adorn through all the years: in you the holy church of God shines mightily, on you the Son of the heavenly Prince, famous through the ages, placed the firm foundations of His house.

Your virtue is clear to all, and judgment to the faithful [15]. You stand as prince among your twelve brothers, and new laws are given to you from on high—by which you tame the fierce hearts of men, you soothe hearts, you teach all to be Christians throughout the world—and now by your merits Christ's glory prepares the kingdom [20].

However, after all these things were completed, he died on February 11. Formerly he was buried in the basilica of the Apostles, before the altar of the blessed apostle Peter under a porphyry stone; now we have carried him out from there and buried him next to the throne of that basilica, and he has been translated through the place which is called At the Strong Arm.[9]

---

8. From Acts 10:11–16.

9. In the early twentieth century a burial covered by an inscription was excavated in the crypt, at the center of the apse, of San Francesco, the former church of the Apostles. The part of the epitaph containing the name was missing; later excavations revealed that the burial and the inscription were later than the surrounding floor, and the burial is thought to be the translation of Neon that took place in the time of Agnellus. "Next to the throne" would therefore refer to the throne of the bishop, which would be located at the center of the back of the apse. See Deichmann, *Ravenna* 2.2:315–16.

30. But you do not know where it is that is called the Strong Arm, or why it was called this. But since there are a few old men who know, I want you to know what place is called this and for what reason it was named.

When you go to the region of the Apostles, not far from the Ovilian wall, you enter the narthex of blessed Peter the Apostle, where the image of our lord Jesus Christ is represented with arm extended, and here on one side is depicted the image of blessed Peter and key bearer, and on the other side the image of the chosen vessel Paul.[10] I have told you where it is; I will now tell you why it is called this.[11]

When two men desired to be joined together by a pact, one said to the other, who had a child, "I pray a small petition of you, and I ask that my request not be turned back empty." To him the other said, "I will not incommode you; let what you wish be done." And he said, "Give me your son, that I might be his father in holy baptism and I might raise him from the sanctified font. Let us be communal fathers, you of his flesh, I however of his spirit." And the other said, "In the name of our lord Jesus Christ let it be done thus." And it was done thus.

And from that day, after the infant had been baptized, they were communally fathers, and they had love for one another in the Holy Spirit and in the kiss of peace, since thus it is proper for those who do such things together, since they place not men, but the Holy Spirit, as mediator between them.[12] And as you know, the spiritual

---

10. This description possibly refers to a picture of the *traditio legis* type, in which Christ would be giving the keys to heaven to Peter (identified here as *claviger*) and the law to Paul (Nauerth, *Agnellus von Ravenna, Untersuchungen*, 63). However, at the end of this chapter, Agnellus mentions a picture of Peter and Paul on either side of a cross, which may be a reference to this same image, in which case "arm extended" would refer to the crucified Christ.

11. The following story, with variations, is told about a picture of Christ in Constantinople, *BHG* 797, as identified by Lanzoni, "Leggende Orientali." The legend is closely associated with the iconoclastic controversy and demonstrates the iconodule concept that images can work miracles; see Deliyannis, "Agnellus of Ravenna and Iconoclasm."

12. The relationship of "co-parenthood" through baptism in the early Middle

father is greater than the carnal, since the latter procreated a son from sin, and in sin is his son born, and in sin that son remains; however the spiritual father, after he has received him from the water of baptism, with the devil and his pomps removed, the son is born spiritually from the holy font. He receives the sanctified son, born again through the water and the Holy Spirit; however much a sinner before, born from sin, so much the more sanctified afterward by the Holy Spirit.

Now it so happened at that time that one of these above-mentioned compadres lent three hundred *solidi* to the other compadre. When they had arrived in the place of which you heard earlier, At the Strong Arm, the one said to the other, "Lend me secretly, I beseech you, three hundred gold *solidi*." To him the other responded, "Tomorrow morning let us meet here, and I will transfer it from me to you."

And when the next day had dawned, they came to the place which they had agreed upon, and with the money counted out, the lender said to his compadre, "Behold, compadre, take what you sought; however make a provision between you and me, how you shall return it to me. You don't want to give me a guarantor. You don't want to call mediators. You don't want to give pledges. Nor do you want anyone to know for fear of censure. And am I to consent to all these things for you?"

The borrower answered him and said, "Such a bond is confirmed between you and me, which we cannot transgress. Give me this money in the name of a loan, you will lose nothing. In the sight of God I say to you: where I stand, I will return it to you."

And the lender, answering, said to his compadre, "Compadre,

Ages is discussed by Lynch, *Godparents and Kinship*, esp. 192–201. Usually the natural parents invite someone more powerful to be a godparent; yet here we see someone asking to be a godparent to the child of someone more powerful, found again in the *LPR* in c. 171. Interestingly, the godparent was considered the spiritual guarantor (*fideiussor*) of the child's behavior after baptism (ibid., 148). Thus there is perhaps some sort of double play on words in this story. I have translated the word *compater* as "compadre," a word that in Spanish represents precisely the relationship of godfather to father; there is, however, no appropriate cognate in English.

let Almighty God be a mediator between us, whose image is depicted here, and let this strong and terrible arm of the Savior be a guarantor, and these two great princes and apostles, namely Peter and Paul, be witnesses between me and you." [The borrower said] "This is the right hand, which led the sons of Israel from the land of Egypt and this Strong Arm, which is today a guarantor for me, that I will return to you this your money."

Therefore with the 300 *solidi* counted out, looking up at the face of the Savior, [the lender] said, "Lord God Almighty, in these words which we have spoken, I give to this my compadre these *solidi*. May You be guarantor, I give them through Your holy arm, so that, if he does not return them to me by the agreement, You will return them to me." And this speech pleased [the borrower].

With the agreement made, they confirmed between them as guarantor the Strong Arm of the Savior, and with the money received he set out immediately to do business. And when he began to do business here and there, he found it quadrupled, and he went to the city of Constantinople, and seeing how the money was multiplied in his hands, he did not want to return to Ravenna; and behold the agreed-upon time arrived for returning the amount, and he didn't come at all.

However that compadre who had lent the money came to the image of the Savior saying, "Lord God eternal, now the day of the agreement has passed, for which You have been guarantor of my compadre; watch over my case, lest I suffer a loss, return to me my *solidi*, which I gave because of Your Strong Arm." That night, that arm of the Savior appeared to [the borrower] in his dreams, saying to him, "Go, return to your compadre the money which you received, for which I am your guarantor, since daily he bothers me." When he did not come, [the lender] went again to the image of the Savior and made accusations as above. And that night the holy arm appeared to him and it protested as you heard above.

It happened on a certain day that he who had given the amount came and he began reproach the holy image of our Lord, "O Lord, why do You not render my justice? You are my guarantor, I gave through Your Strong Arm. You rule the heavens, You control the earth, You govern the seas; can You not compel even one man? You gave me this amount, and if You want to take it, who stops You? No one, since all things are subject to Your power. If an earthly man had been my guarantor, I would have compelled him by a judge, or used force against him, or somehow would have received my amount. You, who are Lord of heaven and earth, unless You order him to return it, what am I to do? Since the heavens are not clean in Your presence, and the sun and moon do not shine, and the angels and archangels tremble, and the earth dissolves, the mountains collapse, all elements are nothing; who am I, that I dare to speak to You? Only let Your pity be upon me, and defend my cause, and return [my money], since here are two witnesses, both apostles chosen by You. In their presence Your Strong Arm became my guarantor, and if I say otherwise, let them bear witness, since they are most true and You have made their tongues the keys of heaven." And with these words he groaned and left.

And finally that night the image of our Savior appeared to the borrower compadre in his dreams, saying, "Return swiftly to Ravenna and give back the *solidi* to your compadre, for whom this My arm is guarantor, since he has reproached Me and I cannot sustain his accusation. And know you, that if you do not go swiftly and he troubles Me further, you will lose all that you have acquired here, and I will give your body to the whips, and you will be in greatest tribulation all the days of your life, and you will fail then. For I will return from My own treasury double the *solidi* to your compadre."

Then he, rising at dawn, negotiated as best he could, and on that day he took ship and returned to Ravenna. When his compadre, who had given the money, heard this, full of joy he went to the borrower's house, as if visiting him. Among other words he began to ask him about the lent money. To him the borrower responded that all his business was finished and his *solidi* were quadrupled.

But the lender said to his compadre, "If that is so, blessed be God! Return to me my *solidi*." But he said to him in answer, "I will do it freely, not today, since it is evening. Tomorrow morning let us go before my guarantor, that is, the Strong Arm, which compelled me strongly in these days. There I will return it to you even in the sight of the two princes our witnesses."

And on the next day the borrower took out four hundred gold pieces. They went to the place where he had lent it, and he gave back the re-counted four hundred *solidi*. The borrower said to the compadre his lender, "You have done well to me, since you raised me from poverty; and Almighty God has blessed my business and has quadrupled my money. Take now three hundred *solidi*, which you lent to me in the sight of my guarantor and our two witnesses, and I pay beyond that a hundred more to you, that I might be innocent, because on the agreed day I was not ready; or also for a gift." And he answering his compadre said, "Far be it from me that I should receive more than I gave. This Strong Arm, which is a mediator between me and you, does not permit me to accept usury at the lace of His shoe."[13]

And the debtor responding said, "I swear to you by this Strong Arm, and I tell the truth, that, however much the money was multiplied in my hands, I would not have returned to Ravenna this year if this Arm had not compelled me three times. But on those nights and the days which followed, it came to me in sleep and protested saying, 'Go, return the money to your creditor which you took, since your compadre is bothering Me, he has worried Me today as your guarantor.' Thus it admonished me on two occasions. Indeed on a certain day of this month this holy image of our Lord came to me at night, and began to rebuke me, saying, 'Why do you not return to give back the money to your creditor and compadre, which you have pledged by My arm to return? That man was quite troublesome to Me today, and lamented before Me, further he said to Me, "That if I had an earthly man as a guarantor he would already have restituted me." Rise quickly, go return it, since I do not sustain his lamentations, they are harsh to Me. And not just for the money, but for this reason also shall you render an account, so that he does not blaspheme because of hardship. Do not delay, but rise, go. Know that if you delay, I will give the *solidi* out of My own

13. Cf. Gen. 14:23 and John 1:26.

alms-chest, and you here will lose this fortune completely, further I will do harm to your body.' Indeed the next day, entering a small boat, with favorable winds I hastened to Ravenna, this city saved by God, to return it all to you; and thus I have done. And now I request that you take these hundred gold pieces, since I deceived you, so that no other injurious charge may be held against me."

To whom the other, answering, said, "I have sworn to you by the Lord and his Strong Arm, which has brought you back here, that I would not accept even a handful of dust, unless by your love alone, which I hold daily. And as you know by these your own words, as you say, when in the night this arm compelled you out of justice to me, it was I who was disturbing you, and blessed be God, who brought you back safe and sound to your own property! And now be innocent of this case in the sight of eternal God and by me, and let Almighty God Himself allow our charity, in the way in which it has been established here, thus remain through eternity. Let us see and act carefully, so that one of us does not defraud the other, since we have constituted this Strong Arm as a mediator between us."

And saying this, they wept for joy and kissed each other. They went in peace, and for this reason, from that day this place was called the Strong Arm up to today, but there are few who know why.

Thence the body of blessed Archbishop Neon was brought and buried, as we have noted above. And you have seen the house which he built, and in that house, you have seen, where the images of the apostles Peter and Paul are made of mosaic, flanking the cross on either side, and you have read a little line of verse, in which it says, "May the Lord bishop Neon be long remembered among us."[14] He sat __ years, __ months, __ days.

---

14. It is not clear which structure is meant by "house." Deichmann, "Studi sulla Ravenna scomparsa," 77, repeats Testi-Rasponi's assertion that the "house" refers to the "house in the episcopium," built by Neon and described in c. 29, although there is no mention of a picture of St. Paul in that decorative cycle. Deichmann bases his argument on the fact that the inscription seems to be an acclamation and belongs in a secular rather than in a religious setting.

CONCERNING HOLY EXUPERANTIUS, C. 473–77

31. Exuperantius, the nineteenth bishop, a man of great age, humble and gentle, wise in good works. What his predecessors built, he held safe.

In his reign the church of St. Agnes was built by Gemellus, subdeacon of this holy church of Ravenna and rector of Sicily.[1] And he endowed it greatly in gold and silver and holy banners, and he built a silver cross for the procession of the birth of this martyr, and it has lasted up to our time.[2]

In his reign Lord Felix was killed at the steps of the Ursiana church in the month of May, and the Lady Eudoxia was made empress at Ravenna on August 6.[3]

Our elders and old men have told me nothing further about his life; he does not have a memorable history. He was a builder of the *Tricollis*, but did not finish it.[4]

32. And if you readers of this Pontifical might have some doubt, and you might want to ask, saying, "Why does he not tell the deeds of this bishop, as of his predecessors?" Listen, it is because of this:

I, Agnellus, also known as Andreas, insignificant priest of my holy church here in Ravenna, asked and urged by the brothers of this see, have composed this above-mentioned pontifical book

---

1. The Ravennate church possessed great land holdings in Sicily, and the rector, an official of the Ravennate church, administered these properties. Agnellus refers to the Sicilian patrimony again, at greater length, in c. 111. For a comprehensive study, see Fasoli, "Sul Patrimonio."

2. The information about Gemellus's patronage must have come from inscriptions in the church and on the silver object, in which the name of Exuperantius is also mentioned.

3. These two events took place in 430–39, long before Exuperantius's reign (c. 473–77).

4. In c. 50 Agnellus tells how Peter II founded the house in the episcopal palace called the *Tricollis*; in all the Lives from Aurelian to Maximian there appears a phrase like "A builder of *Tricollis*, but he did not complete it." In the dedicatory inscription, which is listed in c. 75, Exuperantius is not mentioned. The appearance of the phrase here is obviously a mistake, probably occasioned by Agnellus's confusion over the identities of the two Bishops Peter of the fifth century.

from the time of blessed Apollinaris and after his death lasting almost eight hundred years and more. And when I found out what they certainly did, these deeds were brought to your attention, and what I heard from elders and old men I have not stolen from your eyes. And when I did not discover any history, or what their life had been like, neither from aged and old men, nor from buildings, nor from any authority, in order that there would be no gap in the holy bishops, in the order in which each obtained this see, one after the other, with God aiding me by your prayers, I have constructed their lives; and I believe that I have not lied, since they were encouraging and pure and charitable orators and acquirers of the souls of men for God.

Indeed if by chance you should have some question about how I was able to know about their appearance, know that pictures taught me, since in those days they always made images in their likenesses. And if there might be a controversy over whether I ought to affirm their appearance from pictures, St. Ambrose bishop of Milan, in his *passio* of the blessed martyrs Gervase and Protase, sang of the image of the blessed apostle Paul, saying, "whose face the picture taught me."[5]

33. He finished his pontificate and his life by divine order on May 29, and was buried in the already mentioned basilica of St. Agnes, martyr, in front of the altar under a porphyry stone; some say, behind the altar under a porphyry stone.[6] He sat __ years, __ months, __ days.

---

5. Pseudo-Ambrose, *Epistolae* 2.4: "whose face the picture taught me" (also found in the *Acta Sanctorum*, Iun. 3.821). This passage was cited as evidence of the efficacy of images, at the anti-iconoclastic Council of Rome of 769, of which Agnellus seems to have seen the Acts. The "controversy" in question, then, is the Iconoclastic Controversy. See Deliyannis, "Agnellus of Ravenna and Iconoclasm."

6. The epitaph of Exuperantius, which survives in the Museo Arcivescovile in Ravenna, says: "Here rests in peace the body of holy Exuperantius, pontiff and confessor and archbishop of the holy church of Ravenna" (*CIL* 11.1, no. 303). The appearance of the word "archbishop," first used by the bishops of Ravenna in the middle of the sixth century, shows that this epitaph was not original. Agnellus may not have seen it, since he is not sure exactly where Exuperantius was buried (Deichmann, *Ravenna* 2.2:299).

CONCERNING HOLY JOHN I, 477–94

34. John, the twentieth bishop, very venerable in virtue, sustainer of paupers, adorned by modesty, a lover of purity, at whose prayer the angelic host descended. Of middle height, thin of face, lean from fasting, a giver of alms to the needy.

In his reign the church of the blessed martyr Laurence,[1] which is located in Caesarea, was built by Lauricius the chamberlain of the emperor Honorius;[2] we see that it was adorned with greatest care, with buildings of wonderful size.

35. However I will not remain silent about what I have heard from narrators about this just-mentioned church.

The emperor Honorius ordered this Lauricius to build him a palace in Caesarea. Having taken the money, he came to Caesarea and there built the just-mentioned basilica of the blessed martyr. When it had been completely finished, he returned to his lord, to tell him that the hall he had commissioned was finished.

And [Lauricius] found [Honorius] disturbed, and, sitting in the imperial costume, he began to ask the architect Lauricius in anger if the whole royal hall, which he had ordered him to make, had been completed in all its works. The envious and inveterate fraud of wicked men had assailed the ears of the emperor, saying that blessed Lauricius had not built an imperial dwelling but a church.

Lauricius, responding, said that he had honorably built a great hall, with courts, and that he had placed below these high arches and many *cubilia* at the sides of the house. The anger of the emperor cooled.

1. John I reigned after Exuperantius, from 477 to 494; however, because of Agnellus's misunderstanding of his sources, the events told in his Life cover the years 423–94. The church of St. Laurence was certainly built in the early fifth century, presumably under the sponsorship of Honorius; it is mentioned by St. Augustine in his *Sermon* 322 (Holder-Egger, *LPER*, 298, n. 3). Agnellus tells us below that Bishop John consecrated the altar of St. Laurence, a piece of information he probably learned from an inscription; this may simply refer to the altar, and not to the entire church.

2. Caesarea was a region between Ravenna and Classe. The *maior cubiculi* was an important palace official; I have translated the term as "chamberlain." About the identity of Lauricius, see Deichmann, *Ravenna* 2.2:338–39.

When, after a long journey, the emperor Honorius arrived at Caesarea, seeing the sublime buildings he was very pleased; but when he had entered within it, with a swift movement Lauricius fled behind the holy altar, in order to escape. When Honorius ordered him to be seized, he himself fell on his face flat on the ground, and went into a trance. A most precious gem which had been in the crown on his head was embedded in one of the stones. And raising up only his head, after his sight was restored to his clouded eyes, he saw, behind that altar of blessed Laurence which the most blessed bishop John had consecrated,[3] the above-mentioned Lauricius standing there, and Laurence the athlete of Christ holding his hands over the neck of Lauricius.[4]

Then the emperor judged Lauricius to be more righteous than himself, and his anger was abandoned, and he began to venerate him as a father and considered him second only to himself among everyone in the palace.

36. [Lauricius] lived in the light of this world for ninety-six years;[5] in the days of this emperor he died in good old age. The king followed his bier with his weeping soldiers, and he was buried in the *monasterium* of Sts. Gervase and Protase, next to the above-mentioned church, wonderfully decorated with gold mosaic and different types of stones and pieces of precious materials,[6] joined to the walls.

---

3. Agnellus says *papa Johannes*; he usually uses the word *papa* exclusively to refer to Roman popes. In cc. 44 and 67 he quotes inscriptions that mention "papa Victore" and "papa Agnello," bishops of Ravenna, and thus it is likely that here, too, he saw an inscription commemorating the dedication of the altar. Agnellus uses the word *papa* two other times to refer to John I, and also one time each for Damian and Felix (cc. 132, 144).

4. This story, and particularly the vision of Honorius, may have been derived from a mosaic in the apse of St. Laurence, in which the saint and Lauricius were depicted, in a pose similar to that of the angel and Bishop Ecclesius in the apse of San Vitale.

5. Agnellus must have learned this fact from an inscription on the sarcophagus, which, as he says below, still survived in his day.

6. The meaning of the word *metalla* (materials) is not clear; it can mean metals or minerals or marbles. See Glossary, s.v.

That sarcophagus where his most excellent body rests was so clear, as some assert, that the pious body was seen inside by passersby. And I will tell why it does not look today as it used to look in former times, as I have recently learned.

Some emperor whose name I do not know wanted to drag it away for his own use. On a certain night blessed Lauricius stood before the custodian of the church and said, "Bring ash and water, and smear my tomb and afterward wash it diligently." When this was done, the clarity vanished. But the following day, when the workmen had come to carry it away, they saw the deterioration and they told the chamberlain who was in charge of the revenues; then telling it in the halls of the prince, they sent it back here; and neither earth nor stone would support the sarcophagus.

And before you enter the chamber of the sarcophagus, if you look on the right hand, next to where the images of three boys are depicted in mosaic,[7] there you will find golden letters reading thus:

To Stephen, Protase, Gervase, blessed in martyrdom and who are to him of eternal memory, Lauricius dedicated this on September 29, in the fifteenth year of Theodosius and Placidus Valentinian.[8]

And in the arch of the main apse, in as much as we can read it, we find on one side reading thus, that in four years and six months they had completed the building, all things were finished. And in the entrance of the church we find written that Opilius decorated this facade, and this same Opilius adorned it greatly in silver and gold.[9]

---

7. Testi-Rasponi, *CPER*, 97, n. 2, suggests that the "images of three boys" depicted the three youths in the fiery furnace from the book of Daniel, which has been accepted by most scholars, including Nauerth, *Agnellus von Ravenna, Untersuchungen*, 65. However, Gonin, *Excerpta*, 73, observes that these three youths were probably the three saints to whom the chapel was dedicated.

8. The date is September 29, 435.

9. This information was probably taken from a dedicatory inscription naming Opilius as the sponsor of the decoration. Likewise, the inscription in the main apse, stating that the building was completed in four years and six months, probably also contained names that Agnellus used to create his story, perhaps the name of Honorius.

And if you inquire diligently, you will find that very ornate larger vessels, now carried elsewhere, both crowns and hanging cups, which we see that the Ursiana church has among its ornaments, were brought from this basilica of the martyr.

And this Opilius is buried on the women's [north] side in the middle of the main part of the church.[10]

That gem, which we have described above, was so much more brilliant than other gems, that by its light a man could see to walk through this church by night. Some say that it even shone outside the church, and where it was embedded appears as a mark in the stone up to the present day.

37. Now at that time[11] when the aforementioned blessed John ascended the episcopal throne of Ravenna, it happened that Attila, king of the Huns, devastated the borders of Italy and butchered the bodies of the people with his swords. When he had hastened to the shore of Ravenna, that he might overthrow it and kill its inhabitants with spears, and her enemies lay spread over the beaches like a swarm of locusts, on one day and the next they hastened to Ravenna with breastplates and shields. But the king, wearing a corselet and girded with warlike arms, covered his breast with a shield, and with crested head he marched with his army.

When the most holy bishop John recognized him, he threw himself completely flat on his face with great lamentation and enormous tears, in prayer to the Almighty Lord, and sought death for his soul, that he might not see his sons or daughters and the Ravennate citizens cast out and scattered in exile or death, nor his church contaminated by wicked and cruel men; and that he might not see the destruction of the city in the pillage of looters; that he might not see those souls which he had acquired for God alone from superstitious paganism subjugated at the hands of pagans, and that they should not return again to the error of paganism,

---

10. Testi-Rasponi (*CPER*, 98, n. 2) contrasts *subdita* ("main part" here) with *abdita*, which is found in cc. 96 and 149; see Glossary, s.v.

11. Attila invaded Italy in 450–51, thus during the reign of Peter I or Neon, not John. In any case, the Huns are not recorded as coming anywhere near Ravenna; the story is derived from other legends; see Pizarro, *Writing Ravenna*, 104–11.

and that the most tricky devil might not release the souls to his own authority.

Therefore, while the holy man remained at his vigils the whole night and incessantly besought the Lord on behalf of his sheep, with his knees fixed on the ground and his breast struck repeatedly with blows, his hands stretched out, he besought God with words of this sort:

"Almighty God, Whose wonders are indescribable, hear me, Your humble servant and sinner. Receive my prayer, merciful Father. Let my tears come before the sight of Your pity. Be with me, my God, You Who made heaven from nothing and made the earth solid with a word, Who stood the peaks of mountains on the bulk, Who made man from a liquid element, in Whose creation You were pleased, and You ordered him to fear You alone. Under Your rule, Lord, all things quake, before Your gaze the heavens flee, the earth shakes, the mountains are moved, the waves shake, the angels tremble, the archangels fear, the dominations are in fear, the princedoms and powers fall to the ground, the clouds and winds are scattered, the sun hides its rays, the moon is shadowed in darkness, the clarity of the stars is diminished.[12] Pity us, Creator of the human race, free us with a strong hand and an outstretched arm, save us through Your holy victorious right hand. You are God in the heavens above and the earth below, Who drowned the pharaoh with his chariots and armies in the depths of the sea and protected the Israelite camps, Who overthrew Amalech and scattered the Amorites, Who laid low the camps of the Assyrians, 145 thousands, through Your holy angel.[13] I beseech, Almighty God, that You give us helpers from Your holy heavens, since 'You crush warfare; Lord is Your name.' Through our Lord Jesus Christ, Your son, Who lives with You and reigns as God in unity of the Holy Spirit through all the ages of ages. Amen."[14]

12. Cf. Peter Chrysologus, *Sermon* 6.3, as also in c. 30, above.

13. 2 Kings 19:35; Isa. 37:36. But in the Vulgate both passages give the number as "a hundred and eighty-five thousand."

14. Cf. Ps. 135:10–13, Wisd. of Sol. 10:20, and Jth. 9:6–7 and 10. Judith is praying for her besieged city to be delivered from the enemy, and thus is an appropriate mod-

After his prayer was complete he left the place, damp with tears. On the next day at dawn the most blessed man proceeded as if to celebrate mass, endowed with an angelic form, with the priests and clergy and with censers before them burning incense, with a great light, singing and chanting psalms to God at the same time they hastened toward the above-mentioned King Attila. For there was such divine piety, that not only did it seem that these enticements and shining vestments had laid low the heart of the fierce king, but also that for this holiest man, the king with his armies would have fought against another king, if it were necessary, and would afterward defend those [i.e., the Ravennates] whom he had just come to destroy.

Therefore the king, sitting on his royal throne, wearing purple vestments woven with gold, seeing the bishop approaching him from afar, chanting psalms with his priests, said to his attendants, "Why are these most pure men chanting psalms; from where have they come, and what do they want? For I have never seen such men with my eyes, whiter than snow, more beautiful than everyone and special indeed. And that one, who is at their head, is like an angel of God."

Those who were there, answering the king said, "O unconquered Lord king triumphant, this man, whom you see standing and weeping in the middle of the white-garbed people, comes to supplicate your mighty arm, that you may be merciful; he seeks pity, he asks for your mercy." The king said to them, "For what reason?" And they said, "So that you do not hand over flourishing Ravenna to destruction; so that you restore the citizens of the city to joy." Again the king, asking, said, "And where is he from?" And they said, "He rules the see of this episcopate."

And the king said, "Ask him what he wants for himself, or what consolation hangs over him, or why he has laid himself down in our presence." And answering the king they said, "Everyone has

---

el for John. Testi-Rasponi suggests that this entire prayer was derived from a liturgy "against foreign or barbarian peoples," which existed in Ravenna even in the ninth century (*CPER*, 99, n. 17).

heard that your valor is great and your hand is strong and your arm is most powerful and your troops are robust; therefore this man comes to you and desires to give his soul to death on behalf of his sons, lest he see the overthrow of his city; since your victorious fame has increased in all the earth and is greatly spread abroad."

And the king said to them, "Why do you say an unheard-of thing? You assail my ears with your bitter words. Does worldly law not decree that whoever tells useless things to the ears of a king should be destroyed by the sword? Tell me, all of you who know this case, and I will hear it most diligently and with great care: how can this one man have sired so many sons?"

And some of those standing there, answering the king with great dread and veneration, terrified by fear, said, "It is not the way our lord thinks; but if you want to hear how they are his sons, we will explain it with true assertions and most certain words. They are sons not from conception of the flesh or from the pollution of desire, but spiritual sons, whom he has acquired for Almighty God and brought back from the worship of pagans. For these he desires to die, for these he offers himself as a sacrifice, and before even one of his sheep is killed, he desires that he first be butchered with the sword, by your brandishing arm."

And thus the king, hearing words of this sort, wavered internally for one hour, and his expressions changed, his face was covered with pallor, and his heart was shaken by a great storm, and various thoughts succeeded one another, his mind wandered, his thoughts were taken in different directions, he was senseless in his whole body, he went into a trance, all because such a holy man stood before him, whose merits allowed him to look upon an angelic face, who daily lifted up his mind to the heavens, whose holy praises resounded to the stars, who was like the holy prophets and imitated the renown of the holy apostles, even imitated the Lord Christ, who gave himself for his sheep. But Christ God, the Son of God, separated his soul from his body for us wretches in the crucifixion, and redeemed man, whom He had made long before from mud, from the jaw of the serpent, and afterward returned to his heavenly throne.

And thus when these things had happened, the king's senses returned to him, and where he had just seemed to his men to be mentally paralyzed, by the prayers of the holy man he was returned to his own intelligence. But he cried out, saying, "O good father, who offers himself to die for his sons! O indescribable meekness! O blessed tolerance and bounteous wisdom! He has given himself for everyone, and has borne such uncorrupt faith in his Lord, that he would die before any one of the sheep committed to him might be led away bound. Good shepherd, holiest man, worthy of his God, proven in faith!"

And the king said to blessed Bishop John, "To you, father, all things are conceded. Behold, I will not raise my spear against your people, nor will I send a brandishing lance, nor will the trumpet of my army sound further in your ears. There is just one thing that you should do, since your citizens are very ingenious and very clever, so that they may not say of me that 'we expelled him who was deceived by fraud,' after which censure might arise against both me and my armies. For in the end, it was your sanctity that soothed my heart. Go quickly and lay down your gates to the ground, and open a square opening in the wall, so that I might pass through the middle of the city. The hooves of my horses will trample your gates; we will not kill anyone, nor will we lay any snares, nor will you suffer any injury. Do this, lest some towns might say cunningly, 'He could not demolish or subjugate Ravenna; he is reduced along with his army, he shows his back, he has fled,' and they might have less respect for my powers than for the other kings my predecessors, who ruled for a long time. Now the day is at an end, and since night is bringing out the stars, I will pass the evening here, but at the first rising light of day I will depart from your borders."

Then most holy John returned to his city with great speed, and the gates, shaken loose from their hinges, were cast to the ground, and the entryways lay bare and open to the enemy, and through the whole night his hosts went around the streets of Ravenna, they left together from another part of the city. On the next day at dawn, with the golden sun rising, King Attila entered Ravenna, and sitting on a swift steed, he trod on the above-mentioned entryways of the city; bars and keys and bolts were brought before him, and he wanted to take nothing from there.

The citizens were terrified, struck with great fear, and at once all of their bodies fell down at his fierceness, they were made weak, trembling and groaning, invoking the heavenly Lord with great sighs. But when the king had gone out of the city, they passed before him with great praises, and the city was decorated with all the streets adorned with many types of flowers. Afterward there was great animation, and immense joy among the great as well as the poor and middle class, since the king, who had looked with his own eyes upon the great city, with his fury mitigated by heaven, had left Ravenna unharmed behind his back.

And from that day he did not continue with such cruelty, and without undertaking further war he returned to his own kingdom. And he was not only stronger in physical powers but fought ingeniously, whence it is said about him in proverbs, "King Attila, before he would take up arms, fought with ingenuity." And after all these things he died, carved up by the knife of a most wicked woman.[15]

38. Now let it suffice you for today to have heard of the life of this holy man. For the time is near already, now the sun's shadows are lengthened, the day is darkened and the hour fails.[16] However, whoever wants to ask me with greater diligence from what source I wrote above, how this holy man, placed in a mortal body, looked upon an angelic spiritual image, if after three days I have not become too weak, then seeking divine aid, I will bring to your presence the ancient words that once sounded in my ears, like different vegetables placed in a basket, with large letters engraved by my pen.

---

15. Some of this information is found in Jordanes, *Getica* 36, and Marcellinus, *Chronica*, a. 454. Since there is no other evidence that Agnellus knew either of these works, this information about Attila must have been found in the *Chronicon* of Maximian, which Agnellus cites several times.

16. This is the first of several passages in which Agnellus indicates that he is stopping for the day, and will begin again later. On Agnellus's use of such passages to mask breaks in composition, see the Introduction.

39. Yesterday, confined by a slight bodily illness, I could not narrate to you all the miracles of the above-mentioned holy man; but by divine mercy having pity on your prayers, I will explain today what I heard from the tales of very old men, if I remember the words.

In his reign, after the bridge of Apollinaris in Ravenna was burned on the night of Easter, April 2, Theodoric was engaged against his enemies near the *Strovilia Peucodis,* not far from the city of Ravenna, in the field which is called *Candiani.* After Odoacer, who at that time held the kingdom at Ravenna, had conquered on two occasions, then Odoacer went out to the above-mentioned field with his army, and was overcome on the third occasion, and he fled from before the face of Theodoric, and closed himself within the city. And Theodoric went away to Rimini, and he came back from there with his swift ships to the Lion Port, where afterward he ordered a small palace to be built on that island, not far from the shore of the sea, where there is now the *monasterium* of St. Mary, within a bath, only about six miles from Ravenna.[17]

And now in our day I have ordered my servants to demolish this said palace, and I have brought it into Ravenna for the building of my house, which I have built from the foundations from my maternal inheritance, which is called the Priest's House, in the region which is called *ad Nimphaeos,* next to the church of St. Agnes the martyr, and with the [barracks of the] first flag corps on the other side, not far from the golden milestone.[18]

So long did hunger subdue the armies of Theodoric, that they were driven to eat hides or other unclean and horrible things; and starvation destroyed many bodies which were saved from the

---

17. This palace has been partially excavated; see Bermond Montanari, "La zona archeologica di Palazzolo"; Lusuardi-Siena, "Sulle tracce della presenza Gota"; and Deichmann, *Ravenna* 2.3:267.

18. About this location, see Deichmann, *Ravenna* 2.3:36 and 39–40. The *numerus primus bandus* was one of the military groupings within Ravenna, which is mentioned again in c. 140; Agnellus is apparently using the term here to designate the area in which members of this corps lived. See Deichmann, ibid., 107, and Brown, *Gentlemen and Officers,* esp. 97–98.

sword. And there was a great earthquake just at cockcrow on December 26. And Odoacer gave his son to Theodoric as a hostage on February 26, and after February 27 Theodoric entered the city of Classe.

After this, however, the most blessed man Archbishop John opened the gates of the city that Odoacer had closed, and went out with crucifixes and thuribles and the holy Gospels, seeking peace along with his priests and clergy by chanting psalms, prostrate on the ground he obtained what he was seeking. He invited in the new king who had come from the east, and that peace was granted by him, not only for the citizens of Ravenna, but for all Romans, for whom blessed John had entreated.[19]

And Theodoric entered Ravenna on March 5. After a few days he killed King Odoacer with his associates in the palace At the Laurel. And after Odoacer had been killed at the order of Theodoric, the latter ruled alone and secure in the manner of the Romans.

After all his adversaries were conquered, in the thirtieth year of his reign he sent the Ravennate army to Sicily, he ravaged it and transferred it to his own authority.

In his reign everyone saw the northern sky burning.

The patricians Symmachus and Boethius, related by blood and Roman citizens, were beheaded with axes at the order of Theodoric.[20] And John, the Roman pope, after a delegation to the east with Bishop Ecclesius of Ravenna, was brought to Ravenna at the order of the king, and was confined by Theodoric and kept for so long that he died, and was buried in the public prison in a marble sar-

---

19. In the Roman *LP*, various popes are said to have saved "all Italy" from invaders, particularly Pope Leo I, who repelled the Huns, and Pope Zacharias, who persuaded the Lombards to withdraw from Ravenna. Here, Agnellus's statement is a pointed reversal of this formula, showing a Ravennate bishop saving the Romans from an invader.

20. Agnellus's account of the deaths of Symmachus, Boethius, and Pope John I might have come from the *LP*, Life of John I, although Holder-Egger, *LPER*, 304, n. 5, proposed that this passage was derived primarily from the *Chronicon* of Maximian, since the *LP* does not mention Ecclesius's participation in the delegation.

cophagus. And the above-mentioned patricians were buried in another sarcophagus which remains up to the present day.

Theodoric, however, after thirty-four years of his reign, began to close the churches of God and to restrict Christians, and suddenly incurring a flux of the bowels, he died, and was buried in the mausoleum which he ordered built outside the Artemedorian Gate, which up to today we call At the Lighthouse,[21] where there is the *monasterium* of St. Mary which is called At the Tomb of King Theodoric. But it seems to me that he has been cast out of his tomb, and that very marvelous vessel lying there, made of porphyry stone, was placed before the entrance of that *monasterium*.[22]

I have digressed enough, I have gone through diverse subjects: let us return to our [story].

40. There was great sanctity in the said man John. And when his fame had come to the ears of the emperor Valentinian, for a long time he had desired to see him.[23] (But these [digressions] are not harmful. What I should have explained above, let us note below, lest we miss anything.) Because of this, Valentinian, most noble son of Galla Placidia by his father Constantius, hastened to the holy bishop John, and with the diadem removed from his head he greeted him in a voice of fear and reverence, and having received a benediction from him he went away with a joyous face.

After a few days the same emperor, at the consecration of the blessed bishop John, bestowed fourteen cities with their churches

---

21. The mausoleum, which survives today, was located very close to the coastline in the ninth century; it is possible that there was a lighthouse near it. Pliny the Elder, in his *Historia naturalis*, 36.19, notes specifically in discussing the great Pharus lighthouse of Alexandria that there was a similar one at Ravenna. It is also possible that the term was an imitation of the toponym "ad Pharos," which was attached to a church dedicated to the Virgin in the Great Palace in Constantinople.

22. The porphyry bathtub that is still located in the mausoleum must be the object that Agnellus identifies as an *urna*; for similar examples of such ornamental tubs, see Delbrueck, *Antike Porphyrwerke*, 164–69 and plates 78–80.

23. The Diploma of Valentinian, a mid-seventh-century forgery, links the names of Valentinian and a bishop named John; Agnellus therefore erroneously assigns information about Valentinian and Galla Placidia, who lived circa 425–55, to this Life of John.

under the power of a metropolitan, and up to the present day the fourteen cities with their bishops are subject to the Ravennate church. One episcopal chair is missing, because the city, whose name is Brescello, not far from the city of Bologna, is destroyed.[24] John first accepted from that emperor the pallium of pure wool, as is the custom of the bishop of the Romans to wear over his surcoat, which he and his successors have used up to the present day.

Valentinian in that time held the high citadel of Ravenna, and he ordered a royal hall built in the place which is called At the Laurel.[25] It is called the Laurel for this reason, that some triumphal victory was made there. Such was the rite of the ancients that, if one of them triumphed over enemies or foes, a laurel crown was girded on his head; whence among the ancients they were called "laudis," and if the letter "d" is dropped, and "r" is added, this tree is called "laurus."

And in this royal house Valentinian remained for a long time, and here and there on each side he adorned the streets of the city with great walls, and he ordered iron bars to be enclosed in the bowels of the wall. And so great was his care that the iron bars not only appeared ornamental, but also if at some time some other people should want to threaten this city, and if not as many weapons could be found as were needed, from these bars arrows and lances and even swords could be made; or, as we said, the walls would supply the iron for some other purpose. He added much to this wall of the city, where formerly it had been girded as merely one of the towns.[26] And this emperor made great what was smaller in former times, and he ordered and decreed that Ravenna should be the head of Italy in place of Rome.

41. Meanwhile, when in that time the mother of Valentinian, the Empress Galla Placidia, was building the church of the Holy Cross our Redeemer, her niece, by the name of Singledia, was ad-

---

24. Brescello was destroyed by the Lombards in the early eighth century (Paul the Deacon, *Historia Langobardorum* 3.18 and 4.28).

25. About this palace, see Deichmann, *Ravenna* 2.3:50.

26. Valentinian does seem to have built the walls around Ravenna; see Christie, "The City Walls of Ravenna."

vised one night by a vision, in which a man in white vestments stood there, adorned with a grey-haired head and a beautiful beard, and said, "In such and such a place not far from this church of the Holy Cross, which your aunt is having built, as far as a bow-shot, build me a *monasterium*, as you will find it traced out. And where you find the likeness of a cross in the ground, there let an altar be consecrated,[27] and dedicate it in the name of Zacharias, the father of the Precursor."

Waking at once, she ran swiftly to the place, where its outline had been shown; she found that a foundation had been dug as if by the hand of man. Running forward at once, she told the empress with great joy and requested workmen from her; and [Galla] gave her thirteen builders. And at once she started to build as she had found it drawn out; and in thirteen days she built it all and brought it to completion. And she consecrated it and endowed it with gold and silver and golden crowns and most precious gems and gold chalices, which come out in procession on the Nativity of the Lord, from which we drink the blood of the Lord; from there they came to the holy Ursiana church. And on the lip of a chalice we find it written thus,

I the empress Galla Placidia offer to St. Zacharias.

And this Singledia rests there; her tomb is known to us.[28]

The Empress Galla built the church of the Holy Cross, constructed of most precious stones and with carved stucco; and in the roundness of the arches[29] there are metrical verses reading thus:

---

27. Picard, "Les maîtres d'oeuvre," citing Deichmann, *Ravenna* 2.2:375, suggests that this statement is a transposition of the ceremony of foundation, at which the bishop made a sign of the cross at the site of the future altar.

28. Testi-Rasponi (*CPER*, 118, n. 2) suggests that Agnellus saw the tomb of Sunigilda, who is recorded in a fragment of John Antiochenus as being the wife of Odoacer.

29. Nauerth, *Agnellus von Ravenna, Untersuchungen*, 92, notes that since this expression refers to the cross-shaped church of Santa Croce, any one of the arches at the crossing might be meant, not necessarily the arch of the apse.

John washes Christ at the font in the seat of paradise; where he gives a happy life, he points the way to martyrdom.

On the facade of that temple, entering the main doors, above the depicted four rivers of paradise,[30] if you read the verses in hexameter and pentameter, you will find:

O Christ, Word of the Father, concord of all the world, you who know no end, so also no beginning. The winged witnesses, whom your right hand rules, stand around you saying "sanctus" and "amen." In your presence the rivers run, poured through the ages [5], the Tigris and Euphrates, Fison and Geon. With you conquering, savage crimes are silenced by true death, trodden for eternity under your feet.

Some say that the Empress Galla Placidia herself ordered candelabra to be placed on four round slabs of red marble, which are before the said main doors, with candles of specific measure, and at night she threw herself down in the middle of the pavement, pouring out prayers to God, and she would pass the night praying in tears, for as long as those lights lasted.[31]

42. And if you want to find an analogy to this, read the chronicle of Archbishop Maximian; there you will find many things about her and about many emperors and kings. Also this empress, after she was widowed by a certain Athaulf, was given in marriage by the emperor Honorius to his count Constantius, and the emperor named him as his successor. And Constantius ruled the nations for one year after the death of Honorius; snatched by sickness he lost his life, and he left a young son by Galla, whose name was Valentinian.

When Valentinian was six years and four months old, he succeeded the divine Honorius, his paternal uncle, on the imperial

---

30. The image on the façade of the church of the Holy Cross must have been an apocalyptic vision of Christ enthroned, treading on the two monsters, surrounded by the four symbolic beasts and the elders, with the rivers of paradise at the base; the imagery in the poem is drawn from the Book of Revelation; see Nauerth, *Agnellus von Ravenna, Untersuchungen*, 93–4.

31. The "candles of specific measure" seem to be candles used for marking time; see Glossary, s.v. *manualia ad mensuram*.

throne. Lasting for thirty-one years on the throne, he was killed at Rome in the place which is called At the Laurel. Galla did not see the death of her son, since she had died previously at Rome on November 27.

After these things a star appeared in the sky, burning for thirty days, and Aquileia was captured and destroyed by the Huns.[32] Ravenna burned on March 15, and much wealth was consumed in the fire.

Galla Placidia, as many say, is buried in the *monasterium* of St. Nazarius before the altar, within the chancel screens, which were bronze, but which now are seen to be stone.[33]

And she built the church of St. John the Evangelist. When she was going through the precarious dangers of the sea, with a storm having arisen, the keel tossed by waves, thinking she would be drowned in the deep, she vowed a vow to God concerning a church for his apostle; and she was freed from the fury of the sea. And within the apse of this church, over the heads of the emperors and empresses it reads thus:

Confirm, God, that which you have accomplished for us; from your temple in Jerusalem, kings offer you gifts.

And above you will find another line reading thus:

To the holy and most blessed apostle John the Evangelist, the Empress Galla Placidia with her son the Emperor Placidus Valentinian and her daughter the Empress Iusta Grata Honoria fulfill the vow of liberation from the dangers of the sea.

---

32. Halley's Comet, which passed earth in the year 451; a later appearance of this comet is also mentioned in c. 106 (a. 607). Other comets are found in cc. 90, 98.

33. Galla Placidia is known to have died in Rome and was probably buried there in the imperial mausoleum. In the ninth century the *monasterium* of St. Nazarius was one of the chambers flanking the apse of San Vitale, which contained the burials of Bishops Ecclesius, Ursicinus, and Victor (cc. 59, 65, 68); the church was built a century after Galla Placidia's death. The structure known today as the Mausoleum of Galla Placidia is not mentioned by Agnellus, but it is likely that its identification as Placidia's mausoleum arose from a later misunderstanding of this passage. See Deliyannis, "Bury Me in Ravenna?"

And she also built the church of St. Stephen in Rimini.

43. What now? It is better for me to pass over in silence, than to wander among byways and antiquities. Let us return to the above-mentioned course and speak of our bishops without delay. For his successor now is worthy of being introduced. But who is sufficient to narrate your deeds, O blessed Peter Chrysologus? Even if my voice were made of adamant and my chest of bronze, and my embellishments were connected in verse, even thus I could not narrate all of your deeds.

44. Therefore while the most blessed father, that bishop of Ravenna, the above-named John, sang the celebration of the mass in the basilica of blessed Agatha, when he discharged all things according to the rite of the holy bishops, after the reading of the Gospels, after the protestation, the catechumens, those who were allowed to see, saw miracles.

When the most blessed one began to give the canonical words with supplications to God and to make the sign of the cross over the host, suddenly an angel came from heaven and stood on the other side of the altar, facing that bishop. And after the sanctification was completed, and he took up the body of the Lord, the deacon was supposed to fulfill his ministerial duty, but he did not see that this was to offer up the chalice. Suddenly he was moved aside by the angel, and the angel offered up the holy chalice to the bishop. Then all the priests with the people began to fear and tremble, seeing the holy chalice tilted by itself to the mouth of the bishop and being received back through the air onto the holy altar. The people strained to see; some said, "the deacon is unworthy," others affirmed, "no, but the visitation is angelic." And the angel stood next to the holy man for a long time, until he had finished the celebration of the mass.

After a little while, having blessed his sons, the Ravennate citizens, with eagerness, as if invited to a feast, he finished the day and his life with an eager face, on June 5.[34] He was buried in the above-mentioned basilica of the holy martyr Agatha behind the altar, in

---

34. The epitaph of Bishop John I survives; see below, c. 46 and note.

that place where he saw the angel standing; and daily we see his image depicted above the benches in the apse.³⁵ It appears that he was thin of form with black hair, a few being grey. But he conquered age with sanctity, since the heavenly Lord approves thoughts more than years. Faith is borne in sense, not in years. And in front of his image in a medallion in the Ursiana church, where it is fixed in the renovated church, a candle gleams with clear light the whole night long.³⁶ For I, brothers, as I promised, inasmuch as I could, with God willing, have finished his life. Now I will pass on to holy Peter Chrysologus his successor.

45. But to whom can we compare the life of this most blessed John? If we look into it, with many of the fathers. If it pleases your consideration, do not reject it, and if by chance I stumble, indulge me; for I say these things for the edification of your souls.

We are men and we are subject to human misfortunes. Therefore the prophet, seeing us clothed in fragile flesh, tossed in the punishment of its eddies, exclaimed, "All men are liars."³⁷ But I seek grace in your presence, not swollen with wantonness, but full of humility.

For perhaps I could compare this man with the patriarch Jacob. When Jacob held the angel and did not let him go, the angel said to him, "'Let me go, for the day breaketh.' He answered, 'I will not let thee go, except thou bless me.'"³⁸ And in that place the angel blessed him. For the angel did not bless him, but gave him the body of the Lord with His blood. Oh that in the latter part of my life someone had given me the body and blood of Christ thus sanctified, so that what I was not worthy of receiving in life, I might have deserved at the departure of my soul!

This man imitated David, as you are about to hear. For when

---

35. Agnellus probably derived the story of John and the angel from this depiction, which showed him celebrating mass in the presence of an angel.

36. Deichmann, *Ravenna* 2.1:9, rejects Testi-Rasponi's suggestion that this image was one of a series of pictures of bishops in roundels along the nave of the cathedral, because Agnellus does not mention other such depictions.

37. Ps. 115:11.

38. Gen. 32:26.

David saw that the angel who was slaughtering the people had extended his hand over Jerusalem, he said, "Let thine hand, I pray thee, O Lord, be on me."[39] And when this one [John] had been asked by the king what he wanted, it was revealed that he desired death in place of his flock. Thus the king gave peace, which the bishop had sought.[40] David did this on account of his own sins, since he presumed to obtain a count of those whom God had multiplied as the sands of the sea;[41] this king [Attila], however, had attacked the city on account of the sins of the people, since some were lukewarm in faith; but by his prayers this holy man [John] both appeased the king, and turned the pity of God toward him.

He was also similar to another man by the name of Tobias, to whose wedding the angel Raphael was sent, to visit the father and give him a vision; and thus he visited him and accomplished the fate of his servant.

And finally that great priest Zacharias, whose son, as a prophet of the arrival of our Lord Jesus Christ, was not only equal to but preceded all others; whom the holy gospel records as being righteous before God. Looking upon an angel, he became mute; Bishop John, having regarded an angelic face, remained happy and joyful. Why? Because Zacharias doubted that he would have a son, because his blood had cooled and he was advanced in years. But if he doubted the heavenly messenger, how does the evangelist describe him as righteous? For it says, "Zacharias and Elisabeth were both righteous before God."[42] What is this? How can it be?

Let David speak: "In thy sight shall no man living be considered righteous."[43] And hear Job, "For behold, the heavens shine not; yea, the stars are not pure in his sight. How much less man, that is a maggot, and the son of man, which is a worm?"[44] However Peter, to whom was given the power of loosing and binding in

---

39. 1 Chron. 21:17.
40. This is a reference to either Attila or Theodoric, as above cc. 37 and 39.
41. In 1 Chron. 21, the plague is said to have been sent because David took a census of the people of Israel, contrary to the wishes of God.
42. Luke 1:6.   43. Ps. 142:2.
44. Job 25:5–6.

heaven and earth, and to whom the keys to the kingdom of heaven were delivered, said, "Depart from me, for I am a sinful man."[45] And if the prince of the apostles saw himself as a sinner, how can the Gospels recount that the priest, fettered in marriage, was righteous before God?

Let Manasses come, let him say with the evangelist, "Abraham, Isaac, and Jacob and their seed are righteous; Abraham, Isaac and Jacob, who have not sinned before thee."[46] In this place he says "seed" for this reason, that is, Christ, not "seeds," as was said to Abraham, "In thy seed shall all the nations of the earth be blessed."[47] Seed in the singular, seeds in the plural. For before the eyes of God none is found to be free, as Solomon says, "For there is not a man upon earth, that doeth good, and sinneth not."[48]

Before the face of divine majesty there are terrible sights: for there the angels tremble, the archangels fear, the thrones are afraid, the dominations are terrified, the powers rush, the princedoms dread, the virtues of the heavens are moved, the righteous falter, the earth flees, the elements quake.[49] And man, born from pollutions, and moreover servant of sin, how is he justified? Hear Job, "Who can appear clean before him, that is born of woman?"[50]

I seek by your charity, grant me a little indulgence or favor, since today, tired and weighed down by human business, I have not refreshed my body with sleep; do not trouble yourself too much about these questions, since, if the Lord will grant it, I will explain tomorrow, if life will be my companion. And if some postponement intervenes and I do not quickly loose the knot of the question, imitate the holy gospel, as it says, "Have patience with me, and I will pay thee all."[51] Do not judge me as an ignorant man would, unless I delay.

But in what way is Zacharias righteous? Or how could David throw forth, "No one living is considered righteous before God"?

---

45. Luke 5:8.
46. Pr. of Man.
47. Gen. 22:18 and 28:14.
48. Eccles. 7:21.
49. The angels, archangels, thrones, dominations, powers, princedoms, and virtues are the seven ranks of angels.
50. Job 25:4.
51. Matt. 18:26 and 29.

Or how could Manasses say, "Abraham and the others, who have not sinned before you, Lord"? Or how did Moses intone, "Lord, Lord God, thou art merciful and gracious, yet no one before thee is innocent in and of himself."[52]

In the future sermons I will explain[53] as necessary the manifold things about the latter, who led the people out of Egypt, who made the swollen sea stand as a mass, who fed the people manna in the wilderness, who produced water from a rock, whose hand killed the hosts of Amalech, who went against the king of the Canaanites, who dried up the river Etham, who made the water, bitter and condemned by those who drank it, drinkable by means of a piece of wood, who received in Sinai the ten words of the law on two stone tablets, whose face conquered the shining of the sun, who lifted up the bronze serpent for the Israelite plague in the wilderness, whose enemies the earth absorbed, who broke the golden calf, who talked with God as with a friend face to face, who protected the Israelite armies by means of a column of cloud by day and of fire by night, to whom an angel was given as a guide over all things, the Lord saying, "Behold I send My angel, who will go before thee and watch over thee always."[54] And thus to this holy man John too he sent an angel from the heavens as a guard for his body.

46. But in the following sermon, with the Lord providing, I will gladly tell all these things which I have left above strenuously tied up in knots—how man might be considered righteous, and how he is held in sin and is condemned—so that aversion might not be created in the life of the next holy man.

This most blessed John ruled his church for sixteen years, ten months, eighteen days.[55]

---

52. Exod. 34:6–7.

53. At least one of the following subjects, the drying up of the River Etham, is discussed in another of Agnellus's sermonettes, in c. 55. This is an indication that Agnellus took at least the sermonettes from cc. 45 and 55 from a published series of sermons that he knew, in which all of these topics were considered in turn.

54. Exod. 23:20.

55. These numbers, as well as the date of death reported in c. 44, are found on the

CONCERNING HOLY PETER II, 494-520

47. Peter, the twenty-first bishop, beautiful in appearance, attractive of figure. No bishop before him was his equal in wisdom and none arose after him. He was the author of many volumes of books, and divine wisdom emanated from him daily, like a refreshing fountain; whence for his eloquence I have called him Chrysologus, that is, "golden wordsmith."[1]

He was from the people of the territory of Imola, raised and taught by Cornelius, the bishop of that see; and for the love of his teacher, blessed Peter named that above-mentioned territory, which was then called Imola, as *Corneliensis* from that time forward. But others say that it was called *Corneliensis* because it had been the *Forum Cornelii*.

48. He ruled the throne of the Ravennate church in the times of the most holy Pope Leo I. In those days the most wicked priest Eutyches, incited by an evil spirit, began to arouse a malign heresy against the holy and indivisible catholic faith with his evil thoughts. The most holy Leo warned him in a letter, in the presence of many holy bishops of God, that his superstitious belief could never again be recalled to good intent. Then holy Leo quickly made these things known to blessed Peter, bishop of this city of Ravenna, who

---

epitaph that survives (published in the *CIL* 11, no. 304): "Here rests in peace holy bishop John, who reigned 16 years, 10 months, and 17 days. He was buried on the 5th of June in the consulship of Asterius and Praesidus," i.e., he reigned from 477 to 494. The inscription was found in the pavement of the Ursiana; however, since the epitaph of Bishop Agnellus, which Agnellus quotes and identifies as being in St. Agatha, was also found in the Ursiana's pavement, it seems clear that John must also have been buried in St. Agatha, and that at some time these pieces of marble were reused in the Ursiana's floor. See Deichmann, *Ravenna* 2.2:284.

1. Bishop Peter I of Ravenna, who lived in the middle of the fifth century, was a Doctor of the Church and is known by the appellation Chrysologus. Agnellus got the first two Peters confused; this Peter, who is described as Chrysologus, actually reigned 494–520. The Life by Agnellus contains the earliest known use of the epithet Chrysologus; Benericetti, *Il Cristo nei sermoni*, 65–66, concludes that it was bestowed by Agnellus.

wrote a letter to this heretic, through which he was defeated in the Chalcedonian synod, since he did not agree.[2]

But this most holy Leo sent many exchanges through his writings to the city of Constantinople, not only to the Empress Galla Placidia, but also to Valentinian and Honorius and many others strong in the faith, and at the same time, as I said, he sent many letters simultaneously to the Emperor Gratian and separately to Eudoxia against the aforementioned priest Eutyches; and in that time the heresy was greatly protracted up to the time of the Emperor Marcian.

So, as we said, when a great conflict over the holy inviolate catholic faith had raged for many days, it happened that when the said heretic was brought into the council of bishops, in the presence of all the bishops Bishop Theodore[3] began to contend with him, showing individual books of holy scriptures and various witnesses, [which show] that the holy Trinity is indivisible, and that the Father and the Son and the Holy Spirit are one co-equal God, existing in two natures, of God and of man. Eutyches did not agree. Then with apostolic authority having been proven, he still did not come to his senses.

And the letter of blessed Peter Chrysologus was shown, one part of which contained the following: "Human laws limit all questions of litigation to within thirty years, thus, why after about five hundred years do you presume to rail against Christ with such speech? Truly you should humble yourself to the holy Roman pope and diligently obey his commands. And do not think other than that the blessed apostle Peter himself is now alive and apostolically holds the power of the throne of the Roman see in the flesh."

2. Pope Leo wrote his Tome for the Council of Ephesus of 449, at which Eutyches was vindicated; at the Council of Chalcedon of 451 the Nestorian heresy was declared anathema and Eutyches was excommunicated. By the time of the Council of Chalcedon, however, Peter Chrysologus was dead, and his Letter was probably written before the Council of Ephesus.

3. Several bishops named Theodore are mentioned in the acts of the Council of Chalcedon; see Mansi, *Sacrorum conciliorum*, 6:566–79. Since none of them took an active part in the deliberations against Eutyches, Testi-Rasponi, *CPER*, 142, n. 3, suggests that Theodoret of Cyrene was meant.

After these things, however, this most wicked Eutyches fell in this council; and the rest of the bishops, together with all the Christian people, went away joyful and congratulatory after the dissolution of the council, giving great thanks to God and greatest praises to the emperors who observed the catholic and true faith.

49. Therefore, dearest friends, let us treat the rest of the life of Chrysologus, and ask how or why, in such an orthodox see, the citizens of Ravenna ordained a bishop not from among their own sheep, but from the subordinate church of Imola.[4]

For at that time, after the most blessed aforementioned Bishop John died, the whole assembly of the people convened, together with the priests, as the custom is in the rite of the church, and they elected a shepherd for themselves. And hastening to Rome with him they all came to the holy pope of the apostolic see, that he might ordain the one chosen by them, lest such a church be widowed from its bishop for too many days. On the next day everyone was ready to stand before the holy apostolic presence with the man whom they had chosen.

Therefore that very night, the blessed apostle of Christ and key bearer Peter appeared in a vision to holy Sixtus[5] the bishop of the church of Rome, together with his disciple Apollinaris, and standing between the two the blessed Peter Chrysologus; and blessed apostle Peter, stepping forward a little, said to holy Pope Sixtus, "See this man, whom we have chosen, who stands between us; consecrate him, not any other."

Awakened on that account, the pope explicitly ordered the

---

4. Agnellus presents the election of Peter Chrysologus, not a member of the Ravennate clergy, as the result of miraculous intervention. Testi-Rasponi (*CPER*, 146–47) points out that this story is very similar to that of Samuel's anointing David, told in 1 Sam. 16: David, the youngest son, is not present at the assembly and has to be fetched, whereupon God identifies him as the chosen one.

5. Pope Sixtus III reigned 422–32, and Agnellus's identification of him as the pope who ordained Peter Chrysologus has influenced the dating of Chrysologus's own reign. Given the legendary nature of this entire story, however, it is most likely that Agnellus names Sixtus simply because he was the predecessor of Leo I, with whom Chrysologus was connected, and not because of any definite source that told about the event.

whole people and the man who was to be ordained to be led in at dawn. The holy pope gazed at him for a very long time, and said, "Go, take him from our midst. I do not recognize him. Unless you bring me him who was revealed, I will not ordain anyone." But they began to ask each other what might be the meaning of this; and when they had all been ushered out, they were saddened.

On the next day he ordered that the people with the clerics both important and middling and insignificant be brought before him, and when he did not see the form of the man which had been shown to him, he said, "Ask among yourselves, perhaps you have not all come, or there are more of you?" But they said, "You will not find anyone who is not here with us, lord pope." "Go and get out! I do not see the one chosen by the Lord."

Finally on the third day there again appeared to the pope, who was neither fully awake nor fully asleep, the prince of the apostles with his disciple, as before, holding the most holy Peter Chrysologus between them, saying to him, "We have told you not to place your hands over anyone other than this man, since in his reign the church of Ravenna will grow fat and be illuminated by his learning, as the fat of oil in a lamp illuminates when it is lit by fire."

On the next day all were led in, and he was not found. Then the holy pope of the Roman see said to the bishop of Imola, who at that time had gone to Rome with the Ravennate citizens, "Bring in all your priests and clergy, perhaps there I will find the man who was shown to me." He answered the pope with supplication, saying, "I do not have such a man, except for one deacon, who is in charge of in all my affairs, on whose hands I your servant rely. If you order that he should come into our midst, let him be brought." The most blessed pope said to him, "Let him not come alone, but with all the others; and if I see whom I want, I will take him gladly."

But when everyone had entered, as soon as the holy pope saw the man who had been shown to him in the vision, he saw him as a gleaming jewel, and on either side recognizing in spirit the face of the blessed apostle Peter and the bishop Apollinaris, holding the right and left hand of Peter Chrysologus. And as the holy pope saw all these things, suddenly rising from his seat, he went toward him in the middle of the hall; with willing spirit they greeted each other on their knees. But when holy Peter Chrysologus wanted to withdraw from the pope, the most blessed pope would not allow it.

Suddenly the people began to groan among themselves and send up a great noise to heaven. Some were saying, that "we will not receive a neophyte. He was not from our flock, but suddenly invaded the episcopal throne as a thief. Take him away, take him away from our midst. We will not receive him, since it is not permitted to transfer from a subordinate church to its superior." Others said against this, "This man is righteous, you do not speak correctly. Let us take him, so that our city may prosper, since he is most wise and pure and a good teacher and worthy of all glory. He is of our family, we sense no evil in him, he is full of the fear of the Lord; you want to lose him for no reason."

Holy Sixtus of the Roman see, seeing the people divided on either side in this dispute, told everyone of his vision, as we said above; of how he ought to consecrate him through apostolic advice. "And if you do not want this father, all of you recede from me and alienate yourselves from the holy catholic Roman church."

Then, as with one voice, they began to shout and say, "Let him be ordained, let him be ordained!" Quickly they wrote a decree, and through the laying on of hands he received the Holy Spirit and was ordained as bishop, and returned with glory to the see of Ravenna. From that day everyone began to venerate him as an angel of God.

50. This most blessed man built a baptistry in the city of Classe next to the church that is called Petriana, which Bishop Peter founded. This baptistry was wonderful in size, with doubled walls and high walls built with mathematical art.[6]

---

6. While this may be just a rhetorically exaggerated description, Agnellus also describes this baptistry as "square" *(tetragonus)* (c. 67), unlike the other baptistries in Ravenna, which were octagonal. Unfortunately, this makes the "doubled walls" *(duplicibus muris)* even more difficult to interpret, while the "mathematical art" *(arithmeticae artis)* may refer to some system of proportion or scale, or may just be a rhetorical flourish. Lazard, "De l'origine," 265, notes that the word is used by such authors as Vitruvius, Boethius, and Cassiodorus, and seems to have been a widely diffused technical term.

And he also founded a house inside the episcopal palace of the Ravennate see, which is called *Tricollis*, because it contains three *colla*, which building is constructed inside with great ingenuity.[7] And not far from that house he built the *monasterium* of St. Andrew the apostle, and his image is depicted in mosaic inside this *monasterium*, over the doors. Indeed he decorated all the side walls with proconnesian marble,[8] and outside, over the threshold, in the entrance of the doors, he placed metrical verses reading thus:

Either light was born here, or captured here it reigns free; it is the law, from which source the current glory of heaven excels. Or the deprived roofs have produced gleaming day, and the enclosed radiance gleams forth as if from secluded Olympus. See, the marble flourishes with bright rays [5], and all the stones struck in starry purple shine in value, the gifts of the founder Peter. To him honor and merit are granted, thus to beautify small things, so that although confined in space, they surpass the large. Nothing is small to Christ; He well occupies confining buildings [10], whose temples exist within the human heart.

A Peter is the foundation; and a Peter the founder of this hall. The master is the same as the house; what is made is the same as the maker, in morals and in work. Christ is the owner, who as a mediator uniting the two renders them as one [15]. Let one coming here joyously pour out the tears which will produce joy, making firm a contrite mind in his beaten breast. Let him not lie sick, but prostrate himself on the ground and reveal his hidden illnesses before the feet of the doctor, since the cure is approaching. Often the fear of death becomes the cause of a blessed life [20].

7. About possible interpretations of the phrase "because it contains three *colla*," see Glossary, s.v. *collum*. The dedicatory inscription of the building, in which all the bishops who helped to build it are named, is found in c. 75; the founder was the late-fifth-century Peter II, not Peter Chrysologus.

8. This chapel is now known as the *capella arcivescovile*. Nauerth, *Agnellus von Ravenna, Untersuchungen*, 23–25, has closely analyzed this passage and concludes that some of the information was taken from a written source and some from Agnellus's own observations. However, Nauerth does not compare Agnellus's descriptions with those found in the Roman *LP*, which often contain both iterative statements of patronage and subjective descriptions. On Agnellus's use of the term "proconnesian", see Glossary, s.v. *proconnisus*.

51. He wrote many volumes and was very, very wise.

He and Projectus were both consecrated as deacons together in the same hour by blessed Cornelius of the church of Imola. Afterward, by divine providence, both held episcopal thrones: Peter of the church of Ravenna, Projectus was allotted Imola. After the former was ordained bishop, in turn the latter was consecrated by him as bishop of the church of Imola.

In the time of the Empress Galla Placidia, as we have found written, the same Peter Chrysologus with the above-mentioned empress preserved the body of blessed Barbatian with aromatics and buried him with great honor not far from the Ovilian gate. And he consecrated the church of Sts. John and Barbatian, which Baduarius built.[9]

52. However, after these things, most blessed Peter recognized in his soul the end of his life.[10] He went to the church at Imola, and having entered the basilica of blessed Cassian, he presented gifts, that is, one gold vessel and also a silver paten and great gold votive crowns decorated with most precious gems. He touched all these things to the body of St. Cassian and they were placed on the altar of that church. And standing over the crypt next to the altar, with hands outstretched he blessed all the people, priests and populace; he prayed, saying:

"You have given, Lord God, a soul into this body; receive it again in mercy, since I am Your creation. May the most wicked devil not attack me, but may Your holy angel take up my soul and may You order it to be placed in the bosom of the patriarchs, where light remains to the end and joy is immense. And now, Lord, I acknowledge You with lips and heart, You Who have created

---

9. Baduarius may have been the brother-in-law of the emperor Justin II, and the commander in chief of the armies of Italy in 575–77; if he built the church, it was obviously much later than the time of Galla Placidia, and would have been dedicated by Bishop Peter III (570–8). Deichmann, "Studi sulla Ravenna scomparsa," 68–69, suggests that Agnellus saw an inscription with the names Peter and Baduarius, and thus attributed the work to Peter Chrysologus.

10. Legends about saints knowing the time of their deaths and bidding lengthy farewells to their followers are common in early medieval hagiography.

everything from nothing, You Who alone know past, present and future. Give this people a teachable heart, that they may fear You and know that You are God in the heaven above and in the earth below, who has restored the salvation of the human race through Your holy Son, in whom we believe as God and Lord of the angels, You Who are blessed in the ages of ages. Send them, Lord God, a true shepherd, who may gather Your sheep, not scattering them, but congregating them in the sheep folds of the church. May he not as a mercenary lull them to sleep, may he not be a foreign guard of sheep, but a true shepherd, who will bring untouched back to Your sight the sheep with the lambs committed to his care; and may that greatest fierce wolf, tempestuous desire, who seeks to take loot, not drive away their excited hearts from You their shepherd; may he not tear away the wool of the faithful sheep, may the holy church not groan with bleating voices.[11] You, good Shepherd of shepherds, give to this people a mild shepherd, not an assailant but a nurturer; not to attack, but to defend; not scorning but recalling, not a taker but a benefactor, not to tear, but to restrain; not greedy but a giver; not proud but humble; not harsh but smooth. Guard them—it is Your people—and the sheep of Your hands, You who are blessed in the ages."

To the grieving people he said, "Dearest sons, hear me. I am leaving and 'going into the way of all the earth,'[12] where is found the house of all the living. Now, sons, be comforted and be wise men. The Lord God will give you a shepherd and ruler, as it is written, 'The Lord does not cast off His people at the end and does not abandon His inheritance.'[13] Listen to him; he will teach you, he will lead you through pleasant pastures, he will refresh you with the nourishment of his word; listen to him, do not be thrown into confusion. And raise not my remains against him in swelling of heart; do not chose with tumult and quarrel a shepherd, a father of this land who obtains this see with money, but esteem him whom the Lord chooses. Be perfect sons. Preserve yourselves from

---

11. Cf. John 10:11–13.
12. Cf. Josh. 23:14 and 1 Kings 2:2.
13. Ps. 93:14.

all heresy, beware of the Arian dogma, keep to the holy and uncontaminated catholic faith. Keep your bodies from pollution, since they are valued as the temples of God. Keep and do these things, that you may be worthy with your shepherd to prepare the road of the holy sheep pleasing to the heavenly Lord. Keep his precepts sufficiently. Obey him, that he may pray for you, since the Almighty God does not want mirth, but receives a contrite heart and a humble spirit. May the blessing of the Almighty Lord God be on you and on your sons, in generation and progeny, now and forever and in the ages of ages."

And when they had all answered "Amen," turning to the altar of blessed Cassian he said, "I beseech you, blessed Cassian, intercede for me. I was as a servant in your house, nourished by Cornelius of this see in the bosom of this church. Having returned to you again, I give my soul now to almighty God, however my body I commend to you."

While he was saying these and similar things, as if bursting forth, rejoicing and exulting, with all who were there in tears, he rendered up his spirit on December 3. The workmen quickly prepared a tomb behind the throne of that church in the place where he had ordered, and there his holy body was received; and it remains up to this day. He sat for __ years, __ months, __ days.

CONCERNING HOLY AURELIAN, 521

53. Aurelian, the twenty-second bishop, a notable man, young in age, older in sense and more elegant in every grace, raised above every evil deed, humble among the people, kindly to his flock.

He built on to the foundation of the house which most blessed Peter had founded, now called *Tricollis*, but he did not complete it.[1]

And know, O most beloved, that you have placed greatest weights on my neck. Of this man I could not find any facts, except this one thing, that he acquired the property which the Ursiana church holds in the territory of Comaclo, in the place which is

---

1. This information taken from the inscription in c. 75, below.

called *Ignis and Baias*—that is, by the names of idols—not far from where the church of St. Mary *in Pado uetere* is located. And in his reign this said *monasterium* was built.

54. But because of your request that his history not seem short, let us recount, without any trepidation, what human sense can do, relying on heavenly aid and our knowledge, inspired by the Lord, with you praying that the Creator and Lover of men, Who gave the breath of life and fixed our spirit in our vitals, Who gave us senses and reason and docile hearts and delighted in His creation, might enlarge such intellect in us, that we might be able to fulfill your request, and you might take this volume with desire and read it with love, rather than unroll it with disgust or carelessness.

But I, sick in part of my body, can hardly explain it further today; however as much as I can, with the Creator of all aiding me, let us begin.

Do not do as you did yesterday; your eloquence has impelled me enough. See, do not burden me greatly, since in the words of Solomon, "he that violently squeezeth the paps bringeth out blood";[2] thus may your wisdom consider me. Think this: this gift is not mine, but a gift from the Almighty. Oh poor me, whipped daily by you with hard questions. Do not do this! However, if you want to abuse me further with your words, so that I might be constrained to complete this pontifical book and give it into your hands quickly, consider your fragility first and know mine only later. Today it has been thirty-two years and ten months since I came forth from the womb of my mother and received light;[3] I have never suffered such whips, never been thus confined, as I was yesterday by you. And if you have this desire to beat me and to drag me hither and thither by my earlobes and to lead me fettered with hands tied behind my back, and to whip me on my back and chest and to lay blows on my shoulders, I will consent; do what you want! And after all these things leave me and go away, grant me forbearance and remove yourselves from me; and keep as much as

---

2. Prov. 30:33.
3. This passage tells us that Agnellus was born between 794 and 799.

has been written about the life of the bishops, you will hear nothing further from me.

But let me complete the life of this Aurelian and then be silent. What else is left to me, except only resignation? What good does it do? Why do you upbraid me? If the Lord will not give me the tongue of scholarship, let Him do with me what He will.

Intoning through Ezechiel He said, "And I will make thy tongue stick fast to the roof of thy mouth, and thou shalt be dumb." And to Moses, "Who made man's mouth? did not I?" And his son David, "All wisdom is from the Lord God." And Daniel, "The kingdom and wisdom and fortitude are his."[4]

Behold why do you rage? Inasmuch as that Artificer, Who has created me from dust with His hands, permits me, I will speak; I cannot do otherwise. I have told you all these things; hold them fixed in your mind. I want you to know that if I abandon this pontifical book because of your torture, the time will come when you will read and you will find half of it up to here; you will remember afterward with a groan those things which were said by me to you; but it won't do any good. And if later you want to ask me to finish the work, I will not listen. I want my labor to be completed through the dispensation of God Almighty; you want me to abandon it, through too much haste. I will not do it.

For I remember the words, beloved friends, where in the life of blessed John I said that I was your debtor,[5] and cleverly fleeing the presence of your flaming eyes I hid; since now you have found me, I am not able to hide. And if you do not know my debts, after you have compelled me, before you have examined me, most truly I will reveal them. I am your debtor over this question of the river Etham.

55. For it is written, "Thou hast broken up the fountains and the torrents: Thou hast dried up the Etham river."[6] Behold my debt. But let us see why He dried up the river Etham.[7]

---

4. Ezek. 3:26; Exod. 4:11; Ecclus. 1:1; Dan. 2:20.
5. See above, c. 45.
6. Ps. 73:15.
7. Gregory the Great (*Moralia in Iob* 33.10.20) comments on this passage but inter-

Hear the prophet saying, "Behold I have made a new way in the wilderness, saith the Lord, and rivers in the desert."[8] And if the Lord made all the rivers, and even the seas, why therefore did He dry up only the river Etham, as the prophet says, "Thou hast broken up the fountains and the torrents: Thou hast dried up the Etham river"?

Some want the river Etham to be understood allegorically, as the race of Esau, because he did not propagate progeny like the sons of Jacob, Isaac their father saying to Jacob, "Mayst thou increase to thousands of thousands and mayst thou multiply as the sands of the sea and the stars of heaven and as the dust of the earth, may you sprout as the green grasses, thou shalt spread abroad to the east, and to the west, and to the north, and to the south";[9] but to Esau, "What shall I do for thee, my son, since I have appointed him thy lord? Thou shalt live by the sword and shalt serve thy brother."[10]

We should investigate historically what sort of river this Etham was. We read in Exodus that when the sons of Israel were brought across the Red Sea, after a few days they came to a place which is called Mara, for there the waters were quite bitter; *mara* indeed means "bitter."[11] Because it was too bitter the people could not drink from it, but, parched with thirst, they found the river Etham and drank its drawn-up waters, and their bodies became infected with disease. Some say that not only were the waters of the river Etham bitter, but also those drinking it were infected with disease, and their insides were disrupted. Then they raged against Moses, and Moses with them to the Lord: and the Lord dried up the river Etham.

And it can be understood another way. The river Etham means

---

prets it as referring to the drying up of false doctrines. Ann Moffatt, "Sixth-century Ravenna," 240–41, notes that "what seemed a digression to pad out the text proves to be a homily especially appropriate to the reign of the Arian Theodoric," in whose lifetime Aurelian was bishop.

8. Isa. 43:16, 19.   9. Gen. 24:60, 22:17, 13:16, 28:14.
10. Gen. 27:37, 40.
11. Exod. 15:23.

"the devil,"[12] who indeed raises up poison and necks swollen with pride. He always shoots arrows full of poisonous juices against the servants of God, a goad to incitement. But Christ the Word, coming through the Virgin, dried up the river Etham, that is, He fettered the devil, the prince of death, He restored the world and pitied the human race.

And if God made man, according to what we read, and created the whole world by Himself, why therefore was it necessary to relieve man and to restore the world again? First He made man in the flesh from the dust of the earth and gave him breath; after much time He regenerated him through grace. Is there any way God could not have led man from the trap of death, without using virgin flesh? He could, and I believe He could without doubt. And why did He not do it? Now you have heard above, "Who hath known the mind of the Lord? Or who hath been His counselor?"[13]

But in as much as I can, I say reverently with great awe: earthly man had been placed beyond flesh in paradise as prince of all creation, and all things subjected to him. The devil, seeing such wealth given to him in spiritual form, swollen with pride, enraged with furor, thus said, "I was cast out of heaven, I lost angelic dignity and, although I am still a spirit, having lost heavenly and earthly delights I have nothing. This one however has suddenly been created, all good things are given to him, in addition to the joys of paradise. What should I do?" With this envy, dearest friends, the devil was continuously inflamed against the first man. Thus, having thought out his malice, he entered the bestial throat of the serpent and through this mouth he persuaded the man, and after Adam spurned the commandment, he lost everything; and the devil not only rejoiced but also mocked him. Behold the fatal transgression in Adam, if you consider with great wisdom the question which is placed before you; but with the help of the Lord I will solve it.

---

12. M. Lapidge (personal communication) points out that Etham does not mean "the devil" but "strong," according to Thiel, *Grundlagen und Gestalt*, 307.

13. Rom. 11:34.

The devil had conquered the son of the virgin earth; it was necessary that he be conquered by the son of the virgin Mary. Earthly, carnal man was made from the dust and substance of the earth; that man both carnal and spiritual was made from the word of God and the virgin womb. The devil tempted the earthly man and seduced him; he tempted the heavenly one, and he withdrew confounded. Thus it was necessary that he who had conquered the son of a virgin should be conquered by the son of a virgin, so that a virgin might again restore him whom earlier a virgin had produced through God.[14]

Why did He lay low the king of the demons not through the angels or through any army of heaven, but by Himself? The devil did not see the spiritual form in Adam, but the carnal; again Christ allowed himself to be tempted in the flesh, so that the cunning seducer might not say, "Adam had one form, Christ has another." Seeing the form of Christ, he thought of Adam: equal in form, but not equal in virtue. Christ had the form of man, but godlike virtue.

In many places in the Holy Scripture we can find that where Adam sinned, Christ restored. Adam sinned through gluttony, Christ conquered the devil through abstention. Adam was made from the virgin earth, Christ from the virgin Mary. The earth is called *terra* from its *terendo* [destruction] by the feet. "Maria" means "mistress," or "star of the sea," or "illuminatrix"; and if by chance by some other way you might pronounce "Maria," that is, shortening the "I," you would say "Maria," it means "plenitude." Adam was persuaded by a woman; Christ, born of woman, restores the church. Adam was deceived through wood, Christ saved the world through wood. Adam was cast out of paradise, Christ on the cross introduced a thief into paradise. Adam was cast into hell, Christ dragging him out of hell. Behold what a similarity between them! Man lost himself, and the Son of God delivered all, Who is blessed in the ages.

---

14. Series of parallels between Adam and Christ are a common *topos* of early medieval sermon writers.

56. However, this man Aurelian, after the passing of a few years, died in peace on May 26. Keeping the precepts of blessed Peter Chrysologus, he did not incline away from them. Indeed he left the buildings of the house incomplete. He was buried in the church of the Apostles next to the ambo, not far from the tomb where blessed Neon rests, before the body of Neon was translated by us to the apse. He sat for __ years, __ months, __ days.

CONCERNING HOLY ECCLESIUS, 522–32

57. Ecclesius, the twenty-third bishop, a holy vessel, of middle stature, he was neither stretched tall nor cut short, having a head full of hair and bushy eyebrows, slightly grey-haired and pleasing in form.

In his reign the church of the blessed martyr Vitalis was founded by Julian the banker together with this bishop. And this bishop on his own legal property built the church of the holy and always inviolate Virgin Mary, which you see, of wonderful size, the vault of the apse and the façade decorated with gold, and in this vault of the apse the image of the holy mother of God, the like of which can never be seen by human eyes. With these [eyes] that man himself dared to contemplate the image for the longest time, which contained metrical verses under its feet, namely:

> The hall of the Virgin shines, she who received Christ from the stars, with an angel from the heavens announcing it to her before [his birth]. O mystery! The mother of the Word and perennial virgin, made parent of the Lord her Creator. Truth, the magi, the lame, the blind, death, life confess her [5]. Ecclesius dedicates these holy rooftops to God.

The beginning of the building of the church was prepared by Julian, after the said Bishop Ecclesius had returned with Pope John to Rome from Constantinople with other bishops, sent by King Theodoric in a legation, as you have heard above.

He built *Tricollis*, but left it unfinished.[1]

---

1. See the inscription cited in c. 75.

58. Alas for you flocks, what shepherds they used to be! How different they were from these! They were true lamps in the church, the light of which lamps daily gleamed on those who were in the house of God, as the Lord says, "The light of thy body is thy eye. If thy eye be single, thy whole body shall be lightsome. But if thy eye be evil thy whole body shall be darksome."[2] Let these things suffice for today, so that, with this admonition, we might introduce another bishop.

59. But, as I said above, in his reign the church of the blessed martyr Vitalis was built by Julian the banker. No church in Italy is similar in structures and in mechanical works.[3] As for the expenses for the church of the said martyr Vitalis, as we find in the inscription of the founder Julian of blessed memory, twenty-six thousand gold *solidi* were spent. Therefore [when] this most blessed man [Ecclesius] died, he was buried in the church of the blessed martyr Vitalis, in the *monasterium* of St. Nazarius before the altar, in the central place, next to the bodies on the one side of the blessed Bishop Ursicinus and on the other side of blessed Victor, in the middle of them.

60. It happened at that time, when a dispute arose between blessed Ecclesius the bishop and the priests over certain affairs of the church, they went to the holy Pope Felix of the city of Rome, that he might decree just means of governance between them. He, having summoned the Ravennate bishop with the whole clergy, soon made decisions between them, declared and confirmed in the following:

Letter of Pope Felix:

"Felix IV[4] bishop of the city of Rome. The care of our predecessors for ecclesiastical peace and quiet should be praised. It was decreed that the shepherd by his vigilance ought to restrain legal actions, either condemning or correcting them. It is fitting that similar things be looked at by those of us who walk on the same

---

2. Matt. 6:22–23.
3. For the meaning of "mechanical works" *(mechanicis operibus)*, see Glossary, s.v.
4. Pope Felix IV (526–30).

path with [our predecessors]; since through the mercy of God we hold their places, it befits us to follow their examples. From envy the priests of the church of Ravenna have done things which are known to have saddened the souls of all catholics: altercations, seditions, depravities, which strive to disrupt all ecclesiastical discipline. Again, having true fear of God before our eyes, lest we give courage to illicit excesses, and so that we do not cast out by our decree what it is right to ordain, in the words of Solomon: 'Give no crossing to the water.'[5] Therefore reviewing the documents offered to us by our brother Ecclesius and by the priests and deacons and clergy and notaries of the church of Ravenna, with our brother and priest Ecclesius and his clerics present as designated below, we advise what we see they have agreed by reason:

"That those ought to undertake the office of cleric whose life and manner of living cannot be impugned, by the authority of the holy canons. According to the ordinances of the holy fathers, we order that in the stated times, as far as pertains to priests and deacons, that clerics willing as well as unwilling be solemnly promoted. Let the ancient custom be kept in the church of Ravenna and Classe. Let clerics or monks not need the patronage of the mighty to obtain owed rank or place, for which the bishop would seem either ungrateful by not acting, or unjust by acting.

"Let a quarter of the patrimony of the Ravennate church, that is, three thousand *solidi*, be used for the appropriate payments to all the clergy or to whomever it is supposed to be paid. If, however, any of the pensions or inheritances should happen to increase, by the will of our Lord, with that Lord mediating, its fourth part should be used for the same; thus however, according to the ordained decrees, so that it might not be possible to conceal what is distributed to each person, according to merit or according to rank, since God has established all things according to justice and measure. Thus let each, beyond the requirements of illness or other appropriate cause, vigilantly observe all things in his office. We decree that the following should be accounted to the bishop: ac-

---

5. Ecclus. 25:34.

quisitions of property or of family money distributed from inheritances, or gifts that are offered by different people, and the banquets which it is necessary for him to hold, either for the honor of his rank, or merit, or for the reception of guests.

"None of the clergy should try to make any conspiracy, or any association, within the church of God which could not remain unpunished if they were the persons of the laity. For even as we hope that by divine mercy such a one might not be allowed to be lost, if anyone should try, let him feel the authority of the canons and ecclesiastical discipline, according to the words of the apostle, 'Them that sin reprove before all: that the rest also may have fear.'[6]

"Let those who are vigilant in the works of God deserve praise for their good zeal; let those who are seen to enhance their way of life through obedience know the affection of their bishop; let those who through their obedience in their offices do not desist from works pleasing to God be glorified by the love of their pontiff, as the divine words say, 'The laborer is worthy of his hire.'[7]

"To the patrimony of the church by the judgment of their bishop[8] ... let persons from the clergy, chosen with care, whom the bishop shall have attested worthy through his knowledge, whose faith and industry are proven, be sent under a suitable guarantee so that the alms-giving to the paupers may not suffer fraud and the amount of the patrimony of the church may not be hidden; and let each and every cleric from among these, under fear of God and his own bishop, faithfully explain the accounts which have been committed to him.

"It was not fitting for us to say or to explain in words that which should be cursed in a completely religious way of life. News has reached us that some of the clergy are present at public spectacles, which is such a horrible thing that it arouses the souls of the catholics for their execration, that they see those whom they should hear reciting the divine words in the house of God meeting

---

6. 1 Tim. 5:20.
7. Luke 10:7 and 1 Tim. 5:18.
8. A blank space of about eight letters was left in the manuscript.

against orders at the spectacles. In these things discipline is confused, the divine precepts are trodden underfoot. Wherefore the bishop for his part should take care that if they do not do it now, they will not do it in the future, and if they do do it now, they should be corrected according to ecclesiastical discipline.

"If any one of the clergy holds urban or rural estates belonging to the church, we ordain by the same decrees made under a just estimation of the payment that it should be collected by this calculation, that they should keep from it what they are supposed to receive as remuneration, while they bring in what is left for the benefit of ecclesiastical profit. As regards urban or rural estates and other moveable property bequeathed by the faithful for the redemption of their souls to various named churches, let the old custom be kept.

"Let the notaries in order of office, the *primicerius*, the *secundicerius*, the third, fourth, fifth, sixth and seventh,[9] maintain the ecclesiastical documents in their legal register in the sight of the priests and deacons according to a list of precise inventories; let them give and receive them so that, whatever case requires it, they may be faithfully presented. However we order them to do all things with the order and decree of their bishop. For again, all the ecclesiastical documents should be copied, lest in some way those received should disappear, or at the time they are needed for the uses of the church they cannot be produced. However let these notaries, vigorously observant in their office, follow without deviation the usages provided for them by their elders in antiquity. For, as reason requires and precedent has ordained, let them provide books signed by the hand of the bishop for the security of those whose concern is the whole ecclesiastical patrimony.

"Property under ecclesiastical jurisdiction, both rural and urban, has been given to certain men of secular way of life through no necessity of friendship; by the care of the bishop through those

---

9. This organization seems to imitate the Roman administration, which included seven regional notaries, headed by a *primicerius* and a *secundicerius;* see Noble, *Republic of St. Peter,* 219.

clergy he has commissioned, let him recall this property to the dominion of the church, nor then, because of the reason stated above, let him presume to give it again. Let Mastalus, archdeacon of the Ravennate church, receive the usages assigned in that same place by ancient custom, without the least diminution, so that he thus makes clear those things that followed before him.

"Let monasteries[10] of men or of handmaidens of God be established by the bishop, so that reason, justice, peace and discipline may be kept by all. A consideration of our position requires us not to be silent: it behooves our brother Ecclesius to guard these things, for when justice is observed by the canons it generates peace. Charity proceeds from justice, through which we see God and through Whose grace we can observe these precepts. Therefore it is fitting to be negligent in nothing, but vigilant in all things, so that we might return that talent which has been given to us, augmented by good works, to that Giver of all good things.[11]

"We, Caelius, have read [this document].[12]

"I, Felix, bishop of the catholic church of the city of Rome, have signed this decree between the two sides.

"The names of the priests, deacons, or clerics of the church of Ravenna, who came to Rome with the bishop: Patricius priest. Stephen priest. Constantine priest. Servandus priest. Honorius priest. Exuperantius priest. Clemens deacon. Ursus deacon. Felicissimus deacon. Vigilius deacon. Neon deacon. John deacon. Stephen deacon. Gerontius subdeacon. Honorius subdeacon. Peter subdeacon. Vitalis subdeacon. Julian acolyte. Faustinus acolyte. Romanus acolyte. Severinus acolyte. Andrew acolyte. Peter reader. Mark reader. Asterius reader. Another Peter reader. Andrew reader. Marinus

---

10. One of the few cases in the *LPR* in which the word *monasterium* means monastery; see Glossary, s.v. *monasterium*.

11. A reference to the parable of the talents, Matt. 25:14–30.

12. Testi-Rasponi (*CPER*, 155, n. 2, and 171, n. 3) notes that in the sixth century many bishops took the name *Caelius* as an honorific; thus this is the signature of Ecclesius. The future bishops Victor and Agnellus may be among the signers of the letter; see c. 84, where Agnellus says that Bishop Agnellus was consecrated deacon in the time of Ecclesius.

defensor. Majoranus notary defensor. Hermolaus senior defensor. Honorius cantor. Tranquillus cantor. Anthony cantor. Melitus cantor.

"The names of the priests, deacons, who came to Rome with the priest Victor and the deacon Mastalus: Laurence priest. Rusticus priest. Victor priest. Thomas priest. Mastalus deacon. Magnus deacon. Paul deacon. Agnellus deacon. Maurus subdeacon. Stephen acolyte. Vincemalus acolyte. Vindemius acolyte. Colos acolyte. Cassian acolyte. Laurence acolyte. Stephen acolyte. Thomas reader. Laurence reader. Florus reader. Reparatus reader. Luminosus reader. Calumnios reader. Isaac reader. Laurence superintendent of stores. Peter dean. Stephen dean."

61. After these things blessed Ecclesius recovered and was with his sheep like a father with his sons; and he gave all the things to his clerics about which he was censured by the Roman pope, and even more amply was his gift made; and after these things he ruled his church in peace and he heard no word of murmuring except praises from his priests. And this decree remained for his successors for a long time.[13]

He was buried, as we said, in the church of San Vitale. And in the atrium at the front of this hall he ordered metrical verses to be written with silver tesserae containing the following:

The lofty temples rise to the venerable rooftop, sanctified to God in the name of Vitalis. And Gervase and Protase also hold this stronghold, whom family and faith and church join together. The father fleeing the contagions of the world was to these sons [5] an example of faith and martyrdom.

Ecclesius first gave this stronghold to Julian, who wonderfully completed the work commissioned to him. He also ordered it to be maintained by perpetual law that in these places no one's body is permitted to be placed [10]. But because tombs of earlier bishops are established here, it is allowed to place this one, or one like it.

He sat ten years, five months, seven days.

13. In c. 118 Agnellus reports that many copies of this document were burned by the late-seventh-century Bishop Theodore.

CONCERNING HOLY URSICINUS, 533–36

62. Ursicinus, the twenty-fourth bishop, a humble man, with a ruddy face and big eyes, tall of stature, thin of body, holy in holy deeds. He was a builder of *Tricollis*, but did not finish it.[1]

In the reign of this bishop, King Athalaric died at Ravenna on October 2, and on the next day Deodatus was elevated to the kingship and deposed Queen Malasuintha, and Deodatus sent her into exile to Volsena on April 30. And, as some say, she ordered a house to be built on her own legal property, where now the *monasterium* of St. Peter which is called Orfanotrophium is built.

After a few days King Deodatus went to Rome, and on returning, was killed by the Goths at the fifteenth milestone from Ravenna in the month of December. And in the month of March[2] of that year Lord Belisarius entered the city of Classe, and he entered Ravenna. Having returned from there to Sicily, he laid it waste. The Empress Theodora died in Constantinopole on the twenty-seventh day of the month of July. And the chancellor Narses entered Ravenna with a great army in this said month, on a Thursday; and he fought with King Totila and he died, and the multitude of his army fell to the sword, and the remainder fled, wounded. And the Goths raised over themselves a king by the name of Teia, in Pavia, and there was a brief respite.

Now let these things suffice for today; it is now time for us to return home, and to explain the life of this bishop and faithfully narrate what is left when we have the leisure.

63. This holy man ordered and saw to it that the church of blessed Apollinaris be founded by Julian the banker and finished. With him soon fulfilling the orders, by the will of God, it was

---

1. From the inscription in c. 75.
2. The manuscript has *Madio*, which is an error for either *Maiio* (May) or *Martio* (March). Many scholars have accepted the date as May, but others have pointed out that, according to Procopius's chronology, this event took place in March (B. Croke, personal communication), and the text has been restored accordingly in the edition on which this translation is based (see Deliyannis, *CCCM* edition of *LPR*, note at c. 62).

built by that holy man. No church in any part of Italy is similar to this one in precious stones, since they almost glow at night just as they do in the day.

Therefore this holy man daily dismembered the holy body of the Lamb over the Lord's altar with his hands and, weeping, expiated the sins of the people.[3]

64. But since today by your nobility you want to turn aside into my house, what should I do, since I am the keeper of a house of poverty and am in need of sustenance? Neither my table nor the storeroom of my heart are such, that they might restore your bodies. But I have a most fat lamb, whose body, though consumed, never diminishes, but always remains whole. For it is not right that, after you have passed the entrance of my *monasterium*, the house of St. Bartholemew,[4] you should not receive a blessing from that apostle, and that you should return fasting.

Let four legs be brought, and place a table above them. The four stable feet are the four evangelists, who uphold the whole square world by their preachings; the table above is the holy altar, that is, the cross, where Christ lay down and was offered as the sacrifice for the Father for the salvation of the world. Just as there are four feet, thus there are four corners of the table. Have you reclined at it? Eat the bread. That one is placed here as bread, who said, "I am the living bread which came down from heaven."[5] You eat not carnal food, but heavenly; not earthly bread, but angelic.

That bread, of which David sang, "He had given them the bread of heaven, man ate the bread of angels."[6] How do angels eat, who are incorporeal? Are they endowed with flesh? They do not eat with bites, but are satiated with the abundance of divinity, which is living bread in the ages of ages.

Let this Lamb come placed on a platter, wrapped up, as He was placed in the holy sepulcher, applied to the fire but not burned. He

---

3. Presumably this means that he performed the Eucharist, which is the subject of the following allegorical analysis.
4. One of Agnellus's two *monasteria*.   5. John 6:41.
6. Ps. 77:24–25.

descended to hell, extinguished the flames of Gehenna, destroyed Death, killed the Lion, shattered Tartarus, brought out the righteous, obliterated the bronze doors and threw down the adamantine bars, according to the prophet, "O death, I will be thy death; O hell, I will be thy bite."[7] He rose again from the tomb, left his flesh for us; walking on the wings of the wind, he trod on the heads of the clouds, he was received in the heavens, he sits at the right hand of the Father. Eat of this flesh of the immaculate Lamb. If you eat his flesh and drink his blood, you will remain in him, and he in you, as he says, "He that eateth my flesh, and drinketh my blood, abideth in me, and I in him."[8]

Does not the law which was given through Moses teach that no blood of an animal might be eaten, since the blood is its soul?[9] It teaches, and it teaches truly. But this Lamb is not ordinary, not earthly, but alone, alone and immaculate, alone of alone, true of true, who has borne our [sins], although he has none of his own. And thus the Hebrew people, when they left Egypt, besmeared their doorposts with the blood of a lamb, that they might not be killed by the smiting angel, and where there was no gore of the blood of a lamb, the house was struck, since the Lord passing through the middle of Egypt divided the chosen from the wicked. Behold the flesh of the Lamb which we eat daily, and it does not diminish, rather it increases and gives eternal life to those who eat it.

Now let drink follow after food. Drink the clearest wine from that Vine, who said, "I am the true vine, and my Father is the husbandman."[10] Let this wine come with canticles and organs, with lyres and choruses, songs and harps, horns and cymbals and concerts, since it is worthy of great honor and much honesty.[11] The canticle is spiritual praise, the organs indeed are our jaws, the lyre is the human heart, which daily we smite before God (since, just as we strike the lyre with chords, thus we strike our chests with the

7. Hos. 13:14.
8. John 6:57.
9. Deut. 12:23.
10. John 15:1.
11. Cf. Ps. 150:3–5 and 2 Chron. 5:12–13.

beat of the heart),[12] the chorus indeed means the battleline of priests, the trumpet is our voice (since in the voice we render praises to the Father), the harp from the singing of psalms (since they have as a motif the whole Trinity and inseparable unity), the cymbals and the concerts are the voices chanting psalms in a chorus in a great noise, with which the readings shake the whole church, day and night they do not cease to invoke God.

65. That blessed Ursicinus, completing these things during his reign, by divine order his soul was separated from his body, his body went back to its origin. And he was buried in the basilica of St. Vitalis the martyr, before the altar of St. Nazarius. He sat three years, six months, nine days.

CONCERNING HOLY VICTOR, 538–45

66. Victor, the twenty-fifth bishop. Why is he a "victor"? By divine inspiration, from the wish of his parents it was his surname, from his own acts indeed it became his nickname, in that he frequently, through his many virtues, conquered the camps of the devil by praying and by fasting. He had a beautiful face and an eager expression.

He was a builder of *Tricollis,* but did not finish it.[1] However he made a silver canopy of wonderful workmanship over the altar of the holy Ursiana church, which is called by the name of its builder. Some say that [he made it] together with the people; and others state that in the times of the elder Justinian the orthodox, the emperor proposed that [Victor] make such an object, so that he might offer help. Moved by mercy, he gave to blessed Victor all the taxes of Italy from that year.[2] When he had received it, he built the work, as you see, which, in place of the old wooden one, was con-

---

12. A pun on *chordis* (chords)—*cordis* (heart).

1. From the inscription in c. 75.

2. Brown, "The Church of Ravenna," 6, suggests that this statement actually refers to the remission of the tax payable on the church's property for the year.

structed of a hundred and twenty pounds of silver in exact weight. And above the arches of the canopy these verses were written:[3]

The priest Victor with the people discharges this vow to Christ, Victor who increased faith among the people with love. The holy band of angels encircling these holy places ministers to the bishop who fulfills his vows to Christ; the antiquity taken away marvels at the noble work [5], which returns better with a more noble appearance. If any lover of Catholic law should come here, he will go away restored by your body, Christ.

With the rest that remained, he provided various vessels for the table of the bishop, of which some part remain up to the present day. And he made, over the altar of the holy Ursiana church, an altar cloth of pure gold with silk threads, very heavy, being scarlet[4] in the middle; and among the five images there we see his, and under the worked feet of the Savior these letters are written in purple:

Bishop Victor, servant of God, offers this ornament for the day of the Resurrection of our Lord Jesus Christ, in the fifth year since his ordination.

And he restored the bath next to the ecclesiastical residence, clinging to the side walls of the episcopal palace where he lived,[5] which washes wonderfully up to today, and he attached most precious marbles to the side walls, and he composed various different figures in gold mosaics, and a tablet written with gold mosaic letters, on which we have laboriously taken care to read and thus find these hexametrical cataletical verses written on it:

Victor, priest secure in apostolic virtue, first putting aside the small old baths made by earlier labor, then restored them with wonderful newness, so that more beautiful and greater worship might rise from their depths. He also decreed that it be held by perpetual custom [5] that for two days

---

3. Testi-Rasponi suggests that each pair of lines was found on one side of the canopy (*CPER*, 182, 9).
4. For the meaning of the word *cocca* (scarlet), see Glossary, s.v.
5. Recent excavations have uncovered a bath complex next to the *episcopium*, dating to the fourth or fifth century, which is probably the one restored by Bishop Victor; see Rizzardi, "Note sull'antico episcopio," 725–29.

the clergy of this city should wash for free, to whom is granted Tuesdays and Fridays for washing.

67. He ruled his church for a short time, but the effort with which he held his see is apparent from his great labors. Indeed he decorated the tetragonal baptistry, which most blessed Peter Chrysologus built in the city of Classe next to the Petriana church, and in the middle of the vault, on the men's side, under the arch there is a small medallion, which even today contains the following, "by our holy lord," and facing on the other side, the women's,[6] there is found another little medallion, as above, with gold letters in turn on its side, reading thus, "father Victor."[7]

68. These things, as I said, he indeed completed; but now it is destroyed by evil men, since the devil hardens their hearts so that the temple of God, which was built by holy priests and most faithful Christians, is destroyed by false Christians.

Why so? Because the finish, the end and destruction of the world is near. But according to the apostle these are "dangerous times, and men are lovers of themselves."[8] The world finishes in evil. However great the joy at the beginning of the world, there will be much more wailing at its end. Before the world can be consumed, according to the gospel, there will be pestilence and hunger and terrors from heaven, angers, quarrels, dissensions and strife. Nation will be raised against nation, and kingdom will rage against kingdom, and the youth will outrank the old man, and the younger generation will render no honor to their elders, but sons will despise their fathers, and will not only deride them, but even subjugate them.[9] These things according to the holy gospel. Woe unto you, miserable ones! We have seen all these things. But You, immortal and terrible God in the highest, save us by the power of

---

6. The north and south sides, respectively; see Glossary, s.v. *pars mulierum* and *pars virorum*.

7. Cf. the inscription in the same baptistry cited in c. 91, which begins, *Saluo domno papa Agnello*.

8. 2 Tim. 3:1–2.

9. Lanzoni ("Il 'Liber Pontificalis,'" 366) read this passage as a reference to the wars between the sons and grandsons of Charlemagne.

Your hand! We have foreseen all these things, earthquakes in places, and signs in the sun and the moon. But just as it says, we do not know the hour of the end, which is not revealed to the holy angels; but we know that it is near, and we recognize it, as when an old man is just about to die, and we see the sign of death in him. We do not know on what day or hour it will happen; and thus although all the signs which truth predicts are coming forth, the day or hour is hidden from us.[10] But to You, Who understands thoughts and scrutinizes hearts,[11] all things are known and possible.[12]

This most blessed man, after he finished his life on the February 15, was carried out to the casket, and then, with linen cut, he was buried in the church of San Vitale in the *monasterium* of St. Nazarius next to his predecessor. He sat six years, eleven months, eleven days.

CONCERNING HOLY MAXIMIAN, 546–57

69. Maximian, the twenty-sixth bishop. Of venerable stature, with a thin body, lean of face, bald of head, he had few hairs, grey eyes, and was adorned with all grace. He was not from this flock, but an alien sheep from the church of Pula, ordained as a deacon by its bishop.[1]

70. But I will explain why this foreign-born man held the episcopate of this city;[2] I will not conceal it, but will publicly reveal it just as I heard it from those telling it from the distant past, and it is the truth beyond any doubt.

One day when Maximian was digging in the earth, when *tonsa*

10. Cf. Matt. 24:7–36.   11. Cf. Wisd. of Sol. 1:6.
12. Cf. Matt. 19:26.

1. The church of Ravenna owned land in Istria and thus had close connections with the Istrian city of Pula (Croatia), throughout the Middle Ages; see Fasoli, "Il patrimonio," 394–95.

2. Cf. Agnellus's account of the election of Peter Chrysologus, c. 49, where he must also justify the presence of a foreign bishop who was particularly illustrious.

cesalis was first putting forth its seeds,[3] he suddenly found a large vase filled with gold and many other kinds of riches. He, thinking to himself that it could not remain hidden, ordered a great cow to be brought and killed, and he commanded that its stomach, emptied of muck, be filled with gold coins. Likewise he summoned the cobblers, who made foot coverings, and commanded them to produce great boots from the skins of goats, and he filled these with gold *solidi*. He brought the remainder with him when he went to the city of Constantinople, and gave it to the Emperor Justinian. When the emperor saw it, after thanking him he inquired searchingly if there was more. But Maximian, under oath, answered the emperor: "By your health, lord, and by the salvation of your soul, I do not have more of it than what I lavished on stomach and boots." The emperor thought that he spoke of food for the body and coverings for the feet; Maximian of course was referring to that which he had hidden. Justinian considered what sort of reward he should give for such faith as Maximian had shown him.

It happened at that time that Victor, bishop of this city of Ravenna, died, and the citizens of Ravenna, the priests together with people, went to the emperor, seeking the pallium for their candidate. After hearing them, the emperor ordered the petitioners to wait. Having considered the matter, he ordered blessed Maximian, the deacon from Pula, to be consecrated by Pope Vigilius in the city of Patras in Greece,[4] on October 14 of the tenth indiction, five years after the consulship of Basilius the younger,[5] in the forty-eighth year of Maximian's life, and having given him the pallium sent him to Ravenna.

Since the Ravennate citizens did not want to receive Maximian so speedily, he waited outside the gates of St. Victor, not far from the stream that is called *fossa Sconii*, in the basilica of St. Eusebius, in the episcopal palace which the bishop Unimundus had built in

---

3. The meaning of *tonsa cesalis* is unknown.
4. Pope Vigilius was on his way to Constantinople, having been arrested by Justinian; see Roman *LP*, Life of Vigilius.
5. The year 546.

the time of King Theodoric; and also in the episcopal palace of the church of St. George, which was built in the time of the Arians. And the said episcopal palaces lasted until our own day, and were demolished almost twenty-six years ago, by the order of Bishop Valerius, from which he ordered a house to be built, which is now called the New House, or sometimes the Valerian House.[6]

71. Since the people, as I said, did not want to receive him, men in the bishop's entourage wanted to send legates to the emperor reporting that his orders had been flouted, and that, persisting in their abominable pride, the Ravennate citizens did not want to receive their ordained bishop, and with the church widowed, the flock wandered hither and thither. Most blessed Maximian did not agree with these men, but he overrode them with his words, saying: "Cease, brothers; do not accuse others, do not rejoice in the ruin of another. What sort of shepherd am I, if I do not spare my sheep? Do you want me to tear them to pieces? That is not good advice. Leave them, there will be no evil through me. Let the will of the Lord be done. I beseech you, for a few days give them a truce."

After a few days he sent a faithful messenger from among his men; he called on one of the priests and one of the leaders of the city and invited them to lunch with him. When they came, he made merry with them, and after the food and drink he gave them gifts from the gold that he had found before. Having made peace with them, he sent them back into the city of Ravenna with his blessing, and asked them to visit him often. And on the next day he sent out and invited other leaders, and acted as before, and did the same on the third day.

Then they discussed among themselves the things of this sort, and they said: "What is it that we want to do? This man is good and wise. We plot injuries against him, but he does not wish to render evil to us for evil. We cannot be without pontiff and father. Behold the priests are straying, the people stumble, the church is

---

6. Miller, "The Development," 165–66, and *The Bishop's Palace*, 57–58, notes that remains of this structure still survive within the present bishop's palace.

declining. Let us rise at dawn, let us bring him into the city and worship his footsteps."

Then, at the rise of dawn, they all went together as one man, and opening the gates of the city, with crosses and banners and flags[7] and praises led him honorably into this city of Ravenna, and they kissed his feet and embellished the decorated streets of the city with various adornments. And all of the buildings were wreathed, there was happiness among the soldiers, and gladness among the private citizens, both the young and old rejoiced, those in the middle were glad. And they asked him to sit in the apse of the church and they heard mass from him, and they made it a day of solemnity along with great joy and everlasting happiness.

72. After these things he was like a father with his sons toward his sheep.[8] And he built from the foundations the church of St. Stephen, deacon and martyr, here in Ravenna, not far from the Ovilian gate; he enhanced it with wonderful size and furnished it most beautifully, and in the vaults of the apse his image is fixed in multicolored mosaic, and is surrounded by wonderful glasswork, and he established there many relics from the bodies of the saints, whose names you will find thus written:

In honor of holy and most blessed first martyr Stephen, Bishop Maximian, servant of Christ, by God's grace built this church from the foundations and dedicated it on December 11 in the fourteenth indiction, in the ninth year after the consulship of Basilius the younger.[9]

And he rejoiced in the Lord, who performed such good things for him as no man might be able to tell fully.

He placed here the relics of apostles and martyrs,[10] namely St.

---

7. *Bandus* (flag) refers to a military banner or *vexillum;* the word is used several times elsewhere in the *LPR* to refer to troops within the local militia, and apparently to the regions of the city that corresponded to these troops.

8. The same thing was said about Ecclesius, c. 61; see Pizarro, *Writing Ravenna,* 47–52.

9. The year 550.

10. It is possible that this list of saints was derived from depictions of them in this church, perhaps similar to the processions of martyrs and virgins in Sant'

Peter, St. Paul, St. Andrew, St. Zacharias, St. John the Baptist, St. John the Evangelist, St. James, St. Thomas, St. Matthew, St. Stephen, St. Vincent, St. Laurence, St. Quirinus, St. Florian, St. Emilian, St. Apollinaris, St. Agatha, St. Euphemia, St. Agnes, and St. Eugenia; may they pray for us. And in the triumphal arch of the apse you will find metrical verses, containing the following:

The temple of Stephen shines, holy in relics and in name, he who first performed the exceptional act of martyrdom. The same palm is given to all for holy blood; however he benefits from it more who was earlier in time. He himself now assisting your faith and your vow, great priest [5] Maximian has completed this work. For the hand of man alone could not so soon have made such a hall from its foundation walls. When the gleaming moon was new for the eleventh time, the church which had been begun shines established in beautiful completion. [10]

At the sides of this basilica he added small *monasteria*, which all appear marvelously with new gold mosaics and various other stones fixed in plaster; and above the capitals of all the columns the name of this Maximian is carved. In the *monasterium* on the men's [south] side you will find six mosaic letters; they lead the ignorant into error, for the knowledgeable understand that there is written MU.SI.VA.[11]

73. Some say that one day the bishop summoned the *archiergatus*, that is, the master of the work, and asked him why he had not finished the building of the said church. But the *archiergatus* made it known, saying: "Because you, O our lord, had sailed to the region of Constantinople, cement and bricks were lacking, nor do we have enough stones to have been able to work." Then, at the order of the bishop, in one night so much building material was brought,

---

Apollinare Nuovo (Nauerth, *Agnellus von Ravenna, Untersuchungen*, 97); or perhaps Agnellus saw an inscription in which they were listed.

11. Testi-Rasponi, *CPER*, 192, n. 6, proposes that these *litterae lithostratae* were a monogram of Maximian, in which Agnellus did not recognize all of the letters. In that case the monogram must have been different from the one that Agnellus reports on the column capitals just above, which he had no trouble recognizing. See Glossary, s.v. *lithostratus*.

and the suppliers prepared plaster and tiles, rocks and bricks, stones and wood, columns and stone slabs, gravel and sand,[12] in one night, as I said, that they would hardly be able to fashion in eleven months.

74. And during the reign of that most holy bishop, when a disagreement arose over the woods which go by name of Vistrum, located in Istria, again he took himself to Constantinople, so that the presence of the Emperor Justinian might eliminate such strife. Both were by that time furnished with grey hairs; most bitterly together they began to mourn about all the things they remembered, cut off from youth and united in old age. Then this worthy emperor and *augustus* Justinian established an injunction for him about that forest, that it be perpetually and legally part of the holy church of Ravenna, which he had recognized it belonged to justly and rationally.

75. In his reign he completed all the buildings of the *Tricollis*, and there he is depicted with his predecessors; if you want to read, looking up, you will find written thus:

This younger Peter, following the commands of Christ, displayed by his holy practices what He taught. Also he founded this citadel with wonderful structures; he gave these monuments his name. After his death Aurelian bore the honors [5], after him Ecclesius was bishop; then was Ursicinus, Victor followed in order, finally the youngest, Maximian, is here. He was from Pula, a sincere deacon of Christ, merciful in the law of God and good in faithfulness [10]. God himself adorned this man with the holy summit and placed him as bishop over his church; however, he knows that he did not merit the apostolic summit by his own deeds, but by the faithfulness of God.

76. And he built the church of St. Mary which is called Formosa, in Pula, where he was a deacon, of wonderful beauty, and he decorated it with various stones. He built a house where the rector of that church lives when he is in this city, and gave all his wealth to the Ravennate church, which we possess up to today.

---

12. In this account of construction, many terms for building materials are used; cf. c. 130, and, for the specific terms, see Glossary, s.v.

He decorated with all diligence the church of St. Andrew the apostle here in Ravenna, not far from the Hereulana region; having removed the old wooden columns made of nut trees, he filled the church with columns of proconnesian marble.[13] Then he tried to bring the stolen body of that apostle to Ravenna.

When the emperor in Constantinople knew of this, he ordered blessed Maximian to come to Constantinople and to bring with him the venerable body of the apostle. The emperor, amused, said to him, "Don't be displeased, father, that one brother keeps Rome in first place, this one is to convey second place. The cities are both sisters, and the apostles are both brothers.[14] I do not want to give him to you, since it is fitting that there be the body of an apostle where the imperial seat is."

But most blessed Maximian said, "Let it be done as you command; however I request that I with my priests might pass this night in psalmody over this holy body." And the emperor agreed at once. Then they spent the whole night in vigils, and after all things were completed, seizing a sword and saying a prayer, he cut off the beard of the apostle up to the chin. And from the remains of many other saints he took relics with the emperor's agreement; and from there he returned to his own see.

And it is a true thing, brothers, that if he had buried the body of blessed Andrew, brother of Peter the prince, here, the Roman popes would not thus have subjugated us.

77. He consecrated the church of the blessed Bishop Apollinaris located in Classe and of the blessed martyr Vitalis in Ravenna and of the blessed archangel Michael here in Ravenna, which Bacauda built with Julian the banker of blessed memory,[15] in the

---

13. Testi-Rasponi, *CPER*, 195, n. 1, suggests that the replacement of wooden columns with marble ones referred to the canopy over the altar rather than to the nave columns, comparing this passage to one found in c. 66. Deichmann, "Studi sulla Ravenna scomparsa," 62, suggests that Agnellus knew of a restoration of this church by Maximian through an inscription.

14. St. Andrew was the brother of St. Peter, the apostle buried in Rome; see Matt. 4:18, etc.

15. Julian is also called *sanctae recordationis memoriae* in c. 59, where an inscription is

region which is called *Ad Frigiselo*.[16] And there you will find in the vault of the apse the following:

Having obtained the beneficences of archangel Michael, Bacauda and Julian have made from the foundations and dedicated [this church] on May 7, the fourth year after the consulship of Basilius the younger *vir clarissimus* consul, in the eighth indiction.[17]

And, as some assert, this Bacauda was the son-in-law of the said Julian, and rests in a stone sarcophagus not far from that church of the archangel in the Tower of Bacauda.

And in the apse of San Vitale the image of this same Maximian and of the emperor and empress are beautifully created in mosaic. However long we could tell of the goodness of this holy man, the time for narration is lacking to me. He labored in all things more than the other bishops his predecessors.

In his reign was built near my house the barracks of the regiment which is called the First Flag,[18] not far from the golden milestone, and we find his name stamped on the tiles thus, "Maximian bishop of Ravenna," which I have seen and read.

And in the narthexes of Sant' Apollinare and San Vitale you will find tablets written with majuscule letters containing the following:

Julian the banker built the basilica of the blessed priest Apollinaris from the foundations, authorized by the *vir beatissimus* Bishop Ursicinus, and decorated and dedicated it, with the *vir beatus*[19] Bishop Maximian conse-

---

being quoted. For more about the inscriptions containing the name of *Julianus argentarius*, see Deichmann, *Ravenna* 2.2:3–33.

16. Later known as *in Africisco*.

17. The year is 545.

18. A *numerus* was a military unit of 200–400 men; see Brown, *Gentlemen and Officers*, 56. Here Agnellus seems to be referring to a building connected with this specific *numerus*; see ibid., 97.

19. Maximian was the first bishop of Ravenna to use the title "archbishop," which can be found in the inscription quoted below, c. 80. Deichmann, "I titoli dei vescovi ravennati," proposes that the designation of Maximian as *vir reverendissimus* in this inscription dating to 547, but *vir beatissimus* in the inscription dating to 549 indicates that the change in Ravenna's ecclesiastical rank occurred between these two dates.

crating it on May 9,[20] in the twelfth indiction, the eighth year after the consulship of Basilius.

In the narthex of blessed Vitalis you will find thus:

Julian the banker built the basilica of the blessed martyr Vitalis from the foundations, authorized by the *vir beatissimus* Bishop Ecclesius, and decorated and dedicated it, with the *vir reverendissimus* Bishop Maximian consecrating it on April 19, in the tenth indiction, in the sixth year after the consulship of Basilius.[21]

This holy man preserved the body of blessed Probus with the other bodies of the holy bishops with aromatics and placed them fittingly, and on the facade of that church he decorated the images of blessed Probus and Eleuchadius and Calocerus with various mosaics, and under their feet you will find . . . [22]

78. Now this most blessed man had previously sailed in eastern parts, as he says in his volumes, saying:

In Alexandria there is no external cause of evil, but because the race of men is fierce, there is always seditious unrest, civil war arises among them; aroused, not on account of virtue, nor for defense, but for the sake of slaughter and the killing of citizens, they all killed their prefect within the church, because previously some others had likewise killed their bishop, accusing him of heresy. When this was discovered, the emperor, moved to anger, ordered the city to be completely overthrown. Finally, having sent another prefect by the name of Laudicius, he crucified forty men through each region in that city. But then Dioscorus, bishop of that same city, labored hard, and visibly placed his own life for his sheep; and selected monks hastened from the wilderness to the emperor and pleaded indulgence for the excess of the citizens. Then the emperor gave in to the priests and from that time forward ordered them to beware of such things. Timothy succeeded this bishop in Alexandria, whom I saw administering well in his city when I sailed to the East. But not much later the city of Nazarba in Cilicia fell to earthquake, in which they say that more than thirty thousand men perished.[23]

20. The year is 549.
21. The year is 547.
22. An inscription that was once part of the text is missing.
23. The earthquake of Anazarbas is mentioned by Evagrius Scholasticus, *Ecclesiastical History* 4.8; the earthquake happened around the year 525.

These are the words of the bishop. After blessed Jerome and Orosius and other historians he worked on chronicles, and following them, through their different books about most noble leaders, not only emperors but kings and prefects, he wrote his own chronicle.

79. In his reign a battle was fought between the Goths and the soldiers of the army of Narses on October 1 in Campania; and the Goths were slaughtered, and there were many dead bodies of Gothic men, and Teia, king of the Goths, was killed by Narses. And he returned in peace and came to Lucca, whence he expelled the Goths in the month of September. And the city of Imola was restored by the prefect Antiochus. And again the said Narses came to Ravenna with great victory; then he went to Rome, and he proceeded to Campania to the camp of Cumae and remained there.

After these events, however, the heresy of the Manichaeans arose in the city of Ravenna, which the orthodox Christians overcame, they threw [them] out of the city, they stoned them in the place that is called *Fossa Sconii,* next to the river, and they died in their sins, and evil was cast out of Ravenna.

After the third year a red sign appeared in the sky on the eleventh day of the month of November; and Pope Pelagius died on the third day of the month of March. Then Lord Narses with his army proceeded to Rome. And in that time there were many signs and prodigies around Ravenna, so that many put marks upon their property and homes and vessels, so that they might be recognized again later; and visions appeared to many during the day, like men speaking with them face to face. And they fought against the citizens of Verona, and the city of Verona was captured by the armies on the twentieth day of the month of July. And another great and terrible sign was seen, behold in the air as if men were fighting among themselves, brandishing weapons as if in battle, on July 25, in the third hour of the day, on a Monday; and after this many were terrified.

It is now time to close this reading, so that tomorrow we might hear what follows.

80. And he made two small vessels for holding chrism, one of which had a weight of fourteen pounds, of wonderful sculpted

workmanship, but it recently perished before its time, in the reign of Archbishop Petronax; the other remains up to the present, most beautifully made, on which is read:

> The servant of Christ, Archbishop Maximian, made this vessel for chrism for the use of the faithful.

He ordered an altar cloth made of the most precious fine linen, the like of which we have never been able to see, made with embroidery, containing the whole story of our Savior. On the holy day of Epiphany it is placed over the altar of the Ursiana church. But he did not finish the whole thing; his successor completed one part. Who has been able to see its like? It is not possible to otherwise appraise these images or beasts or birds which were made there, than to say that they all are living in the flesh. The images of this Maximian are excellently made in two places, one great and the other small, but there is no difference between the greater and the smaller. On the smaller there are letters inscribed, containing thus, "Magnify the Lord with me, who has raised me from the dung."[24]

And he made another altar cloth from gold, on which are all his predecessors; he ordered the images to be woven in gold. And he made a third, and a fourth with pearls, on which it is read, "Spare, O Lord, spare thy people,"[25] and remember me, a sinner, whom you have raised from dung into your kingdom."

He ordered a great cross of gold to be made and he decorated it with most precious gems and pearls, jacinths and amethysts and sard and emeralds,[26] and in the middle part of the cross, set in gold, he placed some of the wood of our holy redeeming cross, where the body of the Lord hung. And it is a very great weight of gold.

81. And he had all the ecclesiastical books, that is, two bibles, beautifully written, which he read long and most cautiously and

---

24. Cf. Ps. 33:4, Ps. 112:7, and 1 Sam. 2:7.
25. Cf. Joel 2:17.
26. It is possible that Agnellus was naming stones found in biblical lists of gems (Exod. 28:17–20, Apoc. 21:19–21) rather than actually naming stones on the cross.

left to us without error, which we use up to today. And at the end of the Gospels and the letters of the apostles, if you want to investigate, you will find his letters reporting, "I have emended most cautiously with Augustine's comments, and according to the Gospels which blessed Jerome sent to Rome and arranged for his followers, only that they should not be corrupted by illiterate or evil scribes."[27]

And he produced missals for the whole circle of the year and for all the saints; for you will find everything there without doubt, for ordinary days and for Lent, or whatever pertains to the rite of the church, a great volume wonderfully written.[28]

We have few of his writings; they were taken to Rome, and they are known there, the Romans who see the twelve books written in one volume.[29]

82. We have said a few things out of many; you will find more about him than you have read here.

He never ravaged his sheep, never hurt them, never struck them, but refreshed them with words, fed them with food, warned the wandering, recalled the errant, collected the dispersed, ministered to the needy, condoled the one in trouble. I marvel at how this one, who was from another see, thus behaved with his sheep, that no one ever raised up any word against him. Now that we have pastors from among ourselves, after they obtain the see, they want to devour us with their teeth, nor do they know how to have any mercy.

---

27. The word used for "Bibles" is *septuaginta*, which means "Old Testaments," but from the next sentence the volumes seem to have included the New Testament also. From this statement Maximian is credited with making Jerome's Vulgate the standard Bible used in Ravenna.

28. It is not clear why *volumen* is in the singular; it was more traditional to have a missal in two volumes, one for the *temporale* and one for the *sanctorale*, as Agnellus seems to be describing. Perhaps by his day they had been bound together in one volume.

29. This passage is confused. Cf. Paul the Deacon, *Historia Langobardorum* 1.25: "For all the laws, which formerly were found in many volumes, he collected into twelve books and ordered that that volume be called the *Codex* of Justinian." Perhaps Agnellus is garbling this passage, and saying that Maximian introduced Justinian's *Codex* into Italy, since he knew that Maximian and Justinian knew each other.

They seek secular heights rather than heavenly glory; they do not participate with their sheep, but they devour the possessions of the church alone; and fed from this wealth become such as do not serve the church, but rather depopulate it, nor do they pour out prayers to God for the soul of him who disposed of these possessions. Then these sheep daily cry in mourning to the Lord, saying, "Free us, Lord, from the captivity of the teeth of our shepherd, since he has not the place of a mercenary, but the cruelty of a wolf; he consumes us all in aggrandizing his own possessions."

This most blessed Maximian never did such things, but with kindness he humiliated the hearts of his enemies, that he might fulfill what is written, "Be not overcome by evil, but overcome evil by good," and again, "In your patience you shall possess your souls."[30]

He died on February 22 and was buried in the church of St. Andrew the apostle next to the altar, where he had placed the beard of the said apostle; but now in our times he was buried next to the seat of the church of that apostle.[31]

83. In the fifteenth year of Archbishop Petronax,[32] when we were each urging him with words that the said body of blessed Maximian should be brought from under the earth and placed in an elevated place, on a certain day attending to it itself, he ordered all us priests to hasten together with him to the church of blessed Andrew; with a prayer made in our hearts, he ordered the cover slab to be lifted up by the workmen, but doing it carelessly, it was broken.

Rather angry, the bishop began to revile the workmen; then he said to the tenth priest in order of the see, by the name of Agnellus who is called Andreas (who was at that time filled with the skills of all the arts), "Stand here, tell the workers what they should do, lest the sarcophagus or stone which is placed over it be

---

30. Rom. 12:21 and Luke 21:19.

31. *Sedes* (seat) refers to the area around the main altar and the apse of the church; see Glossary, s.v.

32. This would be around the year 833.

broken." With the stone laid aside, the workers prepared all things according to the order of the priest, and the stone with which the sarcophagus was closed was raised, the bones of blessed Maximian appeared, under water, for the vessel was full of water.

And as we saw this, we began to wail loudly together with our bishop, and wailing we said to each other: "Where are your sheep, O shepherd Maximian, where your flock, where your people, which you have acquired for the Lord? Where the advice, where the sweet words, where the holy preaching, where your doctrines? If we should say, 'you are our shepherd,' would we thus cast away the one who is present? Behold you are both our shepherds together, both you who lie dead, and he who wails, to whom we owe obedience. Your example will bind our flesh. Behold we need and search for you; how much more beloved must you have been to all those who knew you!"

After we had all wept long and bitterly, satiated with grief, a small bronze vessel was brought to us, which in the vulgar tongue we call a *siculus*, and *siculi* were drawn out full of the water which was in the sarcophagus over the bones of blessed Maximian, 115 in number, all of which I myself counted in front of everyone with my own mouth. All the raised bones were wrapped in a shroud, which was on the altar of the blessed apostle Andrew, and with the shroud tied up, the bishop marked the seal from the side of his ring. After this the sarcophagus was cleaned up without a scratch and washed; we replaced it carefully.

All the whole bones that we found were thin, but long, and were located exactly in their places as if they had been separated from the flesh almost for a year; none were missing, except one tooth on the right side. Therefore the bones, washed with choice wine, honorably embalmed in spices, with chanting of psalms, in the presence of the bishop, all were placed in the same sarcophagus and with great grief were lovingly enclosed within the tomb. To those of us who saw it, for many days there was such fear and trembling, as if blessed Maximian himself stood in our sight.

He sat __ years, __ months, __ days.

CONCERNING HOLY AGNELLUS, 577-70

84. Agnellus, the twenty-seventh bishop, had a ruddy face, a full form, few hairs on his eyebrows, red skin on his head, uplifted eyes; he had a double chin under his beard. He was well-proportioned in stature, beautiful in body, perfect in deeds; but after the death of his wife, putting his military belt aside, he devoted and offered himself completely to God. In the time of Archbishop Ecclesius he was consecrated as deacon,[1] he served in the church of blessed Agatha, where he was a deacon, and he became the priest of that church, and his house clung to the wall of the said church, which we recognize up to the present day. Sprung from noble stock, wealthy in possessions, rich in animals, abounding in wealth.

At the end of his life, when he was close to death, he left as his heir, after the death of her mother, his granddaughter, the daughter of his daughter, leaving her, when his death occurred, among other wealth five silver ornamental vessels for the table and many other things, since it is not our task to digress about diverse wealth.[2] But it should be asked by us why this married man obtained such a noble see. As you know, the author of the apostles says the husband of one wife and who has children[3] can be ordained a bishop, with true providence, and the canons confirm this. But let us return to the sequence and discuss women later.

85. In his reign the Emperor Justinian of the true faith granted to this church and to blessed Bishop Agnellus all the property of the Goths, not only in the cities, but also in the suburban villas and hamlets, and their temples and altars, slaves and handmaids, whatever could pertain to their jurisdiction or to the rite of pagans, he

1. At the end of the *constitutio* of Pope Felix IV, which Agnellus quotes in c. 60, one of the signers is "the deacon Agnellus." As Testi-Rasponi (*CPER*, 214, n. 9) points out, Bishop Agnellus's epitaph (given in c. 92) says that he was eighty-three when he died in 570; thus at the time of Ecclesius and Felix IV (521–30), he would have been between thirty-four and forty-three, the right age to be a widower with a child.

2. The information comes from Bishop Agnellus's will, which Agnellus must have seen.

3. Cf. 1 Tim. 3:2–4.

presented and granted all to him and confirmed it through privileges and had it handed over physically through a letter, part of which contains the following:[4] "The holy mother church of Ravenna, the true mother, truly orthodox, for many other churches crossed over to false doctrine because of the fear and terror of princes, but this one held the true and unique holy catholic faith, it never changed, it endured the fluctuations of the times, though tossed by the storm it remained unmovable."

86. Therefore this most blessed one reconciled all the churches of the Goths, which were built in the times of the Goths or of King Theodoric, which were held by Arian falsehood and the sect, doctrine and credulity of the heretics.

He reconciled the church of St. Eusebius priest and martyr, which is located not far from the Coriandrian field outside the city, on November 13, which Bishop Unimundus built from its foundations in the twenty-fourth year of King Theodoric. And likewise he reconciled the church of St. George in the time of Basilius the younger, as is told in its apse.[5] He reconciled the church of St. Sergius, which is located in the city of Classe next to the *viridiarium*, and that of St. Zeno in Caesarea. Indeed in the city of Ravenna the church of St. Theodore, not far from the house of Drocdo, which house together with a bath and a *monasterium* to St. Apollinaris, which was built in the upper floor of the house, was the episcopal palace of that [Arian] church.[6] And where now there is a *monasterium* to the holy and always inviolate virgin Mary, there was the baptistry of the church of the said martyr. But I report regarding what this name "Cosmi" might be in Latin, over which not only Latins, but also Greeks have had some disputes among themselves; for without any censure, in Latin "cosmi" means "ornate," while among the Greeks the world is called "cosmos."[7]

---

4. This chapter, and c. 86, are based on the document, which Agnellus quotes, in which Justinian gave the property of the Arian church to the bishops of Ravenna.

5. There must have been an inscription of the type found in c. 77, in which a date *p.c. Basilii iunioris* (after the consulship of Basilius the younger) was given.

6. The Arian cathedral of St. Theodore is now known as Santo Spirito.

7. The church was known as Santa Maria in Cosmedin.

Therefore the most blessed Bishop Agnellus reconciled the church of St. Martin the confessor in this city, which King Theodoric founded, which is called the Golden Heaven; he decorated the apse and both side walls with images in mosaic of processions of martyrs and virgins; indeed he laid over this stucco covered with gold, he stuck multicolored stones to the side walls and composed a pavement of wonderful cut marble pieces. If you look on its facade on the inside you will find the image of Emperor Justinian and Bishop Agnellus decorated with gold mosaics.[8] No church or house is similar to this one in beams and coffers of its ceiling. And after he consecrated it, he feasted in the episcopal palace of that confessor. Indeed in the apse, if you look closely, you will find the following written above the windows in stone letters: "King Theodoric made this church from its foundations in the name of our Lord Jesus Christ."

87. Let us tell what we have heard concerning the said church, why the marble pavements are crushed. There was in that time a certain king of the Vandals,[9] not perfectly orthodox, who wanted to tear up the pavement from that church and carry it off to his own home. Indeed, when everything had been prepared for the lifting of the stones, suddenly the day became darkened by a storm, indeed in the night following that day a strong wind raced through this church, bringing with it loud noises, a great sound was made throughout this church. Then indeed all the marbles there crashed together, they were broken and crushed as if by people wielding hammers.

88. You can see this on the wall: there, as I said, two cities were made. From Ravenna the martyrs lead forth, on the men's [south]

---

8. The mosaic head of Justinian still survives in Sant' Apollinare Nuovo; it is not clear whether these depictions of Agnellus and Justinian were part of larger scenes, as those in San Vitale (cf. c. 77), or were individual figures; see Nauerth, *Agnellus von Ravenna, Untersuchungen*, 22–23.

9. By the reign of Archbishop Agnellus there were no more kings of the Vandals, and none is known to have come to Ravenna. Agnellus seems to be using the term generally for "destroyers," perhaps as a comment on the depredations made by the Carolingian rulers.

side, going to Christ; from Classe the virgins proceed, proceeding to the holy Virgin of virgins, and the Magi going before them, offering gifts.

But why are they depicted in different clothing and not all wearing the same garment?[10] Because the artist followed divine Scripture. For Caspar offered gold in a reddish garment, and in this garment signifies marriage. Balthasar offered frankincense in a yellow garment, and in this garment signifies virginity. Melchior offered myrrh in a multicolored costume, and in this costume signifies penitence.[11]

He who went first, wearing a purple mantle, through it signifies the King who was born and suffered. He who offered his gift to the Newborn in a multicolored mantle signifies through this that Christ cares for all the weary, and was whipped by the various injuries and diverse blows of the Jews. Of Him it is written, "He hath borne our infirmities and carried our sorrows: and we have thought him as it were a leper," etc., and then, "He was wounded for our iniquities, he was crucified for our sins."[12] He who offered his gift in white signifies that He exists in divine clarity after the resurrection.[13]

For likewise the three precious gifts contain divine mysteries in them, that is, by gold is meant regal wealth, by frankincense the

10. The current mosaic is a modern restoration, above the legs, largely based on this passage in the *LPR*. It is assumed that the colors he mentions were those in the mosaic; however, if Agnellus's entire passage is borrowed from elsewhere, the colors might also have been lifted wholesale from his source.

11. The identification of the three gifts with marriage, virginity, and penitence is found in only one other sermon, a homily for Epiphany in an early-fifteenth-century Irish manuscript called the *Leabhar Breac* (ed. Atkinson, pp. 238 and 475), whose author quotes extensively from "Augustine": "*Et apertis thesauris suis:* this denotes . . . the three gifts offered to Christ by the Church, *i.e.* virginity, penitence, and lawful marriage," cited by McNally, "Three Holy Kings," 688–89.

12. Isa. 53:4–5.

13. Interpretation of the colors of the clothing of the magi is unusual; see, for example, the eighth-century Irish Pseudo-Bede, *Excerptiones patrum* (*PL* 94.541). See McNally, "Three Holy Kings," 670–71 and 685–86, and Kaplan, *The Rise of the Black Magus*, 26–28. A very similar description of the costumes of the magi is found in a sermon for Epiphany from the *Leabhar Breac*, cited above.

figure of the priest, by myrrh death, thus through all these things they show him to be the one who undertook the iniquities of men, that is, Christ; and thus in their mantles, as we said, these three gifts are contained.[14]

Why did not four, not six, or not two, but only these three come from the east? So that they might entirely signify the perfect plenitude of the Trinity, for the love of whom that most blessed Agnellus decorated part of the fine linen altar cloth, as we made mention above, which his predecessor Maximian had not finished, decorated it perfectly with the story of the Magi, and his image was inserted with embroidery.

89. And he reconciled [to orthodoxy] the baptistry of the church of St. Martin and decorated it with mosaic; but the apse of that church, greatly shaken by an earthquake,[15] fell in ruins in the reign of Archbishop John V the younger. Afterward he adorned the buildings of the vault with colors.[16]

Blessed Agnellus made a great cross of silver in the Ursiana church, in which his image prays with extended hands, over the seat behind the back of the bishop.[17]

And he acquired the estate which is called Argentea for the

14. Analyses of the gifts of gold, frankincense, and myrrh as representing king, God, and death are common. The interpretation in the *LPR* deviates slightly from these, interpreting the frankincense not as God but as the priest who sacrifices to God; this explanation is also found in the Carolingian collection known as pseudo-Bede, *In Matthaei evangelium expositio*, 1.2 (*PL* 92.13); Holder-Egger, *LPER*, 335, n. 5.

15. This earthquake occurred in the mid-eighth century; Agnellus mentions it again in c. 151.

16. The "vault" *(camera)* could be the new apse in St. Martin, rebuilt after the earthquake (c. 86), or it could refer to the baptistry, decorated by Bishop Agnellus.

17. Cf. the similar description of the portrait of Peter I in c. 27. Mazzotti, "La croce argentea," agrees with Testi-Rasponi that the picture of Bishop Agnellus must have been found in the apse of the church, not on the cross itself. However, Nauerth, *Agnellus von Ravenna, Untersuchungen*, 37, n. 79, cites Gonin's argument, *Excerpta*, 93, that the apse wall of the Ursiana must have been already decorated in the time of Bishop Agnellus, and argues for a literal reading of the passage as it stands, referring to an image of the bishop on the cross. Furthermore, Deichmann, *Ravenna* 2.3:317, points out that the silver-gilt cross in the Treasury of St. Peter's in the Vatican contains the images of its donors, Justin II and Sophia, as *orantes* on the cross arms, and thus it is possible that Bishop Agnellus was depicted on the cross he donated.

church of Ravenna, and on this estate he built the *monasterium* of St. George from the foundations, when he was placed in old age; and his image is wonderfully depicted on a tablet, and before the entrance of this *monasterium* there are metrical verses, which I could not clearly see.

90. In his reign the Franks were expelled from Italy by Lord Narses. And after this a comet appeared in the month of August up to the first of October. And Emperor Justinian died in Constantinople in the fortieth year of his reign, and there was great grief everywhere and great sorrow for such an orthodox man. And red signs appeared in the sky, and the city of Fano was burned down by fire, and a multitude of men were consumed in the flame, and the camp of Cesena was devoured by fire.

And in the third year of Emperor Justin the younger, Lord Narses was recalled from Ravenna; he left with all the wealth of Italy, and had been the governor for sixteen years and conquered two kings of the Goths and butchered dukes of the Franks with the sword.

91. In the reign of this bishop there was great abundance and order among the people of Italy. Indeed he ordered that the *monasteria* of St. Matthew the apostle and St. James, which are joined to the sides of the baptistry of the Petriana church in the city of Classe, be decorated with mosaic. And you will find in the vault of the apse of the apostle Matthew the following:

> By our holy lord father Agnellus. This apse has been decorated in mosaic from the gifts of God and of his servants, who have given them for the honor and adornment of the holy apostles, and the remaining part was decorated from the sum of the servants who had been lost and were found with the aid of God.

92. It is time to close the mouth and stop it up with bolts. Let us sign the keys with the cross, so that no thief may come, find the doors open in the depths of the heart, sow nettles, deride and destroy it.[18] Again, "set a watch, O Lord, before my mouth: and a

---

18. Cf. Matt. 13:25.

door round about my lips; incline not my heart to evil words,"[19] but help me, that I might finish the life of this Agnellus.

He died on the first day of August, and was buried in the church of St. Agatha the martyr, before the altar. And in letters carved in marble you will find his epitaph over his body thus:[20]

> Agnellus by the virtue of God did not squander the repose of the bishop ceded by heavenly gift. He deserved to know the hoped-for peace of light. He preserved the temple of his body as it was. Righteous, he will rise with the saints to Christ who heals [5]; thus also will he who did such things rejoice for his merits.

> Here rests in peace Archbishop Agnellus, who sat for thirteen years, one month, eight days; who lived for eighty-three years; he was buried here on the first of August, in the second indiction.

He sat for thirteen years, one month, eight days.

CONCERNING HOLY PETER III THE ELDER, 570–78

93. Peter the elder, the twenty-eighth bishop. He was advanced in age, an elder in feeling and body, decorated with grey hair on his head; he led a holy and humble life. He was truly a *Petrus*, since on a solid rock [*petra*] he built the temple of his body.[1]

In the times of Symmachus the pope of Rome he sat in council.[2] And he founded the church of St. Severus the confessor of

---

19. Ps. 140:3–4. Lanzoni, "Reliquie dell'antico Officio Divino," notes that these words make up the last prayer in the part of the liturgy known as the *completorium*.

20. The epitaph survives in damaged form, with the right side partly missing, and was discovered in the paving stones of the Ursiana (*CIL* 11.1.305).

❧

1. Cf. Matt. 16:18; cf. also the epitaph of Bishop Agnellus in c. 92: "the temple of his body."

2. Symmachus was pope from 498 to 514; this piece of information belongs to the Life of Bishop Peter II. Cf. Mansi, *Sacrorum conciliorum*, 8:252 and 268, in which a Peter, bishop of Ravenna, is listed at councils held under Symmachus.

Christ, but with his death intervening, he left it [unfinished],³ in the former city of Classe, in the region that is called the District of Safety.

In the second indiction he was consecrated at Rome without fasting on October 15, and having returned in peace, with great joy the citizens of Ravenna received him; the [populace of] Classe hastened to meet him on the way, at the ninth mile. Then everyone rejoicing sang the acclamation: "God has given you to us, may his Divinity preserve you." Then the boys went before him with prayers, as not only the old but also the young were friendly toward him.

94. In that year the Veneto was occupied by the Lombards and invaded; [the Romans] were expelled without war. In the fifth year of the Emperor Justin II there was a pestilence among cows and there was the death of cows everywhere.

Afterward Tuscany was plundered by the Lombards; they overran Ticinum, which city is also called Pavia, where Theodoric built a palace, and I have seen an image of him sitting on a horse well executed in mosaic in the vault of the apse.⁴

There was a similar image of him in the palace that he built in this city, in the apse of the dining hall that is called By the Sea, above the gate and at the front of the main door that is called Ad Calchi, where the main gate of the palace was, in the place which is called Sicrestum,⁵ where the church of the Savior is seen to be.⁶ In the pinnacle of this place was an image of Theodoric, wonderfully

---

3. Rossi, *Historiarium Ravennatum*, 178, records a dedicatory inscription from this church, naming Bishop Peter and his successor John the Roman as patrons.

4. Agnellus tells of his trip to Pavia in c. 171; it probably took place around 837–39. The picture of Theodoric in Pavia is apparently referred to again in a document from 906–10, where a judgment is rendered in the palace, *in laubia ubi sub Teuderico dicitur.* The *laubia* refers to a colonnaded courtyard; see Ward-Perkins, *From Classical Antiquity to the Middle Ages*, 160.

5. The word *sicrestum* itself is thought to be a degeneration of a word like *sacristia, secretarium*; the words imply some sort of official government function; see Testi-Rasponi, *CPER*, 228, n. 5, and Deichmann, *Ravenna* 2.3:51.

6. About the location(s) described here, see Duval, "Que savons-nous"; Deichmann, *Ravenna* 2.3:51–52; Porta, "Il centro del potere"; and the Introduction, above.

executed in mosaic, holding a lance in his right hand, a shield in his left, wearing a breastplate. Facing the shield stood Rome, executed in mosaic with spear and helmet; and there holding a spear was Ravenna, figured in mosaic, with right foot on the sea, left on land hastening toward the king.[7] O misery, and everywhere having suffered envy, citizens between themselves with greatest zeal . . .[8]

In their[9] sight a base of square stones and rhombus-shaped bricks, in height about six cubits; on top of it a horse of bronze, covered with gleaming gold, and its rider King Theodoric bore a shield on his left arm, holding a lance in his raised right arm. Birds came out of the spreading nostrils of the horse and of its mouth, and in its belly they built their nests. For who could see anything like it? Whoever does not believe [me], let him make a journey to the land of the Franks, there he will see it.[10]

Some say that this said horse was made for the love of the Emperor Zeno. This Zeno was an Isaurian in origin, and the Emperor Leo took him as a son-in-law because of the great speed of his feet, and he received greatest honor in the house of the emperor. He did not have kneecaps in his knees, and he ran so quickly that,

---

7. It is sometimes proposed that Agnellus was describing two pictures, both in Ravenna, one in a dining room and the other in a lunette *(pinnaculum)* over the main gate to the palace. In a mosaic depiction labeled "palatium" on the south nave wall in Sant' Apollinare Nuovo, an image in the pediment above the door was removed during the reworking of the mosaics under Bishop Agnellus. This image is generally assumed to be the equestrian picture of Theodoric mentioned by Agnellus; see Deichmann, *Ravenna* 1:43–44 and 172, and 2.3:52. Deichmann suggests that Agnellus is describing two different figural compositions, one mosaic in a *triclinium* depicting Theodoric on horseback, and another over the main gate showing Theodoric standing, flanked by personifications of Rome and Ravenna. However, Agnellus quite specifically mentions only one picture, analogous to a mosaic in Pavia, and there is no reason that the text could not refer to one picture of Theodoric armed, on horseback, flanked by Ravenna and Rome. If there were only one picture, in a dining room, then the interpretation of the mosaic in Sant' Apollinare Nuovo would not be supported by the passage in the *LPR*. See Introduction, above.

8. Part of the text seems to be missing here, but there is no gap in the manuscript.

9. Perhaps the "citizens" just mentioned, or perhaps someone else from the missing section of the text.

10. Agnellus's account of the equestrian statue is confirmed by Walahfrid Strabo, whose poem "De imagine Tetrici" describes the statue in the palace at Aachen.

having started running, he caught up on foot with chariots. After the death of his son, who had succeeded his grandfather Leo in the kingdom, this Zeno was made emperor; he ruled the nations for sixteen years. For him this most excellent horse was made of bronze and decorated with gold, but Theodoric embellished it with his own name.

And now almost thirty-eight years ago,[11] when Charles king of the Franks had conquered all the kingdoms and had received the empire of the Romans from Pope Leo III, after he had offered the sacrament at the body of blessed Peter, while returning to Francia, he entered Ravenna, and seeing the beautiful image, the equal of which, as he swore, he had never seen, he had it brought to Francia and set up in his palace which is called Aachen.

95. Let us return to ancient history, what was done, as some say, in the reign of that Bishop Peter. For in that time, after the placing of the foundation of the church, all Italy was agitated by the greatest disturbance. Then in those days, in Caesarea next to Ravenna, a fence was built by the prefect Longinus in the form of a wall on account of fear of the enemy. Then little by little the Roman senate failed, and afterward the liberty of the Romans was laid low with triumph. For from the time of Basilius holding the consulate up to Lord Narses the Roman provincial citizens were everywhere reduced to nothing.

After these things the Lombards went forth and invaded Tuscany as far as Rome, and setting a fire, they burned Furlo in the conflagration. And the said Lombards built Imola, and the city was completed by them. In those days the Avars were aroused; they arrived in Pannonia. And Lord Narses died at Rome; after he had won many victories in Italy, with the plundering of all the Romans of Italy, he rested in his palace; he died in the ninety-fifth year of his life.

96. Then in the sixth year of the reign of Justin II, the nephew of Justinian, Alboin king of the Lombards was killed by his own

---

11. Charlemagne was crowned in 800 and visited Ravenna in 801; therefore this passage must have been written in 839.

men in his palace, at the order of his wife Rosamunda, on June 28.[12] The cause of his murder, which we know, I will not leave out, but will eagerly put forward, that you may beware.

On a certain day, while he merrily passed the lunch hour, and the royal food had been removed from him, and the drunkenness of wine had followed, among other cups he ordered the skull of his father-in-law, the father of Rosamunda, to be brought in. When it arrived he ordered it to be filled to the top with wine, and he drank it all down; and everyone, made merry with wine, drank at the same time. Then the king ordered the wine bearer to fill the skull up to the top and that it be given to Rosamunda his wife. This skull had been bound with the best gold and set with pearls and various very precious gems.

With this extended to her, the king said, "Drink it all down." As soon as she took it she groaned, but with a calm face said, "Let me swiftly fulfill the orders of my lord." After she drank, she returned it to the wine bearer, but she doubled the grief in her heart, keeping hardness in her breast.

Let us not wander through many things, let us reveal the murder. There was a man in those days in the palace of the king, a strong man, by the name of Helmegis, who enjoyed copulation with the chambermaid of the queen. Having summoned him, the queen urged him to kill the king. Refusing this request, he said, "Far be it from me to raise my hand against my lord the king. You know that he is a very strong man, and I cannot overcome him." And she said, "Although you won't do it, you won't let anyone know?" And he replied, "Surely this word will never come from my mouth. Find another killer, I will not do it. Since you wanted to do this, you should not have married him, but now that he has become king, keep faith." Then she returned raging to her chamber; she began to think how she could put an end to her husband.

Having thought about it, she called her chambermaid and said to her, "Swear to me that you will not betray me nor reveal my

---

12. The year is 572. For a detailed analysis of Agnellus's version of the story of Rosamunda, see Pizarro, *Writing Ravenna*, 119–41.

counsel, and whatever I tell you, do it." After she had sworn as you heard, the queen said, "Every day I battle with myself in spirit for love of that youth who cohabits with you. Make an appointment with him in a secret place, when he might sleep with you, and say to him, 'Enjoy intercourse quickly, since I am in a hurry and cannot delay,' and I will wear your clothing, and since I will be in a dark place, I will not be recognized."

On a certain day, when he wanted to sleep with the chambermaid, as he was accustomed, she said as instructed, "Unless you come at such and such an hour in a concealed place, we cannot exchange embraces, since I am frequently summoned, and cannot be away from the sight of the queen." He, agreeing, said, "Let it be thus." She did as she had been instructed, and reported all these words to the queen.

When the hour became dark, Rosamunda put on the clothing of her servant, and stood in the place where the sin was supposed to take place; then he came, and when he began to kiss her, in a feigned and soft voice she said to him, "It is time for me to return to my mistress, lest by chance I might be sought after, and get into trouble." Then he remained with her in that place, casting down himself with her. After they had done the dirty deed, she said to him, "Who am I?" He said, "The chambermaid of the queen." To which she rejoined, "Am I not Queen Rosamunda? Did I not say to you that what you did not want to do of your own will, I would compel you unwilling?"

He, when he recognized that she was the queen, began to wail and say, "Woe is me, why have you laid this sin upon me? Why have you killed me without even a sword? Who has stained the bed of the king or oppressed the queen, as I, unfortunate, have done?" Then she began to offer consoling words and said, "Be quiet! These things are done for your advantage; however [now] such a dispute is brewed up between you and King Alboin that either you must punish him, or he will behead you with his sword. Before these things are revealed, first you must rush upon him; and when the day is fitting, I will send for you; you come to the appointed place, and kill him!"

One day, with the royal lunch prepared, the king made merry by prolonging the banquet, and he drank more wine than he had drunk in a long time, with his wife urging him on. And after he had lain down on his bed, Rosamunda having entered began to part the hair of the head of the king to one side and another, and to rub his skin with her nails, as if this were a delight to him. He was soon seized by sleep, compelled by the wine; she touched him twice and three times, to make sure that he had fallen into a very heavy sleep, and sent for the companion in her wickedness to come swiftly. Then she took the two-edged sword, which we call a spatha, which was at his head, which was used at the king's side, and she bound it tightly to the posts of the bed with the straps which girded the loins of the king, so that it was fixed in its sheath.

When the murderer arrived, wanting to escape from such wickedness, that he might not put his hand to it, she reproached him, "If you tell me that you are weak in strength and you can not kill him, I will use my own hand against him. Say that you are weak in courage; then you will see what the fragile sex is made of." This argument between them lasted almost an hour.

And when she was hectoring him, and he was getting up the energy to kill the king, she added, "His sword, which you fear, is completely wrapped up and strongly bound." And he said, "You know that this man is a warrior and is strong in energy and most mighty with his hands. He has won many wars, has subjugated many peoples, he has destroyed the camps of the enemies, and having ravaged his enemies, he has added the towns of others to his territory. And how can I alone butcher him who has shattered all these things without fear of any other person?" But she said with sadness to him, "You can pin no crime on me. Recall the evil that you have done; since if you were revealed, you would die; for everyone esteems me more than the king. If anyone knows of this deed, secretly I will have you killed."

He, confounded by these words, entered the chamber, where the king was lying partly digesting his wine; and he approached the bed of the king, he drew his sword to kill him. [The king], becoming aware, waking up, arose from sleep. He wanted to draw his sword, and he could not, because it had been strongly tied by the hands of his wife. Then, seizing the footstool on which he was accustomed to place his feet, he used it for a shield and defended himself somewhat; but although he shouted, there was no one who could hear him, because at the order of his wife, as if for the repose of the king, all the doors of the palace were shut. And overcome, the king was killed.

The Lombards wanted to put an end to this murderer and the queen with him; but with this counsel known, she went to Verona, until the furor of the people should subside. But with the Lombards contending strongly against her, to destroy the palace, she came to Ravenna with a multitude of Gepids and Lombards, in the month of August, and was honorably received with all the royal wealth by the prefect Longinus.

However after several days the prefect sent to her saying, "if she were united to me in love and wanted to cling to my side and be joined in marriage, she would be greater afterward than she is now as a queen. Would it not be better for her to hold the kingdom and principate of all Italy, than to lose it and to lose the kingdom?" She however sent a message to him, saying, "If he wants, it can happen in a few days."

One day, when she ordered a bath to be prepared, the man who had killed her husband entered the washroom after he left the bath, in that fever of the body which heat induces. Rosamunda offered him a cup full of liquid, fit for a king; but it was mixed with poison. Then he, taking the vessel from her hand, began to drink. But when he knew that it was a potion of death, he removed the cup from his mouth and gave it to the queen, saying, "You drink with me." She did not want to; and with his sword unsheathed he stood over her and said, "If you will not drink from this, I will cut you down." Willy-nilly she drank, and in that hour they died.

Then the prefect Longinus stole the whole Lombard treasury and all the royal wealth, which Rosamunda had brought from the kingdom of the Lombards, he sent them together with the daughter of Rosamunda and King Alboin to the Emperor Justinian[13] in Constantinople; and the emperor rejoiced and gave the prefect many things.

97. Therefore you men who are husbands, be nice to your wives, lest you suffer worse things than this one. Calm their rages and silence your quarrels.

There are women who say, "What I command will stand; what you say will not happen. If you are enraged, turn within yourself; I don't care." I will not believe that you have not tasted such a cup; but you have remained silent because of wickedness and shame. And if you are embarrassed by someone, you readily reveal: "She my wife, for whom you deride or mock me, does not desire the destruction of my house, she keeps my property well, her management pleases me." You cannot speak other than with peaceful words, because if your spouse does not hear them, she is inflamed for a long time arguing, her speechless husband wanders hither and thither for fear of his wife.

That one [Alboin], who held the kingdom, who laid low his enemies, who won battles, who depopulated cities, who poured out blood, who overturned cities, who humiliated his enemies: see how he was killed by caresses and his body struck by blows. What man can offer evil in pestiferous counsel, in the way this evil sex can?

For there are some who do not receive in their house even a friend or a relative without the consent of their spouses, since the woman holds primacy over the man; willy-nilly they conform to the will of their wives. In crime consider the Egyptian [wife of Potiphar, or Hagar], in falsehood Jezebel, in seduction Delilah, in murder Jael, in rejection of man Vasthi, in flightiness Herodias, in rage the Shunammite woman, in anger the handmaid of the prince [Peter] at the threshold.[14] I say this to you, that we find many such men, and we have derided and grieved over them in particular.

Brothers, we are men, we perish like grass;[15] but if we can, be-

---

13. Really Justin II.

14. Respectively, in Gen. 39:6–20 or Gen. 16, 1 Kings 21, Judg. 16, Judg. 4:21, Esther 1:17, Matt. 14:3–12, 2 Kings 4:8–37, and John 18:17.

15. Cf. Ps. 36:2 and 1 Pet. 1:24.

fore death comes, let there be no evil report of us, since thus your holy preachers taught, and with them this great bishop Peter, in whose reign these things were done.

However, he died in good old age on August 17, and was buried, as some say, in the narthex of St. Probus the confessor in the former city of Classe. There he was placed in a great stone sarcophagus, next to the church of St. Euphemia which is called By the Sea, which Bishop Maximian decorated wonderfully with various mosaics, which is now demolished. Thence this sarcophagus was removed and placed in another location. He sat eight years, two months, nineteen days.[16]

CONCERNING HOLY JOHN II THE ROMAN, 578–95

98. John the Roman, the twenty-ninth bishop. John means "grace of God."[1] He was not of this flock, but from the Roman people.[2] He was middling in stature, neither tall nor short; optimal in body, not thin, nor very fat; curly, with the hairs of his head mixed with grey.

After the loss of blessed Peter, this one finished the incomplete work which he had left, that is, the church of St. Severus, and brought it to completion, and he dedicated the body of St. Severus confessor in the middle of the temple. . . . He decorated it in appearance with wonderful size.[3] The holy body was taken up by him from the *monasterium* of St. Rophilius, which is attached to the side

---

16. There seems to be an error in either the date of death or the length of reign, or possibly both; see Deliyannis, CCCM edition of *LPR*, appendix.

1. Cf. Isidore, *Etymologiarum* 7.9.12: "John, received his name by merit of his prophecies; for it means 'in whom there is grace,' or 'grace of the Lord.'"

2. John II was a contemporary of Pope Gregory I, and several of the letters between the two survive, dated between March 591 and November 594; see *Registrum* 1.35; 2.25, 2.34, 2.38; 3.54; 5.1, 5.11, 5.15, 5.24.

3. Part of the text seems to be missing in this sentence, although there is no gap in the manuscript.

of this church, on the men's side, and he placed it in the middle of the church.[4]

In his reign in the month of January a comet appeared morning and evening, and in that month the said bishop died, and the star receded.

He, as I said, was born in Rome, sent here from that see, at once preached the doctrine of the apostle, that all might turn away from sin.

However after he died this most blessed John was buried on the eleventh day of the month of January in the church of St. Apollinaris in the city of Classe outside the walls, in the *monasterium* of Sts. Mark, Marcellus, and Felicula, which he built from the foundations and decorated with mosaics, and finished it all. And over the doors of the said *monasterium* you will find metrical verses containing the following:

The celebrated thresholds gleam in the temple of Sts. Mark, Marcellus and Felicula. Rome had the former as bishops, the latter is considered a martyr. Pope Gregory gives their relics, which John sought, bishop by merits and spirit [5], he is ready to return these small gifts for the highest.

Full of such virtue, he established the oratory whose structure exists thanks to his authority. In the fourteenth year of [his] holy crown, in which he rules the church with watchful management [10], he also added this ruling[5] stronghold of the venerable building and carried it to its final conclusion. Suddenly suspending the roof with wondrous skill, he repairs the curved wall on each side.[6]

Fortunate Smaragdus, inspired forever by these merits [15], whose wealth participated in this foundation.

He sat sixteen years, one month, nineteen days.

---

4. The church of St. Severus has been excavated, and the complex of small chambers to the south of the west end of the church has been identified as the *monasterium* of St. Rophilius. See esp. Bovini, "Il recente rinvenimento."
5. In other words, the sanctuary governs the rest of the building as John governs the church; see Pierpaoli, *Il libro di Agnello istorico*, 117, n. 281.
6. The architectural implication of these two lines is unclear; perhaps some spe-

CONCERNING HOLY MARINIAN, 595–606

99. Marinian, the thirtieth bishop. He was of the Roman people, his appearance was red, with a long thin face, his grey eyes shone, and in all things he was very comely; he was the nephew of the said John his predecessor.

He was consecrated by most blessed Gregory at Rome and by him was sent here.[1] And since he wanted to escape from this episcopal chair and not become bishop, he said that he could not bear the weight of such an honor. Then most blessed Pope Gregory began to offer him consoling words, saying, "I will make a small book for you. Hold it daily in your hands, always direct your thoughts toward it, observe the words of this book and be safe from all dread." And he wrote the "Book of the Shepherd" and sent it to him, saying, "Dearest brother, I have made this book for you; keep it diligently, teach your flock as it says. Act in such a way with your priests and with the whole people, that you may safely say on the day of judgment, 'Behold me, Lord, and my people with me.'" And blessed Marinian accepted it, and was daily reading and observing it.[2]

100. He was not like others, who devour the possessions of the church for episcopal honor, who even take bribes of another, and become debtors. And if a dispute arises between two persons, they so traffic in the dignity of their honor, as to sell out one of the

---

cial sort of engineering was required to attach the roof of the *monasterium* to that of the rest of the building.

1. There are many letters from Pope Gregory I to Marinian, dating between August 595 and October 603; see *Registrum* 5.61; 6.1, 6.2, 6.24, 6.28; 7.39, 7.40; 8.16, 8.17, 8.18, 8.20; 9.118, 9.132, 9.139, 9.149, 9.156, 9.178, 9.189; 11.21; 13.28; 14.6. From the early letters it appears that the election of Ravenna's bishop after the death of John II in January 595 was controversial; Gregory refused to consecrate either of two candidates from Ravenna and instead chose his own candidate, Marinian, in July, several months after the death of John (see esp. 6.2).

2. Gregory's *Regula pastoralis* was considered by his biographers to have been dedicated to Bishop John II of Ravenna; Agnellus must have seen a personal dedication to Marinian in a copy of this book.

parties. And they send spies between each other, to find out how much money the other wants to give. And when one announces perhaps five hundred *solidi*, the other laughs at it, since it is too few. "I," he says, "will give a thousand. Pray, tell my lord ruler, it is better for him to accept a thousand *solidi* than these few." Wretches, they do not know that they follow the Simoniac heresy. And how do they not know, when the bishop publicly declares, "Take care that you are not like Simoniacus through giving and promising," and he forbids it.[3] Are [the bishops] not aware of their own crimes and those of each of the others? Secretly they give and receive, and openly they deny it before everyone.

Why do you not remember, wretches? What you deny in the presence of men will be revealed before divine eyes, before angels and archangels, and princedoms and powers, before thrones and dominations, before the heavenly hosts and virtues: all hidden and secret things will there be made public. Do you want to arrive at the summit of dignity? Behold the labors of the contest. How does it benefit you to wear precious garments, when your soul is caught in the trap of the devil? Do you think that to hold the governance of the church is not enough?

If you want to consider, a bishop is greater than a king. The king in purple and gold, sitting on a royal throne, always thinks of death, aware of the sword, always thinks of how he may pour out blood. But the bishop is mindful of the salvation of the soul, of the punishments of the wicked, of the joys of paradise. See the contrast between them: the king [thinks] that bodies may be destroyed, the bishop that the soul may be crowned; the king that he might lead rebels captive, the bishop that he might purchase, redeem, and release captives; the one, that he might pass a quiet

---

3. Testi-Rasponi, *CPER*, 144, n. 8, and 251, n. 3, cites a document (unreferenced) from the tenth century of a text that goes back to the ninth century, called *De eligendo episcopo*, which consists of the formulaic questions and answers involved in choosing a new bishop; Agnellus apparently knew of this formulary or one like it, as his text is very similar to the charge to the new bishop: "See that you do not [act] through giving [*per dationem*] or promising [*per repromissionem*], since it is simony and against the canons." Cf. Gregory the Great, *Homiliae in Evangelia* 1.17.13.

night in sleep, the other that he might last the whole night in divine prayers. And what more? Just that the king asks the bishop to pray to God for him. Let these things suffice; I have said enough to you of these things, not as a lesson, but for recalling it to memory. See how humbly he who was not of our flock held the metropolitan see, taught by apostolic dogma.

101. Therefore in his reign those dwelling around the marine shores and especially in the city of Ravenna were devastated by a disastrous plague.[4] And at the turn of the year a strong and fatal illness consumed the citizens of Verona. After this a terrible sign was seen in the sky, like bloody hosts battling through the whole night, and the clearest light shone. And in that year Theudebert, king of the Franks, with Lothar, his paternal cousin, brought war, and his army was severely weakened. After some time had passed, the monastery of father Benedict, which is located in the citadel of Cassino, was destroyed at night by the Lombards, in the time of the Abbot Boniface.

And in the midst of these events, the daughter of King Agilulf with Godescalc her husband were captured by the army of Lord Gallicinus, from the city of Parma, and the captives were led to this city of Ravenna. He [Gallicinus] being deprived of life, Smaragdus was ordained lord, who later was cast out of the patrician honor by Gallinicus, who assumed the dignity for himself. Then the indignant Ravennate citizens cast out impudent Gallinicus and restored Smaragdus to his former place.

102. The Emperor Maurice, after he ruled the empire for twenty-one years, was killed with his sons Theodosius and Tiberius and Constantine by Phocas, who was the groom of Lord Priscus.

Then, as we said, there was continual war between the Ravennates and the Lombards, and a great discord because of his daughter, who had been captured by the Ravennates. And because of his great anger the city of Cremona was captured and destroyed by the said king, and Mantua was greatly harassed and disrupted.

---

4. The following passages are taken from Paul the Deacon, *Historia Langobardorum* 4.14–28.

In the second year of the reign of Phocas, in the eighth indiction, blessed Gregory migrated to the Lord, and Savinian succeeded him. And in that time there was a great frost; harvests were laid waste by mice, and others struck by blight. And in that year a serious famine arose among the people, since self-restraint was rarely to be found, as it is now in our times. Now this happened so that through serious famine it might be shown by God as a sign of the lost preaching from the death of blessed Gregory, since preaching is the divine food of the soul, as self-restraint is of the body.

103. Therefore, as we said, this most blessed man [Marinian] died on October 23 and was buried in the narthex of St. Apollinaris, outside the walls of Classe, with great lamentations. And his epitaph is written there thus:

Always sanctifying by your warnings, notable priest, you lie placed in this tomb, O Marinian. Although you have died in body, your fame lives on; though your limbs rest in the earth, the light holds your deeds. Coming to these walls as bishop from the city of Rome [5], you preserved holy Ravenna with your prayers. Governing all the world in a more peaceful time, [Gregory], dutiful, gave you to the people, at the request of Christ. Such a tomb proves that you merited a grave in these temples, that you pleased God [10]. And since as a priest you carried on his duties correctly, may you have holy rest in his grounds.

He sat __ years, __ months, __ days.

CONCERNING HOLY JOHN III, 606–25

104. John III, the thirty-first bishop. He was full in body, beautiful of figure, fat of face, having great eyes, with an eager countenance, comely in appearance. He was not like a master, but like a kindly father of his sheep, he lived meekly with them, beloved by all, an irreproachable man, father to orphans, consoler of the tears of widows, defender of wards, benefactor to the needy, exalter of the destroyed, freer of captives and follower of all good, indeed glorious in the praises of God.

O how [different] they are now from what was he like! He did not ravage his sheep, but his flock was always refreshed with the fruit of his table, and they ate in joy, he rejoicing with the priests and the whole people. But today they are not like this. Therefore what are they like? Are they not bishops like those ones, receiving the Holy Spirit in the hour of ordination like them, and similarly sanctified as bishops? But they are very different from those ones, since those daily gave prayers to God with lamentations for the souls of those who offered the greatest part of their property to the churches and endowed churches, and those redeemed captives from that money, and for such good deeds their sins were expiated, and daily they entreated the merciful Lord in their prayers.

But now these are not at all like those ones. There are some who feed dogs with a gift of a sort formerly given to the church, they cast out paupers but govern as spies, they encourage the greedy and they enjoy scurrilous songs; they cast out priests, they turn away the officials of the church and they stifle all assemblies of the church; and what is worse, they sell the grain and oil and dewy wine of the church, and from this they accumulate masses of silver and gold and they give it to princes and the powerful, that they might suppress their priests and the whole people. Those, as you have heard above, gave for redemption, these give now for killing.

They are not mindful of the words of that prophet, who said, "Thy princes in thy midst as roaring lions and souls consumed through power."[1] Who are these princes but the wretched bishops, who devour the property of the church and spurn their priests, who remove their [the priests'] property when the opportunity arises, and give no solace to them, but even remove what is theirs?[2] [The priests] do not share in the wealth of the church, but lose their own. Hear the charge against you, the words of Solomon, "As a roaring lion and a hungry bear, so is a proud prince over the humble people."[3]

---

1. Zeph. 3:3 and Ezek. 22:27.
2. These sentences may refer to the attempt by Bishop George to take away one of Agnellus's *monasteria*.
3. Prov. 28:15.

Why do you not recall, overseers, bishops, leaders of the church, what it says in the gospel, "because at what hour you know not your lord will come"?[4] Why do you not live piously and give an example to the living, that they might be taught by you and live piously in Christ?

If however *we* want to bring someone to trial, suddenly he reproaches us with a voice full of derision, "Who are you? Are you better than such and such a bishop?" Behold, I have seen such an overseer giving bread from his table to dogs, I saw such a one running with a horse behind his dogs and a hare, I saw him holding a hawk with his hands; and *you* preach to *me?* Behold when we hear these and similar things, we recede confused from them. Tell me, overseers: from where do you have your wealth? Was it from your relatives? No, but the churches are rich from the bequests of dead men. Why did they make this bequest, except that God might cleanse and wash their souls through your intercessions for them?

Why do you transgress the rule of the holy fathers, and abandon what they taught, saying, "Let bishops use the things of the churches as if lent to them, not as their own"? Tell me: when you have left your bodies, if they have not complained against you, will God also cleanse you of this sin? Even if you have given charity from that property, what fee will you take? It did not come from your property, but from the wealth of your predecessors.

For just like a master, who calls his steward and asks him to pay out to his family a hundred bushels of wheat, and the steward keeps some for himself and does not give all of it, and those who are his fellow slaves tell his master about him who did not give all, but fraudulently kept some; he is whipped by his master, who removes him from his estate or casts him out; or, since he did not fulfill his mission, he is sent to prison.

Thus the evangelist offers such an opinion of you, saying, "But if that servant shall say in his heart, My lord is long acoming; and shall begin to strike the menservants and maidservants, and to eat and to drink, and be drunk; the lord of that servant will come in the day that he hopeth not, and at the hour that he knoweth not,

---

4. Matt. 24:44.

and will separate him, and shall appoint him his portion with unbelievers."[5]

O wretches! These words are said of you, who have undertaken the governance of the church, who ought to be irreproachable, without any stain. And when you are seized by death in such negligence, it will be your doom, since the bishop will be seized for punishment, and the people will be invited into the kingdom, since "the day of the Lord shall so come like a thief in the night."[6] But, my fathers, act not incautiously, you are in the place of the apostles, you hold their positions; follow their paths, that you may be numbered in their ranks.

But this most blessed John, who ruled the pontificate humbly, led joyous days for all of his life. He ruled his church in peace, fulfilling the divine mandates. He died in body, he was buried, I think, in the narthex of St. Apollinaris. He sat five years, ten months, eighteen days.

CONCERNING HOLY JOHN IV, 625–31

105. John IV, the thirty-second bishop, a kindly and humble man, wise of heart, prudent in his words, had beautiful eloquence, he led an honest life and good habits with his honeyed speech. He kept the teachings of his predecessors uninjured and safe.

However, some say that he redeemed the citizens and city of Classe from an enemy people with much wealth of the church on three occasions, not only the city but, as I said, he redeemed those living in it with all its suburbs.[1]

For observing the words of the gospel,[2] daily he directed his

---

5. Luke 12:45–46.
6. 1 Thess. 5:2.

1. John IV reigned circa 625–31, during which time no attacks by the Lombards on Classe are known from other sources. It is probable that this passage refers to an event in the reign of John V (*LPR*, cc. 151–53), who ruled 726–44 (Holder-Egger, *LPER*, 346, n. 5).

2. The first part of this sermonette seems to belong together with the sermonette in c. 116.

thoughts to what is said, "But learn what this meaneth, I will have mercy and not sacrifice."[3] Hear therefore through the prophet, "Shall I eat the flesh of bullocks? or shall I drink the blood of goats?"[4] And hear another prophet, Isaiah, the son of Amos, "When you stretch forth your hands, I will turn away my eyes from you: and when you multiply prayer, I will not hear."[5] Why? What then of those words of David: "Call upon me in the day of trouble: I will deliver thee, and thou shalt glorify me."[6] And indeed another prophet: "They will call in the day of trouble, and I will hear."[7] Now what? What then of the prophecy of Isaiah, which you said, "Thus saith the Lord: when thou shalt cry, he shall say to you, Here I am."[8] And he says on the other hand, "I will turn away my eyes from you."[9] One voice cheers us, the other saddens. And why will God not hear us invoking him? On the contrary, he will hear us, but we die.

Listen: "Why are your hands full of blood? Wash yourselves, be clean, take away the evil of your devices from my eyes; seek judgment, relieve the oppressed, defend the widows, come now, and then come, and accuse me, saith the Lord."[10] And again, "Woe to you that justify the wicked and for gifts take away the justice of the just. Woe to you that call evil good, and good evil, since there is no joy for the wicked, saith the Lord. But if you remove from you all bands of wickedness and words of discontent, and deal out thy bread to the hungry from your soul and satisfy the afflicted soul," Isaiah says, "thy God shall be with thee always and shall not turn away from thee. Then shalt thou cry, and the Lord shall hear: and he shall say to you, Here I am."[11] See how quickly God will hear those observing his commandments! Again hear David say of the righteous, "I have been young, and now am old; and I have not seen the just forsaken, nor his seed seeking bread."[12]

---

3. Matt. 9:13.
5. Isa. 1:15.
7. Ps. 85:7.
9. Isa. 1:15.
11. Isa. 5:23; Isa. 5:20; Isa. 58:6–10.

4. Ps. 49:13.
6. Ps. 49:15, esp. the *Vetus Latina* version.
8. Isa. 58:9, esp. the *Vetus Latina* version.
10. Isa. 1:15–18.
12. Ps. 36:25.

However, what is written of sinners? "But to the sinner God hath said: Why dost thou declare my justices, and take my covenant in thy mouth?" etc., up to, "Understand these things, you that forget God; lest he snatch you away, and there be none to deliver you."[13] O beloved friends, this sermon ought to stand before your eyes daily, so that, as much as we may have been disturbed by fear, so much may it profit us for salvation. Woe to that soul which is seized the way a hawk seizes birds. In the hour of the exit of the soul we carry nothing with us except the sins which we have committed. We are mocked by malign spirits, we are derided by them, and they harass us without mercy. When we are drawn along in an ill fashion, they say, "This Christian is false, we do not find the works of Christ in him. Behold this judge has been captured; or this king has slipped. Has not this priest fallen into the depths like one guilty person?" Before human eyes the body lies quietly, but it is not seen how the soul is dragged to its punishment by evil spirits.

And the overseers of the church are judged not only for themselves, but for their sheep and for all the people who have been assigned to them.[14] A man of the people perhaps suffers punishment for his own soul, the overseers for their whole flock. If one should be sent into the shadows of the void, because he did not bring a soul to Christ, where ought that one be sent who actually lost Christian souls? You did not preach, you were silent. You have not acquired them; you have harassed those acquired and those who serve God. Why have you afflicted them? Why, when you sat in judgment, have you been aware of perjury? Why are you the author of crime? Why aware of homicide? Does not the canon teach that a bishop should have no worldly care for himself, except that he has time for reading, that he assiduously read and teach the gospel? But if you do not want to follow the canon, then imitate this holy man, equal this blessed John: redeem captives, rescue, following the prophet, those who are led to death, preach, teach, raise up the wandering sheep, do not separate yourself from your righteous

---

13. Pss. 49:16 and 49:22.
14. This part of the sermonette seems to follow from the one in c. 104.

brethren, that together with them you might be blessed and the grace of God might not be lacking in you.

106. In his reign[15] Agilulf king of the Lombards made peace with the *patricius* Smaragdus, which held for one year. And after the end of the year Bagnoregio and the city in Tuscia called Orvieto were invaded by the army of the Lombards. And in the month of April and May a comet appeared in the sky. And again the Romans made peace with the said king for three years.

After these events, Naples was invaded by John; a few days later Eleutherius killed him [John], after having expelled him. And then when he returned with victory, he scorned the patriciate with the fasces; although he was a eunuch he took up the ruling of the empire. Having left Ravenna he wanted to go to Rome; he was killed with the sword by soldiers in the camp of Lucceoli; his head, placed in a bag, was brought to the emperor at Constantinople.

And also in that time the said King Agilulf sent his notary Stabilissinian as a legate to the Emperor Phocas. Then returning with legates of the emperor, peace was made between them; Italy was quiet for several years.

107. Therefore, as we said, with Maurice and his sons dead, Phocas invaded the kingdom of the Romans, and held the principate for a period of eight years. At the request of blessed Pope Boniface, he decreed that the Roman church was the head and seat of all the churches, where before the church of Constantinople was called first.

And again the said pope sought from him, that the old shrine which the Romans called the Pantheon, with the filth of the idols destroyed, might become a church of the holy and inviolate Virgin Mary and all of the saints of God, martyrs and confessors; and it might be confirmed that where all assemblies of demons used to be gathered, there the memory of all the saints and chosen of God might be venerated.[16]

---

15. The events in this chapter are taken from Paul the Deacon's *Historia Langobardorum* 4.32–36.

16. The account of the rededication of the Pantheon was widely known; cf. *LP*,

Meanwhile war was stirred up in eastern lands and in Egypt. With the Prasinians and the Venetians smiting each other with very heavy battles in civil war, [the Persians] captured many Roman provinces and even Jerusalem itself, and destroying the churches reduced them to nothing, and they took away the wealth and ornaments of the church, and removing the banner of the holy cross by which we were redeemed, they plundered and took [everything] with them.

Indeed Heraclian, who in those days ruled in Africa, rebelled against this Phocas, and coming with his army deprived him of the kingdom and of life; Heraclius, his son, undertook the rule of the Roman republic.

And with these things done, this most blessed man died and was buried, as I suspect, in the narthex of blessed Apollinaris. He sat eighteen years, six months, eight days.

CONCERNING HOLY BONUS, 631–42

108. Bonus, the thirty-third bishop, he was good in name and in deeds, with a thin and red face, a head full of hair adorned with grey, and full of all grace. And if perchance someone might wonder, might say or ask others, "how or from where could he know what the faces of those holy men were like, whether fat or thin?" let there be no doubt about it, since pictures inform me of their faces.[1]

109. From his reign the troubles of the nations began to increase and the waves to dash against them; but he, accustomed to praying, did not cease to give prayers assiduously to God. He prayed for the faithful, that they might conquer; for the infidels, that they might come to grace; since, before the world is destroyed, all will come together to Christ.

Life of Boniface IV; Bede, *Historia ecclesiastica* 2.4; Paul the Deacon, *Historia Langobardorum* 4.36.

1. Agnellus here repeats what he has said in c. 32, which should be understood as an oblique reference to iconoclasm; see Deliyannis, "Agnellus of Ravenna and Iconoclasm."

Hear David: "All the tribes of the earth shall remember, and shall be converted to the Lord, and shall adore in the sight of the gentiles."[2] See, how before the day of judgment all the world will follow Christ, and will adore God alone living in the ages of ages. And say other things, O king, "And all kings of the earth shall adore him: all nations shall serve him."[3] And Paul the apostle cries, "Until the fullness of the Gentiles should come in, and so all Israel shall be saved."[4] And why do they not yet believe? Since their hearts are hard and their vitals are shut. That veil, which Moses had over his face, is fixed in their hearts.

And if they have a veiled heart, how therefore did Ezekiel cry, "I will take away the stony heart out of your flesh, and will give you a heart of flesh, and you shall know that I am the Lord"?[5] Hearts of flesh are given to them, but hardness always increases in them. Hear the apostle, "But according to thy hardness and impenitent heart, thou treasurest up to thyself wrath, against the day of wrath, and revelation of the just judgment of God. Who will render to every man according to his works."[6] Listen to this truth about their hardness, "God is able of these stones to raise up children to Abraham."[7] "With God all things are possible."[8] And why has He not raised them up? If He wanted to, what prevented Him?

Since by Himself the Master of all raised up the holy apostles, who were descended from Abraham, whose imitators you are and whose faces you wear, remember, I ask solicitously, overseers of the holy church, although you hold the highest seat, you are nevertheless mortal, always cautious, always fearful. Hear through the prophet: "But you like men shall die: and shall fall like one of the princes."[9] And the son of the said prophet: "Blessed is the man that is always fearful: but he that is hardened in mind, shall fall into evil."[10]

However this most blessed leader died on August 26 in ripe old

2. Cf. Ps. 21:28.
3. Ps. 71:11.
4. Rom. 11:25–26.
5. Ezek. 36:26 and 36:38.
6. Rom. 2:5–6.
7. Luke 3:8.
8. Matt. 19:26.
9. Ps. 81:7.
10. Prov. 28:14.

age, and was buried in peace in the basilica of St. Apollinaris priest and martyr, in Classe. He sat __ years, __ months, __ days.

CONCERNING HOLY MAURUS, 642–71

110. Maurus, the thirty-fourth bishop. He was energetic; he was deacon and steward of this church and was abbot for the *monasterium* of St. Bartholemew, where now, as you see, I am abbot, God willing, from the bequest of deacon Sergius, my paternal cousin.

This above-mentioned bishop, as I said, had many troubles with the Roman bishop, many contests, many disturbances, many altercations. He went to Constantinople on many occasions, so that he might free his church from the yoke or domination of the Romans. It was done thus, and the church of Ravenna was withdrawn, so that no future pastor of the Ravennate church need ever afterward go to Rome to the bishop of the Roman see for consecration, nor that he should have the pope's rule over him, nor that he should at any time be under the dominion of the Roman bishop, but might consecrate his choice [for episcopal office] with three of his own bishops; and he brought back the pallium from the emperor in Constantinople.[1]

If we digress through many and long journeys, I could tell you in order how this was done and for what reason and by what ingenuities. If we want to do this, to digress through all these things, I will expend parchment and ink, and you will be delayed in waiting for me.

---

1. The privilege of Emperor Constans II regarding the autocephaly of the Ravennate church was given to Maurus on March 1, 666; it is found in the *Codex Estensis*, fol. 43v, and is published in *RIS* 1.2, ed. Muratori, 583, and ibid., 2.1:146, as well as by Holder-Egger, *LPER*, 350–51, n. 8. Agnellus no doubt saw this document; what he says here, as well as below, refers directly to the following section: "WE ORDAIN further that [the church of Ravenna] shall remain safe and free from any superior episcopal authority and shall be vacant only by rescript of our imperial command, and shall not be subject for any reason to the ancient patriarchate of the city of Rome, but shall remain autocephalous . . . and consecrated by its own bishops, using fittingly the pallium."

He was deacon and steward of this church, he ruled the *monasterium* of the blessed apostle Bartholemew, where I am seen to be abbot.

111. Therefore he sent his *manipularius*, whom he wanted to make rector of Sicily, to his [current] rector of Sicily, a deacon by the name of Benedict, who at that time was in charge of taking care of the legal and business affairs of the church of Ravenna,[2] saying in a letter, "Your service has pleased us enough. You have grown old; return to the holy mother church, where you were raised. It is time for me to see you; so confirm this man, our *manipularius*, as rector after you. If possible, let our admonition not be unpleasant to you; but if it is unpleasant to you, see that you send him back to us."

[Benedict] however, once he knew the will of the bishop, honored [the *manipularius*] with various presents and gifts: gold and silver, desirable vases and many other things. And when the two men had been brought down to the boat, they kissed one other and said farewell, and [Benedict] gave [the *manipularius*] three hundred gold pieces and sent him back rich to his bishop.

Then the said deacon Benedict came back to Sicily, where he loaded the long ships with fifty thousand *modia* of wheat, not counting many other grains and vegetables, reddened hides of rams and purple robes and decorated silk episcopal vestments, wool and other garments, vases of brass and silver, and thirty-one thousand gold *solidi*. From these he sent fifteen thousand to the palace in Constantinople and sixteen thousand to the archive of the church.[3] This payment was made every year, but the wheat always [went] to the table where the bishop ate. The *manipularius*, having returned, told the bishop all the things which had been done, and showed the gifts which he had given him, and thanked the absent man.

    2. About the patrimony of the Ravennate church in Sicily, see esp. Fasoli, "Sul Patrimonio," and Fasoli, "Il patrimonio." This story seems to be taken from a letter that Agnellus saw in the archive; however, the biblical language used, particularly to describe the items of tribute, imply that many of the details were invented by Agnellus.

    3. In c. 134, Agnellus says that the *archivus ecclesiae* burned down, implying that it was a separate structure. The *archivus* may also have contained the treasury, since here it says that the money was sent to the archive.

After three years [the bishop] again sent [the *manipularius*] who had gone before back to Sicily to the said deacon; with the excuse that [the *manipularius*] should acquire land for a garden that Benedict owned, so that again [Benedict] might give him gifts. And so that [Benedict] would not be able to guess the reason, he instructed: "Hasten to Constantinople and supplicate the emperor, lest anyone should usurp it."

[Benedict] indeed, after he read the letter sent to him, received [the *manipularius*] honorably and said to him, "Say to my lord that I own the garden in question. Tomorrow let us go and stay there and I will do that thing for which you were sent, so that you will never again desire to come to Sicily." He gave him much silver and several weights of gold. And beyond this it was not necessary for [the *manipularius*], after he reached Ravenna, to return to Sicily.

112. It happened in that time, that the Roman pope sent a legation to [Maurus] telling him to hasten to Rome, wanting to subjugate him to his dominion. Having received the letter, [Maurus] read and folded it, saying to the legates of the apostolic see, "What is this, what do you strive to do? Is there not an agreement and confirmed obligation between us that neither he should raise trouble against me or my church, or his successors against my successors? He has my signed pact by him, and I keep his, as well as all things written between us and confirmed by the signatures of my priests and his. In his hands the received document is confirmed; you have written your letters there for yourselves. I do not agree to these orders. Return to him who sent you, and tell him what you have heard."

Having returned, they told the sequence of events. Then the indignant pope ordered written a letter of obligation, wound about with the chains of anathema, and he signed it with his own hand; [saying] that if Archbishop Maurus would not come to the apostolic see, he would not have permission to sing masses, nor might any man approach him for communication, nor might any cleric cling to him nor approach the sacrosanct altar with him, nor offer any oblation with him or for him.

However [Maurus] was bold, he did not accept that he was

bound with the chains of the Jews and cast out from the kingdom of God. The legates of the Roman see brought all these things inserted in a letter, they offered it to Bishop Maurus of the city of Ravenna. Bishop Maurus, accepting it, read the unhappy words. And he was filled with anger, not with outward fury, but like an irrevocable rage, and he wrote a letter similarly sending restrictions of anathema, so that the pope would not have license to sing the mass, as he did not; he ordered his to be written corresponding to the Roman letter and sent it to Rome to the said pope.

Having read it [the pope] cast it away from him, and again ordered [Maurus] to be brought. After this [the pope] wanted to send legates to Constantinople to the emperor, that he might coerce Archbishop Maurus to go to the council at Rome, telling how he had dared to send a letter of obligation to his master.

Indeed in such obligation both died. And from that day they did not offer oblations for [Maurus] at Rome, nor for [the pope] here;[4] but every week, on Thursday after the office of vespers was completed, the priests, deacons, subdeacons and clergy gathered, they entered the *secretarium* and divided among themselves a round loaf of bread and individual sausages, a vial of wine; and the priest or whoever was first in rank said, "May the Lord God give eternal rest to the soul of him in whose commemoration we have eaten this," and the others said, "May God order it"; and with these words they retired.[5]

Some say that long after their deaths this case was discussed at Rome in a council.[6] By the providence of the bishops, as if for their burial, they cut the top of the fetter of the right foot.[7] Thus for the one, thus for the other.

113. However in the hour of his death he called all his priests,

---

4. The Roman *LP,* Life of Leo II, records that the death of Maurus was not commemorated at Rome "and that the anniversary and requiem of the former Bishop Maurus should not be observed."

5. The meaning of this passage is not entirely clear; it seems to refer to an unofficial celebration of a memorial mass.

6. There is no record of this in any of the councils whose acts survive.

7. A strange phrase, the meaning of which is not clear.

weeping before them, seeking their forgiveness, and he said to them, "I am entering the path of death, I call to witness and warn you, do not place yourselves under the Roman yoke. Choose a pastor from yourselves, and let him be consecrated by his bishops. Seek the pallium from the emperor. For on whatever day you are subjugated to Rome, you will not be whole." And with these words he died; and he was buried in the narthex of blessed Apollinaris, in a wonderful tomb.

There was a porphyry stone before the said sarcophagus, most precious and very shiny like glass. And with the doors which look out onto the church of St. Severus open, whoever looked at this stone as if in a mirror could see images, men and animals or birds or whatever things were passing by there, just as in a mirror.

But almost twelve years ago, in the time of Bishop Petronax, the Emperor Lothar ordered it to be removed, and he enclosed it in a wooden chest on wool and carried it off to France, and placed it on the altar of St. Sebastian, as if it were a table. It was commanded me by the bishop, that I go there, lest the workmen should act carelessly and break it; but since my heart was full of grief I withdrew to a different place.[8]

114. He brought the body of blessed Apollinaris, which was for some time in the narthex of that [church] founded by Bishop Maximian with Julian the banker, out of there and placed it in the middle of the temple; and he set in silver sheets the history of that martyr.[9]

You will find his epitaph written above [his sarcopahgus] containing the following:[10]

8. This event took place in 829–30. From this passage we learn both about Agnellus's role as *magister caementariorum* and about spoliation in the ninth century.

9. Classe was sacked by the Saracens around 858, and probably at that time whatever silver sheets Agnellus saw were plundered. It is not clear in any case whether the "history" *(historia)* on these sheets was a text or a series of pictures; two silver plates were discovered in 1173, and the text written on them contains several phrases that correspond exactly to those used by Agnellus (contained in the twelfth-century account entitled *De inventione corporis beati Apollinaris martyris*). For more on the date of these plates, see Deliyannis, *CCCM* edition of the *LPR*, introduction.

10. As pointed out to me by R. Johnson (personal communication), this poem is a

Faith first, and the Father had promised should one day be seen by our eyes and called by the voice of the law [*Apo.* 374–75]; it proclaims Christ, and sounds Christ's name, all things Christ [*Apo.* 391].

O sweetest name of Bishop Maurus! Light and glory, our protector, O certain rest from labors [5], sweet savor in the mouth, fragrant odor, flowing spring, pure love, beautiful appearance, genuine delight.

If a deaf people should deny itself such commendation of you, so many voices of nature and so many elements [10] [*Apo.* 393–98], you have seen on high with companies of angels [*Apo.* 532] the final one, which extends through infinite space [*Apo.* 813], running in the steps of kings and sitting [*Apo.* 998], carrying the worthy awards which they joyously brought to you, you were, by comparable merit of being first in eloquence [*Comm.* 14.1].

You have as high a peak of family, as you have glory in speaking [15] [*Comm.* 14.7], looking at the inviolate rewards of a pure life [*Par.* 19.5]; fitting in speech, good in ingenuity, and eloquent in everything [*Par.* 14.7]. Your vows are approved favorably by God through your holy merits [*Par.* 8.13]. Everything that you wanted you saw was prosperous; whatever you hoped, it happened as you wanted [20] [*Par.* 1.5–6], and you believed in healing the lives of men with reason [*Par.* 1.13].

Thus this reverence remains for your completed life [*Par.* 1.15]. By your virtues you revealed your see to the summit, holding the apostolic garlands, you arranged them by their own laws. And now you lie tranquil, removed from dutiful care [25] [*Par.* 19.13], and now you live under the honor of a lasting tomb [*Par.* 8.15]. As a child, born in filthy corruptions of putrid flesh [*Apo.* 816], you will find Christ, the parent of your heart [*Apo.* 999].

And in front of this sarcophagus on the pavement you will find written in mosaic containing the following:

---

compilation of lines from three different sources: Prudentius's *Liber apotheosis (Apo.)* Ausonius's *Commemoratio professorum Burdigalensium (Comm.)*, and Ausonius's *Parentalia (Par.)* as indicated in the translation. There are many problems with the language and meter of the verses; the translation reflects these difficulties, especially as many lines are part of longer sentences in the original poems, the rest of which have been omitted.

Here rests in peace Archbishop Maurus, who lived for very many years, sixty-seven, who in the time of the lord Emperor Constantine liberated his church from the yoke of servitude to Rome.

He sat twenty-eight years, ten months, eighteen days.

CONCERNING HOLY REPARATUS
(671–77)

115. Reparatus, the thirty-fifth bishop. He was older in age, and his thin image was in the church of St. Peter.[1] He was ordained bishop at Ravenna by three of his suffragan bishops, as is the custom of consecrating the bishop of Rome. He was called from the *monasterium* of St. Apollinaris here in Ravenna, not far from the Ovilian gate in the place which is called the Public Mint;[2] there he was abbot. And he was steward of this church, he held the next rank after the bishop.

In the reign of Emperor Constantine the Greater, father of Heraclius and Tiberius, he went to Constantinople, and whatever he asked of the emperor, he got. Among other things [the emperors] ordered confirmations to be written of the following mandate: that no priest or any cleric whatsoever should have to pay tax to the public [treasury], that no one should exact from them either shore tax or gate tax or sales tax or customs tax. And again he stated and decreed that neither the church nor those from a *monasterium* nor the tenants of the church nor the servants nor the cross bearers might be subject to any judge or exactor or any power except to the bishop or *rector* of the church. And he decreed this, that at the time

---

1. Although the phrase "ecclesia beati Petri" could refer to the Church of the Apostles in Ravenna, Nauerth, *Agnellus von Ravenna, Untersuchungen*, 44, notes that Agnellus uses a past tense *(erat)* for the state of this picture, and thus it is likely to have been located in the Petriana church in Classe, which no longer existed in Agnellus's day. This would mean that Agnellus would have known about the picture from a document or oral legend; his reference to Reparatus as "thin" *(macilentus)* must be based on the portrait in Sant' Apollinare in Classe, described below, which still survives today.

2. Cf. c. 164. About the *moneta*, see Deichmann, *Ravenna* 2.3:54–56.

of consecration the elected bishop might delay in Rome no more than eight days.[3]

And [Reparatus] ordered that their images and his be depicted in the upper wall of the apse of St. Apollinaris and decorated with multicolored mosaic, and below their feet two metrical verses to be written, containing thus:

This Reparatus, that he might be a comrade to the saints, made new decorations for this hall, to blaze through the ages.

And over the head of the emperor you will find the following, "Constantine the senior emperor, Heraclius and Tiberius emperors."[4]

116. As a true shepherd he lived dutifully with his sheep. He did not subjugate himself to the Roman see.[5] He raised the priests from poverty, he endowed and increased the clergy, and did not

---

3. The emperor was Constans II. The specificity of these rights indicates that Agnellus saw documents containing these privileges; see Brown, "The Church of Ravenna," 20–24. The statement "and he decreed ... eight days" contradicts the right of the bishop of Ravenna to be consecrated by his suffragans, and indicates that these autocephalic rights were being eroded after the election of Reparatus, despite what Agnellus says.

4. This image, which survives on the north wall of the apse of Sant' Apollinare in Classe, is often said to represent the granting of privileges by the Emperor Constantine IV, and his brothers Heraclius and Tiberius, to Bishop Reparatus. However, Deichmann, *Ravenna* 2.2:273–80, identifies this as a depiction of the grant of autocephaly made to Bishop Maurus by the Emperor Constans II, installed by Reparatus to commemorate his role as the ambassador who obtained the privilege. The bishop shown between the emperor and Reparatus would be Maurus, while the other three people to the left of Constans are his sons, Constantine IV, Heraclius, and Tiberius. Deichmann explains Agnellus's confusion over the emperors as indicating that by the ninth century part of the inscription was already missing.

5. Agnellus here contradicts the statement in the Roman *LP*, Life of Donus, where it says: "In his time the church of Ravenna, which had separated itself from the Roman church to achieve independence, brought itself back into subjection to the ancient apostolic see; as it pleased God, that church's prelate, named Reparatus, instantly died" (Davis, *Book of Pontiffs*, 73.) The statement in the *LPR* echoes the phraseology in the *LP*; Agnellus must have interpreted the passage in the *LP* to mean that some members of the Ravennate church submitted to Rome but that Reparatus was not among them, an indication of dissension that resulted in the election of Theodore as the next archbishop.

take from them, as they do now, but gave to the lesser members of the church and augmented the more important ones. The sheep rejoiced in the church, doctrine flourished, he kept watch day and night. He was not full of cupidity, not timid, not proud, not envious, not a lover of gluttony, repelling greed, he refused vainglory, he fled sloth, he scorned pride.[6] He was such a one, as the Lord says, "A true Israelite, in whom there was no guile."[7] How do we report that our elders spoke of the goodness of bishops, when now we see many evils in them? Those who ought to mend a broken vessel, break a whole one. Alas how many lamentations envelop us, how many griefs, and with how many tears and weeping and sobbing are we surrounded! And those who ought to pray to God in simplicity of heart,[8] blaspheme him greatly, and they demand that sins be committed to free them from their evil pastors.

This prayer against sin is according to the Bible: "and may his prayer be turned to sins."[9] But it is better to be freed by God through daily appeals, than to be brought down under the hands of the wicked by remaining silent. For it is written: "Thou callest upon me in affliction, and I delivered thee,"[10] and elsewhere: "And call upon me in the day of trouble: I will deliver thee, and thou shalt glorify me."[11] Let us keep firm hold of these promises, since God hears and frees those seeking him in time of difficulty. Moses by crying out was freed from the hand of Pharaoh; Ezekiel by crying out merited an angel from the heavens, who laid low for him a hundred-and-eighty-five thousand from the camps of the Assyrians; Peter by praying was removed from the hand of Herod. Who prays to God not falsely, but with all his might, and is not deliv-

---

6. Muratori, "Agnello e il suo libro," identifies *gastrimargia*, *philargiria*, and *cenodoxia* as γαστριμάργια, φιλαργυρία and ξενοδοχία Cf. also Lazard, "De l'origine," 263.

7. John 1:47.

8. I.e., the priests, who should be humble but want to be freed from the evil bishops.

9. Ps. 108:7.

10. Ps. 80:8.

11. Ps. 49:15, *Vetus Latina* version; the same use of the *Vetus Latina* version of this passage is found in c. 105.

ered from the hands of his enemy? Hear the Lord saying in the gospel, "There was a judge in a certain city, who feared not God, nor regarded man. And a certain widow in that city was bothered, and she came to him, saying: Avenge me of my adversary, etc. However the Lord himself said, 'And will not God revenge his elect who cry to him day and night?'"[12] Thus it is fitting always to pray and not to cease, just as that holy bishop obtained all things by his prayers rather than by bribery.

He died and was buried in the church of St. Apollinaris. His epitaph is destroyed. He died, as we said, on July 30. He sat five years, nine months, ___ days.

CONCERNING HOLY THEODORE, 677–91

117. Theodore, the thirty-sixth bishop. He was young in age, terrible in form, horrible in appearance, and full of all deceit. He was consecrated by his bishops in the church of the Apostles here in Ravenna. Our elders recount many evils of him. I marvel at how he was once able to obtain the see, given all of his bad actions. The statutes of the church which were made in the time of Pope Felix between the priests, clergy, and archbishop lasted up to his appearance. Let us explain his cruelty.

He stole their quarter from the clerics.[1] The written statues of the church, which . . .[2] he ordered to be burned on a pyre. He established weights for bread, he diminished the measures of wine. Then he added many other hardships, which here I cannot describe with my tearful pen, since I am trying to go on to other things.

118. In those days there was a heavy famine in all this land, and

---

12. Luke 18:2–7.

1. In the *constitutum* of Pope Felix IV, quoted in c. 60, it is mandated that a quarter-part of the income of the church be distributed to the clergy. Testi-Rasponi, "Note marginali," 252–57, identifies Agnellus's characterization of Bishop Theodore as a thinly disguised portrait of the hated Bishop George.

2. A few words seem to be missing here, but there is no gap in the manuscript.

he devoured the grain of the whole region. When the priests could not find enough to buy, they went to him, beseeching that he help them. He however said to the archdeacon by the name of Theodore and to the archpriest similarly named Theodore, whom he had summoned: "Say to the priests of the church and to the whole clergy: 'Why does the exigency of famine consume you? If you will send to the church your whole quarter and receive so much for the quarter as a gift through the circle of the year, according to the providence of the bishop, then I will relieve your need.'" Long castigated, with hunger growling, they agreed; and from that time to the present day their quarter is given up by the clergy of this church.

The usages of the church, which were written in individual volumes in each office, he removed and destroyed by fire. One day, when the murmur of the priests and clerics was against him concerning a usage of the church, about how much one might have according to his office, sitting on his episcopal throne of dignity and seeing that he was worsted, he said to everyone, "Believe me, sons, that I do not usurp your usage in all things, but rather I increase it." And with a pledge given in the assembly of the church, [he ordered] that all of these usages, wherever they were found to be written, should be brought before him.

When many documents had been brought before him, in the evil machination of his heart he was pleased. He received them as if with joy, with a serene face before all, but in his heart there was a most savage wound. He said again to them, "Seek them out again, that you may find more, and let an agreement be made between me and you, that quarrels may never arise between you and my successors."

They again went away and searched diligently, and as soon as they could find things they brought them to him. He pretended to copy all the documents and said to them, "Go now, that I might consider which to confirm, and that this case may never be repeated." And collecting all the things he had received in one volume, he burned it in the fire in the furnace of his bath.

He did such wrongs for a bishop with his sheep, and his evil seduction deceived them. Would that he held not the episcopal throne of a shepherd, but the place of a mercenary! In his see he was like a wolf among the flock, a lion among quadrupeds, a hawk among birds, a storm in the ripe crops. What use was it to him to be a bishop? Even up to today, when the clerics mention his tomb, where his body lies buried and destroyed, even after the passage of perhaps 180 years,[3] they say curses and insults. And others who do not know say to those who know, "Tell us, where does that most wicked leader rest?"

119. In his reign the *monasterium* of St. Theodore the deacon was built by the *patricius* Theodore,[4] not far from the place which is called *ad Chalchi*, next to the church of St. Martin the confessor which is called the Golden Heaven, which King Theodoric built, but restored under the power of that bishop. The said *patricius* and exarch made three gold chalices for this holy church of Ravenna, which exist up to the present day.

And daily he went to the *monasterium* of St. Mary which is called *ad Blachernas*, where by the will of God I am abbot, and there he rests with Agatha his wife. And he made a most precious purple covering over the altar of the Virgin, having on it the story of how God made heaven and earth and the creatures of the world and Adam and his progeny. Who has seen its like? God being favorable, it remains up to today.

The church of the blessed apostle Paul was placed near Wandalaria; he with that bishop raised it up and increased it, since formerly it was described as a synagogue of the Jews.[5]

120. In the time of that exarch, in his palace here in Ravenna, the man by the name of Johannicis[6] began to grow in wisdom. We will report the reason why to you, we will not keep it hidden.

---

3. This number must be incorrect, since Theodore reigned 679–93, and this part of the *LPR* was written in the 840s.

4. Deichmann, "Studi sulla Ravenna scomparsa," 71, notes that Theodore was the exarch from 678 to 687.

5. Agnellus probably learned that the church of St. Paul had been a *sinagoga* from a document about its foundation, since *discribebatur* implies that some written source has "described" it as a synagogue.

6. Johannicis was an ancestor of Agnellus and reappears in the Lives of Damian

It happened at that time that the notary of the said exarch by divine order died, for whom the exarch grieved, not only for his death, but moreover because he did not have a similar wise man in the palace who could compose imperial letters or complete other written charters which were necessary.

However, when he indicated his sadness to his attendants, they said to him, "Let our lord have no doubt in this case. There is here a youth, one Johannicis by name, most skilled in writing, learned in scriptures, fruitful in wisdom, wise in counsel, truthful in word, cautious in speech and full of all knowledge, sprung from noblest birth. If at once you will order him to come and stand before your sight, he will please you, he has been instructed in Greek and Latin letters."

Uplifted at having heard this speech, he ordered him to come. And [Johannicis] stood before him, and [the exarch] despised him in his heart, for he was short in figure and unpleasant in appearance. He was horrified at the visible things, but later he was pleased with the invisible. "God hath chosen the weak things of the world to confound the things which are mighty."[7] However the exarch, conferring with the leading men of this city, said, "Do you think that he could maintain this palace through his knowledge? I do not think so." And they said to him, "Let our lord order him to be interrogated; if he cannot do it, let him go away again."

And the exarch ordered a letter to be brought, which had come to him from the emperor, written in Greek, and said to him, "Read it." But he rose from lying at [the exarch's] feet and frowned, and said, "Do you order, my lord, that I read it in Greek, as it is written, or with Latin words?" since he used Greek as well as he used Latin, and held Latin as Greek. Then the admiring exarch, together with the leaders and assembly of the people, ordered a charter to be brought written in Latin letters, and ordered him, saying, "Take this charter in your hand and read it in Greek words." Taking it, he read the whole thing in Greek. Then the exarch was pleased at the

---

and Felix. Except in one case in this passage, his name is spelled in the manuscript as "Iohanicis."

7. 1 Cor. 1:27.

knowledge of this Johannicis, and he praised God, who had taken away one soul, but had replaced it with a living body. And he ordered that [Johannicis] should on no account move his feet outside the palace without [the exarch's] knowledge, but daily should stand in his presence.

With these things done, after three years the emperor in Constantinople ordered a letter to be written to this exarch, saying thus: "Send to me that man who produces such compositions and poems which you have sent to me." [The exarch], burdened by necessity as if by oaken beams, sent him to Constantinople. And when the emperor had looked at him, he did not [at first] believe in [Johannicis's] knowledge. After a few days [Johannicis's] learning shone forth, and [the emperor] placed him among the leading men.

121. But Bishop Theodore of this city did not recede from the infinite wickedness which he had begun.[8] When he embraced the priests, he would repel all the deacons; after the accustomed punishment he would again love the deacons and hate the priests. This most wicked planter was sowing such dissensions between them, and was then soothing on either side.[9]

After he had brought everyone to poverty and afflicted them with great need, out of great necessity they were all outraged with great anger. On the day of the vigil of the nativity of the Lord the priests went together to Theodore the archpriest and to Theodore the archdeacon, and said to them, "Tell our lord bishop that he acts badly against us, he punishes or goads us too much, he places many hardships on us, which we cannot tolerate at all. He has taken the opportunity to steal our quarter from us, he has broken apostolic statutes, he has burned the laws of the church, he takes away our offices, he repels us from the bosom of the church, he conceals the Gospels, he afflicts bodies, he seizes property, he removes resources, he tries to make us subject to taxes. We cannot tolerate his anger."

8. It is possible that the story in cc. 121–23 was based on a document pertaining to this conflict, naming the principals; Pizarro, *Writing Ravenna*, 52–60, discusses the dramatic elements found in this story.

9. Ibid., 54, notes that he was pursuing a policy of divide and rule.

They went to tell the words of the clergy into the ears of the bishop. He, having heard all the words, as if taking up a javelin, suddenly angered, said to them, "You are stirring up the clerics, you are placing these words in their mouths. Surely those who said this will never advance to better things." And turning to the archpriest, he said, "You are the author of this verbal crime, you are the head of the uprising of the priests, you most clearly are my bitterest enemy, you the exciter of the people, you are the most wicked adversary anywhere. After this festival I will make sure that you never again harm another with your voice."

In this anger all hastened to the church of St. Mary ever virgin to celebrate vigils. And after the Office was completed they reported the words of the bishop to the whole clergy; and they were indignant, and taking counsel with each other, each went to his own home.

Then Theodore the archpriest went to Theodore the archdeacon, his maternal cousin, in the *monasterium* of St. Andrew the apostle, which is found not far from the church of the Goths, near the house which is called *Mariniana*. When he knocked on the door, the servants of the house came to the entrance, to ask who was knocking on the door. He said to them, "It is I." They swiftly went to tell [the archdeacon], saying, "Theodore the archpriest is knocking on the door, he wants to see you."

Immediately another came and said that [the archpriest] was in the *monasterium*. And the archdeacon said, "What good will our talking do, since we will not arrive at an answer?" His servants said to him, "What is this, that you are angry? He is your own flesh; since he is your relative, speak with him, do not be separated. If the bishop had raged against you, would he bring forth words on your behalf?"

So [the archpriest] having entered the said *monasterium*, they spoke to each other; and before they separated, they said to each other, "How will our counsels, which we have spoken, be confirmed?" The archpriest said, "May Almighty God and this his apostle be mediators between us, and if one of us betrays the other, on the day of judgment God will require the cause of his deception." And the archdeacon answered, "Let it be done, let it be done thus. Such a bond has been confirmed between us, which neither of us will be able to transgress."[10]

[The archpriest said,] "Let all the priests of this see assemble at my *monasterium,* you convoke all the deacons and others of the church. Let us go to the church of St. Apollinaris, and entering the house of the man from Antioch, let us stand there and there hear masses. Let no one minister with [the bishop] today. Let us cast him off, that he might not be our shepherd." With these words, he left.

That night everyone went to the church of the blessed Virgin Mary to celebrate the rituals of the mass; and speaking secretly with each official, they agreed and said, "Would that it had been done earlier, that we might not have fallen into such need." With the masses completed in the church of the Apostles, with the rising of the dawn, when the Phoebean lights had brightened the earth, everyone hastened with one mind to the church of St. Apollinaris, which is located in the former city of Classe; and crying out they wailed with bitter spirit.

However it happened, after the ray of the sun had shone forth on the earth, that the said bishop sent his notary according to custom, to call the priests that they might proceed to the church and celebrate the mass. When he came, he found none of them; and having returned he told [the bishop]. But he said, "Perhaps they sleep, because last night they were tired, they are still sunk in slumber." Restraining him for about one hour of the day, again he sent the notary, and he did not find any of them, and he told [the bishop] that they were all gone. And [the bishop] said, "What is this? What time is it now? If they have not all come, let at least some of them come." But those attending him answered, one of them said to him, "Let not our lord master think otherwise than what I say: you will find none of your priests today to approach the altar with

---

10. The oaths "May almighty God" and "Such a bond" may be legal formulae; they are very similar to oaths taken in the story about the miraculous image *ad Brachium Forte,* told in c. 30; ibid., 99.

you in this celebration." And [the bishop] said, "Why?" And he said again, "Because all have traversed the paths of Caesarea, they have gone to St. Apollinaris, and there the priests, deacons, subdeacons, acolytes, *hostiarii,* readers, and singers are celebrating mass; with the rest of the clergy they have walked there; not even one of them is left; the church is empty, there is no keeper. They said that they were heavily afflicted, so they left."

Then he rose from the chair where he was sitting, he gave himself a blow on the forehead, saying, "Alas, I am conquered." Dragging sighs from the depth of his chest, lamenting to himself, he withdrew to his chamber. The people in the church, however, marveled, not knowing the cause of this.

122. With these things being laid in place, immediately the bishop sent noble men with swift horses, so that all, satisfied, might return to the church. [The clergy], when they saw them coming toward them, got up all at once, with their faces cast down to the ground, and in a great voice, before the legates of the bishop had spoken, said:

"Turn back, since we do not have a shepherd, but a killer. When he entered this sheepfold, he promised not to do as he has done. Rise, St. Apollinaris, celebrate with us the mass of the day of the nativity of the Lord. Holy Peter gave you to us as a shepherd. Therefore we are your sheep. We gather around you, save us. You did not receive consecration here, but the apostle himself blessed you with his hands and gave you the Holy Spirit; he directed you to us, and we received your preaching. You were sent to govern, not to destroy. You stand before the most impartial judge; strive for us, break the cruel jaws of the wolf, that you might lead us through the sweet pastures of Christ. If you do not arise and celebrate masses today for this Nativity, we will all together leave your house and hasten to Rome to blessed Peter your teacher, and cast ourselves down before him with lamentations, and with great mourning and immense grief and with great sighs say, 'We went to your disciple, our leader and preacher, whom you gave to us, and he did not want to celebrate masses on such a distinguished day as the birth of the Lord. Either deliver us from him, or give us a new shepherd, who will defend us from the mouth of the serpent who lives within our walls, and will comfort our afflictions. Behold you yourself, a good shepherd, know that many of your sheep have turned astray for great hardship and needy famine, and they have receded from the holy commandments and from your doctrine, with a most wicked leader suffocating them.' And if he will not hear us, then we will travel to Constantinople to the emperor and seek from him a father and shepherd."

And with these words there arose such a lamentation and huge grief on every side that those who had been sent by the bishop could scarcely say anything because of the excessive tears and murmurings of all those priests, and they could not fulfill their mission.

Then Theodore the archbishop, afraid, went sadly to the palace with great haste and told the exarch all that had happened to him with sorrow, saying, "My sheep have abandoned me, I am stripped of pastoral honor and repulsed and scorned. The flock of the Lord entrusted to me seeks another shepherd for itself; they have hastened to Classe, and having entered the church of St. Apollinaris, they accuse me before God and deride me."

The exarch at once sent noble men to call back all of the clergy, and [to say that] he would restore all their usages as they had been before. They however, indignant, began to weep and said, "If we go to Constantinople, we will also complain of this exarch, since he did not want to correct [the bishop] before this. We will not come, but up to the ninth hour we will wait for St. Apollinaris our bishop; but if he delays, we will go to Rome." And returning, pouring our great tears, [the nobles] told the bishop and the exarch what they had heard, and they lamented. They added that such grief and roaring resounded in that church as had ever been either heard or seen in all of Classe, "and hearing the voices of those sorrowing, we wept bitterly with them."

Then the archbishop, strongly struck with remorse, wanted to throw himself at the feet of the exarch; for he said with great grief, "I beseech your mercy, may it not trouble you to go there and to toil on my behalf, that you might engage for me to do all that was promised, as it pleases them, and of the property of the church I will share no more than one of them." Then the exarch ordered trappings to be placed on his horse, he mounted it, he came to the said tomb of the martyr, and calling everyone to him, he poured out soothing and pacifying words, and he brought them back with him, promising to emend all things, as you heard above. And they came and in the same hour celebrated mass and Vespers with the humbled bishop, as it was drawing toward evening.

123. On the next day the exarch came to the episcopal palace, and sat with the archbishop and all the priests, with the deacons standing behind their backs; together with the whole clergy of the church they stood in conflict. When there had been much controversy and words passed between them, the bishop was convicted, and at once all of the honors and dignities were restored, and the wealth of the church was allotted, and there was not one of them who did not have a certain portion of the church; even the bailiffs and suburban estates stolen from the servants of this church. And all joyfully hastened to their *monasteria*, and blessed God. Those things which formerly only the bishop had used, afterward were allotted to all, and from that day the following pact was established between bishop and priests, that before he was consecrated, [he would guarantee] through a formal promise that the servants of the church might have managerial responsibility.

124. After a short time that bishop, retaining the pain in his heart to bring down his priests, and remembering the evil that they had done to him, and since he could not, as he wanted, endow his relatives with the property of the church, he secretly sent a letter to Rome to Pope Agatho, suggesting that [the pope] should order him to come there as if for the purpose of bringing with him the holy churches of God into the catholic faith. [The pope] soon wrote a letter, saying that Bishop Theodore should hasten to Rome on behalf of the holy and inviolate catholic faith.[11] He showed the

---

11. Theodore is listed as a participant in the acts of the synod of Rome of 680, at which the Monothelete heresy was discussed, and he signed the letter from Pope Agatho to the Emperor Constantine. See Mansi, *Sacrorum conciliorum*, 11:235, 314.

letter, reading it in the presence of all his priests, he rolled it up and said to them, "What do you think? Behold you see the apostolic letter, and you know what it contains: how does it seem to you? I will not act outside of your will. Let us have one counsel, brothers, one will, one spirit, shall we go or stay?" They, responding in simplicity, not knowing the secret counsel, said, "It is fitting for us all to undergo the danger of death for the orthodox faith and the holy church of God."

However, when [Theodore] had arrived in Rome, he submitted himself and his church to the control of the Roman bishop. The Roman bishop, pleased that he had acquired what his predecessors had lost, received [Theodore] with thanks and agreed to whatever he wanted, and what [Theodore] sought was given by his will. When Pope Agatho died, [Theodore] poured all flattery on his successor Leo; and they made agreements between them that the priests should send whomever they chose from Ravenna to Rome, and [the pope] would consecrate him; they would remain at Rome in the time of the consecration not more than eight days; beyond this [the pope] might not come [to Ravenna], except on the day of the birth of the apostles he might send a legate from his priests; and the bishop of Ravenna would be quiet; and many other laws, which we cannot write, were confirmed through the hand of Leo with the priests.[12]

Therefore when this most arrogant one died on the eighteenth day of the month of January, with great eagerness of the priests and to the joy of everyone he was buried in the earth, he lies buried in the narthex of St. Apollinaris. I could not read his epitaph clearly. He sat thirteen years, three months, and twenty days.

---

12. Agnellus may have seen these *capitula*. Theodore's reconciliation with Pope Agatho is mentioned in the Roman *LP*'s Life of Pope Agatho. The revocation of the typus of autocephaly is recorded there also, in the Life of Pope Leo II.

CONCERNING HOLY DAMIAN, 692–708

125. Damian, the thirty-seventh bishop, short of body, not very fat, from this flock, he was consecrated at Rome,[1] a humble man, meek and dutiful. When he was ruling the bishopric, there was great peace among the priests and people. Listen to what our elders have reported to us.

It happened at that time, as I have heard told, that a certain woman came with her small infant, for the bishop to give him the Holy Spirit through the laying on of hands and the unction of chrism. He was being shaved, so his attendants said to the woman, "Wait, while he is being shaved." She however cried out, saying, "O what insanity, men! The boy is dying, and you do not want to aid his departing soul or report [to the bishop], and I am to remain silent? Run, tell the lord bishop, so that he might sign with the cross this little one before he dies, since he is close to the end, lest after the death of the boy you might be held culpable." While they went off and delayed, the boy died. Then the woman began to make a fuss and with great voices to cry and to stir up a drama, she spread the news to the crowd as if with the clash of trumpets.

The bishop, hearing these things, began to ask what was going on. And they wanted to cover up the facts of this thing, to turn the bishop from anger, and they could not. The woman exclaimed, "Behold I have been delayed here for many hours, and none of your attendants wanted to announce [to you], that you might sign the body with the cross; now his spirit is not in him. You see the dead body, how can it receive the protection of the Holy Spirit, O best leader?" Then the bishop, taking him in his arms, greatly groaning and weeping, entered behind the apse of the church, and prostrated himself with the infant flat on the ground weeping and praying for the longest time, invoking the heavenly Lord. By his prayers, the soul was returned to the boy in his vitals, and having been signed with the cross, he gave up his spirit.

Now at that time the said Johannicis returned from Con-

---

1. Cf. *LP,* Life of Sergius, c. 13.

stantinople to Ravenna, and his wisdom was famed in all of Italy.

126. Indeed, brothers, we are always on our guard, like soldiers in readiness for battle; and when we hear of the miracles of our Almighty God, we are pleased that he has deigned to raise the sinners to his kingdom; and when we hear that the devil has injured someone and caught him in his traps, we are saddened, since that captive did not strive strongly against the invisible enemy. But no one can threaten [the devil] unless he is fortified by a heavenly shield. If it does not disgust you to stay, you will hear what sort of deeds of craftiness that equivocator, who wanted himself to be the highest and derided the Son of God, sowed in the reign of this bishop in this city.

In former times a custom arose, which up to today is a thing to be abhorred and feared, dragged away, wicked; and it remains up to today.[2] On every Sunday or day of the Apostles the citizens of Ravenna, not only the illustrious but men of different ages, youths and adolescents, middle-aged and young, of both sexes, as we said, after lunch go out through the various gates as a body and proceed to fight. They are delirious and insane, since for no reason they put each other to death.

127. It happened at that time, as we said, that those of the Teguriensan Gate entered the contest against those of the gate [*posterula*] which is called the *Summus Vicus*, next to the *fossa Lamisem*. The Posterulans, having entered in the first wave, were pursued by sling-shooters and ran away. The Teguriensans following them laid many bodies on the ground, and came to the said gate; they threatened those left inside and broke the bolts and bars, after which in their victory they returned home.

And after eight days, on Sunday they exited by each gate again; and boys [were playing] with small hoops, as was their custom, but leaving games behind, rushing on each other broke their heads with staffs. Some killed each other from afar with stones hurled from their hands; others terrified by the noise of the slings fled

---

2. For a complete analysis of the rhetorical devices used in the story in cc. 126–29, as well as the sources for some of them, see Pizarro, *Writing Ravenna*, 141–58.

to different places; others here and there, girded with youthful weapons, entered into battles against old men as if equal in age. And there was not any respite.

On every side the crowd from the side of the *posterula* died, falling by the sword; for some were left half alive, and hot rivers of dark blood flowed from their breasts, and there were others from whose open mouths rosy blood emanated; and many poured gore out of their bodies from very large wounds, and with mouths eating the dirt breathed out their spirits. Whoever asked for life from his enemies, saying, "Alas my soul, my soul," the attack ceased, and he was not killed. And thus even now, he who resigns himself to die and asks life for his soul is allowed to live and is not struck further. And a great blow was struck in that region, as had never been done from former times, as our elders can remember. Behold the first disaster and grief and woe in that region; but the second disaster and slaughter was to cause the greatest lamentation.

128. When these things had happened, after these battles there was a short respite. The most pernicious devil and invisible enemy, envious of the human race, excited the hearts of the Posterulans, like someone knocking on a door, and thus daily their hearts were devoured.

When they had all taken counsel as to how they might kill and completely eradicate the Teguriensan men, each one said to his compadre and his messmate, "Why are we still alive? Behold the Teguriensans have killed all our comrades, and will strive to kill us on Sunday. We leave our sons orphans, we do not know whom they will have to serve; our wives will be widows; our enemies will devour all our property. Why do we yet live? Are we the bravest hearts in war?" And with voices raised they all wept. After their grief was laid aside, they said, "Come, let us ambush them. Let us secretly prepare grievous tricks against them and fashion wicked words and deceive them in false humility."

On the following Sunday, in the Ursiana church, the Posterulan men secretly asked that the Teguriensans should have lunch with them, and they requested that no one should know. With the divine words finished, each one went to his host, and scattered through individual mansions and through various feasts, they approached death. Some were committed to the earth, brought down by daggers; others, struck in the head by axes, were buried in stables under the dung of horses, so that no sign of their murder might be found; some were pierced in the legs by cast spears; and others were thrown into sewers stripped of their fluttering garments; some, rushing on double-pointed swords ended the day and their lives; many, struck by flying spears and cast in ditches, were covered by mud. The miserable Teguriensans were killed by the Posterulans with different punishments, and it was done secretly, so that none of their friends might recognize any sign of murder or burial.

On the next day there was great grief and sorrow everywhere, the whole city was frozen in grief. The baths were closed, the public spectacles stopped, traveling merchants removed their shoes, innkeepers closed their taverns, traders left their business, the priests groaned in the churches, the elders bewailed, all the youths were sorrowing in the streets, every husband raised a lament, and the matrons sorrowed on their marital beds, and the widows were clothed in weeds, the beauty of the virgins was altered, the children shook greatly with sobs, all were afflicted in bitterness of soul.

Some lamented for the unknown death of a father; others looked for their sons, not knowing if they had run away; some were ignorant of the fate of their brothers; others looking for their husbands knew nothing for certain; and each walked here and there on the various streets, and searching they found none of them. These were the words of the mourners, "If indeed the earth absorbed them, perhaps someone would have seen their bodies; if they were drowned in the depth of the sea, the waves would have returned their bodies to us; if beasts had devoured them, they would not have swallowed their bones; if someone had killed them with a sword, surely the gore would show us their death." And the grieving people conjectured many other things, lying on the ground, tearing out hair and beards, biting their fingernails, tearing their clothes at the breast, lamenting brothers and relations, sons and nephews, seeking lost relatives, all the citizens ended the week in lamentation.

129. Then the holy man Damian, seeing this city bogged down in such grief, gave himself up to greatest laments. On that Sunday he declared a fast, and on Monday, Tuesday, and Wednesday he prayed incessantly to God, that this slaughter might be revealed to someone who was helped by divine aid from heaven.

The bishop ordered the people to form separate processions. He stood with the clerics and monks on one side; he ordered the laity, old men, adolescents and boys, together to form one chorus; and the women, married and unmarried, widows and girls, in another part; and the crowd of the paupers separately. They did not all walk together as one, but separately, a stone's throw apart.[3]

The priests, with holy vestments put aside, were wearing sackcloth, and they walked barefoot with ash scattered on their heads. All the nobles and commoners covered themselves with hair shirts, they walked sorrowing with uncombed heads and filthy beards. The matrons, with their pleasant clothing laid by, wore the garments of grief. All cropped their heads and bared their skin. The beauty of the virgins was removed; they took off their changing clothes and capes and cast away from them earrings and rings and bracelets and anklets and necklaces and perfumes and pins and mirrors and crescents and emerald necklets and *laudosias*[4] and ornaments, and all pleasant and desirable things cast away, they were clothed in a song of lamentation.[5]

The infants hung from the breasts of their mothers; the lamentation of men, the crying of children, the weeping of mothers, the roaring of the cows, the neighing of the horses, the bleating of sheep, and [the noise] of other women and animals, all the city cried together.

Three days of this affliction having passed, before the rising of

---

3. A very similar account of a divided procession organized by Pope Gregory I in order to free Rome from the plague is found in Paul the Deacon, *Historia Langobardorum* 3.24. A longer version is found in Gregory of Tours, *Historia Francorum* 10.1. See Pizarro, *Writing Ravenna*, 155.

4. The latter's meaning is unknown; Holder-Egger suggests that it was corrupted from *sandalias*.

5. Cf. Isa. 3:17–24.

the sun the almighty God, who reveals the depths of the shadows and brings hidden things into the light, made miracles, such as have never been heard among the nations. From the amphitheatre, which in former times was next to the gate which is called Golden, up to the said *Posterula* there was a sort of rustling and a great sound, and smoke was raised like a cloud; and the earth opened, showing with a great stench all the dead which had been closed in its bosom, whom the Posterulans had destroyed. Then the people, having heard the sound, running toward the stench, each found their dead in individual houses, with worms feeding in the wounds.

Then they arrested the homicides, they judged that for their deeds it was fit that that region with its buildings be overthrown; and they reduced it to nothing, and they called that region "of the Criminals" up to this day. Not only they, but their wives and sons underwent various kinds of punishment. No one wanted to touch any of their property, but it was given to the pyre at the bridge which is called Milvian, which afterward was broken down, and it was in that region of the Criminals next to the apse of the *monasterium* of Severinus the blessed confessor of Christ.[6]

130. There was in this city of Ravenna a very religious man of good report; and when he came to the Ursiana church, his shoulders clung to the upper part of a column of the temple on the men's [south] side. Before the introit of the mass he sang psalms, he never had discussions with any man, and after the entrance of the mass he always gazed at the face of the bishop.

On a certain day the bishop ordered him to approach for the benediction of St. Apollinaris, that he might be a participant at the table of the bishop. After his stomach was filled with the feast and the fibers of his heart were replete with new wine, but with a sober mind, the bishop asked him why he always looked in his face

---

6. Agnellus makes the story explain the name of this part of the city, much as the story in c. 30 explains the designation *ad Brachium Forte*. However, Lanzoni, "La 'regio Latronum,'" doubts that this event was the origin of the name *regio Latronum* and suggests instead that the word *latro* originally meant "soldier of the bodyguard" and that this area was named because a corps of guards was stationed here.

at church. But he answered, saying, "I do not gaze at you, best of bishops, but rather at him who stands behind your back, whose beauty I can hardly bear. And when you sanctify, he stands next to you. Your face now is not like his, who is always with you at the celebration of the mass and never leaves you."

After a few days [this man] died in peace; and some heard him saying before the time of his death that on a certain Sunday, when at night everyone sang the antiphon to the benedictions and said, "Mountains and hills sang praises before God,"[7] he swore that the stones of the church, columns and slabs and bricks, the roof tiles likewise and even all the marble, also sang the said antiphon along with all the people. Therefore after this man was buried, the bishop ordered the said column to be surrounded by a small screen, lest any part of the base of the column, where the holy feet had stood, should be worn away by unworthy feet, and he ordered a small cross to be fixed there for an eternal memorial, which remains up to the present day.

131. But let us not pass over John, abbot of the *monasterium* of St. John which is called *ad Titum*, located across Caesarea in the former city of Classe.[8]

There was in the times of this Bishop Damian a priest by the name of John, abbot of the *monasterium* of St. John which is called *ad Titum*, which the ignorant rustics call *ad Pinum*. Since he had many altercations and legal struggles with various men over the property of his *monasterium* of blessed John and no end was in sight, but many greatly wanted to unjustly devour the farms of the *monasterium*, this said priest went to Constantinople, and, waiting there for many days, he did not see the face of the emperor.

Pondering various plans, on a certain day he stood below, next to the wall of the chamber where the emperor was sitting above, and spoke about the arrival of the herald of the Lord, "He that is

---

7. Isa. 55:12.
8. Aspects of this story, in particular a miraculous instantaneous transport to Constantinople, is found in the ninth-century *Vita Leonis thaumaturgi, episcopi Cataniae* (*BHG* 981); see Lanzoni, "Ancóra sulle leggende orientali."

to come, will come, and will not delay; in His hand are the kingdom and the power and the empire."[9] The emperor, hearing these things, was taking pleasure in listening. And the doorkeeper went and wanted to remove him from that place; and the emperor from above ordered that no one should disturb him, until he had finished.

And with the whole of the Invitatory finished, he called him up; and he stood before the emperor and he set out in order the case about which he had come. And the emperor ordered an edict to be written, so that the property would belong to that *monasterium* in perpetuity and that this statute should be an eternal law.

After this, the said priest John prostrated himself at his feet for a long time, weeping and saying, "Let my lord order a letter to be written for me to the exarch, so that my guarantor might not incur obligations, since tomorrow will be the day agreed in the document that I should stand with my adversary in debate." And the emperor obeyed his request, and ordered a letter written to the exarch, that there might be no distinction regarding this case: no one might lead him into judgment, nor might the guarantor incur obligations, nor trouble him in any way.

With the letter written, and with the month, the day and the hour sealed, given into his hands, he left and came at twilight to the port of that city of Constantinople, so that by chance he might find the use of a ship sailing to Ravenna or to Sicily. And having asked all the riverboats and chelandia and dromons,[10] he did not find one.

He took a path next to the shore of the sea. Night, stretching her black wings over him, seemed unfriendly. Although the shadows displeased him, nevertheless the moon's thin rays seemed a kindness to him; and the higher she raised herself toward the summit, the clearer the earth appeared.

While he walked along the shore and wondered what he should

---

9. Heb. 10:37; Dan. 7:14; Isa. 62:3. See Lanzoni, "Reliquie della liturgia ravennate," 246.

10. Chelandia and dromons are Greek names for boats.

do, before his eyes appeared three men in black clothing, and they said to him, "Why, abbot John, do you walk with disturbed mind on this shore?" He answered, saying, "All those things that I sought from the emperor I have obtained; but I have lingered much time, there is no ship in which to return to Ravenna, thus I am filled with sadness." The wicked men said to him, "If you do those things which we say to you, tomorrow you will be in your house among your servants." So he said to them, "I will do what you want."

And they said, "Take this wand in your hand and draw in the sand a ship, then a sail, oars, lifeboats and sailors." He did this, as he had been ordered. Again [they] said to him, "Lie in the hull of the ship, in the bilge-water area next to the keel. You will hear the roaring of the winds, after you have entered the sea, you will hear voices warning of dangers, and you will hear storms and horrors, you will hear sounds of waters pouring in; but nevertheless stop up your mouth, and do not let your hand make even the sign of the cross." He lay on the ground looking out at the sea next to him. Behold everywhere suddenly a sound was made like the breaking of the clouds and like a tempestuous storm; the wind roared, the sea shook its own waves. The oars were broken, the masts were felled, the skiffs were released, the blackest sailors gave most terrified groans, and the abbot so held himself in check that no one could even hear his breathing.

At cock-crow he found himself on the roof of his *monasterium*; and seeing himself alone, he cried in a great voice to his attendants, to remove him from off the roof. They, thinking him an apparition, did not want to obey the commands of their lord. Then he cried in a great voice, naming each of them, saying, "Take me down, and you will know that it is I. You know that I was in Constantinople for the benefit of this *monasterium*, and now I am come [back]; do not be afraid, but know that I am cast hither by strong winds." They, having heard these words, swiftly placed ladders, and he descended. He was recognized by them, and having been kissed by them all in order, he ordered them to strike the tablet, saying, "Now it is the hour for matins," and after the divine Office was finished, sleep overtook him.

132. At the dawning of the next day, he left, having traversed Caesarea, and from the Wandalarian gate, which is near the Caesarean gate, having passed the Laurentian palace,[11] he entered the [palace of] Theodoric, and he asked to be presented to the exarch. He received him with joyful spirit, and ordered the edict to be read; and he returned it folded to the priest who had offered it to him, and said to him, "Let this edict be your protection in perpetuity for you and your posterity. I will give the *sponsio* to your guarantor, since you were negligent in having dealings with your adversary." He, responding to these things, said, "The lord our emperor has confirmed his edict in a letter, that all my obligations might be made invalid in court."

Then the exarch, angered, received the letter from the hand of the priest and read it, he found written that which we have said above, and keeping the letter, enraged, burst out, saying, "Tell us, author of falsity, when was this letter written?" John the priest responded, "Yesterday in the ninth hour." The exarch said, "And where could you have got to so swiftly? Because there is no one who can go to Constantinople and return in three months." "How I returned," said the priest, "I will tell my bishop; it remains equally my business and my repentance within me. However if you accuse me of falsity, send your legates with me, and let us hasten there. If these things are found false, hear the matter defined as it appears."

Then setting out from there, he came to the episcopal palace of this church, and having entered the presence of Bishop Damian, he cast himself at his feet and told him all the facts of the case; and he revealed how apparitions had led him through the difficulties of the sea and had placed him on the roof of his *monasterium* and had left him there alone. However at the encouragement of the bishop he made true repentance, and he finished his days in peace.

133. I beseech you, brothers, that it might not trouble you to stay, since one miracle remains.[12]

---

11. The palace here called "Laurenti" must refer either too the *palatium ad Laureta* of c. 40 or to a palace built near the church of St. Laurence by Lauricius, c. 35.

12. Aspects of the following story are found in a legend of the conversion of an Islamic youth, *BHG* 690; see Lanzoni, "Leggende Orientali."

On a certain Sunday after the end of the Sunday prayer, the said bishop broke the body of the Lord with the priests, as they were accustomed to do. A certain Jew, who was accustomed to stand near the virgins in the place which is called Ermolas,[13] ran swiftly, hastening to the holy altar, and said to the bishop, "I beseech you, excellent bishop, give me part of the body of the lamb which now is pulled apart by your hands." To him the high priest said, "It is not permitted to share the body of the Lord with you, since you are not washed with holy baptism." Again the Jew, "I do not seek holy bread from you, father, but the flesh of the lamb, which you pull apart with your hands, which I see you touching on this altar with my human eyes. I seek the lamb which I see; I do not desire bread, since I do not see it." To this the holy man answered, saying, "We cannot give the holy to the unclean, until such a one is cleansed by holy water. Receive the sign of the Lamb, and eat of the Lamb with us."

And at once the Jew gave up his name, and, instructed by the bishop, he received immortal baptism and from infidelity was made a believer.

134. This bishop was from the area near Dalmatia, but his parents offered him to this church. And, learned in sacred letters, he arrived at the summit of this church. He lived in the reign of the Emperor Constantine.[14]

In that time the archive of this church[15] was destroyed by fire, and the flame consumed many documents, and many were seized and hidden by wicked men. Then with all the priests gathered together, the said bishop sat with them in a tavern, and gave anathemas of malediction, that whoever had any of the said documents

---

13. What this location means is unclear, whether "Ermolas" was a location within the church (but then why would a Jew be permitted to stand with the virgins?) or a location in the city that had a convent. Nauerth, *Agnellus von Ravenna: Liber pontificalis*, 485, n. 551, suggests that "Ermolas" is a corruption of "hermula" and refers to a row of herms that once stood outdoors.

14. This is incorrect. Damian reigned 691–707; Constantine IV died in 685, and the emperors during Damian's reign were Justinian II, Leontius, and Tiberius III.

15. The *archivus ecclesiae* is also mentioned in c. 111.

258   BOOK OF PONTIFFS OF THE CHURCH OF RAVENNA

and did not return them, he would be anathema, and whoever returned them, he would be innocent of blame.

This most blessed man died on May 13. You will find his epitaph on his tomb containing the following:[16]

> Always sanctifying by your merits, notable priest, you lie placed in this tomb, O Damian. Although you have died in body, your fame lives on; though your limbs are buried in earth, the light holds your deeds. Blessed bishop coming from the land of Dalmatia [5], you preserved holy Ravenna by your prayers. Governing all the world in a more propitious age, faithful Christ gave you to his praying people.
>
> Such a tomb proves that you merited a grave in these temples, that you pleased God [10]. And since as a priest you carried out his duties correctly, may you have holy rest in his grounds.

We find this written inside the church of St. Apollinaris over his tomb. He sat sixteen years, two months, sixteen days.

CONCERNING HOLY FELIX, 709–25

136.[1] Felix, the thirty-eighth bishop. He had a short body, a narrow face, small eyes, a thin figure, his spirit was full of wisdom and he was a refreshing fountain, an excellent father, a noble preacher, the author of many volumes, fruitful in his holy church.

He wrote the exposition on the Day of Judgment which we still have now, where it says in the gospel, "When you shall see the abomination."[2] And this alone was saved by the priests, for all the remaining volumes he burned with his own hands by fire.[3] He was in charge of the *monasterium* of St. Bartholemew, where I, by God's favor, am abbot, and he held most brilliantly the charge of the of-

---

16. The wording of this epitaph is almost identical to that of Marinian, in c. 103.

1. There is no c. 135 in Holder-Egger's edition, whose chapter numbers are used here.
2. Matt. 24:15.
3. This *expositum* may be included in the *LPR*, as the sermonette in c. 166.

fice of *vicedominus*. After many tribulations which he sustained in Constantinople, as you will hear, the Lord recalled him with the crown of victory to his own see.[4]

And thus it happened to me with my own *monasterium*. I was without cause deprived of this *monasterium* by Bishop George for a few years. Before he had ascended to that high position, we were to each other like two brothers from one womb; and after he accepted the metropolitan dignity he offended God, he brought down all the priests, seizing all the *monasteria*, and he spent all the treasure of the church, which his predecessors had acquired, for the guilt of his own person.[5]

137. In [Felix's] reign, the nose and ears of the emperor [Justinian][6] were cut off by his soldiers, together with some citizens of Ravenna; they reduced the excellence of his body, and, expelled from the palace, he was cast out on the shore, and they wanted to behead him. But after his limbs were mutilated he begged for life, claiming he had forgotten the whole empire. After these events, while he was wandering, maimed, along the coast, having taken counsel with the Bulgarians, he was restored to his throne; and having retaken the empire, he made for himself a nose and ears of gold.

Remembering the anger of the people, he ordered the leaders to be beheaded by the sword. A huge noise[7] was made by the elders,

---

4. In the Roman *LP* Felix is said to have been consecrated by Pope Constantine, who began his reign on March 3, 708. The *LP* says that Felix rebelled against the pope and was punished by being captured by the emperor and blinded (Life of Constantine). Agnellus knew of the *LP*'s account of these events and provides the Ravennate version of them, in the process making Felix appear as a sort of martyr.

5. Agnellus's quarrel with his former friend, Bishop George, here explicitly described, personalized his arguments over the rights of the clergy against episcopal encroachment, and may be responsible for several of the specifically anti-episcopal statements and sermonettes.

6. In the manuscript the name "Constantine" is found here, but the story is about the emperor Justinian II.

7. This narrative contains language that seems to be derived from Vergil's *Aeneid*; for the specific references, see Deliyannis, *CCCM* edition of the *LPR*, apparatus. The most detailed study of Vergilianisms in the *LPR* is Tamassia and Ussani, "Epica

with their youth destroyed, and many lost their heads on their own thresholds; some, shrieking, were stabbed to the hilt in their tangled intestines; some, cast into the sea in sacks, were consumed in the deep; many were burned to the quick in the flames of a pyre; other unfortunates, undone, sought their intestines as lunches;[8] some received lead punishments, the tyrant received many *nicopos* from these;[9] and everywhere cities were consumed.

Pondering, he turned his thoughts back to Ravenna, and thinking many things throughout the night, saying such things to himself: "Alas, what shall I do, and what shall I initiate against Ravenna?" And his mind, looking at his soul, wandering through many ideas, takes him alternately through different thoughts. He secretly calls his faithful commander to fit out a vessel, to lead his comrades to the shore, and to provide expenses. And of what this thing might be, he is to be entirely ignorant; he orders him to dissimulate, until it should be the right time. Then he speaks to him and gives these commands, "Be resolute in obeying my commands, act firmly, and go as my messenger; speak to the Ravennates and quickly report my words. These people inimical to me, through fraudulent counsel, have cut off my nose and ears. Place your tent on the bank of the river Po, and send out kind words and hide anger behind a smooth face, and extend salutatory words from me to them, and give gifts and invite them to celebrations of the table. In their eyes be friendly, in your heart be an enemy."

Having left the city, he got to the ship and ordered the sails to be unfurled, and he sat on the thwart and plowed the salty waves with the keel. Having passed the port of Trapani, he came to Pachino on the coast of Sicily.[10] With the sea raging, with a cloud

---

e storia," although their conclusions about Agnellus's sources for these stories is doubtful; see, most recently, Pizarro, *Writing Ravenna*, 183–88.

8. I.e., were starved to death so that, like Erysichthon, they devoured their own bodies?

9. *Nicopos* is an unknown word. The entire passage is so garbled, and contains so many obscure words, that it is not possible to arrive at a definite reading.

10. These locations are found in the *Aeneid*. Holder-Egger (*LPER*, 368, n. 1) notes that a ship sailing from Constantinople to Ravenna probably would not have passed

over the deep waters, with Orion setting in the sea, the sky immutable, unwillingly he was delayed in that place. When he saw that the sea and waves were calm and the sea tranquil, penetrating the curve of the Adriatic, rejoicing he saw Ravenna, and deceiving with guile, his voice burst forth, saying, "O Ravenna, alone unhappy and cruel, who outside has fields, but hides bitterest venom within! You seem to be leveled to the ground, although your head now touches the clouds."

With these words the ship reached the shore and with oars outstretched it plowed the bank of the Po; and all the people went out of the city with glory, since the commander of the Greeks had come from the noble palace; and he ordered seats to be prepared for them on the greenest grass, and inviting all those noble by birth, he received them in the apparent spirit of a man of good will. On the next day he ordered various hangings to extend from either side to form an enclosed area, for one whole stade, and invited all the leaders who came to his threshold to be introduced to him two by two. And arresting them, they put wooden wedges in their mouths and bound their heads behind their backs, and they were cast into the hull of the ship. By such trickery all the nobles were captured.

And then Felix, bishop of this city, was deceived, and then most wise Johannicis was captured, and then many lesser men were conquered, and none of the citizens could have known this trick sooner, but after they entered the hollow beams of oak, and they tried to flee, then the ruinous trick was revealed. Then the remainder [of the soldiers], entering the city walls, lit a fire beneath the citizens. There were riots of the people, and their roar went up into the sky. There was a great noise everywhere; all were prostrate on the ground. The marine wave does not make similar sounds, nor the

---

through Trapani (*Aeneid* 3.707) in northwest Sicily, even if the sailing route had taken the ship to Pachino (*Aeneid* 3.429) on Sicily's southeast corner. Tamassia and Ussani, "Epica e storia," 19, n. 5, observe that in the Roman *LP*, the man who is sent to punish the Ravennate citizens is Theodore the *strategos* of Sicily. However, below, in c. 145, the same cities are mentioned again, in the context of Felix's return from Constantinople, making it more likely that here too they are rhetorical devices.

clouds with thunder, nor when a great avalanche falls from an Alpine summit, nor when the cypresses are shaken in the mountainous woods by a great wind. Trumpeters wandered through the streets, they gave forth great noises, and they resounded in the earth. With great fear of the present commotion [the people] poured out salty tears; there was no consolation nor restoration to life. Everywhere noise, everywhere sighs, and even the earth groaned at their sounds.

138. One day, while the kidnappers and exiles raced through the glassy seas, fifty [days] after the destruction in the city of Classe, Johannicis said to his brother, "Bring parchment and ink and write, since today in the third hour your sister-in-law, my wife, has died; and I will be punished there, and you will return with greatest wealth."[11]

When they had entered Constantinople, they found the emperor Justinian sitting in a gold and emerald seat, and wearing on his head a crown, which his royal wife had decorated for him with gold and pearls. And he ordered them all to be placed in custody, until he could mete out various punishments against them. And all the more important senators were now killed and destroyed, and he added to his crimes by swearing that he would kill the bishop.

That night, before day had come, before dawn had touched the ocean and had lit the lamps of the sun, while the divine emperor retained peaceful sleep in his breast, a most noble youth stood before him, decorated with all glory, together with Bishop Felix, and said to him, "Spare this one man from the sword." And at once he vanished. Again returning to sleep he saw above the head of this bishop something like the right hand of that man, gleaming here and there with light.

However the emperor, awakened, told this to his attendants; and because of the oath which he had sworn, so that he should not have lied and the city-dwellers might not kill him, he ordered a great tray to be brought made of purest silver, and after sending it

---

11. Is this statement supposed to imply that Felix was Johannicis's brother-in-law? Given the subsequent events, it is possible.

to be heated up on a great pyre, he ordered the bitterest acid to be poured on it; and the bishop, compelled to look at it for a very long time, lost the sight of both his eyes.

139. Meanwhile the Ravennate citizens, also known as the Melisenses, uncertain of their captured ones, exchanged various words, and were greatly sunk in sorrowful grief from the bitterly wicked day.

One day, with dawn arriving, before dewy night had folded her wings, driven off by the [sun's] chariot, while armed men were looking out on the sea, gazing far away over the waves, behold a great ship hastening through the glassy expanses, and bravely plowing the glassy fields. After the pilot saw the walls of the city, he turned his rudder, he began to turn around the course of the ship, he passed by the harbor, clinging to the shore of the Po.

At its arrival all the men went out of the city carrying weapons, wearing armor on their bodies. Fear striking their hearts, all colors gone pale, they recognized the captives, and both sides wept. And they asked a man from among them, who was in charge of them all, and they said to him, "We charge you by your head and your soul, do not fabricate lies, since faith is not complete in this time, but fraud and perjury rule in this present age."

Then, extending his hands to the stars and turning his eyes to heaven, he spoke with a great groan, "I call to witness heaven and earth through the undefiled faith and the inviolate heavenly kingdom, I do not fabricate lies or speak false nonsense—the liar and wicked one always esteems lies." He spoke, and everyone, intent, became silent, their faces were hanging around him, and all the rows [of people] around were watching him; he explained to them what he had seen, all fatal words. And they wept with raised voices; the noise struck the heavens, and the earth groaned and the mountains resounded.

140. Then the Ravennates chose a man outstanding among them, the legitimate son of Johannicis, by the name of George, who at that time was wise in speech, provident in counsel, true in words and very fine in all grace. And they all devoted themselves equally to his commands, and anyone who was disobedient was

punished. Seated on a dun-colored horse, having crossed the parts of Italy outside [the city], he returned at the sixth hour, and said to his companions:

"Let us place guards in the cities through which we have just passed. For I confess that we have all drunk foul poison from the mouth of the serpent, which was brought from the Byzantine sea. And let us not flee from the Greeks, who are swollen in heart. Be faithful! If necessary, prepare your spirits and present brave and iron breasts to the battle; encourage your comrades and make a noise with the terrible trumpet. Go quickly, tell the citizens; under cover of night let our allies come down from the mountainous places. Put poison on your weapons, stretch the twisted sinews of the stag, throw javelins and flying wood in clumps. Let youth first break camp with youthful arms; let the weapons resound, let shining shields glow on arms, throw spears, let the waters of the sea shine with their gleam. Spare the aged bodies of your parents, and pity the old age of the elderly. Let the church be their refuge, their part be prayer, let them go in with the priests, let them seek heavenly aid and burn frankincense at the altar and bear the host to the holy altar. Through the day the fire-formed one [the sun] stands against us on the ramparts, crimson at its birth, but then carried in the air, leaving the ocean; but when it is present pouring out fiery rays in the sky, when it returns to earth in its chariots, then seek poplar trees and fall on them with bare iron, let some take the double-edged axes, cut unshorn viburnum trees, weave their woody twigs and mix in the oak; give work to the tent-makers.[12] Protect your heads from the heat. Let no one be cowardly; when the first sign is given, no fear or thought will betray anyone.

"Let all the factions of Ravenna and everyone [else] lay aside their quarrels. He who is strong in running and he who has heartfelt daring in his powers, let him not be lazy, nor lukewarmly cast his arrows. Seeing this, they prepare their allied spirits for battle. Do not be afraid to defend the walls with your right hands; allies will come to you from all the suburban districts, in order to defend

---

12. About Agnellus's use of the word *scenofactor* (tent maker), see Glossary, s.v.

our stronghold and save our city. Let the coasts be secure and the ports guarded by all. Let Sarsina keep watch; let Cervia stand at arms by the sea at Nova, Papia at the sandy curve which is called Cesena; let the men of Forlimpopoli keep to the port of Savio, let them take a stand next to the marine waves; let the tax-paying farmers keep watch next to the port of Candiano; let the neighboring men of Forli place themselves in the curved shore; at the old stream of Beden to let the troops of Faenza watch behind the port of Lacherno and the banks of the Po; let the soldiers of Imola cover the Coriandrum Field and all the places around it; let the armed divisions of Bologna, having crossed the Po, keep watch over the palisade of the Lion Port."[13]

With these things done, everyone sent their voices to the stars, they blessed to the heavens and made the earth resound with praises. Then George gestures with his hand, he orders the loud voices to be silenced. After this the religious men of Ravenna asked him that, just as the city was fortified with a ring all around it, thus he might place watchmen inside. And he agreed to their petition and divided the people of the city in eleven parts; the twelfth part was reserved for the church. And each soldier is to march according to his militia and cohort, that is: Ravenna, First Banner, Second Banner, New Banner, Unconquered, Constantinopolitan, Strong, Joyful, Milanese, Veronese, Classensian, and the parts of the bishop with clergy, those not worthy in honor or family, and servants or others belonging to the churches. And this ordering remains up to the present day.[14]

141. Let us turn our pen back to the other city and tell in order about our lost citizens.

Justinian, having become enraged, ordered Johannicis to be brought into his presence; as if ignorant he asked him ironically,

---

13. For an analysis of what the places named in this passage tell us about relations between Ravenna and the subordinate cities in the region in the eighth and ninth centuries, see Guillou, "Esarcato e Pentapoli," 298–99; and, with a map showing the locations, Fabbri, "Il controllo delle acque," 22 and plate 4.

14. About the military organization of Ravenna, see esp. Deichmann, *Ravenna* 2.3:104–7, and Brown, *Gentlemen and Officers*, 90 and 97.

"Is this indeed Johannicis the scribe?" And when he answered that it was he, the imperial rage rose yet higher. He ordered a reed to be brought and he ordered that it be forced under all the nails of his fingers[15] up to the second joint.

He then ordered parchment and pen to be given, that [Johannicis] might write. When he received it, he forced the pen between two fingers. He did not write with ink, but with the blood which flowed from his fingers, he wrote letters containing the following, "God, be my helper. Lord, hasten to my aid. Free me from my enemies, my God, and from the hand of this wicked emperor." And he threw the page in the face of that emperor sitting on his throne, saying, "Take this, wickedest one, and satiate yourself with my blood." So the emperor threatened him, saying, "What are you doing, you who are about to die? Your audacity will perish."

And he ordered the servants to lead [Johannicis] to the place of execution, and he ordered the herald to cry, "Johannicis the Ravennate, that eloquent poet, since he was against the most unconquered emperor, he shall die a mouse's death between two arches." Those chosen [for the job] having surrounded his neck, putting bars in iron rings, struggling they raised a stone over him. He however turned his flaming eyes to heaven, extending his hands, bloody with gore, to the stars. Having finished his prayer, he said to his killers, "Tomorrow, in the same hour as it is now, you will kill your emperor, and he will stand with me before the most righteous judge. You will tell him so." And with his body stretched out on one rock, yet living, with his neck stretched out, another slab on top of him broke his body, and they left him dead. In such torment and martyrdom he finished his life.[16]

142. On the next day, at the hour which he had predicted, the people, not tolerating his wickedness, rushed on the emperor and

---

15. Tjäder, "Die Bestrafung des Notars Johannicius," notes that having a reed pen thrust up the fingernails is a very appropriate punishment for a scribe.

16. For discussions of the Life of Johannicis, see Hartmann, "Johannicius von Ravenna," Tjäder, "Die Bestrafung des Notars Johannicius," and most comprehensively, Pizarro, *Writing Ravenna*, 171–88, who points out the many similarities between this story and that of Boethius and Theodoric.

killed him. Some thrust lances in his side into his intestines, others pierced his groin and kidney with spears. He vomited blood, and with his hair scattered in the hall, with feet bound with tow, dragged down a slope, mangled, gloomy death rushed his frigid body into the shadows. Various people looked around at each other; one of them snatched a sword, clutching the hair in his hand, struck off the imperial head, making a terrible noise with the vibrating iron, he threw the body to the ground. And having discussed it among themselves, they put [the head] in a sack and sent it through all of Italy.

And the sister of the said Johannicis, hearing this, asked the heavenly Lord with tears only that she might see the head of Justinian severed, as rumor had it, and at once she would fall down in death. It happened, however, when the said head was led through each of the streets, fixed on the point of a lance, it was announced to the above-mentioned woman that the cut-off head would be brought there. She at once went upstairs in her house; looking out of the window, she asked the bearer to stand still; and when she had gazed on it for the longest time, as tears welled up, she filled her heart, giving thanks to God, that she had seen what she desired. And when she wanted to turn away from the window, she fell backwards and died, shattered.[17]

143. After the death of the emperor Justinian, the Greeks raised up a new emperor over them, and they made him lord of the whole earth, and the empire was confirmed in his hand.

He said to Bishop Felix, "Return to your land and your see." The bishop, responding to him, said, "Wherefore shall I return, or where shall I go?" And the emperor to him, "And why not? For what reason?" The bishop replied, "I have lost the sight of my eyes. All the wealth of my church was destroyed here, and they took away what your predecessors, faithful princes, gave in ornaments to the church; they were brought within this city, and nothing remains there except the circuit of the walls." The emperor said

---

17. This peculiar story seems as though it should have a moral, but it lacks one; in fact, it is similar to another story in c. 163.

to him, "Who took them away? If you no longer have your own property, take from ours." And Bishop Felix said to him, "My own property will suffice, if you order returned those various things which various people took away."

Then the emperor, moved by pity, ordered the herald to cry through the whole city that whoever had anything from the church of Ravenna should swiftly bring it to the palace. And vases and hangings were brought, and the bishop received all the ornaments of the church. And nothing was missing from them except one candelabrum. After these things, the emperor asked the bishop to receive some gift from his palace. Answering him, [Felix] said, "Your grace has been more than generous. However, if for the remission of your soul you wish to offer gifts to my church, you have crystalline gems in such and such a place in the treasury of this palace, which would be wonderful for the adornment of the church and best for decoration." Having heard this, the emperor sent the most faithful men of the Greeks, that he might discover if they were in that place as the bishop said, and they were found. He ordered all the vessels which were found there to be brought out and given to [Felix].

From the list[18] made of them: one crystalline bowl, large and decorated with gold and gems, and two other bowls made of onyx, and decorated with gold and gems; one great container on which were images of men and various birds, of clear glass, like crystal; wine ewers, one of them beautifully carved; a water pitcher shaped like a hand; and a hand-washing basin with such a covering of silver on top as can no longer be seen by the sight of man in this time; two wine ladles of crystal; one crown of ordinary gold, but having such precious gems, that in our day, when a Jewish merchant was asked by the emperor Charles how much he could sell it for, he stated that if all the wealth of this church and all the ornaments and houses were sold, he could not make up the price. It disappeared at the time of George.

144. When these things had happened, when he wanted to leave

---

18. Agnellus must have seen a list, or *descriptio*, of the gifts given to Felix by the Emperor Philippicus.

the city, a person at the entrance of the port, pretending that he was blind and that all his limbs were weak, so that he might receive a gift, exclaimed, saying, "Fortunate Felix, help this injured body." However the blessed father standing there said to him, "Son, why do you pretend to be what you are not? Why do you play with me? Although I am deprived of my external eyes, however the gleaming internal ones are open within me, through the grace of Christ." And he took his hand, saying, "Rise, get up, go, and do not again mock the servants of God." However the men of the city, who were with him at the gate, began to cross themselves, and terrified said to each other, "This man is righteous."

And having left the walls of the city, while he was still a little farther from the ships, *dimorae*[19] waited for him, that they might get something from him.[20] And having taken wicked counsel among themselves, they said, "They say that this seer, the man from Ravenna, is charitable and has hands generous for giving. Let us test if this is true about him. Let one of us lie on the ground pretending death, and let us ask for funeral gifts and let us divide whatever he gives us." With this done, when the bishop was passing by, they raised up wailings, fictitious voices, tears, sorrowing, and saying, "Aid us, good shepherd, give something to us that we might bury our dead."

But he, taking off his chlamys, which he was wearing, gave it to them, saying, "Take it; if you truly have a dead man, bury him." Falsely wailing, rejoicing and rejoicing yet more, they took it. However, when the bishop had gone on a little, the *domidae* thought of their colleague who lay on the ground pretending to be dead. They said to the man lying lifeless, "Rise, get up, behold we have the chlamys of the bishop." His own death, which he had invited to himself by mocking and pretending, had come upon him! They shook his sides here and there, but he was moved by no false mourning, nor did he see their tears; they turned away, he remained motionless. This story swiftly filled the royal city.

When the emperor heard it, he ordered blessed Felix to return

---

19. Below, these men are called "domidae"; both words are unknown.
20. Lanzoni, "Novelle orientali," discusses sources for this miracle story.

from the ship, and took him into a house made of wonderful marble, and asked a blessing from him and gave him many gifts, that is, two great dishes of crystal and cantharus vases of the same and other vessels for the decoration of the church. And he ordered all privileges to be written according to the petition of the bishop, and whatever he asked from him, he received. And the emperor ordered the ships to be prepared and all things necessary and desirable to be done; and kissing him, saying farewell to him, having received a benediction from him, he left. And he ordered privileges to be written, as [Felix] wanted, and he exalted him much more, as he had been before. And joyous and rejoicing he sent him back to his own see.

145. Meanwhile, with the royal city left behind, he ordered the sails to be opened to the winds and the blades of the oars to stretch out, plowing the sea, the salty keel creaks. He passes the port of Trapani, he reaches the shores of Sicily. Having been delayed here a few days, arranging the property of his church, having reached Palermo, he was delayed there for a few days; he arrived at Tindario. Having crossed from there, he arrived at the shores of Pachino. And when the sun scatters new rays on the level earth, he orders the fleets to proceed, with the port left behind without rowing, they left the shores, they twisted the foam and they sweep the deep blue sea, running over the glassy fields.[21] Breathing the gentle airs, with the gulf of the Adriatic crossed, he reaches the port of the Po; and having entered the city of his see, crying eagerly he received its inhabitants.

After three years he built a house in the episcopal palace, which he named the House of Felix after himself.[22]

146. Before these battles and the wickedness had been done, in [Felix's] reign the most wise Johannicis shone forth. He was asked by the bishop to set forth all the antiphons which we sing now on the Sundays of the cross or of the holy apostles or martyrs or con-

21. This passage contains the same Vergilian overtones found in c. 137.

22. The *domus Felicis*, built on the northeast side of the cathedral, next to the baptistry, still existed in the twelfth century, and was destroyed between 1207 and 1262; see Miller, "The Development," 162, and Miller, *The Bishop's Palace*, 57.

fessors and virgins, not only in Latin speech, but also in Greek words, since he was a great orator in both tongues.

From this tree and from his generosity we have branchlets and great-grandsons. Johannicis bore Agnes, Agnes produced Andrew. From Andrew of Basilius was born Basilius,[23] who bore Andrew the priest, the author of this pontifical book.

But we will set forth what his notary, by the name of Hilarus,[24] who, taught by him, was afterward the secretary of this holy church, told of him to his grandson, the son of his daughter, Andrew by name, as we said, my grandfather, the father of my mother.

147. Since each night he walked through the churches of the saints of God and returned late to his house, his notary, whom we have named above, wanted to look into forbidden things which were none of his business.

In the silence of the night, in the hour of quiet, rising from his soft bed, [Johannicis] went to the church of St. John the Evangelist. And his notary came with him, to see what he did. For he said to himself, "I will see, if this man secretly by night takes counsel with the exarch, or by chance enjoys himself with harlots, or why he walks alone."

And when the said Johannicis had arrived before the entrance of that church, suddenly the doors were opened, and the bars and bolts on the other side were silently pulled back. And praying for a long time before the face of the Savior, he entered the narthex of the church of this apostle, and with all the closed doors opened, he prayed prone on the ground. After the prayer he left, and the doors were closed, all their bolts moved, each back to its place.

Seeing all these things Hilarus, as if mad, became speechless and hid himself in the corner of the entranceway, where, as he lat-

---

23. The statement "From Andrew [son] of Basilius was born Basilius" is confused and contradicts Agnellus's later statement that Andrew was the father of his mother; perhaps something was left out, perhaps a whole generation. See Introduction, above, for Agnellus's family tree.

24. Although Agnellus cites Hilarus as the source of this story, it is actually an imitation of a miracle told by Gregory of Tours, *Liber vitae patrum* 7.2.

er attested, he ordered his body to be placed in a marble tomb after his death. And when [Johannicis] had reached the place, he softly sent out his voice, saying, "Hilarus, why do you hurry and want to hide? Do not tell anyone what you have seen, as long as I live. Because if you tell while I am still alive, at once you will die."

And [Hilarus] attested to other things about him, that one day in a certain place during winter he saw a pauper, and when he saw that he was sick, he ordered a dinner to be prepared for himself, and when they brought it before him, that he might taste it, he pretended catarrh, and ordered it all to be put aside until the next day. That night he visited the sick man, he brought the dinner which he had commanded to be put aside, he gave it to the sick man. And after the sick man had recovered his strength, he walked secretly through the churches of God, and returned to his own only later.

148. The *monasterium* of St. Andrew the apostle which is called *Jerichomium* was his house. He left there vessels with a weight of five hundred pounds of bronze for the use of that *monasterium*, and over the altar, where the crown hung from bronze chains, he placed at the front a cord of gold, like those the most noble virgins of Ravenna use. And where the crowns hung from bronze chains, he ordered women's gold belts to be hung.

By speaking of this man, not so much for the glory of his descendant,[25] but that we might reveal his works, we have wandered through many byways far from the bishop. But what we have once begun, we cannot relinquish, until we have explained [it all].

I have sought for [Johannicis's] tomb, I have found it firmly and certainly, as the deacon Maurus told me almost thirty days ago, who coming from Constantinople said, "At the gate which is called the Golden Gate, there is his small church, and there I was and in that temple I poured out prayers to the almighty God."

149. Therefore that most blessed Felix, behind the shrine of the church, placed many relics and extruded sheets of silver, and in the curve of the arch verses containing thus, . . .[26]

---

25. I.e., Agnellus himself.
26. An inscription is missing, but there is no gap in the manuscript. It is not quite

And he placed many relics of saints there, and a chest of cypress wood was put in the altar, and [it lasted] up to the time of Bishop Petronax.

Later the deacon Sergius, abbot of the *monasterium* of St. Bartholemew the apostle (where the said bishop was abbot and deacon and steward of this see, where, by the aid of God, after the said deacon Sergius, through his generosity, now I am the abbot with divine aid) removed the altar of proconnesian stone, with various wonderful marble ornaments, among which I also have decorated things.

This most blessed Felix made an entrance chamber, from which the bishops, up to today, proceed at the Introit of the mass into the presence of the watching people. And over its doors you will find written the following:

The form of the place formerly was squalid and accessible only to the people; now it is seen to be renewed by the merits of the bishop.

He planned the area around the church, whence by day the crowd of priests here proceeds better into the halls [5]. The shepherd is not separated off to one side; with [the bishop] walking through the middle of the people, reverence increases, when he pours out over them the familiar words to God.

Now they might observe the ceremony, whatever priest is coming; for the path, which is in the middle, can remain fixed [10].

This happy[27] and worthy priest repairs these things by his merits, so that the pontifical apex might have no end; talkative fame alone will never retain such honors.

For formerly the entrance door was the western exit.

---

clear which church is meant here, or, in the following statements, whether St. Andrew q.v. *Jerichomium*, the church in Constantinople, or some other church whose name has been lost. I would suggest that it is St. Andrew; see Glossary, s.v. *proconnisus*. The *paginas* (sheets) that Felix *extruxit* (extruded) were associated with relics and may have been similar to the *laminis argenteis* placed in the tomb of Apollinaris by Bishop Maurus; see Glossary, s.v. *laminis*.

27. "Felix," a pun on the name of the bishop? Or did Agnellus perhaps ascribe the rebuilding of the *salutatorium* to Bishop Felix because he saw that word in the inscription?

150. When his death approached, he made the priests and clergy promise that whoever might have homilies or any other words spoken by him, they should bring them before him. When all of these had been brought before him, at once he ordered a pyre to be prepared, and burned them all in the fire. When he was asked by the priests why he had done this, he said, "I, deprived of my eyes, can see nothing or retract what I wrote in those books. Perhaps I might have overlooked something, or a scribe might have made a mistake; may no one come after me and find evil in my words. You have the books of Peter Chrysologus, which you see; he wrote ingeniously and most brilliantly; hold him, use him, as you please."[28]

However with these things completed, he died on the twenty-fifth day of the month of November and was buried in the church of St. Apollinaris, not far from the *monasterium* of St. Felicula. Going there you will find his epitaph containing the following:[29]

Among the kind praises and triumphs of the virtues, with which leaders worthy of God are crowned, Felix was a lover of highest patience. Excellent in his habits, he led an honest life, he flourished most magnanimously at the pastoral summit. With his whole soul the bishop had regard for all the people, nor could he bear to see any sadness. Subtle in ingenuity, intelligent, wise and serious, equal to his predecessors. He knew how to dwell greatly at the apostolic summit, relying on its wealth he drove away profane dogmas. Fluent of speech, accustomed to saying many things, learned, erudite, a memorable color to be seen in his words.

As leader he suffered great hardships for his country: exile, injuries, hunger, nudity, violence, dangers, contempt, banishment, terrors, chains, cudgels; and his highest episcopal honor underwent derision. Snatched from his borders, he was deprived of his see. Lacking sight in his body, divine light arose there. He was taken to a narrow cliff in the land of Pontus, where he was lacking the necessities of life, but Christ was there

---

28. Felix edited the sermons of Peter Chrysologus; his edition is the one that has survived today, and Agnellus knew it also; see Benericetti, *Il Cristo nei sermoni*.

29. Although written in the *Codex Estensis* with line divisions, as if it were a poem, actually Felix's epitaph is not a poem at all; at least, the lines that result are not, for the most part, correct hexameter or pentameter.

as bread, buried in which with his whole body and virtue, the bishop was consoled by the highest grace of God, and was raised from the heavy prison on the island of Pontus.

At last he was borne to the port of his beloved country. Having lost everything, he was endowed with his first see, where with a pure heart offering up the host to the Lord, he remained on earth for twelve years. Here the holy one was placed in the tomb you see; lamentation for whose fate now is counted among his blessings.

He sat sixteen years, seven months, twenty-four days.

CONCERNING HOLY JOHN V, 726–44

151. John V, the thirty-ninth bishop. He was very patient, humble and meek. In his reign the Petriana church fell in an earthquake, after the celebration of the Sunday mass was completed.[1]

And when King Liutprand was ruling the Lombard kingdom, by his army the said city [Classe] was surrounded by a siege and destroyed, betrayed by its own citizens, through false deceit, from the gate which is called the Vicus Salutaris, which was next to the river Pantheus.[2] All the citizens assembled there, but one of them, hostile toward his own citizens, having been promised money, brought the keys and lifted the bars from the gate which leads to the area of the Lepers, where there is a bridge made of bases.[3] With all the locks unbolted and the gates opened, the enemies entered the city and overthrew it. But by the judgment of God, the one who was the betrayer of his citizens and opened the closed doorposts did not receive the promised money, but gave his blood

---

1. Agnellus has mentioned this earthquake already, in c. 89.

2. The *LP*, Life of Gregory II, c. 13, says that the Lombards besieged Ravenna, and "carried off many captured ships [*classes*]," which Agnellus may have interpreted to mean that the city of Classe was destroyed. Paul the Deacon, *Historia Langobardorum* 6.49, on the other hand, says specifically that Liutprand destroyed Classe, and thus is the more likely source for this passage. This event took place around 718–19, therefore during the reign of Felix and not John V.

3. Does this mean a bridge made of column bases? In c. 130, *basis* does mean the base of a column, but the use of the word here is unclear.

before everyone else, because he died first, pierced by a wooden post, nor was he buried in the earth.

152. Then the Ravennate citizens, angry at this bishop, forced him into exile to Venetian territory, and he was an exile for one year. Then Epiphanius the secretary, seeing the downfall of this holy church, and that the father of the country was being kept in untimely discomfort and affliction, recalled him to his own see by means of the exarch of this city.

But after he was restored to the pontifical throne, on a certain day the said secretary Epiphanius said to him, "Lord father, do not shy away from going to the palace to the exarch and offering him a great *palarea*[4] of silver; and ask him to bring to justice those men who sent you into exile, that we ourselves might be avenged upon them. And what you give, I will restore tenfold from them. You keep the pontifical customs, I will bring the charges against them, and I know that with the Lord's aid I will bring back a triumph over our enemies." And it was done as you have just heard, whereupon Bishop John withdrew into the maternal bosom of the church.

On the next day, the author of the advice, the same Epiphanius the secretary, standing in conflict against each man, said the following, "You have a written edict of property, [which says] that you will never act or mutter with your mouth against this holy church or against the bishop of this see for whatever reason.[5] Say now, what sort of sheep are you, that you have butted against your shepherd, while he fed you and led you through grassy fields, and that you wrote a testimonial against him?" They were convicted by the judge; he collected the twentieth part, which he gave to the exarch. With these things done, all unanimously came humbly to [John], seeking mercy; and no one afterward brought him down in bitterness.

153. In the reign of John, the commander came again to Ravenna

---

4. An unknown word.

5. Agnellus may have seen a document relating to the settlement of the controversy; see Tamassia, "L'enfiteusi ecclesiastica."

to destroy it, thinking that he would escape as before.[6] Having recognized him, the Ravennates went out against him to the Coriandrian Field, where it was customary to fight. Pretending flight, giving their backs, when they arrived at the *stadium tabulae*, where as a sign a stone boundary is fixed,[7] turning around they began to strongly threaten the front of the Greeks; and there was no rest from slaughter on every side, the greatest massacre of the Greeks, cut down by the sword.

And the priests, together with the bishop and the elders, prostrate on the ground, wearing hair shirts, sprinkling ash on their heads, were praying to Almighty God. And the elders, covered with sackcloth, with uncombed and filthy heads, tearful eyes, were crying out to heaven. And likewise all who were left in the city, male and female, waited for aid from the Almighty.

The rest, girded with the sword, taking on the arms of young men, slaughtered the enemy without pause. Then, as we have heard from those telling of it, there appeared between the two armies a sort of image of a great bull and it began to scatter dust with its feet against the army of the Greeks, and soon a voice intoned—whence it had come or whose it was, no one knew—it resounded in the ears of all, saying, "Go Ravennates, fight strongly! Victory will be yours today!"

The Greeks, seeing that their flank was broken, began to flee into the ships, thinking to escape. Then the Melisensians, that is, the citizens of Ravenna, surrounded them with skiffs and riverboats, and rushing on the Byzantines, killed them all and threw their bodies in the river Po. And thus it was that for six years no one ate any fish from the Badareno.

Now this happened on the day of Sts. John and Paul, and they began to make that day like the festive day of Easter, decorating the streets of the city with various banners and walking in pro-

---

6. The following account of a battle between the Ravennates and the Greeks seems to refer to the struggle that broke out in Italy when the Byzantine emperors began to promote iconoclasm in 727.

7. Reference to the "stadium tabulae" is also found in c. 22.

cessions to their church, blessing God in the ages of ages, amen.

And [John] died and was buried in the basilica of St. Apollinaris. You will find his epitaph over him containing thus: ...[8] He sat eight years,[9] __ months, __ days.

CONCERNING HOLY SERGIUS, 744–(69)

154. Sergius, the fortieth bishop. Young in age, short of body, smiling of face, pleasing of form, with grey eyes, sprung from most noble family. He was a layman and had a wife.[1] After he took up the rule of the church, he consecrated his wife Euphemia as a deaconess, and she remained in that condition.

Since in his day the priests were experiencing jealousy and altercations, and were not united in spirit, the multitude was split; and after he was consecrated at Rome, the priests spurned him, and refused to act as assistants for him, and there was no one who would accompany him to the holy altar.

The city was troubled by Lombards and Venetians. We cannot digress through these things, since [the book] grows too long; however, let us reveal the situation in brief.

The bishop sent to the deacons and to the remaining assistants of the church, that they all should gather together in the bosom of the church. But they, hardened against him by the stimulus of grievance, refused. Then, having considered things, he consecrated [new] priests and deacons. And those who were hard of heart, hearing this, came and went with him on Sunday to the celebration of the mass. And the new sheep, who thought that they should stand higher, were repelled by the old priests, and closed

---

8. An inscription is missing from the manuscript.
9. This number must be an error; the correct number is eighteen.

1. Much of the information in this Life, including the mention of Sergius's marital state, is derived from various passages in the Roman *LP*; however, most of the information does not match what is told in the *LP*. For discussions of how Agnellus used the material from the *LP* in the Life of Sergius, see Bertolini, "Sergio arcivescovo"; Savigni, "I papi e Ravenna," 332–37; and Deliyannis, "Agnellus's Life of Sergius."

their mouths, ashamed. Then the bishop, sweetly and softly soothing the older priests, poured sweet words around them until he brought them back them from anger to meekness. Then discussing many things, they afterward set out a truce of peace over the new consecration, that the deacons, having left off the dalmatic, might wear the *superhumeralis* after the Greek custom and might remain around the altar. And from that day the deacons began to multiply, although the canons, buttressed by apostolic authority, forbid it.[2]

155. Now in that time the Roman Pope Zacharias, having left Rome, reached the borders of Francia, requesting protection and troops for expelling the Lombards from the Roman borders, since King Aistulf was harshly oppressing Italy. But with the other king cast off the throne of the Franks, Pepin took the scepter of the kingdom and was blessed by the hands of the pope and was anointed with holy chrism by him; and [Zacharias] returned to Rome.[3]

And before he returned to Rome, he celebrated mass in the church of St. Apollinaris, and donated an altar cloth of alithine purple wonderfully decorated with pearls, and his name is written there.

But as King Aistulf saw that on all sides evils were weighing down on him, he sought the hands of the Italians, since time was not on his side, and he went to the threshold of the blessed prince [of the apostles] Peter and donated gifts and many presents; then returning to Ravenna, he placed the chlamys painted with gold, which he was wearing, on the holy altar of the Ursiana church. He voluntarily wanted to rebuild the Petriana church, which had been completely destroyed in the earthquake, and erected bases all

2. This episode is sometimes seen as an indication of conflict between the Greek and Latin clergy of Ravenna; see esp. Guillou, *Régionalisme et indépendance*, 172–73, and Sansterre, "Monaci e monasteri greci."

3. Although Zacharias did save Ravenna from the Lombards, and also visited Sant' Apollinare in Classe on a different occasion (*LP*, Life of Zacharias, cc. 12–16), it was Pope Stephen II who went to Francia and crowned Pepin (Life of Stephen II, cc. 24–39).

around it, and set up columns, which remain up to today, but he did not finish it.

156. Shall I speak of the name of this said king, why he was called Aistulf, or shall I remain silent? All right, I will tell.

His mother bore five infants in one hour, in one birth, from one womb. When this was told to the king and the miraculous thing was made known, having taken new counsel, he ordered them to be brought before him in one great basket. And seeing them, he wanted to cast them on a dung heap; he was horrified to be the father, he who had been the procreator. He ordered the royal spear to be brought, saying to his attendants, "Whichever of them catches the spear with his hand, he shall live." As soon as the spear was placed in the middle, among the other brothers this one grasped the spear with arm outstretched. Then his father called him Aistulf.[4] Let us return to our previous narrative.

157. When the Roman Pope Paul journeyed to Francia through Tuscany, this man, Bishop Sergius, did not go to meet him; and the indignant pope went out of the valley which is called Calle Collata, which is commonly called Galliata, with great anger.[5] With the kingdom of the Lombards crossed, with the highest points trodden, [Paul] crossed the summit of the mountain of Jove;[6] then he took the road to Francia, and whatever he asked of King Pepin, he received.

Then having returned, he began to harass Archbishop Sergius.[7] [Sergius], however, trusted in the king, that the king would offer him support; and [Aistulf] betrayed him, and [Sergius] was led to Rome by his citizens, deceived by trickery. And when the bishops

---

4. The preceding story is taken from Paul the Deacon's *Historia Langobardorum* 1.15, where it explains the origin of the name "Lamissio." Here the etymological point of the story has been lost.

5. Agnellus may have seen a bull from Pope Paul I, restoring the monastery of St. Hilarius Galliatensis to the Ravennate church.

6. The pass through the Alps known as the Grand St. Bernard, between Mont Blanc and the Matterhorn.

7. About the trial of Sergius, and the similarities with the trial of the antipope Constantine in the Life of Stephen III in the Roman *LP,* see Deliyannis, "Agnellus's Life of Sergius."

had gathered together at the order of the pope, they wanted both to deprive him of honor and to expel him from the episcopal ranks.

The apostolic representative proffered the following charge against him: "You are a neophyte, you were not of the flock, nor did you advance through the ranks of the Ravennate church according to the canons, but you suddenly invaded the throne like a thief; and you repelled your priests, who deserve to enjoy the gifts of the church, and you obtained the see through secular favor, efficaciously however."

To these things the bishop of Ravenna said, "Not by my own presumption, but the clergy and the whole people chose me. You asked about all these things according to canonical custom, and everything about me was revealed to you, how I was a layman and had a wife and arrived at the priesthood, and it was made known to you; and you said that there could be no obstacle to me. If afterward you have thought such things of me, why did you consecrate me?"

However the bishops considered the various charges among themselves, and within each chamber of their hearts a great storm was raging. For all of them said, "How can we, since we are disciples, judge our master?" Hearing these things the pope, becoming furious, stated that on the next day he would with his own hands remove the priestly stole from [Sergius's] neck.

Then Sergius, bishop of Ravenna, that night lay with tears at the altar of St. Nicholas and completely gave himself over to great lamentations. With his body prostrate he poured out tears for so long that he moistened the place where he was sorrowing and produced rivulets.

By the judgment of God, on that same night Pope Paul died, he was unexpectedly seized, suddenly he lay silent, and his attendants kept it secret until morning. Indeed with the dawn of the day approaching, before the ray of the sun could shine forth and Phoebus could fill the earth with his rays, Stephen, a deacon of the city of Rome, the brother of the said pope, came to the prison where Bishop Sergius was. He said to him, "What will you give to me, if you return with peace to your house and you are increased in all honor and dignity?" Having heard these things, the bishop, freeing himself as if escaping from a trap, said, "I promise to give no small gifts to you, if I do not do what you are hearing. Come yourself to Ravenna and enter the episcopal palace in that church and examine diligently all the treasures of that house, gold, silver, vessels or coins; all may be given to you, and however many you want to take away for a blessing, take them." On these words they swore to each other.

And on that day the same brother of the dead pope was elected to the apostolic throne,[8] and at once he released all captives and conceded indulgence to all offences. Then he ordered Sergius the bishop of Ravenna to come with all honor and glory; and when he saw him, he raised himself from the chair where he was sitting, and when [Sergius] had sought the ground prostrate and with his face cast down, he was raised up with elevated hands, and [the pope] fell on his neck, kissing him, and he ordered a seat to be brought next to his seat, and they spoke peaceful and sweet words to each other, and he allowed him to return to his see with great joy and speed.

So after three years [Sergius] entered Ravenna, and with his people receiving him, there was a little congratulation and a little peace. Bishop Sergius went to the *monasterium* of the blessed virgin Mary which is called *Cosmedin*. After the mass was celebrated he prostrated himself before the altar of St. Nicholas, praying for the longest time and pouring out tears, which appear up to the present day.[9]

158. Now in that time the Roman Pope Stephen, leaving Rome, took a journey to Francia; hastening hither to Ravenna, he was welcomed in its episcopal palace. However the priests, knowing

---

8. Actually, it was Pope Stephen II who was succeeded by his brother Paul I, who was in turn succeeded by Stephen III.

9. Lanzoni, "Il 'Liber Pontificalis,'" 428–29, suggests that this piece of information is intended to account for the perpetual dampness in this structure, the former Arian baptistry.

that he was examining the treasures and seeing that he would devour all the wealth of the church, exchanged unpleasant words among themselves. Some were saying, "Let us suffocate him," others, "No, let the fortunes of the church be saved." There were disparate voices in the crowd.

Then Leo, deacon and *vicedominus* of this house,[10] said to the priests, "When he begins to plunder everything, let us call him secretly as if to show something to him, and let us cast him down, so that, drowned in the deep water, he might never be found." This was their plan, and words unpleasant and pleasant were passed and concluded. Some, since it seemed as though this might be done, were thinking about putting the blame elsewhere.

Hearing these things, Uviliaris, the archdeacon of this see of Ravenna, from the *monasterium* of St. Bartholemew (he at that time was the abbot here, where with God's favor I am now the fourth after him), he ran with greatest speed to the episcopal palace of the church and saw all the priests in such machinations of discussion and considering various plans among themselves; knowing that he stood in opposition, clapping his hands he spoke against them, "O what insanity, brothers! If you think to kill this bishop, you do not have good plans in your hearts. Agree with me, that the pope should leave here honorably, and keep your hands from crimes, and let us keep uninjured the vow of our bishop. When black night begins to fall, and when the bodies of the Romans are full from feasting and from clearest wine, in their first sleep they will lie like the dead; let all the lamps of the hall be extinguished, so that not even the flames of candles stand out as comforts in the night, and what we can remove secretly, let it all be hidden in underground places, with our bishop kept ignorant; and when the places of wealth are opened, let the Roman pope remove what he finds."

And this plan pleased everyone, and they decided that this opinion of Uviliaris was better than the one offered by the mind of the others. And the priests, having entered each of the treasur-

---

10. Probably the Leo who became the next bishop of Ravenna.

ies, hid as much as they could. In the darkness of the night, the said Pope Stephen came. All the keys were brought before him by the officials of the church, and all the entrances were unbolted for him. He took the relics, which they had not been able to hide quickly, nine full weights of gold, several silver vessels and spoons of silver, large vases, one *quaternaria* and various other things of gold and silver, and thus he hastened to Francia; indeed he sent one of the spoons to Rome.

Then, after the pope had gone, when the plundering of the church was known to the Ravennate citizens, they wanted to chase after the wagon which carried the treasure, but the frightened drivers went instead to Rimini, and the Ravennates returned to their own city.

159. Therefore [Sergius] had jurisdiction over the whole Pentapolis, from the borders of Persiceto up to Tuscany and the river Volano, he ruled everything like the exarch, just as now the Romans are accustomed to do.[11]

Indeed when Pope Stephen returned to Rome from Francia, having previously formed a plan with the archbishop, he sent very many enticements and propitiatory letters to certain noble Ravennate judges, urging that those who had agreed to the murder of the pope should come to Rome (the grandfather of my father was among them), and they were imprisoned at Rome for so long that they all died there.[12]

And after these things the bishop made an alliance with the Venetians, lest presently worse might come than what had already happened to him, since the king of the Lombards had deceived him, and he did not believe him any more; and in money given to the Venetians he paid seven weights of gold to their noblest men.

---

11. Guillou, "Esarcato e Pentapoli," 298, reads the "Romani" as referring to the Byzantines; but Bertolini, "Sergio arcivescovo," 73, correctly notes that it refers to the popes. See Savigni, "I papi e Ravenna," 334. On this geographical definition of the Pentapolis, see Alfieri, "Appunti di topografia altomedioevale."

12. The taking of hostages to Rome by the Carolingian *missus* Fulrad is told in the Roman *LP*, Life of Stephen II, c. 47, and may refer to the event in which Agnellus grandfather was involved.

He built that *cella* of St. Apollinaris on the men's side,[13] where the monk stood,[14] and he left there many possessions . . .[15]

CONCERNING HOLY LEO, C. 770-78

160. Leo, the forty-first bishop. He was from this flock, not very outstanding in stature, very thin, but strong in energy.

He first showed to the Franks the route into Italy, through his deacon Martin, who ruled the church fourth after him;[1] and King Charles, invited by him, came to Italy. He plundered the kingdom of the Lombards, and their King Desiderius, his father-in-law, was brought to Francia as a hostage. Adelgisus, the son of the said king, together with his army, turned their backs before him and fled to the region of Epiros; and after lingering for a few days at Salerno, when Charles had come to Rome, afraid, he went from there with his few faithful men to Constantinople.[2]

---

13. The meaning of *cella* here is unknown (see Glossary, s.v.). Moreover, it is not clear whether this was a *cella* dedicated to Apollinaris on the south side of an unknown church, as it has been translated here, or a *cella* on the south side of the church of Sant' Apollinare in Classe. The structure built around the original tomb of Apollinaris on the south side of Sant' Apollinare in Classe, discovered through excavation, is identified by Mazzotti as this *cella*; see Deichmann, *Ravenna* 2.2:233–34, and Mazzotti, "S. Apollinare in Classe."

14. Is this the same monk who is said to have stood "on the men's side" in the Ursiana in c. 130? In that case, the description would refer to a chapel to St. Apollinaris in the Ursiana church, but this is merely conjecture.

15. The text of the Life of Sergius stops here in the manuscript. The date of Sergius's death, August 25, 769, is known from the Roman *LP.*

◈

1. The future Bishop Martin, whose Life is found in cc. 167–70.

2. The text of the Life of Leo ends here. He is known from other sources to have died around 777–78; his election was a matter of great controversy, and is described at length in the Roman *LP,* Life of Stephen III, cc. 25–6.

CONCERNING HOLY JOHN VI, C. 778-85

161. John, the forty-second bishop, young . . .[1]

Having heard these bitter words, the bishop changed his expression, and his heart became like the raging of a lion, and he said to his archdeacon, "O what insanity you excite in your body! Help him, if you can." Then with anger piling upon anger, like a cloud raising itself in the sky, or swelling waves raised to the highest point and striking the shore, thus various hearts of the priests were beating.[2]

Then the archdeacon said to the archpriest, "Do you want us to go, that we may take him outside?" And he said, "Let's go." And they said to the rest of the priests, "Let us go, brothers, let us visit our brother, let us suffer with him. He is our limb and our flesh, we are from one flock, we have one Father and one incorrupt mother, washed in one font."

And all went to the Cuthine door, and with knees straight, the archdeacon together with the archpriest broke the door of that prison, striking it with a stone, and they brought him outside, and everyone went into the church with him, and they sat in the *sacrarium*, until the time when the messenger came back, he asked that they all go in [to the church], as is the custom. And they found the bishop arguing and raging loudly, but his priests were not terrified by his threats.

162. Then one day, when the said bishop was sitting behind the apse of the church[3] with the priests and many of the people, suddenly John, the abbot of the *monasterium* of St. Donatus which is called *in Monterione*, outside the gate of St. Laurence next to Wan-

---

1. The beginning of this Life is missing, and the narrative takes up in the middle of a story, but there is no gap in the manuscript.

2. It is difficult to know what this story is about, although, like several other stories in the *LPR* (cc. 118-23 and 158), it seems to pit the bishop against the archdeacon, the archpriest, and the rest of the clergy. Holder-Egger, *LPER*, 382, n. 1, notes that Gratiosus, the next bishop, was the archdeacon in the time of John VI, as Agnellus tells in c. 164.

3. Since the episcopal palace was located behind the cathedral, this presumably refers to a location within the palace.

dalaria, not far from the *monasterium* of St. Mary which is called *ad Blachernas* (where God willing I am abbot) fell forward to the ground and went into ecstasy, and his spirit went out from him.

And, returning to his own senses, asked by those standing around why it had happened, he, standing up, said to them, "If I tell you, death will consume me." Then in front of everyone the bishop asked him, "For what reason has this happened to you?" And he answered, "Leo *ipatus*[4] is suddenly dead, and I saw his soul wrapped in the cleanest linen by an angel who was carrying it with an eager face to heaven."

All those present were amazed, those standing around marveled, and in order that the truth might be proved, the bishop immediately sent one of his attendants to find out the truth; and he found him dead in that hour. And indeed that abbot died after eight days.

163. I will hasten to tell you of the death of the bishop. Stand and behold the divine and just judgments of God!

There was in this city my mother's uncle, the son of a most noble man, who after the death of his father held possession of the *monasterium* of St. Martin which is called *in Aqua Longa*.[5] The bishop plotted continuously to be able to take control of the said *monasterium;* and since he could not bring force against him on account of the nobility of his parents, he fell on him with the sword of malediction and with blasphemous words.

On the day of the birth of St. Apollinaris, that boy, whom he was cursing, offered to him an oblation, which the bishop refused, but cursed him, saying after the curse, "Let me see your death and at once I will die." He went away weeping, repulsed and offended. Indeed after the celebration of the mass was complete, he went to his mother, widowed of her husband, and told her everything

---

4. Holder-Egger, *LPER*, 382, suggested that either this word is for the Greek ὕπατος (consul), or it is part of the name "Leopatus," perhaps the name of the priest who was freed from prison in c. 161. The point of the story seems to be that John VI was so bad that he would force someone to do something that he knew would cause their death.

5. Agnellus's grandfather Andrew was the brother of this man; he and Agnellus's father, Basilius, are mentioned below.

weeping and thus announced "that he would not even give me the body of the Lord."

However it happened after these things by divine will that Deusdedit, weakened by an illness of the stomach, died in the villa which is called the Aurelian, at a distance of twelve miles from the city, next to the aqueduct near Herculis.[6] All his house was in tumult.

And after they washed his body, they placed it on a wagon, and there, lifeless, it was lying as if in a tomb. The many bereaved were filled with tears. By day his mother lay prostrate on the ground; some people beat their breasts, others disfigured their faces with their fingernails; some wove basketry of willow-withies, others peeled the branches of willows, which covered the bier; some looked for growing grasses to put on top, others plucked up elder and beech trees, they removed the rocks that the wheels might run more swiftly; others on each side lopped off little twigs of willow; some chased cows away with a goad, others indeed strewed grassy flowers on the body.

The people of Herculis, animal herders and litter bearers who tickled the ribs of bulls with twigs, preceded the heavy animals, which went with open nostrils through the road, led by their milky horns by youths, and they arrived at the bridge of Odio. Then Andrew, brother-in-law of the dead man, ordered the body to stop and ordered the youths to form a circle. And they decorated the lifeless body with various banners, and he was tied up from chin to head with a fringe, which his mother had sent for him from the gold of Basilius.

Then everyone from great to small went out of the city, nobles and commoners, grandmothers and unmarried girls, and there was great lamentation and grief everywhere, and they grieved not only for the buried body, but for the mother deprived of her son. Then raised on the necks of men, he was brought into the *monasterium* of St. Euphemia in *sancto Callinico*, where they buried him.

---

6. Holder-Egger, *LPER*, 383, notes that this *regio prope Herculem* is not to be confused with the *regio Herculana* inside the city.

Then the grieving crowd entered the city, and they sent their hoped-for voices into the ears of the bishop. And he asked what was going on. And a messenger, who had seen it, said to him, "Deusdedit, the son of the tribune Peter, is dead." He sent another messenger back, to know for sure; and he came back saying the same thing.

And while he sat at the table, behind the apse of the church above the *vivarium*,[7] with his hands raised up, looking at the face of the Savior, he said, "I thank you, Lord Jesus Christ, and you, blessed Apollinaris, since you have heard me. I have always desired this day." And he said to his wine steward, "Mix, since, thanks to God, I have been heard." Then the wine pourer, taking a *dimia* of glass filled with unmixed wine, gave it to the bishop. Taking it, he drank the half of the cup, and, suddenly struck with a pain in his left side, quickly gave the chalice to his servant, and ordered the meal to be removed, and the joy of the feast was turned to sadness, and he went to bed; on the seventh day after the death of the youth he died. And the mother, deprived of her child, rejoiced just as he had rejoiced at the death of the youth. Behold divine vengeance!

He was buried in the church of St. Apollinaris the confessor. You will find his epitaph written over his tomb. He sat seven years, one month, three days.

---

7. This may mean that the dining hall was located in an upper storey, above the *vivarium*. Deichmann identifies the *vivarium* as the pool or *nympheum* containing fish for the episcopal table, and summarizes the archaeological evidence for the discovery of such a *nympheum* in 1919 at the base of the building containing the Capella Arcivescovile ("Studi sulla Ravenna scomparsa," 108–11; a reconstruction drawing, as well as a discussion, is provided in *Ravenna* 2.1:207 and fig. 151). About the location in the *episcopium* that contained the episcopal *mensa*, see Glossary, s.v. *triclinium*. There is a peculiar insistence in the Life of John VI on the fact that he sat "behind the apse of the church"; the phrase recurs in c. 162. Since this bishop is depicted by Agnellus as uniformly bad, his sitting here may be some indication of additional malfeasance, explained in the part of the Life that is lost.

290   BOOK OF PONTIFFS OF THE CHURCH OF RAVENNA

CONCERNING HOLY GRATIOSUS, C. 786–89

164. Gratiosus, the forty-third bishop. He was humble and meek, beautiful of appearance, somewhat balding, with a neck extended in size, big eyes, a pleasing form, and sweet eloquence. He was the abbot of the *monasterium* of St Apollinaris, which is found not far from the church of the holy redeeming Cross at the old Mint, whence most holy Reparatus also came.[1] He was truly "Gratiosus," since he was filled with the grace of God; he was archdeacon of this see.

In his reign a terrible sign of a deadly disaster appeared, that, in whoever's clothes or garment or glove or boot appeared three poisoned drops, on the third day he would be seized by death; and bodies were strewn over the ground, which the living were hardly able to bury.

165. And in those days Charles king of the Franks came to Ravenna;[2] and, invited to feast there, he came gladly. And the priests said to their bishop, "Lord, keep your simplicity and beware lest you say anything which might not be appropriate." He answered them, "No, sons, no, but I will keep my mouth closed."

When they were eating and drinking, the bishop began to speak to the king, saying, *"Pappa,* lord my king, *pappa."* And the king, amazed, asked, "What is this word, which the holy man is saying, *pappa, pappa?"*

Then some of the priests standing around said to him, "Let our lord king not think that the word might be some injury or irony, but persuasion. This man your servant and orator is of great simplicity; but as a mother, who soothes her sons and persuades them for great love to eat something, thus he, with great clemency, has asked your clemency that you might eat and be merry." Then the king commanded everyone to be silent, and he burst into speech, saying, "Behold an Israelite indeed, in whom there is no

---

1. Cf. c. 115. About the *moneta,* see Deichmann, *Ravenna* 2.3:54–56.
2. Charlemagne visited Ravenna in 787 and again in 801.

guile."[3] After these things, whatever the bishop requested from him, he obtained.

I will explain another fearful sign which was made in the sky. At that time in which Charles received the Lombard kingdom, many men saw in the sky, after sunset, horses with their riders contending against each other, and there was motion everywhere.

166. Therefore, O best beloved, do not be lazy, but stay and listen to what the Lord will say through my mouth, that you might know what things are to come.[4]

I am not a prophet, but that Spirit which spoke through the prophets can likewise pour itself into our hearts. That Holy Spirit cries through Joel, "I will pour out my spirit upon all flesh"; and says to Jeremiah, "I have made my words in thy mouth"; and saying to the patriarch Jacob, "Gather yourselves together, O ye sons of Jacob, hearken to Israel your father, whence he may tell you the things that shall befall you"; and even the Son of the eternal Father says, "I will give you a mouth and wisdom."[5]

What is the marvel, if before the incarnation the Holy Spirit filled the hearts of the prophets, that He might foretell the things to come, that now, after He has become our comrade in the flesh, He has given us all His words in the fullness of His grace, with the evangelist saying, "His fullness we all have received"?[6] If therefore the Spirit has spoken through the mouths of gentiles and infidels, such as through the cruel tyrant King Nebuchadnezzar and the poet of the gentiles Vergil and the Sibylline seer, and has predicted the future, why therefore should this divine majesty not speak now through a Christian man and one redeemed by the blood [of Christ]? For if this Spirit dwelt in the fragile sex, namely in Anna and the Sibyl, you may not therefore doubt the words of the gospel which say, "The Spirit breatheth where He will."[7]

---

3. John 1:47.

4. It seems likely that the sermonette in c. 166 is the *expositum* on Matt. 24:15 by Bishop Felix, identified by Agnellus in c. 136.

5. Joel 2:28 (*Vetus Latina* version); Jer. 5:14; Gen. 49:1–2; Luke 21:15 (*Vetus Latina* version).

6. John 1:16.   7. John 3:8.

But I say to you, my brothers, my fellow soldiers [in Christ], citizens of Ravenna, that the time will come such as no one dwelling there will be able to remember. And [the city] will be diminished of all its gifts, and it will be completely consumed by its citizens, and there will be various wars and quarrels between them, envying each other, thinking evil thoughts, speaking peaceful words from their mouths but having swords in their hearts. The head of all[8] is under siege, and her enemies will trample her underfoot; and everywhere there will be devastation in her, and they will rise against their enemies and, seeing them, will return terrified. And they will snatch booty from the neighboring cities, and they will trample underfoot and plunder the churches of the saints and apostles.[9]

And there will come from western parts clean-shaven men for her defense, but they will greatly damage her. And there will be in that time a great famine, much devastation. And there will be serious pestilence around the marine shores, and the ocean with swollen waves will violently devour her beaches, and the sea will rise against its creation, it will cast up its fish which now it gladly finds in its waters. Every race will destroy its own seed.

[God] will even dim the fair weather in the sky and will hold back dew at its proper time. And its moderation will draw together the clouds with rain, but with sun's ray hidden, it will show a shadowy day. That prophecy will come true, which is written, "The sun shall go down at midday";[10] which Christ said, from the "sun of justice," Who ascended the cross at midday. However this is understood spiritually and carnally. And the moon will lose its light,[11] that means, the holy doctrines of my church will be less-

8. Ravenna, as suggested by Pierpaoli, *Il libro di Agnello istorico*, 180, n. 518? Or the eastern empire?

9. Lanzoni, "Il 'Liber Pontificalis,'" 369 and 576, reads this passage and the passage below about the invasion of the "Agareni" as a reference to the Saracen sack of Rome of 846; however, the verbs are in the future tense, as befits prophecy; in any case, if the sermonette was written by Bishop Felix in the early eighth century, it would have some other meaning.

10. Amos 8:9.

11. Cf. Matt. 24:29.

ened through evil and ignorant priests. Thus that most evil time will come in this church: youths will go before old men and will deride the doctrines of the elders and the holy church. Those who are learning, if they are wise, will be stupid, according to the words of the apostle, "ever learning, and never attaining to the knowledge of the truth."[12] These are idiots and greatly depraved and hard of heart, who act in such ways. They can in no way drink the ecclesiastical milk. They are not really sons, but stepsons.

Ravenna little by little will become divided. Four men will not be found in her having one will, and if three are found in one house, jealous of each other they will bite each other. And there will be a savage and dreadful plague against men and beasts, and the earth will not give forth its fruit, and the mother of all will be [no mother, but only] an aunt; and the edible fruit will be lacking, and all joy will be turned to sorrow. And what is now the empire of the Romans will be laid waste, and kings will sit on the imperial throne. And there will be Christians judging other Christians, and no one will have mercy upon his neighbor.

This will be the beginning of these signs: when the priests begin to be proud and greedy and will grant no honor to their predecessors. Because of evil bishops the church of Ravenna will lie open, for their own honor they will give away the treasure to the church and scatter bribes, and afterward they will consume all the ornaments of the church, they will give away the estates. And the time will come that they will serve at the table of the church with wooden vessels, and shepherds will kill their sheep. They will not attend to the things of God, but will love the world more.

And there will come around the shores of the sea people ignorant of God, and they will kill Christians and will plunder their regions, and those who had lived there will be their tributaries. And Christians will rise against Christians, and they will horribly oppress them, and they will snatch their property, and they will afflict their bodies, and for their great weakness they will blaspheme to heaven. The whole world will be stirred up against itself. And the

---

12. 2 Tim. 3:7.

people of the Agareni [Arabs] will rise from the east and will plunder the cities located in the seacoasts, and there will not be anyone to get rid of them. For in all the regions of the earth there will be kings needy and desiring wealth, and they will oppress the peoples subject to them, and the empire of the Frankish Romans[13] will perish, and kings will sit on the imperial throne, and all things will diminish, and slaves will surpass their masters, and in these things the earth will roar, and the elements will lie open, and each person will trust in his sword, and all the hearts of the world will tremble, and the elders will be eclipsed, and the youth will be raised up, and they will not remember the ancient precepts, but each will walk in the path of his own depravity.

And the stars will be removed from the sky, and there will be a disaster against nature and against cattle and beasts of burden, and many will groan, sustaining great penury, and the bodies of many will fail because of the need of hunger, and the Roman nobles will wander as captives in alien lands on account of their wealth. Rome will be plundered by its own people and burned with fire. And all the earth will be sterile, and there will not be fruit in it, and whoever esteems peace or authority will be abominated. And justice will not be remembered, and there will be perverse judgments, and bribes will make the eyes [of the judges] blind, and they will stifle the cases of the poor, and they will joke about the widows.

And monasteries will be disrupted, and they will destroy the churches, and thus the devil will disturb the holy churches, which will be demolished by faithful Christians, and the house of God will be shadowed, and the ministers will remove the incense from the holy altar, and they will not minister; and many will disturb the services, since the priests will not be honored by men, but when the [priests] desire to admonish anyone, they will be derided by them. The offering will not be pleasing to God, if the priest is not completely cut off from the greed of this world; if he does not remove anger from his soul, the gift will not be immaculate.

 13. Other than this one place, there is no reference to the Franks in this sermonette, only to the Romans. Perhaps Felix's original sermon said "empire of the Romans," and either Agnellus or a later copyist added "Frankish."

And this will happen in the above-mentioned days: slaves will marry with the daughters of their masters and the lowly with the nobility, and they will bring forth sons and daughters, and judges and leaders will be born from this defilement, and they will overthrow the earth. And many who do not bear reproach will leave their cities and their homes and will wander in alien lands, and the camps of the church will be overturned and the priests scattered and the nuns, willingly and unwillingly, will be oppressed by individual men, and some will have abortions, lest the fruit of their womb becomes both witness and betrayer.

These few things, brothers, derive from the depths...[14]

... since I am consumed by a pain in the head, "but however," according to the words of blessed Job, "who can withhold the words he hath conceived?"[15] Stand, most wise, and struggle with the most pernicious enemy; may your head not suffer pain, may your eye not cloud over, may your ears not become deaf, may your mouth not be quiet, may your tongue not be silent, may your hands not rest from [making] the sign of the cross, may your arms not wither, may your heart not swell, may the spirit of your chest not freeze, may your stomach not be extended double, may your knees not lock, no bent back, no unbending knees, no lazy feet, but may your stable body be entirely strong. Be, God willing, perfect, just as this most blessed Gratiosus was all the days of his life.

He died on the twenty-third day of the month of February, and was buried in the church of St. Apollinaris, priest and martyr of Christ, in the city of Classe. He sat three years, eleven days.[16]

CONCERNING HOLY MARTIN, C. 810–18

167. Martin, the forty-sixth bishop. He had a tall stature, a large head, and was bald, exceedingly fat, from the *monasterium* of St. An-

---

14. Several words seem to be missing from the text, although there is no gap in the manuscript.
15. Job 4:2.
16. The life of the next bishop, Valerius, is missing from the manuscript.

drew which is located not far from the church of the Goths; he was archdeacon of this see, and obtained his see almost eighty years ago,[1] he was consecrated in Rome at the hands of Pope Leo III. When he had returned from Rome, he sent his messengers to Francia, to the Emperor Charles, and the emperor was pleased.

He gave the *monasterium* of St. Mary which is called *ad Blachernae* to the priest Andrew, who was still a boy;[2] and the said bishop received from him two hundred gold *solidi* for the use of his church; and he made from it a small gold liturgical vase, using more gold, in the shape of a seashell, and it is used for the chrism up to the present day.

He was so huge in his body, as I said, that the said two hundred *solidi*, which I gave him in both my hands, he held in his left hand alone; and the Ravennate leaders of this city, together with the priests, were amazed at seeing this.

168. This bishop restored the church of St. Euphemia which is called *ad Arietem*, which was formerly covered by water.

In his reign Pepin, king of the Lombards, died, and with the passing of time the Emperor Charles died on the thirtieth day of the month of January, and Louis, his son, took over the empire in his place.

Now in his reign Leo, bishop of the church and city of Rome, sent his attendant, by the name of Chrisafus, and other workmen, and he restored the roofs of St. Apollinaris,[3] everything with beams and panels of fir, and all the coverings of that martyr; together with his expenditure all the suburban cities brought all the beams and roof-tile supports and all fir beams and whatever else was necessary, with the Ravennate citizens working in corvée labor with ropes and other devices. And the workmen arranged the

---

1. Martin was bishop circa 810–18; "almost eighty years ago," indicating a date of around 770, must refer to the time in which Martin came to Ravenna, perhaps from elsewhere, or was consecrated as a priest. Or perhaps the number is an error.

2. This is, of course, Agnellus himself.

3. Agnellus may have known Chrisafus personally, since he mentions him by name. This restoration is also mentioned in the Roman *LP*, Life of Leo III, c. 106.

beams on top of the side walls, and all things were completed; and this bishop ordered the floors to be laid with *hypocartosis*.[4]

169. After some time Pope Leo, angry with Bishop Martin, sent his legate to Francia to the Emperor Louis, wanting to take action against the said Bishop Martin. Then the Emperor Louis agreed to his wishes and sent John, bishop of Arles, ordering him to go with Bishop Martin to Rome and treat with Pope Leo. The said John, bishop of the see of Arles, came to Ravenna, and taking counsel with the archbishop, he compelled him by means of a guarantor to make the said bishop of Ravenna go to Rome, and men gave two thousand gold *solidi* as surety that he would go, except in case of physical illness.

Ten days after having left his see, he was traveling that he might hasten to Rome, and he came to Nova,[5] about fifteen miles away from Ravenna, where there once was a city, now abandoned; he delayed there for fifteen days in the church of St. Stephen. And he sent the legate to Rome, who was to report that he had left the city, wanting to come, but was ill, for he was not able to ride a horse, since his body was weakened; he was in part pretending infirmity. Having heard this, the Roman bishop was very upset, since he could not summon [the bishop] to him, to really compel him. Then he left him alone and ordered him to return together with the legate of the emperor to his own see.

After these events, with the legation completed, the bishop of Arles entered Ravenna, and Bishop Martin received him with great joy and much eagerness, and replete with feasting, the bishop of Ravenna [gave] a table, made in the form of a plane tree, entirely filled with silver vessels, which was in his palace from the bequest of Archbishop Valerius, which he made during his reign, and small gold covers of the Gospels, made with skillful craft . . .

170. In that time Pope Leo died, whom Stephen succeeded in the see. And this pope, having helped the Emperor Louis in Fran-

---

4. The meaning is rather unclear; see Glossary, s.v. *hypocartosis*.
5. This location, a town between Ravenna and Rimini, is also mentioned in c. 93 and possibly also in c. 140.

cia, received whatever he asked from him; and he came to Ravenna, and both bishops kissed, the Roman and the Ravennate. And the Roman bishop celebrated mass in the Ursiana church, and displayed the sandals of the Savior, which all the people saw. And having left the city, he joyfully returned to his own see.

Then in the reign of this Martin the Emperor Louis sent to Bishop Martin of this see of Ravenna, as a bequest from his father Charles, one table of pure silver, without wood, having engraved on it the image of all of Rome,[6] together with square silver feet, and various silver vessels, and one cup of gold, which cup sits in the holy golden vase, which we use daily . . .[7]

CONCERNING HOLY GEORGE, C. 837–46

171. George, the forty-eighth bishop. He was young in age, with curly hair on his head, big eyes. He was consecrated by the Roman Pope Gregory IV.[1] But after he had received the sacrament from the body of blessed Peter, having left Rome, at once he stood in opposition to the one who had ordained him.[2]

After he received the authority, he destroyed all the treasures of the church and broke open the crypts and dragged out the treasures of his episcopal predecessors.[3] And he paid out great wealth

---

6. This gift is mentioned in Charlemagne's will as recorded by Einhard, *Vita Karoli Magni*, c. 33. See Deliyannis, "Charlemagne's Silver Tables."

7. The text of the Life of Martin breaks off here in the manuscript, and the life of the next bishop, Petronax, is also missing.

❧

1. Testi-Rasponi, "Note Agnelliane, la data della elezione," establishes the date of George's accession as 837, by noting that he is known to have been bishop in 838, from a document (Fantuzzi, vol. 2, no. 2, 5–7), but that Agnellus does not mention, among the natural events in c. 172, the passing of Halley's comet in February 837, which was very visible. Testi-Rasponi concludes that Agnellus must have recorded this comet in the lost Life of Petronax.

2. The implication is that George pursued an antipapal, pro-imperial policy, as is also seen in later events; see Brown, "Louis the Pious and the Papacy," 305. Agnellus's personal hatred of George seems to have overshadowed any approval he might have felt of George's antipapal policies.

3. Agnellus has already told us several times, most notably in c. 136, that George

from them so that he might raise the daughter of Lothar from the font.[4] In that year he went to Pavia; and after having given all the gifts to the emperor, he bought baptismal vestments for fifty gold pieces from the palace of the same emperor,[5] of fine white linen decorated with gold; and he received the daughter of the said emperor, by the name of Rotruda, whom he handed to me, and with my hands I clothed her and decorated her feet with shoes ornate with gold and jacinth,[6] and afterward he celebrated mass for the emperor. Likewise the Empress Ermengard, attended by her maids, wearing a shining robe, surrounded by a gold fringe, hair bound with fillets, with blue gems, her face veiled, her appearance dripping with sard, emeralds, and gold. And before the beginning of the mass he confessed that he was burning with thirst, and he drank secretly a vial full of foreign wine, and after this he participated at the heavenly table in the palace of that city, in the *monasterium* of St. Michael.

172. At that time, on the seventh day of the month of May, at the dedication of the basilica of St. Michael here in Ravenna, it rained blood, in the second Indiction; on the eighth day of the same month, in the watches of the night there appeared in the sky

---

tried to take one of his monasteries. For this reason, Agnellus portrays George in as bad a light as possible.

4. By acting as godfather to Lothar's daughter, George became the *compater* of Lothar, a relationship that implied certain responsibilities and loyalties between the two; cf. *LPR*, c. 30 and note. The most notable example of such a spiritual/political bond created by *compaternitas* in this period is Pope Hadrian's sponsoring of the sons of Charlemagne. It is no doubt because of this relationship between George and Lothar that George is treated so harshly by Charles, below.

5. Romano, "A proposito di un passo di Agnello Ravennate," says that this passage indicates that there were workshops attached to the palace, from which George bought the baptismal vestments, and explains the economic organization centered on palaces in this period.

6. It is not clear whether Agnellus, by dressing the infant after baptism, could also claim some sort of baptismal relationship to Lothar, or whether he simply includes this information to show that he was a witness to the event. This event probably happened shortly after George became bishop around 837–38, when Lothar is known to have spent time in Pavia; in c. 94, Agnellus mentions having seen the palace there. Nothing else is known about Rotruda.

a miraculous sign: a most swift coursing through the stars from the east to the west, and again from the east to the west on the twentieth day of the moon.

And on the fifth day of the month of May, in the third Indiction, the sun became very dark at midday throughout the whole world until the ninth hour. And a star flaming like a torch appeared in the sky, exceeding the power of the sun, with another small one about two paces under it; they went from east to west. And after the power of the sun shone again, their brightness [remained] in those stars. And the Emperor Louis died, as some say, on that day.

And Lothar, his son, succeeded after him. And before the emperor died, he divided his empire among the kings his sons: Emperor Lothar [received] the greatest part, Pepin the kingdom of Aquitania, Louis [the kingdom of] Bavaria. These were the sons of Ermengard. To Charles he gave the most fertile and best part, and Gisela, his daughter, he gave in marriage to a most pious man by the name of Eberhard. These two had been given birth by the empress Judith. However with Louis dead, there was always war between the brothers, or there was but unstable peace.

173. After these events, Archbishop George thought that legates of the apostolic see ought to go Francia to make peace between the brothers; he sent his messengers to the emperor Lothar, [asking] that [Lothar] might tell Pope Gregory to let [George] go with the Roman legates to Francia. And it was done thus; and he went with the apostolic curse.

And George, thinking that he held apostolic office, went with three hundred horses, which carried various burdens: and he took with him much gold and silver, having plundered the treasury of the church, and gold crowns which the blessed bishop Peter had made, and chalices and patens of gold and various vessels of both silver and gold, and he carried with him gems which he extracted from cross and crowns, so that he might give generously to everyone. And thinking that through this he might change the hearts of the emperors, so that he might escape from under the power of the Roman bishop, he carried along all the privileges which Maurus and other Ravennate bishops had received from holy princes.

174. And he came to the emperor with the Roman legates, and they found him in a battle camp in the place which is called Fontenoy, fighting against Charles.[7] And they say that the size of the army of Lothar was so great that no quadruped or even the smallest bird could escape or pass through it. When the struggle began on the Sabbath day after the day of St. John the Baptist, they each threw shining spears at each other. Weapons resounded, splendid shields were brandished on shoulders, many trembled in spirit, gave their backs, fearful hearts and immense sighs, their bodies fell by the sword.

Lothar, armed, plunged into the midst of the enemy, seeing his followers, conquered, fleeing everywhere, nor was there a respite from the slaughter of bodies with swords. Having arrived, as I said, in the midst of the weapons of his enemies, there were none from his side who could offer aid, but alone, fierce, he destroyed many corpses with his spear. Alone, he conquered in war, but all his followers fled. Sitting on a crested horse, decorated with trappings colored with purple, he struck the horse with his heel, devastating his enemies with its biting. Thus alone among the enemy, [he fought] as if he were ten men, so that the empire might not be divided, nor [have] such kings on its thrones.

However, the victory turned into the hands of Charles. Louis, his brother, king of Bavaria, aided him. But afterward King Pepin of Aquitania, son of Pepin the nephew of Lothar, came and strengthened the army of Lothar, and war was again waged, and some fell on the side of Charles, since they were wandering around. Collecting themselves, with the struggle begun, on the side of Lothar and Pepin there fell more than forty thousand men.

Then Archbishop George was captured, and they rudely threw him off his horse and took away the ecclesiastical robe with which he was covered, and they compelled him to go to his enemies before his horse, like one of the beasts; and when he had no power to proceed on foot, they struck him with a sharp lance. Then one of

7. The Battle of Fontenoy took place on June 25, 841.

them placed him in mockery on a beast of burden with a shattered back, without a saddle, its ears and tail cut off and very deformed, and he miserably went along. And another came, threw him off of that one, and made him ride another beast, stretched out beyond the flasks and food bag, tied to the saddle, and they led him to King Charles, and he ordered guards to detain him for three days.

All his priests were scattered, and the wealth of the church was destroyed by the hands of looters. The legates of the Roman bishop, who were three, having taken flight, went to the city of Auxerre. Then Charles, moved by pity, ordered that when the priests or clerics of the church of Ravenna were found, they should be brought before him unharmed and safe and honorably. Judith, the mother of Charles, gave to these priests one small silver vase, asserting that she did not have any more, saying, "Take this vessel, relieve your penury."

Charles and Louis, brothers born from one father, hearing of the wickedness of George, because he was savage and very bad, wanted to send him into irrevocable exile. But although he had been bad, his priests had argued for him for a long time, when the Empress Judith, the mother of Charles, moving his spirit to pity, swiftly asked her son and his stepbrother to send George back to his see. Then Charles ordered [George] to come before him.

[George] was prostrate on the ground, groveling at his feet; the king stood, wearing youthful arms, wearing a purple robe girded with gold brooches, on his left side were hanging gold amulets set with emeralds and gleaming with jacinths, his arm protected with a shield, wearing a breastplate, holding a spear in his hands and an attached lance of iron, standing fierce in arms, head crested for the battle-line;[8] before everyone he burst forth with a voice sent from his heart, "O shepherd, if this is still your name, why did you leave the church and people assigned to you, whom you have afflicted rather than revived, and why have come through a long journey in

---

8. This scene should be contrasted with the scene of the saintly Bishop John I and Attila, told in c. 37, above; in both the king is regally attired and is addressed by the bishop as a suppliant, but the outcomes are very different. For a discussion of the symbolic and literary aspects of this scene, see Pizarro, *A Rhetoric of the Scene*, 10–15.

order to see the battle? Why was it necessary to plunder your church, and why have you lost in one hour the possessions which were received by your predecessors from Christian princes or emperors? I know that if you live a hundred years, you will not recover."

Then Bishop George groaning, hearing such a reproach, cast his eyes sideways to the ground and at once witless became dumb and stood speechless in confusion, nor could he respond to the king clad in purple. And with his face cast down to the ground, he said with large tears, "We came to seek peace, not to bear arms against you."

To these things Charles responded, saying, "As I see, you are irreverent and stupid. Say now to me, face to face, were you not yesterday saying in your tents, that "when Charles has been conquered and his arms bound with thongs, after he is stripped of his honors, I will make him a cleric and carry him off to my parish"? Why do you deny your own words? Behold two evils: one, that you have said inextricable things; the other that through fear of a man you have dishonored God and have perjured God living in heaven, Who has delivered you from our hands. When He comes again, let Him render to you according to your own merits. Behold, as my mother has ordered, I will release you. Return to your own see."

Then, at the order of the kings, relics of the saints were brought and the holy wood of the cross of the Lord and the holy Gospels, and with everyone sent outside, afterward some relatively young men were led in, and Bishop George of the see of Ravenna offered the sacrament, as it had been commanded him, and at once [Charles] released him. And whenever parts of the property of the church were found by [Charles], at once he ordered them to be returned. One of the clerics, having Gospels with gold covers under his shirt, pretending grief, lay on top of it, doing this for five days and nights he saved them. The ancient privileges, in which it was stated that he should be removed from the power of the Roman pope, were cast into the mud and were pierced by sharp lances. And the gold crown from the church of the blessed martyrs John and Paul was captured there, having most precious gems, and likewise a golden vase for consecrated hosts, and chalices set with gems, and many other things were lost there.

And the priests and other people, who did not end up in the hand of Charles, lost everything in affliction by their enemies: inasmuch as they were sent out in linen clothing, and had previously been riding horses, afterward were made pedestrians, and like pilgrims they all sought alms along the roads.

In that hour when he was received by his own people, he firmly promised the needy priests, in the presence of God, to emend everything and not to do the evil things which he had formerly done. But when some of the *solidi* were found by those who had fled, and when he had revived himself with food and drink, reversed by his evil conscience, after retreading the mountain of Jove covered with a cloud and the trodden roads in those parts, he lied about everything that he said, and did not remember his oath, which he had promised to the Lord. The priests, reduced to nothing and consumed by hunger, said to him, "Lend us some money so that we may live. We will go to Ravenna, give us double." He did not agree to their petition, but his cruelty increased.

175. And in his reign, one Sunday the bread crackled in the oven of a certain judge, and all the bread was found dirty and all the offerings were as black as soot; and likewise in the oven of this bishop. And many leaders had to lend bread to their neighbors, and a lamentation was made in that city.

But in these things, brothers, what else was shown than the shady works of the priest, that it might be revealed what he was like, and what sacrifice he ought to be offering? This proves that although his sheep did not dare to speak against the malignity of their shepherd, the offerings themselves, which he was accustomed to break apart carelessly, cried out against him and rejected him as their sacrificer. Such signs ought to be marveled and wept over, my brothers, when a thing is changed into a different form because of our deeds. For when we are not moved to emend our ways, when we do not follow the holy Scripture testifying to us nor the commanded Gospels, we are warned through nature that we should recover our senses.

Meanwhile [George] became more and more ill of a sickness, and some say that he gave up his soul badly, which it is not necessary for me to say, since it is better to pass over the deeds of evil ones, than to be silent in praise of the just. He died on the twentieth day of the month of January, and is now buried, as is the custom, by his priests, but when he was brought out . . .

THE BISHOPS OF RAVENNA

Name	LPR cc.	length of reign	dates
Apollinaris	1–2	28, 1, 4	?
Aderitus	3		?
Eleucadius	4		?
Marcian	5		?
Calocerus	6		?
Proculus	7		?
Probus I	8		?
Datus	9		?
Liberius I	10		?
Agapitus	11		?
Marcellinus	12		?
Severus	13–18		c. 340's
Liberius II	18–19		?
Probus II	20		?
Florentius	21		?
Liberius III	22		?
Ursus	23	26, __, __	c. 405–31?
Peter I	24–27		c. 431–50
Neon	28–30		c. 450–73
Exuperantius	31–33		c. 473–77
John I	34–46	16, 10, 18	477–94
Peter II	47–52		494–520
Aurelian	53–56		521
Ecclesius	57–61	10, 5, 7	522–32
Ursicinus	62–65	3, 6, 9	533–36

Victor	66–68	6, 11, 11	538–45
Maximian	69–83		546–57
Agnellus	84–92	13, 1, 8	557–70
Peter III the Elder	93–97	8, 2, 19	570–78
John II the Roman	98	16, 1, 19	578–95
Marinian	99–103		595–606
John III	104	(18, 6, 8)	606–25
John IV	105–7	(5, 10, 18)	625–31
Bonus	108–9		631–42
Maurus	110–14	28, 10, 18	642–71
Reparatus	115–16	5, 9, —	671–77
Theodore	117–24	13, 3, 20	677–91
Damian	125–35	16, 2, 16	692–708
Felix	136–50	(16, 7, 24)	709–25
John V	151–53	[1]8, —, —	726–44
Sergius	154–59		744–(69)
Leo	160		c. 770–78
John VI	161–63	7, 1, 3	c. 778–85
Gratiosus	164–66	3, 0, 11	c. 786–89
Valerius	(missing)		c. 789–810
Martin	167–70		c. 810–18
Petronax	(missing)		c. 818–37
George	171–75		c. 837–46

Almost every date in this table is controversial, and most are based on unreliable data and speculation. The table is based on a detailed examination of Agnellus's dates, which can be found in Deliyannis, *CCCM* edition of the *LPR*, appendix; other studies of particular relevance to the chronology of the bishops are Holder-Egger, *LPER*; Zattoni, "Origine e giurisdizione"; Stein, "Beitrage zur Geschichte von Ravenna"; Testi-Rasponi, *CPER*; and Orioli, "Cronotassi dei vescovi di Ravenna."

GLOSSARY OF ARTISTIC AND ARCHITECTURAL TERMINOLOGY

As discussed above, Agnellus uses language, particularly terms for art and architecture, in different contexts for different purposes. In descriptions of patronage and decoration, for example, he uses terms found in the Roman *LP* and the Vulgate. In narrative passages, such as those found in cc. 26, 39, 111, 127–29, and 161, he chooses unusual terms, found nowhere else in his text, as a way of embellishing the language of the story. In two places, cc. 73 and 130, the narratives are specifically about construction, and so he lists building materials. In some cases, such as cc. 52, 143–44, 158, and 170, he copies items from documents or lists; often these words are found only once in the text. Some terms have specific connotations: for example, porphyry is mentioned only in funerary contexts. Finally, descriptions can be compared to surviving monuments. All of these factors must be taken into account when considering the meaning of terms and the reasons they are mentioned by Agnellus. A few terms have been the subject of scholarly controversy, and for these, longer discussions of the various meanings proposed have been provided.

At the end of the Glossary there are lists indexing terms by the following categories: types of buildings, locations within buildings, building elements, construction materials, pictures, church furniture, vessels and objects, fabric objects and vestments, decoration of objects, and workmen.

abdita (cc. 96, 149): Shrine; concealed or reserved place. Holder-Egger suggests that this word is written for *adytum* or *aditum*,[1] from the Greek ἄδυτον, which had a meaning similar to βῆμα.[2] Testi-Rasponi notes that in c. 36, a part of the church, the location of a burial, is identified as the *subdita*; he suggested that this latter area is for the congregation, while the *abdita* is for the clergy.[3] In c. 96 Rosamunda says that she will meet Helemchis *in abdito*, which refers to a concealed location.

1. Holder-Egger, *LPER*, 374, n. 1.
2. Du Cange, *Glossarium*, s.v. *aditum*.
3. Testi-Rasponi, *CPER*, 98, n. 2.

abiegnus (c. 168): Fir; cypress. The word is used to modify *laqueares* and *ligna* (s.v.). It is used only in c. 168, which is connected in both style and substance to the Roman *LP*, as well as to the biblical description of the temple of Solomon.[4]

absida (cc. 91, 125): Apse. Although *absida* was a common medieval word for apse, as for example in the Roman *LP*, where it is the only word used, in the *LPR* Agnellus preferred the word *tribuna* (s.v.), which is not used in this way by other authors. Indeed, in c. 91 Agnellus identifies the location of the inscription with his usual phrase *camera tribunae* (s.v.).[5]

aculis [factus] (cc. 80, 88): [Made] with needles; embroidery. These two passages describe the same object, an altar cloth with a depiction of the magi on it. The needles in this case must refer to embroidery needles,[6] as Isidore of Seville defines embroidery as *acupicta uestis acu textilis uel acu ornata*.[7]

aedificator (cc. 28, 31, 41, 62, 66): Builder; patron. In the contexts of patronage, *aedificator* means the sponsor of the construction; however, in the narrative in c. 41, Singledia asks for *operarii* (s.v.) and is given *aedificatores*, in this case, surely, workmen.

alapae (cc. 27, 169, 174): Clasps or covers of a gospel book. This word is unusual; usually, *alapa* means "a blow." Testi-Rasponi interprets it to mean the covers of a gospel book, coated with sheet gold, since Agnellus always says that these *alapae* are made of gold.[8] It could equally refer to gold clasps or fibulae for such books.[9]

alithinus: See *blattus alithinus*.

altar (passim),[10] *altarium* (passim),[11] *ara* (cc. 35, 52, 63, 64, 85, 133, 154): Altar. Altars appear frequently in all sorts of contexts in the *LPR*, but Agnellus does not seem to make much distinction among the different

---

4. 1 Kings 5:24, 6:15, 6:34; 2 Chron. 3:5.
5. Nauerth, *Agnellus von Ravenna, Untersuchungen*, 20, n. 37.
6. See Cabrol, Leclerq, and Marrou, *Dictionnaire d'archeologie chrétienne*, s.v. broderie.
7. Isidore, *Libri Etymologiarum* 19.22.21.
8. Testi-Rasponi, *CPER*, 75, n. 15.
9. Du Cange, *Glossarium*, s.v. alapae.
10. *LPR*, cc. 23, 27, 29, 33, 35, 44 (2), 52, 60, 119, 121, 140, 149, 154.
11. *LPR*, cc. 23, 41, 42, 59, 65, 66, 80, 82, 83, 92, 113, 133, 148, 149, 155, 157, 166.

words used for this object, and indeed sometimes uses them interchangeably in the same story. Only *ara*, which appears less frequently, seems differentiated, for it appears only in narrative passages.[12]

ama (c. 143): Liturgical vessel for holding wine.[13]

amula (c. 167): A small *ama*; liturgical vase.[14]

anaglifa operatione (c. 80), *anaglifte* (c. 170): Sculpted, carved in low relief. For *anaglyptus*, a very widely used word in the Middle Ages.[15] In both cases the carving is done on metal.

ambo (c. 56): An elevated reading desk, like a pulpit.

aquimanile (c. 143): Wash basin for the hands.[16]

ara: See *altar*.

arca (cc. 1, 26, 36, 39, 77, 83, 97, 113, 114): Sarcophagus. Many notable people were buried in sarcophagi made of stone (*saxea*—cc. 1, 77, 97) or marble (*marmorea*—c. 39). Most of these sarcophagi seem to have remained above ground, as Agnellus describes seeing them and even opening one (c. 26). Only the original sarcophagus of Maximian was underground, or perhaps in a crypt, as Agnellus says that when opened it was full of water, "next to the altar." This would seem to mean either that the sarcophagus was located below the floor next to the altar or that it was in

---

12. It is noted in Cabrol, Leclerq, and Marrou, *Dictionnaire d'archeologie chrétienne*, s.v. *autel*, that Cyprien's distinction between the *ara diaboli* and the *altar Dei* was used by Chrysologus and many other patristic authors, and that *altar* was thus much more common during the early period.

13. Davis, *Book of Pontiffs*, 108: "The people would bring their offerings [of wine] in *amulae* (small flasks); a deacon would pour the wine from these into the larger *amae*, and return the *amulae* to their owners. The rather smaller quantities of wine actually needed for the mass would then be poured (through a strainer) into a cup or chalice (*calix*) which would stand on the altar.... The wine consecrated in the large chalice would be poured into a number of service chalices (*calices ministeriales*) . . . for distribution to communicants. The *scyphus* . . . was for additional wine to be placed on the altar when it was foreseen that the main chalice would not hold all that was required to be consecrated."

14. Du Cange, *Glossarium*, s.v. *amula*, where he cites the *LPR*; Davis, *Books of Pontiffs*, 108.

15. Lazard, "De l'origine," 268.

16. Cf. Davis, *Book of Pontiffs*, 114.

a crypt under the main altar. Perhaps this is also the location of other burials said to be located *iuxta altare*.

archiergatus (c. 73): Master of the works; person in charge of construction work. Lazard notes that the word is a transliteration of the Greek ἀρχιεργάτης; it must not have been in common use, as Agnellus feels he has to define it as the "master of the work" *(princeps operis)*.[17]

architectus (c. 35): Person in charge of construction. Here *architectus* does *not* mean architect in the modern sense of the term, nor does it mean patron, as it often does in early medieval literature, but refers to the person who carries out the patron's instructions.

arcus, -us (cc. 41, 67, 72), *arcus, -i* (cc. 36, 66): Arch. Agnellus uses these words interchangeably, although they can mean different things in other texts.[18]

ardica (cc. 8, 25, 30, 77, 97, 103, 104, 113, 114, 124, 147): Narthex. A corruption of the Greek word for narthex, in the accusative, ναρθήκα,[19] this word is used only in Ravennate sources, only up to the thirteenth century, and is not found elsewhere in the Latin West.[20]

argirius (cc. 138, 152): Silver. This word is found only in the *LPR* in medieval Latin; it comes from the Greek word for silver, ἀργυρίον. Agnellus uses it only twice; much more common is *argenteus*. Lazard suggests that because it is found within a dialogue in c. 152, it must have been part of the spoken vocabulary of Ravenna.[21] However, in the passage, the word occurs in the phrase *ex argiriom palarea*, the meaning of which is unclear. Tamassia suggests that the phrase means literally a "shovelful of silver," in other words, a large amount of silver,[22] but the word *argirius* seems

---

17. Lazard, "De l'origine," 290; ἀρχιεργάτης is not found in the dictionaries, but its meaning can be inferred as a combination of ἀρχι-, "chief," and ἐργάτης, "workman."

18. As, for example, in the Roman *LP*, where *arcus, -i* apparently refers to a small decorative structure of precious metal on the top of a shrine. Davis, *Book of Pontiffs*, 109.

19. Holder-Egger, *LPER*, 282, n. 7; Testi-Rasponi, *CPER*, 37, n. 1.

20. Lazard, "Les byzantinismes," 366.

21. Ibid., 366–67.

22. Tamassia, "L'enfiteusi ecclesiastica," 111, noted by Pizarro, *Writing Ravenna*, 70, n. 45.

more likely to refer to an object made of a silver substance than to silver in the abstract. Since at least part of that story is based on some documentary source, it is possible that these two words were also contained in some document that Agnellus saw and perhaps misread. In c. 138 the object is a large dish.

artifex (c. 83): Workman.

atrium (cc. 35, 36, 49, 61, 158): Hall; forecourt. In the *LPR*, *atrium* refers generally to "rooms in a palace," or more specifically to "audience halls" rather than to courtyards.[23] In only one case (c. 61) does the word refer to the forecourt of a church.

aula (cc. 25, 35, 40, 50, 57, 61, 72, 115, 137, 142, 149): Hall; building. Used several times to mean palace, from the meaning of royal hall (the meaning given by Isidore of Seville)[24] and also to refer to churches.

auricalcus (c. 111): Brass. The word is found in a narrative that appears to be based on a document but actually contains several words found in Isidore or the Vulgate.[25]

auro textilis (cc. 37, 80): Cloth of gold; embroidered with gold.

balneum (cc. 39, 66, 86, 96, 118, 128): Bath.

basilica (cc. 1, 3, 6, 7, 8, 12, 29, 33, 35, 36, 44, 52, 65, 70, 82, 109, 153, 163, 172): Church. Agnellus uses the words *ecclesia* and *basilica* somewhat interchangeably; while there are some churches that are only called *ecclesia*, there are none that are only called *basilica*. The distinction between *basilica* as a funerary, extramural church, and *ecclesia* as an intramural cathedral or parish church, does not seem to have been retained.[26] Lazard has suggest-

---

23. Cf. Isidore, *Etymologiarum* 15.3.4: "An atrium is a large building, or a large and spacious house; and it is called an 'atrium' because three porticoes are added to it on the outside."

24. Ibid., 15.3.3: "An aula is the house of a king, or a spacious habitation surrounded by four porticoes."

25. Although *auricalcus* for "brass" is rare in the Vulgate, found in, e.g., 1 Kings 7:45 and Ecclus. 47:20; more common in *aeramentum*.

26. In some early Christian sources, *ecclesia* seems to refer only to the main intramural, episcopal churches, while *basilica* is used for suburban structures; see Pietri, "Bâtiments et sanctuaires." Weidemann, *Kulturgeschichte der Merowingerzeit*, 62–66 and 97–99, confirms that in the works of Gregory of Tours, the word *ecclesia* refers to

ed that *basilica* was reserved for more solemn usage, in fixed formulas, but it is difficult to detect a consistent pattern.[27] Curiously, *basilica* is not used in descriptions of patronage or decoration.[28]

basis (cc. 130, 151): Base; column-base.

bisalis (cc. 73, 94): Rhombus-shaped bricks. The Latin word *besalis*, which means two-thirds, was translated into Greek as βησσάλον, which came to mean a type of brick and was then translated back into Latin with the same meaning.[29] *Bisalis* is very rare in medieval Latin, although it is common in Greek in the fifth and sixth centuries.[30] While modern scholars have identified several different types of bricks used at Ravenna in the fifth and sixth centuries, it is unlikely that Agnellus was making the same sorts of distinctions when he used terms like *bisalis*.

bissinus (cc. 80, 88, 171): Made of fine flax; linen. This word is common in description of altar cloths in the Roman *LP*; since every use of it in the *LPR* occurs in the context of patronage, Agnellus may have borrowed it from the *LP* as a topos for a fine altar cloth, rather than necessarily implying that these particular objects were made of linen.[31]

blattus alithinus (cc. 119, 155): Purple; red-purple. These words are very common in the Roman *LP* in the same context, but they are never used together, as they both mean some sort of purple.[32] Given Agnellus's use

---

cathedrals or churches *intra muros*, or parish churches in the towns; *basilicae* all lay outside the walls and were mostly located on cemeteries, over the body of a saint.

27. Lazard, "Les byzantinismes," 367.

28. In the Roman *LP* both words are used, more or less interchangeably, in accounts of patronage. In the earlier part of the work, *basilica* is used almost exclusively, but later it is alternated with *ecclesia*. Davis, *Book of Pontiffs*, 109, notes that in the *LP basilica* is sometimes used to distinguish the churches that were not *tituli*, but that this usage is not consistent.

29. Lazard, "Les byzantinismes," 368. Vitruvius mentions a type of small brick which he calls *besalis laterculus* (*De architectura* 5.10.2 and 7.4.2); see Callebat, Fleury et al., *Dictionnaire des termes*, col. 92.

30. Du Cange, *Glossarium*, s.v. *bisalis*; Lazard, "De l'origine," 291.

31. The use of this word in the *LP* probably derives from biblical descriptions of hangings in theTabernacle andTemple: e.g., Exod. 25–28, 35–36, and 39; 2 Chron. 2–3; Esther 1:6; Apoc. 18. The most common phrase is "uelum de hyacintho et purpura coccoque et bysso retorta." Isidore, *Etymologiarum* 19.22.15, mentions "Byssina candida confecta ex quodam genere lini grossioris."

32. Davis, *Lives*, translates *blatta* as purple and *alithina* as crimson. Isidore, *Etymologiarum* 19.28.8, lists *blatteum* as a color of fabric.

of the two words together, it is possible that he misunderstood the meaning of one of them. In these two descriptions of altar cloths, he does not use any word to tell the type of fabric, as he uses *bissina* (s.v.) elsewhere. Perhaps he was using *blatta* to mean linen.

caementarius (cc. 36, 52, 83, 113, 168): Workman; construction worker. Found in a variety of contexts, including several that Agnellus probably experienced himself. In four of the five cases, the *caementarii* are associated with tombs; however, in the final case (c. 168), they are constructing a roof. This parallels the meaning in the Vulgate, where *caementarii* are the workmen who built Solomon's temple.[33]

caementum (c. 73): Cement.

calathus (cc. 38, 156): Basket.

calix (cc. 36, 41, 44, 96, 97, 119, 163, 173, 174): Chalice; goblet. Used by Agnellus to refer both to vessels used in the mass (see *ama*) and for goblets used for secular purposes.

calx (cc. 25, 72, 73): Plaster. In one case (c. 25) an image of the Savior is made of *calx*; possibly an image in some sort of relief. In the other two cases, the *calx* seems to be plaster as a building material, for holding *tesserae* and other decorative features in place.

camera (cc. 28, 67, 89): Wall and ceiling zone at and above the level of the windows; *camera tribunae* (cc. 23, 72, 77, 91), *camera tribunalis* (cc. 57, 94, 115): Wall and ceiling zone of an apse, at and above the level of the windows. In classical and late antique Latin, *camera* means vault or ceiling.[34] In the *LPR* there are two distinct zones of the wall in an apse: the *camera* and the *paries*, but these do not correspond exactly to the vault and the wall; rather, Agnellus uses *camera* more loosely to mean any part of the

---

33. E.g., 1 Kings 5:18; 2 Kings 12:11 and 22:6.

34. In the Vulgate, 1 Kings 7:3, *et tabulatis cedrinis vestivit totam cameram quae quadraginta quinque columnis sustentabatur*, clearly referring to the ceiling. Paulinus of Nola also uses *camera* to mean ceiling, including vaulting; see *Epistola* 32.10–11, and Goldschmidt, *Paulinus' Churches at Nola*, 96–97. Isidore, *Etymologiarum* 15.8.5–7, provides the following discussion of this term: "Camerae sunt uolumina introrsum respicientia, appellatae a curuo; kavmour enim Graece curuum est. . . . Absida Greco sermone, Latine interpretatur lucida, eo quod lumine accepto per arcum resplendeat." Hence *camera* is apparently essentially the same as *absida*, both meaning curved space. Earlier, Isidore has defined *tribunal* as the raised platform from which the priest teaches (15.4.16).

wall surface at or above the window zone. This can be seen most clearly in the cases in which Agnellus is talking about apses (s.v. *tribuna[l]*), using the phrase *camera tribunae.*

The three cases in which *camera* is used alone all probably refer to baptistries. Agnellus says about Bishop Neon's decoration of the Orthodox baptistry, "he set up in mosaic and gold tesserae the images of the apostles and their names in the vault *(camera)*, he girded the side walls *(parietes)* with different types of stones" (c. 28). The pictures of the apostles are in the vault of the surviving structure, and the *camera* is contrasted with the *parietes* (s.v.), or walls. The passage in c. 67, about the Petriana baptistry, probably describes an arrangement similar to the Neonian baptistry, and refers to mosaic decoration. The third use of the term (c. 89) is found in a garbled part of the text; Agnellus might be talking about decoration of the apse in St. Martin (Sant' Apollinare Nuovo), or about the baptistry of the same church.

While these examples certainly refer to vaults, the broader meaning of the term as used by Agnellus can be seen in two appearances of the phrase *camera tribunae* for which the monuments survive: a portrait of Bishop Ursus (c. 23) and a mosaic of Bishop Reparatus receiving privileges from the emperor (c. 115). Both pictures are found in Sant' Apollinare in Classe at the level of the windows in the apse, not in the vault proper. Of the seven other occurrences of this phrase, three more refer to portraits of bishops, two to inscriptions, another to a picture with an inscription beneath it, and the last to a picture of Theodoric on a horse in a palace in Pavia.[35] All of these items could be found in the zone around and above the windows in an apse, as well as in the vault. The contrast with *paries*, the area below the window level, can be seen in the combination *paries tribunali*. Agnellus uses this phrase in one case (c. 27) to identify the location of a mosaic portrait, and he defines it quite precisely: "behind the back of the bishop, over the seat where the bishop sits." In this case the portrait must have been set into the level below the windows, at the back of the apse where the bishop's throne would be.

The interpretation of *camera* as the wall surface at or above the window zone, rather than the vault alone, is distinct in early medieval literature, yet is not the only case in which *camera* does not mean vault. In the Roman *LP, camera* appears several times, often meaning either a small

---

35. *LPR*, cc. 23, 72, 115 (portraits); 77, 91 (inscriptions); 57 (picture with inscription); 94 (Theodoric).

chamber of some sort, perhaps the entire apse, or a decorated wall or ceiling surface.[36] Although *camera* is often translated as apse-vault, for both Rome and Ravenna this definition needs to be reconsidered. A *camera* need not be in an apse, nor need it refer to a vault.

cancellus (cc. 42, 130): Screen.

candela (cc. 16, 44, 158): Candle.

candelabrum (c. 143): Candelabrum.

canistrum (cc. 143, 174): Container; dish. According to Du Cange, either an ecclesiastical basket-like vessel in which the bread of the Eucharist is distributed, or a dish placed under a lamp to catch drips.[37]

cannata (cc. 144): Type of vase.

caput (c. 72): Column capital.

capsa (cc. 26, 113, 149): Chest; crate.

casa (c. 129): House.

casula (c. 111): Long robe; priestly vestment.

cella (c. 159): Cell? Monastery? Chapel? This word is used once, in a passage that breaks off in the middle; it is not clear what structure is

---

36. Geertman, *More veterum*, 192–93, suggests that throughout the *LP*, *camera* means a finished ceiling, either flat or curved, made of wood or plaster, rather than the roof or vaulting per se. However, the various contexts of the word make it difficult to assign one definition to it. In many of the cases *camera* is used in the context of some sort of pictorial or painted decoration (Life of Gregory III, cc. 8, 11; Life of Hadrian I, c. 74, Life of Leo III, cc. 10, 92), while there is little evidence to restrict it to the apse. However, work on the *camera* is mentioned along with repairs to the roof, *tectum* or *sarta tecta*, in only a few cases, (Life of Gregory III, cc. 8, 11; Life of Leo III, c. 92), while in the other passages, all that is said is that a *camera* is made or restored. It is even possible to translate *camera* in each case as an independent small room, especially since in one passage the *camera* is *mirae magnitudinis*, an appellation more likely given to an architectural structure than to a ceiling (Life of Leo, III c. 6). In other passages, the *camera* is mentioned in parallel with other architectural spaces (Life of Symmachus: "et cameram fecit et matroneum"; Life of Leo III, c. 4: "simul etiam in cameram . . . et in quadriporticu"; Life of Leo III, c. 9: "aedificauit . . . cameram decoratam seu presbyterium," and c. 10: "camera cum absida de musibo").

37. Du Cange, *Glossarium*, s.v. *canistrum*; Davis, *Lives*, 237.

meant.[38] Since Agnellus says that Sergius left in this *cella* many possessions, perhaps he took this information from a document or will, in which the structure was called a *cella*.

cereostatus (cc. 27, 41): Candelabrum. In the manuscripts, this word is used for *cereostatum*, found frequently in the Roman *LP*.[39]

chlamys (cc. 14, 155): Chlamys; cloak. One use of this word (c. 144) occurs in a story that may be derived from some Byzantine source, but the other refers to an item that Agnellus probably saw, the cloak of Aistulf that was supposedly donated to the Ursiana to be used as an altar cloth. Perhaps Agnellus took this piece of information from a document recording this donation, because it is extremely unlikely that Aistulf would have been wearing a Greek chlamys.

chrismatarium (c. 80): Vessel for holding chrism.

ciatum (c. 112): Bowl? *Cyathi* are found in the Vulgate, as liturgical dishes for the tabernacle.[40]

civorium (c. 66): A canopy above an altar, supported on columns; *ciborium*.

coccus (c. 66): Scarlet. Holder-Egger suggests that this word should be *coccum*, a purple piece of cloth. In the phrase in which it is found—*endothim . . . mediam habens coccam*—the *coccam* could be either a substantive object in the middle or the color of the middle part. The word *coccinus* is found in the Roman *LP* describing an altar cloth; Davis translates it as scarlet.[41] Furthermore, the word *coccus* occurs frequently in the Bible in the context of liturgical fabrics.[42]

coclearium (c. 158): Spoon.[43]

---

38. It has been suggested that the structure built around the original tomb of Apollinaris on the south side of Sant' Apollinare in Classe, discovered through excavation, was this *cella*; see Deichmann, *Ravenna* 2.2:233–34.

39. See Davis, *Book of Pontiffs*, 115.

40. E.g., Exod. 25:29.

41. *LP*, Life of Sergius; Davis, *Book of Pontiffs*, 86.

42. Cf. above, s.v. *bissinus*. Isidore, *Etymologiarum* 19.28.1 mentions "κόκκον *Graeci, nos rubrum seu uermiculum dicimus*."

43. The word was fairly common in early medieval Latin; cf. Lazard, "De l'origine," 271, and Du Cange, *Glossarium*, s.v. *coclearia*.

coenobium (c. 101): Monastery. Used only once, in a passage copied directly from Paul the Deacon's *Historia Langobardorum* 4.17; cf. *monasterium*.

collum (c. 50): Gable? Story? Testi-Rasponi suggests that the word *Tricolli* is a corruption of *triclinium*,[44] but Agnellus says specifically that the *domus* in the *episcopium* was called *Tricolli* because it had three *colla*.[45] Du Cange provides a meaning for *collum* as the *fastigium*, or gable, of a temple. The Capella Arcivescovile is mentioned in the same passage in the *LPR*, founded at the same time by Peter II, as *non longe ab eadem domo* (i.e., the *Tricollis*), and is located in a three-story structure. De Angelis d'Ossat suggests that the Greek word κῶλον, meaning "part of construction," referred to stories and thus that *tria colla* refers to the three-story building; when Agnellus says that *quae aedificia nimis ingeniosa interius structa est*, he is referring to the system of vaulting within this structure.[46]

Deichmann suggests that the name *Tricolli* comes from the Greek τρίκωλος, meaning tripartite, and thus refers to some sort of internal division of the building.[47] Rizzardi goes a step further and says that the *Tricolli* was built to house the clergy, and the division indicates the three canonical orders of clergy that existed at that time.[48] This does not, however, explain the fact that Agnellus specifically identifies some feature that he calls a *colla*, of which the building has three. Most recently, Miller has suggested that *colla* should be read in its usual meaning of "neck," and that the *Tricolli* was a three-necked house, a triconch, or three-apsed hall.[49] Κῶλον also means the "side or front of a building";[50] could it possibly refer to a building with three sides?

coloribus (cc. 29, 28, 89): Colored decoration; painting? The three passages all describe decoration of buildings, and in each case mosaics *(tessel-*

---

44. Testi-Rasponi, *CPER*, 148, n. 4.
45. Gonin's statement that the phrase *eo quod tria colla contineat* is a later gloss is unfounded (*Excerpta*, 79).
46. *Sulla distrutta aula*. Rizzardi, "Note sull'antico episcopio," 725, and Miller, "The Development," 152–53, note that the Capella is not said to be in the *Tricolli* but only near it, and thus the structure of the building containing the Capella is not relevant to the name.
47. Deichmann, "Studi sulla Ravenna scomparsa," 102–3, and Deichmann, *Ravenna* 2.1:198.
48. Rizzardi, "Note sull'antico episcopio," 725.
49. Miller, "The Development," 153; also Miller, *The Bishop's Palace*, 30–31.
50. Liddell, Scott, and Jones, *A Greek-English Lexikon*, s.v. κῶλον.

lis) are not mentioned. It is tempting to state that this usage is Agnellus's way of describing wall paintings;[51] but caution should be used because each of the statements is rather general, and none of the buildings survives.

columna (cc. 23, 72, 73, 76, 130, 155): Column.

corona (cc. 36, 41, 143, 148, 173, 174): Votive crown.

crapula (c. 96): Wine cup. Lazard identifies this word as one found only in Christian literary sources, not in everyday language.[52]

crater (cc. 52, 143, 170): Large vase for wine.

crips (c. 52), *cripta* (cc. 158, 171): Crypt. Agnellus describes Peter Chrysologus as standing "over the crypt next to the altar," so clearly the crypt referred to is located under the altar. In both cases, the *criptae* are places to hide or store treasure rather than liturgical spaces within churches such as the one called a *crips*.

cristallus (cc. 143, 144): Crystal.

crux (cc. 31, 39, 71, 80, 89, 130, 173, 175): Cross; processional cross.

cubiculum (cc. 36, 96, 121, 131, 157): Chamber; bedchamber; niche.

cubilium (c. 35): Side chamber. Given the context, *cubilia* probably means small cells or *monasteria* (s.v.), attached to the side of the church.[53] Its use here is puzzling, as Agnellus uses *monasterium* frequently for this type of structure.

cuppa (c. 170): Cup.

dalmatica (c. 154): Dalmatic; priest's robe of white with a reddish-purple border and long sleeves.

diadema (c. 52): Crown. This is an alternative word for the more commonly used *corona* (s.v.).

---

51. Testi-Rasponi, *CPER*, 77, n. 9.   52. Lazard, "De l'origine," 263.

53. *Cubile* generally means the same as *cubiculum*, "bed chamber," as defined by Isidore, *Etymologiarum* 15.3.9 (*Cubile autem cubandi locus est*). However, *cubiculum* is used once by Agnellus with the meaning of a small side chamber or niche in a church (see above, s.v. *cubiculum*). Paulinus of Nola uses *cubiculum* to mean side chapels; see *Epistola* 32, and Goldschmidt, *Paulinus' Churches at Nola*, 106.

diplois (c. 40): Mantle; surcoat. Found in a passage based on the document known as the Diploma of Valentinian, and describing the custom of wearing of the *pallium* (s.v.) over the *diplois*. Lazard notes the word comes from the Greek διπλοῖς, which was borrowed from Greek into Latin sometime around the fourth century but remained in use only among the educated upper classes.[54]

discus (c. 144): Disk; dish.

docaria (c. 168): Beam. Du Cange suggests that this word originated from the Greek δοκος, meaning beam, wooden post; the *LPR* contains the only known use of the word.[55]

domus (passim):[56] House; dwelling place. Found in a great variety of contexts, *domus* means dwelling place, although it often does not mean simply house; for example, three of the structures in the *episcopium* are called *domus* by Agnellus: the *Quinque Accubitas triclinium*, the *Tricollis*, and the *Domus Felicis*. However, the word does not seem to mean anything more specific, nor is it used to mean church, except in one case, in c. 121.[57]

domus ecclesiae (cc. 66, 123). *Domus ecclesiae* refers to a specific structure connected with the *episcopium* or the cathedral, rather than to the *episcopium* generally. In the first case, a bath is built "next to the *domus ecclesiae*, clinging to the side walls of the *episcopium*," implying that the *domus ecclesiae* and the *episcopium* are two different structures. In the second passage a formal assembly of the clergy and the exarch takes place at the *domus ecclesiae*; this usage makes one think of a sort of chapter house or assembly hall for all the clergy.

ecclesia (passim):[58] Church. See *basilica*.

effigies (cc. 25, 27, 30, 32, 36, 44, 44, 50, 57, 72, 77, 80, 86, 88, 89, 94, 108, 115, 153), *enigma* (c. 23), *figura* (cc. 23, 66), *imago* (cc. 23, 24, 26, 28, 30, 32, 57,

---

54. Lazard, "Les byzantinismes," 397.   55. Lazard, "De l'origine," 292.
56. Cc. 1, 29, 30, 39, 50, 53, 56, 62, 64, 66, 70, 76, 77, 84, 86, 97, 121, 127, 131, 144, 145, 147, 148, 157, 158, 163, 166.
57. See Nauerth, *Agnellus von Ravenna, Untersuchungen*, 84, n. 222; Deichmann, *Ravenna* 2.2:309; and Miller, *The Bishop's Palace*, esp. 56–58.
58. Cc. 1, 3, 4, 5, 8, 9, 14, 15, 21, 23 (3), 24, 25, 26, 27, 28, 29, 31, 34, 35, 36 (2), 39, 41 (2), 42, 50, 51, 53, 56, 57, 59, 61, 63, 66, 67, 68, 70, 72, 73, 76, 77, 80, 83, 84, 86, 87, 89, 91, 92, 93, 94, 97, 98 (2), 107, 113, 116, 119 (2), 121 (2), 122, 125, 128, 130, 134, 147, 150, 151, 155 (2), 161, 162, 166, 168, 169.

66, 80, 86, 94, 143), *istoria* (cc. 29, 29, 29, 80, 88, 114, 119), *pictura* (cc. 24, 32, 108): Portrait; image; picture; figure. Many of the buildings and objects in Ravenna were decorated with pictures of people, things, or scenes. Agnellus tells us about most of them in the context of describing patronage or decoration, although occasionally these images form part of some type of narrative. It has been debated whether Agnellus used these terms specifically for different kinds of pictures or whether he uses them more generally. Nauerth claims that Agnellus uses *imago* to refer to a full-length picture of someone,[59] but this meaning was not unique, as we know that he also referred to such full-length depictions as *effigies* (e.g., c. 77, the *effigies* of Maximian in San Vitale). Agnellus makes only a very subtle distinction between these two terms: *imago* refers to an image as an object made by an artist, while *effigies* refers rather to the appearance of the person depicted, as a portrait. This distinction is perhaps best grasped in Agnellus's own defense of his use of pictures of bishops for information, in c. 32: "Indeed if by chance you should have some question about how I was able to know about their appearance *(effigies)*, know that pictures *(pictura)* taught me, since in those days they always made images *(imagines)* in their likenesses."

Of the other terms, *figura* and *enigmata* mean simply "designs," while *pictura* means "pictures" generally and is borrowed from the passage of Pseudo-Ambrose quoted by Agnellus in c. 32. *Istoria* refers to a scene or scenes depicting a narrative story, i.e., a history.[60] Agnellus's use of these terms is very different from the Roman *LP*, where they are used with quite precise meanings:[61] there, an *imago* is an icon, a moveable representation made of gold or silver; an *effigies* is a portrait or likeness of a person, while a *historia* is a scene depicting a narrative event; a *figura* is a likeness or perhaps a symbol, while *pictura* refers to the procedure of painting, as contrasted with *musiuum*.

endothis (cc. 66, 80, 88, 155): Altar cloth. Comes from the Greek word ἐνδύτης, and appears only in Ravennate texts.[62] Although Testi-Rasponi

---

59. Nauerth, *Agnellus von Ravenna, Untersuchungen*, 21.
60. Cf. ibid., 79.
61. See Andaloro, "Il *Liber pontificalis* e la questione delle immagini," 70–71, although she proposes that *imago*, *effigies*, and *figura* all mean icon, while *pictura* indicates more generally a pictorial narrative representation.
62. Lazard, "Les byzantinismes," 375.

suggests that the word refers to decorative banners that hang around the altar,[63] Bovini points out that in one case, in c. 80, an *endothis* is said to be placed *super altare*, and this must refer to an altar cloth.[64]

enigma: See *effigies*.

fenestra (cc. 29, 86, 142): Window. It is not clear whether this word refers to panes of glass or simply to any type of window opening. In one case Agnellus refers to *fenestra mirifica* (c. 29) but does not explain what is so miraculous about them. See s.v. *uitreum*.

ferculum (cc. 138, 174): Dish; vessel.

feretrum (cc. 36, 68): Bier. The word was commonly used by classical poets, including Vergil, as well as by later authors.[65]

fiala (cc. 171): Flask; carafe. Lazard says that this means cup and reflects a classical Latin borrowing of the Greek word φιάλη.[66] However, it is more likely that Agnellus took the word from the Vulgate, where *phialae* are a common type of liturgical vessel;[67] Isidore defines a *phiala* as a cup made of glass.[68]

figura: See *effigies*.

fons (cc. 26, 28, 50, 67, 86, 89, 91): Baptistry. Agnellus always uses the word *fons*, never *baptisterium* or any other word. Four baptistries are mentioned: one next to the Petriana Church in Classe (cc. 26, 50, 67, 91); one next to the cathedral, decorated by Bishop Neon (c. 28); one next to the Arian cathedral, later rededicated to St. Mary in Cosmedin (c. 86); and one next to the Arian St. Martin, now Sant' Apollinare Nuovo (c. 89). Agnellus uses *fontes* in the plural for the latter three structures, two of which survive and are octagonal in plan.

For the baptistry of the Petriana, Agnellus uses only *fons* in the singular, and in addition describes it in more detail than the others: "This baptistry was wonderful in size, with doubled walls and high walls built with

---

63. Testi-Rasponi, *CPER*, 182, n. 11.
64. Bovini, "Le 'tovaglie d'altare,'" 77–79.
65. Lazard, "De l'origine," 288.
66. Lazard, "Les byzantinismes," 411.
67. E.g., Exod. 25:29 and many other passages.
68. Isidore, *Etymologiarum* 20.5.2.

mathematical art" (c. 50), and as a *fons tetragonus* with a *pars uirorum* and a *pars mulierum* (c. 67). Different plans have been proposed, based on readings of the word *tetragonus* (four-sided). Testi-Rasponi says that it was another octagonal structure, explaining *tetragonus* as referring to the exterior at ground level, as at the Arian and Neonian baptistries, while interpreting *duplicibus muris* as meaning that there was an external ambulatory passage around the building, as has been discovered for the Arian baptistry.[69] While the idea of an ambulatory is convincing, Agnellus does not describe any of the other baptistries as *tetragonus*, and it is thus possible that the Petriana baptistry was literally *tetragonus* in plan, namely basilical or square, perhaps with an arcaded core and central vault.[70] At the least it had some sort of window zone and upper wall surface, since Agnellus describes roundels located "in the middle of the vault . . . under the arch" in c. 67 (s.v. *camera*). Even this part of the description is unclear, however; one must perhaps imagine tympanum arches supporting the vault.[71]

The baptistry had at least two *monasteria* attached to it ("joined to the sides of the baptistry," c. 91), accessible from the inside (Agnellus calls one "within the baptistery," c. 26), dedicated to Sts. James and Matthew, at least one of which had an apse. This elaborate complex, reminiscent of the Lateran baptistry at Rome to which two chapels were added in the mid-fifth century, may have been partly in ruins by the ninth century; on the one hand Agnellus says that the *fons* is destroyed (c. 68), but on the other hand he describes the decoration and furnishing of many of its parts.

frons (cc. 29, 36, 41, 57, 61, 77, 86, 94): Façade; entrance wall. Used consistently to describe the location of some type of decoration or inscription. The decoration could apparently be either on the inner (specified as *intrinsecus*, c. 86) or the outer surface of this wall, or on both surfaces (*interius . . . extrinsecus*, c. 29). It should not therefore be assumed that all of the images so described were located outside the church; even if they were, they were probably located in the narthex or atrium.[72]

---

69. Testi-Rasponi, *CPER*, 148, n. 2, and 184, n. 2.
70. Such baptistries were extremely common in North Africa and were not unknown in the West; see Deichmann, *Ravenna* 2.2:352.
71. Ibid.
72. Nauerth, *Agnellus von Ravenna, Untersuchungen*, 42 and n. 94.

gipsea metalla (cc. 23, 41, 86): Stucco. *Gipsea metalla* is a material that, according to Agnellus, is incised (c. 23), sculpted (c. 41), and imbedded (c. 86). *Gypsum* usually refers to some type of plaster.[73] *Metalla* is a word with many meanings: it can mean metal or gilding but also marble (s.v. *metalla*). Testi-Rasponi identifies *gipsea metalla* as stucco that was gilded or silvered.[74] In the Life of Leo III in the Roman *LP,* mention is made several times of windows made *ex metallo cypsino/cyprino;* Davis translates this phrase as "with the mineral gypsum," noting that it refers to stucco gratings.[75] Although in the *LPR* the phrase *gipsea metalla* is not used in the context of windows, it seems reasonable to assume that here also it means stucco, without assuming that *metalla* must indicate some sort of metallic coating.

glosochomum (cc. 26, 163): Tomb; sarcophagus. Found both times in narratives that contain several words not found elsewhere in the *LPR.* Lazard notes that the word is of Greek origin, from γλωσσόκομον, meaning sarcophagus, and that because it is not found later than the *LPR,* it was not part of the general spoken language of Ravenna but was taken by him from some lost literary model.[76]

harena (c. 73): Sand. Presumably for use in construction, since it appears in a list of construction materials; cf. *sabulum.*

hypocartosis (c. 168): Marble opus sectile. In the manuscript this word is *hypocrastos* and is generally considered to be an error for *hypocartosis,* as suggested by Holder-Egger. Liddell and Scott define ὑποχαρτῶσις as *tectoria,* referring to materials used to cover walls, ceilings, floors, etc.[77] Du Cange defines it as marble incrustation of the side walls and vaults. Geertman, on the other hand, argues that it refers to the finishing of a ceiling with wood or plaster, based on its use in a letter in the *Codex Carolinus* to mod-

---

73. Cf. Isidore, *Etymologiarum* 19.10.20: "Gypsum cognatum calci est, et est Graecum nomen."
74. Testi-Rasponi, *CPER,* 67, n. 2, who identifies a surviving example of this type of work in the Neonian Baptistry.
75. Davis, *Lives,* 195, n. 82.
76. Lazard, "Les byzantinismes," 375 and "De l'origine," 292.
77. Liddell, Scott, and Jones, *A Greek-English Lexikon,* s.v. ὑποχάρτωσις. Although Smith, "The Side Chambers of San Giovanni Evangelista in Ravenna," shows evidence for a fifth-century hypocaust in the church of San Giovanni Evangelista, such heating systems are not known to have been constructed in the ninth century.

ify the word *camaradum*; he specifically mentions this passage in the *LPR* as an example of a *hypocartosis* being required after repairs were made to the roof.[78] Lazard offers yet another explanation: that *hypocartosis* comes from the Greek ὑποχαρτῶσις, which meant the same as the Latin *hypocaustus*, i.e., a type of underground heating system. Indeed, Bacchinius had originally suggested that *hypocrastos* in the manuscript was an error for *hypocaustus*. This meaning seems somewhat far-fetched in the context, given that by the ninth century churches were not provided with hypocaust heating systems.

ialicum (c. 163): Glass. *Ialicum* is a substantive form of *hyalus*, "glass," which comes from ὕαλος, glass. *Ialicus* is found only in the *LPR*; Lazard suggests that its use was inspired by Vergil's use of *hyalus* to mean glass.[79] It modifies the word *dimia*, an unknown word, possibly a scribal error, but it seems to mean some sort of goblet.

ianua (cc. 17, 23, 50, 92, 96, 113, 121, 147, 161): Door. A general term for door;[80] cf. s.v. *ostium, postis, regia, ualua*.

imago: See *effigies*.

introitum (cc. 89, 147): Entrance chamber. Unlike *ingressus* (cc. 36, 50), the *introitum* is a specific entrance porch, perhaps even a narthex or atrium. Since Agnellus commonly uses *ardica* to mean narthex, perhaps the *introitum* was a small porch that was not fully enclosed, or that for some other reason could not be considered a narthex proper. This meaning of the word should not be confused with the entrance of the mass, also called the *introitum*, which may however have given its name to the physical entrance chamber.

istoria: See *effigies*.

lamina argentea (c. 114): Silver pages; extruded silver sheets. In the Roman *LP*, images were made *inuestitas laminis argenteis*, probably silver-coated icons.[81] Silver sheets were found in the tomb of St. Apollinaris in the ear-

---

78. Geertman, *More veterum*, 192–93.
79. Lazard, "De l'origine," 293.
80. Isidore, *Etymologiarum* 15.7.4, notes that *ianua* is the main door of a house, to the outside, while *ostia* are doors within the house. Agnellus does not use the words in this way; in c. 96, for example, the *ianuae* are clearly doors within the palace.
81. See Croquison, "L'iconographie chrétienne à Rome."

ly part of this century; they contained a text and are dated to the late ninth century or later. Thus it is not clear what Agnellus meant or saw.

lapis / lapides (cc. 23, 24, 28, 29, 35, 36, 41, 63, 73, 76, 83, 86, 94, 130, 141): Stone. *Lapis* refers to the material stone generally, but also to various types of precious marbles and other stones, especially those used in revetments (36, 86, 23, 28), and floors or pavements (29, 35, 36), etc. In these cases it is usually modified by an adjective such as *diversus, preciosus,* or *promiscuus,* and is often found in formulaic descriptions of the decoration of a church. This type of usage is very typical of patronage descriptions such as those found in the Roman *LP,* which in turn comes from descriptions of Solomon's temple in the Vulgate.[82] Terms such as these should not thus be taken to indicate particular techniques such as *opus sectile,* although in some cases they may refer to this type of work.

laqueares et trabes (cc. 86, 168): Coffered wooden ceiling system. The *trabes* are the beams, the *laqueares* are the paneling between them; the two words are used together to refer to this type of ceiling.[83] Both *laquearia* and *trabes* are mentioned in the Vulgate as part of Solomon's temple, although the words are not used together.[84]

lasta (cc. 73, 130), *lastra* (c. 87): Thin slab of stone. In c. 87 the slabs are specifically those of a pavement, which may be the case in the other two examples also.

later (c. 130): Brick.

latercula (c. 73): Tile; small brick.

lavacrum (c. 96): Washroom. Used only once, the word is taken from the story in Paul the Deacon's *Historia Langobardorum,* from which this passage was copied.

lichna (c. 158): Lamp. Lazard traces its use to Vergil, and claims that in the *LPR* it is used with this poetic intention.[85]

ligna (cc. 66, 73, 76, 168): Wood (as raw material for construction).

limbus (cc. 138, 163, 171): Fringe, crown. It seems, from the contexts, that a *limbus* is something worn on the head, perhaps a cap or crown of some

---

82. 1 Kings 5:31, 7:9–12; 1 Chron. 29:2.
84. 1 Kings 6:6, 15; 2 Chron. 3:7.
83. Testi-Rasponi, *CPER,* 219, n. 4.
85. Lazard, "De l'origine," 261.

type. An emperor wears it on his head (c. 138); an empress wears a gold one, possibly on her head, as Agnellus describes her hair immediately afterward (c. 171); and the youth Deusdedit wears his *limbus a barba usque ad caput*, a location on the head.

liminare (c. 50): Threshold.

lithostratus (cc. 72, 86, 87): Pavement of mosaic or *opus sectile*. Isidore defines *lithostrota* as "small *crustae* and tesserae tinted in various colours," where *crustae* are marble tablets.[86] The use of the word in c. 72 is more problematic; Agnellus says that "In the *monasterium* on the men's [south] side you will find six mosaic letters [*sex literas lithostratas*] . . . the knowledgeable understand that there is written MU.SI.VA." Testi-Rasponi interprets this to be a description of the monogram of Maximian, in which Agnellus failed to find the letters X and N.[87] This may be true, but it does not explain the word *lithostratas* in connection with *literas*. Although such monograms have survived when carved in stone impost blocks and capitals, in this case it must have been found on the floor, possibly in some sort of opus sectile work, as Agnellus usually uses the word *tessellis* to refer to mosaics, even in the floor.[88] It is therefore also possible that Agnellus is referring here to a fragment of an inscription that commemorated the decoration of the church.[89]

lucerna (c. 27): Lamp.

mansio (c. 128): House.

manualia ad mensuram (c. 41): Candles for measuring time. The use of this term here has given rise to controversy. Holder-Egger identifies *manualia* as prayerbooks.[90] Testi-Rasponi gives a derivation from the modern Greek word μανουάλι, meaning candelabra.[91] Testi-Rasponi's interpretation was combined with his translation of *cereostatus* as large candle; how-

---

86. *Lithostrota: Etymologiae* 15.8.10 and 19.14: *paruulis crustis ac tessellis tinctis in uarios colores*; *crusta*: 19.13: *tabulae marmoris.*
87. Testi-Rasponi, *CPER*, 192, n. 6.
88. Cf. c. 114, where an inscription is *in pavimento tessellis exaratum*. However, Deichmann, *Ravenna* 2.2:373, states that the letters must have been in mosaic.
89. As suggested by Gonin, *Excerpta*, 88, who points out that the word *musiva* is found in the inscription in c. 91.
90. Holder-Egger, *LPER*, 306, n. 3.
91. Testi-Rasponi, *CPER*, 123, n. 4.

ever, since *cereostatus* is a candlestick (s.v.), it makes sense that *manualia* are the candles placed on it. Testi-Rasponi applies *ad mensuram* to the candles and makes the useful observation that Agnellus's statement that "she would spend the night praying in tears, as long as those lights lasted," indicates that such candles were used for marking time.[92]

marmor / *marmores* (cc. 66, 87, 92, 144, 147, 149), *marmoreus* (cc. 29, 41, 76): Marble; stone. *Marmores* in the plural is used every time specifically decorative materials are mentioned, implying that the word means "pieces of marble." In all of the accounts of patronage, *marmor*, like *lapis*, is modified by an adjective such as *diuersus* or *preciosissimus*.

mausoleum (c. 39): Mausoleum.

mechanicis operibus (cc. 59, 169), *mechanico opere* (c. 88): Artistically. Used for a building (c. 59), an altar cloth (c. 88), and *alapas* (s.v.) for the Gospels (c. 169). This phrase indicates that the work was complicated or of a high quality.[93] Hrabanus Maurus, writing at the same time as Agnellus, says: "Mechanica is skill of manufacture in metal and wood and stone."[94]

metalla (cc. 36, 130). The meaning of the word *metalla* in the *LPR* is problematic, as it had several meanings in the early Middle Ages. In the Roman *LP*, *metalla* occurs in several papal Lives of the eighth and ninth centuries; in one case it occurs as *marmorum metallis*. Davis translates *metalla* by itself as metals; in the latter case, he calls it marble minerals,[95] just as he translates *metallo cyprino* as "the mineral gypsum" (see above, s.v. *gypsea metalla*). However, Silva suggests that in the Roman *LP* *metalla* means marble, and that in some inscriptions it also means stone *tesserae*.[96]

In both cases in the *LPR*, *metalla* is found in the plural, as a noun in lists of decorative substantive materials, so that it cannot have the meaning "gilded." In one case (c. 130) it occurs in a list of building materials,

---

92. Ibid., 123, n. 5.
93. Lazard, "De l'origine," 274.
94. *De rerum naturis* 15.1. Cited by Berschin, *Biographie und Epochenstil* 2:156, n. 95: "Mechani<<c>>a est peritia fabricae artis in metallis et in lignis et lapidibus."
95. In Davis, *Lives*, 9 (Life of Gregory II, c. 9), 44 (Life of Zacharias, c. 18), 84 (Life of Paul I, c. 6), and 223 (Life of Leo III, c. 92).
96. Silva, "L'imitazione di Roma," 1 and n. 5. See also Goldschmidt, *Paulinus' Churches at Nola*, 137–38, who notes that Paulinus uses *metalla* to mean marble.

along with "stones, columns, slabs, and tiles"; it is possible that this use of the word *metalla* means marble. However, it is not clear what the *metalla singula* (c. 36), part of a decorative system that includes "gold mosaics and types of various stones," could be; here *singula* indicates separate pieces of whatever it is.[97] Because the terms appear in generalized descriptions of decoration, it is best to read them simply as referring to some rich material.

moenia (cc. 22, 40, 50, 137, 139, 144), *murus* (cc. 4, 21, 23, 24, 37, 40, 50, 66, 84, 95, 98, 103, 131, 140, 143): Walls; city walls. Agnellus usually uses *moenia* to mean city walls, and *murus* to mean the walls making up the outer shell of a building. But *murus* also means city walls several times, either in the expression *extra muros* in the context of burial (cc. 4, 98, 103), or in narrative passages that may have been derived from other written sources (cc. 37, 140).[98] In two cases *moenia* and *murus* are used together in the same contexts: for the city walls built by Valentinian (c. 40), and the *duplicibus muris et altis moenibus* of the Petriana baptistry (c. 50). Occasionally the nature of the *murus* as the outer wall of a building is defined more precisely: as the *muros per circitum* of an incomplete building that was finished later (c. 24), or the *ambitus murorum* left after the looting of churches (c. 143). An inner wall, or the inner surface of a wall, is called *paries* (s.v.).

monasterium (passim):[99] Side chapel; monastery; private chapel. A clear distinction is made between the term *monasterium* and the undifferentiated *ecclesia/basilica*: of the twenty-three structures identified as the former, none is called anything but a *monasterium*. However, although the use of this term might be exclusive, it does not seem to have had only one meaning. In a few cases, the word means monastery as we use it today, but in other cases it refers to a small attached chapel with its own dedication, especially one used for burial. Many of the *monasteria* in the *LPR* seem to have been independent structures, and for most of these Agnellus indicates that someone (including himself, in two cases) lived there or was *abba* there.[100] Others are either *iuxta* (c. 36) or *infra* (c. 26) or even *haerens*

---

97. Testi-Rasponi, *CPER*, 96, n. 9, says that they are the same as *gipsea metalla*, but he does not explain *singula*.

98. Isidore admits that the two words are often confused; *Etymologiarum* 15.2.17–18.

99. *LPR*, cc. 1, 21, 22, 26, 36, 39 (twice), 41, 42, 50, 53, 59, 60, 62, 64, 67, 72 (twice), 86 (twice), 89, 91, 98 (twice), 110, 115, 119, 121, 129, 131, 136, 148, 149, 150, 157, 158, 162, 163 (twice), 164, 166, 167, 171.

100. St. Andrew the Apostle near the *ecclesia Gothorum* (cc. 121, 167), St. Andrew the Apos-

murae (c. 21) of a larger church; some of these small adjunct chambers that Agnellus calls *monasteria* still survive.[101] One other type of structure Agnellus calls a *monasterium:* St. Andrew the Apostle is a small private chapel within the *episcopium*, now called the Capella Arcivescovile (c. 50), and a similar arrangement is probably indicated by Agnellus's description of the *monasterium* of St. Apollinaris in the Arian *episcopium* (c. 86).[102]

Various scholars have attempted to explain why Agnellus used the one word *monasterium* for such a variety of structures. Wickhoff suggests that even the small side chapels were actually monasteries, with monks living in them to be close to the major churches.[103] Wickhoff offers examples of *monasteria* attached to the sides or *atria* of churches in other cities, which were actual monasteries with monks living in them; however, although he notes that some of the *monasteria* in the *LPR* are inhabited, he does not apparently notice that none of the *monasteria* attached to the sides of larg-

---

tle q.v. *Ierichomium* (c. 148), St. Apollinaris at the mint (cc. 115, 164), St. Bartholemew (cc. 64, 110, 136, 149, 158), St. Donatus q.v. *in Monterione* (c. 162), St. Eufemia *in sancto Calinico* (c. 163), St. John q.v. *ad Titum* (c. 131), St. Mary *ad Blachernas* (cc. 62, 119, 162, 167), St. Mary q.d. *ad memoria regis Theoderici* (c. 39), St. Mary *ad palatium Theoderici* (c. 39), St. Peter q.v. *Orfanumtrofium* (c. 62), St. Pulio (c. 22), St. Severinus (c. 129), and St. Zacharias (c. 41). *Monasteria* that are *not* specifically identified as having inhabitants or an abbot are St. Eufemia *in sancto Calinico*, St. Peter q.v. *Orfanumtrofium*, St. Mary q.d. *ad memoria regis Theoderici*, St. Mary *ad palatium Theoderici*, St. Pulio, St. Severinus, and St. Zacharias.

101. At San Vitale, the two chambers flanking the apse are called *monasteria*, and one can probably be identified with that of St. Nazarius (cc. 59, 65, 68, 42). The so-called Mausoleum of Galla Placidia was probably another such *monasterium*, attached to Santa Croce. The church of St. Severus at Classe has been excavated, and the small complex to the south of the narthex, made up of several small chambers, has been identified as the *monasterium* of St. Rophilius (c. 98; see Bovini, "Il recente rinvenimento"). The *monasterium beatae virginis Mariae qui uocatur Cosmiti* (cc. 86, 157) is the baptistry of the Arian cathedral, converted into a chapel connected to the church by a walkway. Other *monasteria* of this type, which no longer survive, include Sts. Gervase and Protase (c. 36), Sts. Mark, Marcellus, et Felicula near Sant' Apollinare in Classe (cc. 98, 150), Sts. Matthew and Jacob next to Petriana baptistry (cc. 26, 91), St. Petronilla (c. 21), St. Theodore the Deacon next to Sant' Apollinare Nuovo (c. 119).

102. A few other uses of *monasterium* do not refer to specific structures, but to monasteries, usually in the plural, in general. It is noteworthy that these uses are found in contexts taken directly from other written sources, such as the *Constitutio* of Pope Felix (c. 60), the *Praeceptum* received by Bishop Reparatus (c. 115), and the sermonette about the End of Days (c. 166).

103. Wickhoff, "Die 'monasteria' bei Agnellus."

er churches are said to have an abbot or anyone living in them. Testi-Rasponi proposes that originally the word referred to a monastery but that over time, with the attachment of monks to secular churches, it came to mean simply a church devoted to private worship rather than public mass, either free-standing or attached to a larger church, and with a cemeterial function.[104] Vassuri lists functions that apparently could take place in *monasteria*, such as burial and the performance of the Eucharist, and notes that all *monasteria* contained an altar dedicated to a saint, although he does not connect the term with any specific function or form.[105] Vasina accepts Vassuri's definition of a *monasterium* as a small chapel with a priest attached to it who assumes the title of abbot, and notes that in some cases these chapels were attached to other churches and in some cases they were not.[106]

That Agnellus calls various different types of structures *monasteria* may merely imply that this was the only such word used by him. Agnellus uses only three other words, once each, that can mean small adjunct chambers: a *crips*, probably a crypt, in a church in another town (c. 52), a *cella* of St. Apollinaris on the men's side of an unknown church (c. 159), and a *sacrarium*, the place "behind the apse of the church," in another unknown church (c. 161). It is perhaps most significant that Agnellus does *not* use any other terms commonly meaning small chambers, such as *oratorium*, *capella*, *porticus*, or *memoria*; nor does he use any other words, such as *coenobium*, to refer to monasteries.[107] If these words were not available to him, there should be nothing surprising in the fact that he used one word with a variety of meanings, and it is perhaps not appropriate to try to discover some precise architectonic or functional meaning invested in the word *monasterium*.

murus: See *moenia*.

musivum (cc. 23, 28, 36, 91): Mosaic. Given the number of mosaics mentioned, this word is used surprisingly infrequently; more common is *tessellis* (s.v.). It seems that the singular form is used to refer to the tech-

---

104. Testi-Rasponi, *CPER*, 61, n. 5. The cemeterial function is also mentioned by Du Cange, *Glossarium*.
105. Vassuri, "I 'monasteria' di Ravenna."
106. Vasina, "Clero e chiese," 545 and 555.
107. The word *coenobium* does occur once in the *LPR* (c. 101), but in a passage copied verbatim from Paul the Deacon's *Historia Langobardorum*.

nique of mosaic *(in musiuoo)*, while the plural (cc. 28, 36) refers to "mosaic pictures" as objects of patronage.[108]

operarius (c. 41): Worker; builder.

orarium (c. 157): Priest's stole. The use of this word in this context is taken from a narrative from the Roman *LP,* upon which the story in the *LPR* is based.[109]

orbita (cc. 27, 44, 67), *orbitella* (c. 67): Disc; circular frame. Found on walls (cc. 27, 44) and objects (c. 44); contain both portraits (cc. 27, 44) and inscriptions (c. 67).[110]

ostium (cc. 121, 158): Door; entrance.

palatium (cc. 35, 39, 94, 95, 96, 111, 120, 122, 132, 143, 152, 169, 171): Palace.

pallea (cc. 31, 153, 163), *pallia* (cc. 137, 143): Hangings. A general word for hangings or banners made of fabric, sometimes referring to the hangings belonging to a church and hung on the walls, between the arcades (cc. 31, 143), sometimes to banners hung or displayed outdoors (cc. 137, 153), and once to cloth objects draped over a corpse (c. 163).

pallium (cc. 40, 70, 110, 113): Pallium; narrow band of white material worn by a bishop; *pallium* (c. 129): Woman's dress. Although *pallium* could mean an article of women's clothing, as in one case here (c. 129, which is taken from a stylized description of a procession based partly on a biblical passage), its other meaning was very significant for Agnellus. The *pallium* was worn by bishops and was given to them by their immediate superior in the ecclesiastical hierarchy; the acquisition of this article was of great importance to the Ravennate episcopacy. Agnellus mentions it in connection with three bishops, each of whom presided over a documented change in the status of the church of Ravenna. According to Agnellus, John I was the first bishop of Ravenna to have metropolitan status, which was recognized in the Diploma of Valentinian by his receiving the *pallium* from the emperor rather than the pope (c. 40). Maximian, apparently the

108. In the Roman *LP, musivum* is the only word used for mosaic; it is used only in the singular, and almost always in the construction *de/ex musivo.*
109. See Deliyannis, "Agnellus's Life of Sergius."
110. It should also be noted that the word *orbitella* occurs in one other passage, meaning pebbles, sling-stones (c. 127).

first bishop to be called an archbishop, is appointed by the emperor when the clergy come to him seeking the *pallium* for their candidate; however, it is not clear whether it is the emperor or the pope who gives the *pallium* to Maximian (c. 70).[111] Maurus was the archbishop who obtained from the emperor the charter of autocephaly stating that the *pallium* would be granted by the emperor rather than the pope; on his deathbed, he urged his clergy to seek the *pallium* from the emperor (cc. 110, 113). Controversy about the archbishop of Ravenna's right to wear the *pallium* on certain occasions is also found in various letters from Pope Gregory I to Bishops John II and Marinian.[112]

paries (cc. 23, 25, 27, 28, 29, 36, 50, 66, 86, 88, 168): Side wall; zone of wall beneath the window level. Most of the references to *paries* indicate either, as Agnellus himself defines it, "where columns are placed in a row up to the wall of the main door" (c. 23), namely, the clerestory walls of a basilica, or merely the side walls of a rectangular room. In some cases they seem to refer more specifically to the part of the walls below the zone of the windows; this is especially true for spaces that were not rectangular, such as apses or centrally planned buildings (esp. cc. 27, 28, 50). See s.v. *camera*. As contrasted with *murus* and *moenia* (s.v.), *paries* is generally used to refer to internal walls or wall surfaces.

pars mulierum (cc. 23, 36, 67): North side (of a church); *pars virorum* (cc. 23, 67, 72, 88, 98, 130, 159): South side (of a church). These phrases are found several times in the Roman *LP*, in the Lives of the eighth and ninth centuries,[113] as well as in a synodal canon written in 853.[114] They seem to have their origin in the separation of men and women during the sacred service; in the *Ordo Romanus*, the south is identified as the side where men stand, while women stand to the north.[115] Note that in Sant' Apollinare

111. See Markus, "Carthage—Prima Justiniana—Ravenna."
112. See Markus, "Ravenna and Rome, 554–604," 574–75.
113. *LP*, Life of Sergius I, Life of Gregory III, c. 6, Life of Hadrian I, c. 84, and Life of Leo III, c. 54.
114. Mansi, *Sacrorum conciliorum*, 14, col. 1014. The Canons of a Synod held at Rome by Pope Eugene II were supplemented at a second synod and published by Pope Leo IV in 853; this statement comes from the supplement: "Et sicuti discrete in eclesia singula videntur exposita, ita virorum pars et mulierum partibus suis contenta sit."
115. Du Cange, *Glossarium*, s.v. *pars*; *Ordo Romanus primus* 1.37: "procedunt qui baptizandi sunt ad ecclesiam, et ordinantur per ordinem, sicut scripta sunt, masculi in dexteram, feminae in sinistram." This part of the *Ordo* dates at the latest to the early ninth century, but may go back to the time of Pope Gregory the Great.

Nuovo, as described in c. 88, the procession of female saints is *parte mulierum*, on the north wall of the nave, and the male saints are *parte virorum*.

patena (c. 173): Paten; dish for chrism.

patera (c. 52): Shallow bowl; dish.

pavimentum (cc. 29, 41, 86, 87, 114): Floor, pavement.

petra (c. 73): Stone.

pictura: See *effigies*.

pila (cc. 41, 147, 151): Doorjamb, door. Usually connected with *ianuae* (cc. 41, 147), the *pila* would be the central pillar between a pair of doors. In c. 151, it is used to mean door. In cc. 41 and 147, it appears as *pili*, a form that does not come from *pila*. Testi-Rasponi (*CPER*, p. 41, n. 2), says that this word is a Latinized form of the Greek πύλη, gate, door, and that *ianuas* was a marginal note explaining it, subsequently inserted in the text.

pinnaculum (c. 94): Summit. Describes the location of the mosaic picture of Theodoric in the *tribunal triclinii* in his palace in Ravenna (see s.v. *tribuna*). It probably refers to the top of the semi-dome of such an apse.

piramis (cc. 94, 155): Base. As used by Agnellus, *piramis* means base, as in the base of a statue or column, whether or not shaped like a pyramid.

pirfireticus (cc. 23, 29, 33, 39, 113): Porphyry. Porphyry was used for the slabs over the tombs of Ursus, Neon, Exuperantius, and Maurus (cc. 23, 29, 33, 113), and for the *urna* in which Theodoric was buried (c. 39).[116] Porphyry was thus connected with burial, and Agnellus's use of the word may have something to do with this connotation rather than every occurrence of the stone in Ravenna. In some cases Agnellus may assume that a bishop is buried under these stones *because* they are of porphyry. For example, in c. 41, Agnellus mentions *rotae rubeae marmoreae*, which are thought to refer to porphyry discs in the pavement (s.v. *rota*), but since it is not a funerary context, he does not specifically use the word *pirfireticus*.

plathoma (cc. 83, 141): Slab of stone. This word is found as *plathoma* only in the *LPR*, although in the Roman *LP* it appears as *platonia*.[117]

---

116. For a complete analysis of literary mentions of and surviving examples of porphyry, in Ravenna and elsewhere, see Delbrueck, *Antike Porphyrwerke*.

117. *LP*, Life of Damasus and Life of Sixtus III; in these cases the slabs bear in-

pluvialis (cc. 111, 174): An episcopal vestment; pluvial.

pocula (cc. 96, 163): Cup, goblet. In both cases, the word occurs in narratives that were derived from other sources.

postis maior (c. 23): Doorpost; door? Agnellus is describing the rows of columns in a basilica, which go up to the wall of the *postis maior*. This phrase must refer to the main door of the church, but it is an unusual use of *postis*, which literally means wooden post.

proconnisus (cc. 26, 50, 76, 149): Proconnesian. Marble from the island of Proconnesos, near Constantinople, characterized by its color—white with grey striations—and found in several of the most richly decorated churches in Ravenna. Agnellus does not identify all the proconnesian marble as such, but only four examples, all related to the veneration of St. Andrew, which he seems to identify with Constantinople and with this type of marble.[118]

pulpitum (c. 14): Pulpit.

purpurus / *purpureus* / *purpuratus* (cc. 37, 66, 88, 100, 174): Purple. This family of words for purple is used to convey the idea of kingship; except for cc. 66 (the letters on an altar cloth), the uses of the word refer to the clothing of kings.

quaternaria (c. 158): Some type of church furnishing. Used only once, in a list of objects derived by Agnellus from a document listing treasure given to Pope Paul. Du Cange cites this occurrence in the *LPR* as the only known use of this word with this meaning.

regia (cc. 24, 41, 94, 149): Main door. The *regiae* were the main doors of a church or other structure.

rota (c. 41): Disk; roundel. The word *rota* had many meanings in the early middle ages; the *rotae rubeae marmoreae* (red marble *rotae*) are thought to be porphyry roundels set into the pavement of the church. Such roundels, called *rotae*, are known from St. Peter's in Rome, perhaps from the Constantinian period, and were frequently used in *opus sectile* floors from late antiquity and from the ninth century.[119] Cf. *pirfireticus*, s.v.

---

scriptions marking the burials of saints. Lazard, "Les byzantinismes," 381; it is also found in Rossi, *Historiarium Ravennatum*, who based his text on the *LPR*.

118. See Deliyannis, "Proconnesian Marble."

119. See McClendon, "The Revival of Opus Sectile," 160–61. The liturgical and

sabulum (c. 73): Sand. Presumably for use in construction, since it is found in a list of building materials; cf. *harena* (s.v.).

sacrarium (c. 161): Small chamber within a church. According to this passage, the clergy were accustomed *(ut mos est)* to gather in this chamber before proceeding to the mass; the function is thus the same as that of the *salutatorium* (s.v.), but it is not clear whether the same chamber is meant.[120]

salutatorium (c. 149): Chamber for the assembly of the clergy before mass. Defined very precisely by Agnellus, "whence up to today the bishops process at the entrance of the mass, in the sight of the watching people." Agnellus says that formerly the clergy entered *de uespertino egressio*; this may perhaps refer to an entryway that connected the cathedral to the episcopium directly, at the east end, and that would therefore also be used for evening prayers, or Vespers, by the clergy.[121] The new *salutatorium* would logically be located farther toward the west, requiring the entering clergy to process through the church in order to reach the altar.

sartatecta (c. 28): Roof; roof works. Found in only one description of patronage, this word is commonly used in similar descriptions in the Roman *LP*,[122] and is also found in the account of a restoration of Solomon's temple in the Vulgate.[123]

scenofactor (cc. 27, 140). Both Holder-Egger and Testi-Rasponi claim that in c. 27 this word comes from the Greek σχοίνος, meaning "rush, stiff reed," and refers to painting with a reed.[124] Since the portrait is ap-

---

symbolic significance of these roundels, based mainly on passages from the *LPR*, is discussed by McClendon and by Glass, *Studies in cosmatesque pavements*, 48–49. Glass makes the useful point that the story of Galla Placidia praying amid the *rotas* may reflect ninth-century rather than fifth-century practice.

120. Deichmann, *Ravenna* 2.1:207–8, assumes that because Agnellus uses both terms *sacrarium* and *salutatorium*, he is distinguishing between two different chambers, but the use of *sacrarium* within a narrative makes it seem more likely that the same space is meant.

121. *Vespertinus* literally means western, which is confusing, because if the clergy entered the church at the west, they would already have to process through the body of the church to reach the altar in the east. Elsewhere (c. 112) Agnellus uses the phrase *post vespertinum officium expletum*, indicating that he is using the adjective to refer to the evening prayers rather than to the direction west.

122. See esp. *LP*, Life of Leo III, passim.

123. 2 Kings 12 and 22.

124. Holder-Egger, *LPER*, 291, n. 3, quoting Du Cange, *Glossarium*; Testi-Rasponi, *CPER*, 75, n. 12.

parently on a candlestick made of some sort of metal, a painted portrait would seem less likely than a relief in a medallion, as for example are still found on the silver cross in the Museo Arcivescovale in Ravenna, known as the Cross of [Bishop] Agnellus. Lazard claims that the word comes from the Greek σχοίνος, referring to a special type of ceramic made by fixing colored reeds to a still-hot ceramic. The same word is used again in c. 140, in the speech of George to the soldiers of Ravenna. However, in the latter case, Lazard claims that the meaning is "makers of triumphal crowns," i.e., in anticipation of the victory.[125] Perhaps in both cases the meaning has something to do with triumphal crowns, and in c. 27 it refers to a portrait surrounded by a wreath. Pizarro notes that since in c. 140 the context is one of warning against sunstroke, the word means tent-makers,[126] which may be the case but which is inappropriate for its use in c. 27.

secretarium (c. 112): Small chamber within a church. Used in a passage with many other unusual words, *secretarium* generally refers to a small chamber close to the altar of a church; it probably means the same thing here, although it is possible that Agnellus is also playing on the word *secretus*, since the events that take place in the *secretarium* in this passage take place furtively.

sedilia (cc. 44, 137, 174): Seats, benches. In c. 44, the benches for the clergy in the curve of the apse, i.e., the *synthronon*.

sedis (cc. 27, 29, 56, 71, 82, 89): Seat. The word *sedis* is used many times in the *LPR* to refer to the office of the bishop; however, in a few cases it refers to an actual object, or to a location in the church. In the two cases referring to decoration, the pictures are located at "the lower wall of the apse, behind the back of the bishop, over the seat *(sedis)* where the bishop sits" (c. 27) and "above the seat *(sedis)* behind the back of the bishop" (c. 89), in both cases clearly referring to a seat at the back of the apse. Furthermore, in c. 71, Maximian is asked to sit *in sede ecclesiae* and to lead the mass, which must also refer to this seat.

In the passages about burial, two translations of the bodies of bishops are described, those of Neon (cc. 26, 56) and Maximian (82). Both bodies are removed from their former resting places *iuxta altarium*, thus

---

125. Lazard, "De l'origine," 295.
126. Pizarro, *Writing Ravenna*, 165, n. 125.

probably underground or in crypts (see s.v. *arca*), and are taken *iuxta sedem basilicae*. Testi-Rasponi, who discusses this question at length, notes that the *sedis* could not be the seat of the bishop in the apse, as there is not room to put sarcophagi there.[127] However, excavations in the crypt of the Basilica Apostolorum have shown that the reburial of Neon, at least, probably was located underground, in the sanctuary of the church, thus indeed close to the *sedis* of the bishop.[128]

sella (cc. 121, 157, 174): Seat.

sepulchrum (cc. 7, 8, 14, 15, 16, 22, 26, 39, 41, 52, 83, 122, 134): Tomb. Cf. *tumulus* (s.v.).

siculum (c. 83): Bronze vessel, perhaps a bucket or vase. Du Cange says that the word *sicula* is often used for some type of vase for holy water, while *sicla* is a vessel for measuring liquids and also a unit of liquid measurement.[129] Either of these meanings would be relevant here.

sindon (c. 68, 83): Muslin; shroud. Lazard notes that although the word is used in the Vulgate to designate the shroud of Christ, its use in the *LPR* is instead a borrowing from the Byzantine word σινδῶν.[130]

stamines sirici (c. 66): Silk warp. From a description of an altar cloth; the fact that this whole description contains several unusual words (s.v. *coccam*) may indicate that Agnellus derived the information from a list of donations rather than from his own experience.

subtegulata (c. 168): Rafter.

supercilium arcus (cc. 72, 149): Curved band on the façade of an arch; zone above the curve of an arch? Agnellus certainly knew the literal meaning of *supercilium* as eyebrow, as he uses it twice in portraits of bishops (cc. 57, 84). In both architectural cases, the *supercilium* is the location

---

127. Testi-Rasponi, *CPER*, 81, n. 7. He interprets the location "next to the seat of the church" as meaning that the new sarcophagi were placed in structures adjacent to the church, such as the narthex. However, Agnellus frequently identifies burials in the *ardica*, and so it is not clear why, if that were the location, he would use a different word here.

128. Deichmann, *Ravenna* 2.2:315–16; excavations published by Mazzotti, "La cripta della chiesa ravennate."

129. Du Cange, *Glossarium*, s.v. *sicla, sicula*.

130. Lazard, "Les byzantinismes," 383.

of an inscription in verse; oddly, in one passage this location is identified as *supercilium arcus*, and in the other as *supercilii arcum*. Testi-Rasponi suggests that, at least in the case of c. 72, this phrase refers to the band between the perpendicular wall and the vault of the apse, a location that often contained inscriptions.[131] However, poetic inscriptions are also known from above the triumphal arch, which seems a more logical application of the phrase.[132]

superiora domus (cc. 86, 142): Upper part; upper storey.

syrius (c. 111): Red. Although Bacchinius suggested that this word should be read as *sericis*,[133] in fact Isidore of Seville explicitly notes that *syricum* refers to a red pigment, while *sericum* is "silk."[134]

tabula (cc. 22, 66, 77, 89, 131, 153): Tablet; plaque; wooden tablet. This word has several different meanings in the *LPR*. In some cases it refers to a plaque with writing or pictures, placed on a wall (cc. 66, 77, 89). In one case it refers to the wooden *tabula* that was struck when it was time for church offices to begin. Twice it is stated as *stadium tabulae*, some location outside the city.

tectum (cc. 131, 132, 168): Roof.

tegula (cc. 77, 130): Tile.

tegumen (c. 26): Cover; lid. The cover of a wooden chest inside a stone sarcophagus.

tegumentum (c. 168): Coverings. Roofs? Or literally cloth coverings of the shrine? The narrative is about a new roof, so this is probably just another word for it.

templum (cc. 1, 2, 23, 28, 41, 61, 72, 85, 98, 114, 130, 134): Temple; church. Although Agnellus uses this word for pagan temples such as those in the Life of Apollinaris (cc. 1 and 2),[135] he also uses it several times to refer to

---

131. Testi-Rasponi, *CPER*, 191, n. 16.
132. Nauerth, *Agnellus von Ravenna, Untersuchungen*, 98.
133. Cited by Holder-Egger, *LPR*, 350.
134. Isidore, *Etymologiarum* 19.17.6: "Aliud est autem sericum, aliud Syricum. Nam sericum lana est quam Seres mittunt; Syricum uero pigmentum quod Syrii Phoenices in Rubri maris litoribus colligunt."
135. Otherwise, pagan temples are not mentioned in the *LPR* except in one other

churches. This use seems to be poetic rather than descriptive, particularly since the word appears in several dedicatory poems and inscriptions.

tessella (cc. 23, 24, 27, 28, 30, 50, 61, 66, 72, 77, 86, 89, 91, 94, 97, 98, 114, 115): Mosaic decoration. Generally found in the ablative plural, *tessellis* is used to refer to mosaic decoration, always in the context of patronage or of description of decoration, and sometimes modified by adjectives such as *argenteis, auratis,* and *variis.* The gold and silver *tessellae* indicate the richness of the decoration, but it does not follow that if gold or silver are not mentioned they were not there (e.g. c. 94, the mosaics in Sant' Apollinare Nuovo).[136]

testudo (c. 23): Vault; ceiling. Used in the context of the decoration of the Ursiana, where it refers to the ceiling or vault of the church.[137] Testi-Rasponi suggested that it means the same as *camera* (s.v.), namely, the vault and also the triumphal arch of the apse.[138] Bovini examined all of the various interpretations of this passage, from nave vault to dome, and concludes that despite the fact that Agnellus usually uses *camera tribunae* (s.v.) to mean apse vault, here he uses *testudo* to mean the same thing. Bovini pointed out that in the tenth-century *Vita Probi*, a crypt under the apse is referred to as *subter testudinem*.[139] However, it is most likely that at one time there existed an inscription in the church, commemorating the decoration by Ursus.[140] The alliterative phrase *totius templi testudinem* is suited to such a poetical inscription. Agnellus is known to have taken words that he does not use elsewhere from inscriptions; therefore, in this

---

instance, in c. 107, where the description of conversion of the Pantheon, called a *fanum*, into a church is taken directly from Paul the Deacon's *Historia Langobardorum*.

136. Cortesi, "Andrea Agnello," 62–65, proposed that the phrase *tessellis auratis novis* in the church of St. Stephen shows that Agnellus knew that mosaics with gold backgrounds first appeared in the time of Maximian, and that he indicated this by the use of the word *novis* (c. 72). The descriptions of mosaics are formulaic enough that the one word *novis* need not indicate a recognition of period style by Agnellus, who does not refer to style anywhere else.

137. Isidore, *Etymologiarum* 15.8.8, defines the *testudo* as the oblique *camera* of a temple, where a *camera* is a curved volume. He says that this meaning arose because, "in modum testudinis veteres templorum tecta faciebant; quae ideo sic fiebant ut caeli imaginem redderet, quod constat esse convexum."

138. Testi-Rasponi, *CPER*, 66, 4.

139. Bovini, "Mosaici parietali scomparsi."

140. Cf. Nauerth, *Agnellus von Ravenna, Untersuchungen*, 73–74.

context the word may not have had a precise, literal meaning for Agnellus.

theca (c. 119): Altar cloth. Du Cange defines this word as a "chest for holding relics," which is accepted by Lazard by analogy with the Greek θέκη, and is often translated in this way.[141] However, the way Agnellus describes this object makes it clear that he is referring to an altar cloth. The *theca* is placed on the altar, *ex blatta alithino* [*s.v.*] ... *habentem historiam, quomodo Deus fecit caelum et terram*. This description, in addition to being similar to those of other *endothes* (s.v.),[142] is also very similar to descriptions of altar cloths in the Roman *LP*, where they are called *vestes*.

trabes: See *laqueares et trabes*.

tractorium (c. 158): Large vase.[143]

tribilon (c. 174): Vase. Du Cange, citing the *LPR*, defines *tribilium* as a vase in which food is placed, derived from the Greek τρύβλιον. Agnellus's is the only use of the word he cites.[144]

tribuna (cc. 42, 72, 77), *tribunal* (cc. 27, 36, 86, 89, 94, 129, 162, 163): Apse; semicircular niche. Except in one case, Agnellus uses *tribuna* or *tribunal* to mean apse.[145] We know that these words mean apse because of one passage referring to the mosaics of Justinian and Theodora at San Vitale as *in tribuna* (c. 77), and they are indeed found in the apse. None of the other *tribunae* mentioned by Agnellus survive, but the word is sometimes modified to refer to a more specific location within the apse, such as *in arco maioris tribunae* (c. 36) or *in supercilium arcus tribunae* (c. 72). Externally, too, the apse is the *tribuna*, as seen by the topographical reference to a region *iuxta tribunal monasterii* ... *Seuerini* (c. 129). *Tribuna(l)* does not only refer to apses in churches; in c. 94, Agnellus describes a picture of Theodoric on horseback, in a *camera tribunae* of the palace in Pavia, which he has recently seen.[146] He compares it with another picture that was once found in Theodoric's palace in Ravenna, *in tribunale triclinii quod uo-*

---

141. Cf. Mango, *The Art of the Byzantine Empire*, 131: "he made a most precious casket (*theca*) [covered] with genuine purple cloth."
142. Nauerth, *Agnellus von Ravenna, Untersuchungen*, 79.
143. See Du Cange, *Glossarium*, s.v.
144. Ibid., s.v. *tribilium*.
145. See s.v. *absida*.
146. In c. 171, he tells of his trip to Pavia, which must have taken place in later 837 or 838; cf. Testi-Rasponi, *CPER*, 228, n. 1. The picture of Theodoric in Pavia is appar-

catur Ad mare. Both of these references must be to apsed niches, such as the *accubitae* (s.v.) in a dining room.

triclinium (c. 29, 94): Dining room, banquet hall. Agnellus describes decorations in two apparently still-functioning *triclinia*, one in the episcopium and one in the Palace of Theodoric.[147] The name of the former is given as *Quinque Accubitas*, a reference to the number of couches the dining room would hold, and thus to the number of apses it had.[148] Most palaces had a notable triclinium with apsed spaces for the couches: the one in the Lateran palace at Rome, built by Pope Leo III in the early ninth century, was called the *XI accubita*, while in the imperial palace in Constantinople the triclinium was called the *XIX accubita*.[149]

trulla (c. 143): Wine ladle.

tugurium (c. 143), *tegurium* (c. 23): House, building. According to Isidore of Seville, a *tugurium* is a type of rough hut or shelter, the same as *tegurium*.[150] In both cases, Agnellus is using the word rhetorically to refer to buildings in general.

---

ently referred to again in a document from 906–10, where a judgment is rendered in the palace, "in laubia ubi sub Teuderico dicitur"; Manaresi, *I placiti del "Regnum Italiae*," vol. 1, no. 122 (a.d. 906/10). The *laubia* may refer to a colonnaded courtyard; see Ward-Perkins, *From Classical Antiquity to the Middle Ages*, 160.

147. The latter possibly the three-apsed room excavated in the palace to the west of Sant' Apollinare Nuovo; Testi-Rasponi, *CPER*, 228, n. 3. On the location of the *triclinium* in the episcopium, see Rizzardi, "Note sull'antico episcopio," 719. She connects the description of the *triclinium* in c. 29, as between the church and the Fossa Amnis, with another passage in the *LPR*, c. 163, in which Bishop John VI is said to be sitting "at the table, behind the apse of the church above the *vivarium*." An area between the Ursiana and the Fossa Amnis would have been "behind the apse" of the church, and thus she concludes that in c. 163 Bishop John was sitting in the *triclinium* of the Quinque Accubita. Deichmann ("Studi sulla Ravenna scomparsa," 107, and *Ravenna* 2.1:206–7), however, suggests that *mensa* refers to a smaller, more private dining chamber. Whichever is correct, the room seems to have had a picture of Christ in it.

148. Agnellus mentions first the *domus* built by Neon within the episcopium and then describes the decoration of the *triclinium*. The mention of both a *domus* and a *triclinium* led Testi-Rasponi to postulate that the *domus* was a house that contained the *triclinium*, and that took its name from that chamber's structure (*CPER*, 78, n. 7).

149. Ibid. See also Rizzardi, "Note sull'antico episcopio," 714–18; and Krautheimer, "Die Decanneacubita."

150. Isidore, *Etymologiarum* 15.2.6 and 12.2.

tumulus (cc. 26, 56, 103, 134, 148): Resting place; burial site; tomb.

turibula (cc. 37, 39): Thurible; censer.

turris (c. 77): Tower.

urceus (c. 143): Pitcher.

urna (c. 39): Urn; vessel; sarcophagus. Agnellus is referring to the porphyry container that still survives in the Mausoleum of Theodoric and that was an imperial bathtub, before it was used to hold Theodoric's body (if it was indeed used as his sarcophagus). There is no good word to describe this object, either in Latin or in English, which may be why Agnellus uses *urna*, a word he uses nowhere else.

valvae (cc. 17, 25, 50, 98): Doors; double doors. Always used in the plural, to mean entrance doors. *Valvae* are probably double doors; Isidore of Seville says that they open inward.[151]

vasa (cc. 111, 143): Vase; jar. Both appearances of this word are in passages that were probably derived from documents seen by Agnellus.

vasculum (cc. 24, 36, 66, 80, 83, 96, 144, 148, 157, 158, 166, 169, 170, 173): Vessel. A word used frequently to mean any kind of vessel, usually in a general sense.

vectes (c. 40): Bars. *Vectes ferrei* are said to have been placed within the city walls by Valentinian; Agnellus probably saw such bars protruding from the walls. *Vectes* is also used several times (cc. 37, 64 [metaphorically], 147) to mean bars, particularly in connection with *serrae* to mean bars and bolts.

vestimenta (cc. 25, 37, 41, 88, 96, 164, 171): Clothing; vestment. A general word for clothing, there does not seem to be any distinction between the use of *vestimentum* and that of *vestis*, which Agnellus always uses to mean clothing (cc. 17, 100, 128, 129, 131, 171, 174) and never to mean altar cloth (cf. *theca*, s.v.).

villa (c. 163): Villa, country-house.

viridarium (c. 86): Garden? Orchard? Used only once, in a topographical context, which means that Agnellus either knew of this *viridarium* per-

---

151. Ibid., 15.7.4.

sonally or that it was mentioned in the document listing the churches reconciled by Bishop Agnellus, which Agnellus used in writing this passage.

vitreum (c. 72), *vitrum* (cc. 113, 143): Glass. In c. 72 the image of Maximian, placed in the *camera* (s.v.) of the apse of St. Stephen's, is surrounded *mirifice opere vitreo*. The image must have been in the window zone of the apse, like the pictures of bishops in Sant' Apollinare in Classe; the *vitreo* could refer to windows made of glass of some special type, found, as Agnellus says, around the curve of the apse.[152] The description of the vessel made of glass (c. 143) was taken from a document listing donations; Agnellus says that a piece of porphyry was as shiny as glass (c. 113).

vivarium (c. 163): Fish pond. Deichmann identifies the *vivarium* as the pool or *nympheum* containing fish for the episcopal table, and summarizes the archaeological evidence for the discovery of such a *nympheum* in 1919 at the base of the building containing the Capella Arcivescovile.[153]

Types of Buildings

aula	ecclesia	palatium	tugurium
balneum	episcopium	platea	tegurium
basilica	fons	pons	turris
casa	lavacrum	porta	villa
coenobium	mansio	posterula	viridarium
domus	mausoleum	templum	vivarium
domus ecclesiae	monasterium	triclinium	

Parts of buildings

abdita	camera	cripta	laqueares et
absida	tribunae	cubiculum	trabes
arcus	caput	cubilium	moenia
ardica	cella	fenestra	monasterium
atrium	collum	frons	murus
basis	columna	ianua	ostium
camera	crips	introitum	paries

152. Nauerth, *Agnellus von Ravenna, Untersuchungen*, 28, n. 55.
153. Deichmann, "Studi sulla Ravenna scomparsa," 108–11; a reconstruction drawing, as well as a discussion, is provided in Deichmann, *Ravenna* 2.1:207 and fig. 151.

pars mulierum	piramis	secretarium	tegumentum
pars virorum	postis maior	supercilium	testudo
pavimentum	regia	arcus	tribuna(l)
pila	sacrarium	superiora	valvae
pinnaculum	salutatorium	domus	

Construction materials

abiegnus	lapis	lithostratus	sabulum
bisalis	laqueares et	marmor	sartatecta
caementum	trabes	metalla	subtegulata
calx	lasta	musivum	tegula
docaria	lastra	petra	tessella
gipsea metalla	later	pirfireticus	trabes
harena	latercula	proconnisus	vectes
hypocartosis	ligna	rota	vitreum

Church furniture

altar	cancellus	pulpitum	tabula
altarium	civorium	sedilia	tegumen
ara	feretrum	sedis	tumulus
ambo	glosochomum	sella	
arca	plathoma	sepulchrum	

Vessels and objects

alapae	cereostatus	diadema	patera
ama	chrismatarium	discus	pocula
amula	ciatum	ferculum	quaternaria
aquimanile	coclearia trac-	fiala	siculum
calathum	toria	ialicum	tribilon
calix	corona	lichna	trulla
candelabrum	crapula	lucerna	turibula
canistrum	crater	manualia ad	urceus
cannata	crux	mensuram	urna
capsa	cuppa	patena	vasa

GLOSSARY 347

Fabric objects and vestments

casula	endothis	pallea	pluuialis
chlamys	limbus	pallia	sindon
dalmatica	orarium	pallium	theca
diplois			

Decoration of objects

aculis factus	bissinus	lamina argentea	scenofactorae
anaglifa operatione	blattus alithinus	mechanico opere	artis stamines sirici
argirius	coccus	orbita/	syrius
auricalcus	coloribus	orbitella	vitrum
auro textilis	cristallus	purpurus	

Pictures

effigies	figura	istoria
enigma	imago	pictura

BIBLIOGRAPHY

Primary Sources

Acta Sanctorum quotquot toto orbe coluntur, vel a catholicis scriptoribus celebrantur. Ed. J. Bollandus et al. 68 vols. Paris, 1863–1940.
Agnellus. *Liber Pontificalis sive vitae Pontificum Ravennatum.* Ed. Benedetto Bacchinius. Modena, 1708. Reprint with an introduction and corrections by L. A. Muratori. *RIS* 2.1. Milan, 1723. Reprinted in *PL* 106:477–750.
———. *Codex Pontificalis Ecclesiae Ravennatis* (CPER). Ed. Alessandro Testi-Rasponi. *RIS* n.s. 2.3. Bologna, 1924.
———. *Liber pontificalis ecclesiae Ravennatis.* Ed. Deborah M. Deliyannis. *CCCM*, forthcoming.
———. *Liber pontificalis ecclesiae Ravennatis* (LPER). Ed. Oswald Holder-Egger. *MGH SS rer. Lang. et. Ital.,* 265–391. Hanover, 1878.
Anonymus Valesianus. Ed. Theodor Mommsen. *MGH AA* 9:306–29. Hanover, 1892.
Augustine. *Sermonum classes quatuor. PL* 38 and 39.
Ausonius. *Parentalia.* In *The Works of Ausonius,* ed. R. P. H. Green, 25–41. Oxford, 1991.
———. *Commemoratio professorum Burdigalensium.* In *The Works of Ausonius,* ed. R. P. H. Green, 41–59. Oxford, 1991.
Caesarius of Arles. *Sermones.* 2 vols. Ed. Germain Morin. *CCSL* 103–4. Turnhout, 1953.
Chronica Minora saec. IV, V, VI, VII. Ed. Theodor Mommsen. *MGH AA* 9, 11, 13. Berlin, 1892–98.
Codex Carolinus. Ed. Wilhelm Gundlach. *MGH Epistolae* 3:469–657. Hanover, 1892.
Davis, Raymond, trans. *The Book of Pontiffs (Liber Pontificalis): The Ancient Biographies of the First Ninety Roman Bishops to AD 715.* Liverpool, 1989.
———. *The Lives of the Eighth-Century Popes (Liber Pontificalis): The Ancient Biographies of Nine Popes from AD 715 to AD 817.* Liverpool, 1992.
———. *The Lives of the Ninth-Century Popes (Liber Pontificalis): The Ancient Biographies of Ten Popes from A.D. 817–891.* Liverpool, 1995.
De inventione corporis beati Apollinaris. Ed. Lodovico A. Muratori. *RIS* 1.2:538–46. Milan, 1725.
Einhard. *Vita Karoli Magni.* Ed. Georg H. Pertz. *MGH Scriptores rerum Germanicarum in Usum Scholarum.* Hanover, 1911.
Eusebius of Caesarea. *The Ecclesiastical History.* 2 vols. Ed. Hugh J. Lawlor, trans. John E. L. Oulton. Cambridge, Mass., 1942–49.

Evagrius Scholasticus. *The Ecclesiastical History of Evagrius, with the Scholia*. Ed. Joseph Bidez and Léon Parmentier. Amsterdam, 1898; reprint 1964.

Gregory of Tours. *De miraculis sancti Martini episcopi. PL* 71, cols. 913–1010.

———. *Liber vitae patrum.* Ed. Bruno Krusch. *MGH SS rer. Merov.* 1.2:661–744. Hanover, 1885.

———. *Libri historiarum X (Historia Francorum).* Ed. Bruno Krusch and Wilhelm Levison. *MGH SS rer. Merov.* 1.1. Hanover, 1951.

———. *Life of the Fathers.* Trans. Edward James. Vol. 1 of *Translated Texts for Historians*. Liverpool, 1985.

Gregory the Great. *Homiliae in Hiezechihelem.* Ed. Mark Adriaen. *CCSL* 142. Turnhout, 1971.

———. *Dialogi.* Ed. Adalbert de Vogüé, trans. Paul Antin. *Sources Chrétiennes* 251, 260, and 265. Paris, 1978–80.

———. *Moralia in Iob.* 3 vols. Ed. Mark Adriaen. *CCSL* 143, 143A, 143B. Turnhout, 1979–1985.

———. *Registrum epistularum.* 2 vols. Ed. Dag Norberg. *CCSL* 140–140A. Turnhout, 1982.

———. *Homiliae in Evangelia.* Ed. Raymond Etaix. *CCSL* 141. Turnhout, 1999.

Hrabanus Maurus. *De rerum naturis. PL* 111, cols. 9–614.

Isidore of Seville. *Etymologiarum sive Originum Libri XX.* Ed. Wallace M. Lindsay. Oxford, 1911; reprint, 1978.

Jerome. *Commentariorum in Evangelium Matthei libri quatuor.* Ed. and trans. Émile Bonnard. *Sources Chrétiennes* 77. Paris, 1977–79.

Jordanes. *Getica.* Ed. Theodor Mommsen. *MGH AA* 5. Berlin, 1882.

Mansi, Giovanni Domenico, ed. *Sacrorum conciliorum nova et amplissima collectio.* 53 vols. Florence, 1759–98.

Marcellinus Comes. *Chronica.* Ed. Theodor Mommsen. *MGH AA* 11, 60–104.

Ordo Romanus Primus. In *Les Ordines Romani du haut moyen âge.* Vol. 2 of *Les Testes (Ordines I–XIII).* Ed. Michel Andrieu. Louvain, 1948.

Paul the Deacon. *Historia Langobardorum.* Ed. Ludwig Bethmann and Georg Waitz. *MGH SS rer. Lang. et. Ital.*, 12–187. Hanover, 1878.

———. *History of the Lombards.* Trans. William Dudley Foulke. Philadelphia, 1974.

———. *S. Gregorii Magni Vita. PL* 75:42–62.

Paulinus of Nola. *Epistolae.* Ed. Wilhelm de Hartel. *Corpus scriptorum ecclesiasticorum latinorum* 29. Vienna, 1894.

Peter Chrysologus. *Letter to Eutyches. PL* 52, 71.

———. *Sermones.* Ed. Alexandre Olivar. *CCSL* 24, 24A, 24B. Turnhout, 1975–1982.

Peter Damian. *Sermones: ad fidem antiquiorum codicum restituti.* Ed. Giovanni Lucchesi. *CCCM* 57. Turnhout, 1983.

Pliny the Elder. *Historia naturalis.* 10 vols. Ed. and trans. Harris Rackham et al. Cambridge, Mass., 1949–61.

Prudentius. *Liber apotheosis.* In *Carmina*, ed. Maurice P. Cunningham. *CCSL* 126. Turnhout, 1966.

Pseudo-Ambrose. *Epistolae ex Ambrosianarum Numero Segregatae. PL* 17, cols. 813–30.

———. *Sermones hactenus sub Ambrosii nomine evulgatos.* PL 17, cols. 605–758.
Pseudo-Bede. *Excerptiones Patrum, Collectanea, Flores ex diversis, Quaestiones et Parabolae.* PL 94, cols. 539–48.
Saxo Poeta. *Annalium de gestis Caroli Magni imperatoris Libri Quinque.* Ed. Paul de Winterfeld. *MGH Poetae Latini Aevi Carolini* 4.1:5–71. Berlin, 1899.
Spicilegium Ravennatis historiae. Ed. Lodovico A. Muratori. *RIS* 1.2:525–83. Milan, 1725.
Strabo, Walahfrid. *Versus in Aquisgrani Palatio editi anno Hludowici Imperatoris XVI. De imagine tetrici.* Ed. Ernst Duemmler. *MGH Poetae Latinae Aevi Carolini* 2:370–78. Berlin, 1884.
The Passions and the Homilies from Leabhar Breac. Ed. Robert Atkinson. Todd Lecture Series 2. Dublin, 1887.
Vita beati Apollinaris martyris archiepiscopi Ravennatis ecclesiae. Ed. Lodovico A. Muratori. *RIS* 1.2:529–33. Milan, 1725.

Secondary Sources

Alfieri, N. "Appunti di topografia altomedioevale: 'usque ad mensam Walani' (Agn. rav. 159)." *Atti dell'Accademia delle Scienze dell'Istituto di Bologna, Classe di Scienze morali, Rendiconti* 62.2 (1973–74): 5–23.
Andaloro, Maria. "Il *Liber pontificalis* e la questione delle immagini da Sergio I a Adriano I." In *Roma e l'età carolingia: atti delle Giornate di Studio, 3–8 maggio 1976,* ed. J. Hubert et al., 69–77. Rome, 1976.
Austin, Norman J. "Autobiography and History: Some Later Roman Historians and Their Veracity." In *History and Historians in Late Antiquity,* ed. Brian Croke and Alanna M. Emmett, 54–65. Sydney, 1983.
Bandmann, Günter. "Die Vorbilder der Aachener Pfalzkapelle." In *Karl der Grosse, Lebenswerk und Nachleben,* ed. W. Braunfels, 3:424–62. Düsseldorf, 1965–67.
Baños Vallejo, Fernando. *La hagiografía como género literario en la Edad Media: tipología de doce vidas individuales castellanas.* Oviedo, 1989.
Benericetti, Ruggero. *Il Pontificale di Ravenna: studio critico.* Faenza, 1994.
———. *Il Cristo nei sermoni di S. Pier Crisologo.* Cesena, 1995.
Bermond Montanari, Giovanna. "La zona archeologica di Palazzolo." *CARB* 30 (1983): 17–21.
Berschin, Walter. *Biographie und Epochenstil im lateinischen Mittelalter.* Vol. 1, *Von der Passio Perpetuae zu den Dialogi Gregors des Grossen.* Stuttgart, 1986. Vol. 2, *Merowingische Biographie: Italien, Spanien und die Inseln im frühen Mittelalter.* Stuttgart, 1988.
Bertolini, Ottorino. "Sergio arcivescovo di Ravenna (744–769) e i papi del suo tempo." *Studi Romagnoli* 1 (1950): 43–88.
———. "Il 'Liber Pontificalis.'" In *La Storiografia Altomedievale,* Settimane di Studio del Centro Italiano di Studi sull'Alto Medioevo 17, 1:387–456, and discussion, 1:707–10. Spoleto, 1970.
Beutler, Christian. *Statua. Die Entstehung der nachantiken Statue und der europäische Individualismus.* Munich, 1982.

Bovini, Giuseppe. "Mosaici parietali scomparsi degli antichi edifici sacri di Ravenna." *Felix Ravenna* 68 (1955): 54–76; *Felix Ravenna* 69 (1955): 3–20.

———. "Le origini di Ravenna e lo sviluppo della città in età romana." *Felix Ravenna* 70 (1956): 38–60; *Felix Ravenna* 72 (1956): 27–68.

———. "Le vicende del *Regisole* statua equestre ravennate." *Felix Ravenna* 86 (1963): 138–54.

———. "Le 'tovaglie d'altare' ricamate ricordate da Andrea Agnello nel *Liber Pontificalis Ecclesiae Ravennatis.*" *CARB* 21 (1974): 77–90.

———. "Il recente rinvenimento del 'Monasterium Sancti Ruphilli.'" In *Studies in Memory of David Talbot Rice*, ed. G. Robertson and G. Henderson, 164–70. Edinburgh, 1975.

Brill, Joseph. "Der Liber Pontificalis des Agnellus von Ravenna. Kulturelles und Sprachliches." Ph.D. diss., University of Münster, 1933.

Brown, Thomas S. "The Church of Ravenna and the Imperial Administration in the Seventh Century." *English Historical Review* 94 (1979): 1–28.

———. *Gentlemen and Officers: Imperial Administration and Aristocratic Power in Byzantine Italy A.D. 554–800*. Hertford, 1984.

———. "Louis the Pious and the Papacy, A Ravenna Perspective." In *Charlemagne's Heir: New Perspectives on the Reign of Louis the Pious (814–840)*, ed. Peter Godman and Roger Collins, 297–308. Oxford, 1990.

Bullough, Donald A. "Early Medieval Social Groupings: The Terminology of Kinship." *Past and Present* 45 (1969): 3–18.

Cabrol, Fernand, Henri Leclerq, and Henri I. Marrou. *Dictionnaire d'archeologie chrétienne et de liturgie*. 15 vols. Paris, 1907–51.

Callebat, Louis et al., eds. *Dictionnaire des termes techniques du De architectura de Vitruve*. Hildesheim, 1995.

Capitani, Ovidio. "Agnello Ravennate nella recente storia della storiografia medioevale." *Felix Ravenna* 105–6 (1973): 183–98.

Carile, Antonio, ed. *Storia di Ravenna*. Vol. 2, bk. 1, *Dall'età Bizantina all'età Ottoniana: Territorio, economia e società*. Venice, 1991.

———. *Storia di Ravenna*. Vol. 2, bk. 2, *Dall'età Bizantina all'età Ottoniana: Ecclesiologia, cultura e arte*. Venice, 1992.

Christie, Neil. "The City Walls of Ravenna: The Defence of a Capital, A.D. 402–750." *CARB* 36 (1989): 113–38.

Clanchy, Michael. *From Memory to Written Record: England, 1066–1307*. Cambridge, Mass., 1979.

Cortesi, Giuseppe. *Classe paleocristiana e paleobizantina*. Ravenna, 1980.

———. "Andrea Agnello e il 'Liber Pontificalis Ecclesiae Ravennatis.'" *CARB* 28 (1981): 31–76.

Croquison, Jacques. "L'iconographie chrétienne à Rome d'après le Liber Pontificalis." *Byzantion* 34 (1964): 535–606.

Dagron, Gilbert. "Holy Images and Likeness." *Dumbarton Oaks Papers* 45 (1991): 23–33.

De Angelis d'Ossat, Guglielmo. "Sulla distrutta aula dei 'Quinque accubita' a Ravenna." *CARB* 20 (1973): 263–73.

Deichmann, Friedrich W. "I titoli dei vescovi ravennati da Ecclesio a Massimiano nelle epigrafi dedicatorie di S. Vitale e di S. Apollinare in Classe tramandate da Agnello." *Studi Romagnoli* 3 (1952): 63–67.

———. *Ravenna, Hauptstadt des spätantiken Abendlandes.* Vol. 1, *Geschichte und Monumente.* Wiesbaden, 1969.

———. "Studi sulla Ravenna scomparsa." *Felix Ravenna* 103–4 (1972): 61–112.

———. *Ravenna, Hauptstadt des spätantiken Abendlandes.* Vol. 2, bk. 1, *Die Bauten bis zum Tode Theoderichs des Großen.* Wiesbaden, 1974.

———. *Ravenna, Hauptstadt des spätantiken Abendlandes.* Vol. 2, bk. 2, *Die Bauten des Julianus argentarius; übrige Kirchen.* Wiesbaden, 1976.

———. *Ravenna, Hauptstadt des spätantiken Abendlandes.* Vol. 2, bk. 3, *Geschichte, Topographie, Kunst und Kultur; Indices zum Gesamtwerk.* Wiesbaden, 1989.

Delbrueck, Richard. *Antike Porphyrwerke.* Berlin, 1932.

Deliyannis, Deborah M. "Agnellus of Ravenna and Iconoclasm: Theology and Politics in a Ninth-Century Historical Text." *Speculum* 71 (1996): 559–76.

———. "A Biblical Model for Serial Biography: the Roman *Liber Pontificalis* and the Books of Kings." *Révue Bénédictine* 107 (1997): 15–23.

———. "Bury Me in Ravenna? Appropriating Galla Placidia's Body in the Middle Ages." *Studi Medievali,* n.s., 42 (2000): 289–99.

———. "Year-Dates in the Early Middle Ages." In *Time in the Medieval World,* ed. C. Humphrey and W. M. Ormrod, 5–22. Woodbridge, Suffolk: Boydell and Brewer, 2001.

———. "Charlemagne's Silver Tables: The Ideology of an Imperial Capital." *Early Medieval Europe* 12 (2003).

———. "Proconnesian Marble in Ninth-Century Ravenna." In *Archaeology in Architecture: Festschrift for Cecil L. Striker,* ed. Deborah M. Deliyannis and Judson Emerick. Forthcoming.

———. "Agnellus's Life of Bishop Sergius of Ravenna and the Roman *Liber pontificalis.*" Forthcoming.

Du Cange, Charles du Fresne. *Glossarium Mediae et Infimae Latinitatis,* ed. L. Favre. 10 vols. Paris, 1937.

Duval, Noel. "Que savons-nous du Palais de Théodoric à Ravenna?" *Mélanges d'Archéologie et d'Histoire* 72 (1960): 337–71.

Elliott, Alison G. *Roads to Paradise: Reading the Lives of the Early Saints.* Hanover, N.H., 1987.

Fabbri, Paolo. "Il controllo delle acque tra tecnica ed economia." In *Storia di Ravenna,* ed. A. Carile, vol. 2, bk. 1, 9–25. Venice, 1991.

Falkenstein, Ludwig. *Der "Lateran" der karolingischen Pfalz zu Aachen.* Cologne, 1966.

Fantuzzi, Marco. *Monumenti ravennati de' secoli di mezzo, per la maggior parte inediti.* 6 vols. Venice, 1801–4.

Farioli Campanati, Rafaella. "Edifici paleocristiani di Classe, Stato attuale delle ricerche e problemi." In *Ravenna e il porto di Classe: Venti anni di ricerche archeologiche tra Ravenna e Classe,* ed. Giovanna Bermond Montanari and Maria Grazia Maioli, 23–51. Imola, 1983.

———. "La Topografia Imperiale di Ravenna dal V al VI secolo." *CARB* 36 (1989): 139–47.

———. "Ravenna, Constantinopoli: Aspetti Topografico-Monumentali e Iconografici." In *Storia di Ravenna*, ed. Antonio Carile, vol. 2, bk. 2, 127–57. Venice, 1992.

Fasoli, Gina. "Rileggendo il 'Liber Pontificalis' di Agnello Ravennate." *Settimane di studio del Centro italiano di studi sull'alto medio evo* 17 (1970): 457–95, 711–18.

———. "Sul Patrimonio della chiesa di Ravenna in Sicilia." *Felix Ravenna* 118 (1979): 69–75.

———. "Il patrimonio della chiesa Ravennate." In *Storia di Ravenna*, ed. Antonio Carile, vol. 2, bk. 1, 389–400. Venice, 1991.

Felletti Maj, Bianca M. "Una carta di Ravenna romana e bizantina." *Rendiconti della Pontificia accademia romana di archeologia* 41 (1968–69): 85–120.

Geary, Patrick. *Furta Sacra: Thefts of Relics in the Central Middle Ages*. Princeton, 1978.

Geertman, Herman. *More veterum: il Liber Pontificalis e gli edifici ecclesiastici de Roma nella tarda antichita e nell' alto medioevo*. Archaeologica Traiectina 10. Rome, 1975.

Gerola, Giuseppe. "Il valore della frase 'ante altare' nello storico Agnello." *Atti e memorie dell'accademia di Agricoltura, Scienze e Lettere di Verona*, 4th ser., 19 (1916): 25.

Giani, Duilio. "Alcune osservazioni per la cronologia di Agnello Ravennate." *Studi Storici di A. Crivellucci* 7 (1898): 399–409 and 461–79.

Glass, Dorothy F. *Studies in Cosmatesque Pavements*. BAR Intl. Series 82. Oxford, 1980.

Goldschmidt, Rudolf C. *Paulinus' Churches at Nola*. Amsterdam, 1940.

Gonin, Henri L. *Excerpta agnelliana: The Ravennate Liber Pontificalis as a Source for the History of Art*. Utrecht, 1933.

Grimm, Herman. *Das Reiterstandbild des Theoderich zu Aachen und das Gedicht des Walafried Strabus darauf*. Berlin, 1869.

Guenée, Bernard. *Histoire et culture historique dans l'Occident médiéval*. Paris, 1980.

Guillou, André. "Esarcato e Pentapoli, regione psicologica dell'Italia bizantina." *Studi Romagnoli* 18 (1967): 297–319.

———. *Régionalisme et indépendance dans l'empire byzantin au VIIe siècle. L'exemple de l'Exarchat et de la Pentapole d'Italie*. Studi Storici 75–76. Rome, 1969.

Hartmann, Ludo M. "Johannicius von Ravenna." In *Festschrift Theodor Gomperz: dargebracht zum siebzigsten Geburtstage am 29. Marz 1902, von Schulern, Freunden, Kollegen*, 319–23. Vienna, 1902; reprint Aalen, 1979.

Haubrichs, Wolfgang. "*Veriloquium nominis* zur Namensexegese im frühen Mittelalter: Nebst einer Hypothese über die Identität des 'heiland'-Autors." In *Verbum et signum. Beiträge zur mediävistischen Bedeutungsforschung*, ed. Hans Fromm, Wolfgang Harms, and Uwe Ruberg, 1:231–66. Munich, 1975.

Heffernan, Thomas J. *Sacred Biography: Saints and Their Biographers in the Middle Ages*. Oxford, 1988.

Heinzelmann, Martin. "Neue Aspekte der biographischen und hagiographischen Literatur in der lateinischen Welt (1.–6. Jahrhundert)." *Francia* 1 (1973): 27–44.

Hoffmann, Harmut. "Die aachener Theodorichstatue." In *Das Erste Jahrtausend*, ed. Victor H. Elbern, 318–35. Düsseldorf, 1962.

Holder-Egger, Oswald. "Untersuchungen über einige annalistische Quellen zur

Geschichte des fünften und sechsten Jahrhunderts, II, III. Die Ravennater Annalen." *Neues Archiv der Gesellschaft für Altere Deutsche Geschichtskunde* 1 (1876): 309–68.
Kaplan, Paul H. D. *The Rise of the Black Magus in Western Art*. Studies in the Fine Arts, Iconography 9. Ann Arbor, 1985.
Krautheimer, Richard. "Die Decanneacubita in Konstantinopel: Ein kleiner Beitrag zur Frage Rom u. Byzanz." In *Tortulae: Studien zu altchristlichen und byzantinischen Monumenten*, ed. Walter Nikolaus Schumacher, 195–99. Römische Quartalschrift für Altertumskunde und Kirchengeschichte, suppl. 30. Rome, 1966.
Lanzoni, Francesco. "Il 'Liber Pontificalis' ravennate." *Rivista di scienze storiche* 6 (1909): 345–70, 425–64, 571–92.
———. "Reliquie dell'antico Officio Divino di Ravenna in Agnello." *Rassegna Gregoriana* 8 (1909): 243–46.
———. "Reliquie della liturgia ravennate del secolo IX secondo il 'Liber Pontificalis' di Agnello." *Rassegna Gregoriana* 9 (1910): 327–38.
———. "S. Severo vescovo di Ravenna (342–343) nella storia e nella leggenda." Parts 1 and 2. *Atti e memorie della deputazione di storia patria per le provincie di Romagna*, 4th ser., 1 (1910–11): 325–95; 2 (1911–12): 350–96.
———. "Leggende Orientali in Agnello Ravennate." *Felix Ravenna* 8 (1912): 318–26.
———. "Novelle orientali in Agnello Ravennate." *Felix Ravenna* 17 (1915): 763–64.
———. "Ancóra sulle leggende orientali in Agnello Ravennate." *Felix Ravenna* 18 (1915): 795–97.
———. "Le fonti della leggenda di Sant'Apollinare di Ravenna." *Atti e memorie della deputazione di storia patria per le provincie di Romagna*, 4th ser., 5 (1915): 111–76.
———. "La 'regio Latronum' di Agnello." *Felix Ravenna* 20 (1915): 866–67.
———. "L' 'ad arietem' di Agnello ravennate." *Felix Ravenna* 28 (1917): 1125–26.
Laqua, Hans Peter. *Traditionen und Leitbilder bei dem Ravennater Reformer Petrus Damiani, 1042–1052*. Munich, 1976.
Lazard, Sylviane. "De l'origine des hellénismes d'Agnello." *Revue de linguistique romane* 48 (1976): 255–98.
———. "Les byzantinismes lexicaux de l'exarchat de Ravenne et de la Pentapole." *Byzantion* 56 (1986): 354–426.
Lehmann, Phyllis Williams. "Theodosius or Justinian? A Renaissance Drawing of a Byzantine Rider." *Art Bulletin* 41 (1959): 39–57.
Liddell, H. G., R. Scott, and Henry Stuart Jones. *A Greek-English Lexikon*. 9th ed. Oxford, 1996.
Longère, Jean. *La prédication médiévale*. Paris, 1983.
Löwe, Heinz. "Von Theoderich dem Großen zu Karl dem Großen." In *Von Cassiodor zu Dante; ausgewahlte Aufsatze zur Geschichtschreibung und politischen Ideenwelt des Mittelalters*, 33–74. Berlin, 1973.
Lucchesi, Giovanni. *Note agiografiche sui primi vescovi di Ravenna*. Faenza, 1941.
———. "Giovanni I Angelopte." *Bibliotheca Sanctorum* 6:927–28. Rome, 1961–70.
Lugari, Giovanni B. *Il culto di S. Pietro sul Gianicolo e il Libro pontificale ravennate*. Rome, 1907.
Lusuardi-Siena, Silvia. "Sulle tracce della presenza Gota in Italia, Il Contributo delle

Fonti Archeologiche." In *Magistra Barbaritas. I Barbari in Italia*, ed. Giovanni Pugliese Carratelli, 509–58. Milan, 1984.

Lynch, Joseph H. *Godparents and Kinship in Early Medieval Europe.* Princeton, 1986.

Manaresi, Cesare, ed. *I placiti del "Regnum Italiae."* 3 vols. Fonti per la storia d'Italia 92, 96, and 97. Rome, 1955–60.

Mango, Cyril. Letter in response to Phyllis W. Lehmann, "Theodosius or Justinian?" and Lehmann's reply. *Art Bulletin* 41 (1959): 351–56, 356–58.

———, ed. *The Art of the Byzantine Empire, 312–1453, Sources and Documents.* Englewood Cliffs, N.J., 1972.

Markus, Robert A. "Carthage—Prima Justiniana—Ravenna: An Aspect of Justinian's *Kirchenpolitik.*" *Byzantion* 49 (1979): 277–302.

———. "Ravenna and Rome, 554–604." *Byzantion* 51 (1981): 566–78.

Mazzotti, Mario. "Per una nuova datazione della 'Passio S. Apollinaris.'" *Studi Romagnoli* 3 (1952): 123–29.

———. "La croce argentea del vescovo Agnello del Museo Arcivescovile di Ravenna." *CARB* 7 (1960): 261–70.

———. "Note di antica topografia Ravennate." *CARB* 14 (1967): 219–31.

———. "La cripta della chiesa ravennate di S. Francesco dopo le ultime esplorazioni." *CARB* 21 (1974): 217–30.

———. "S. Apollinare in Classe: indagini e studi degli ultimi trent'anni." *Rivista di archeologia cristiana* 62, nos. 1–2 (1986): 199–219.

McClendon, Charles B. "The Revival of Opus Sectile Pavements in Rome and the Vicinity in the Carolingian Period." *Papers of the British School at Rome* 48 (1980): 157–65.

McLaughlin, R. Emmet. "The Word Eclipsed? Preaching in the Early Middle Ages." *Traditio* 47 (1991): 77–122.

McNally, Robert E. "Three Holy Kings in Early Irish Latin Writing." In *Kyriakon, Festschrift Johannes Quasten*, ed. Patrick Granfield and Josef A. Jungmann, 2:667–90. Münster, 1970.

Miller, Maureen C. "The Development of the Archiepiscopal Residence in Ravenna, 300–1300." *Felix Ravenna* 141–44 (1991–92): 145–73.

———. *The Bishop's Palace: Architecture and Authority in Medieval Italy.* Ithaca, 2000.

Moffatt, Ann. "Sixth-century Ravenna from the Perspective of Abbot Agnellus." In *The Sixth Century: End or Beginning?* ed. P. Allen and E. Jeffreys, 236–46. Brisbane, 1996.

Muratori, Santi. Review of *Codex Pontificalis Ecclesiae Ravennatis*, by Alessandro Testi-Rasponi. *Felix Ravenna* 30 (1925): 59–74.

———. "Agnello e il suo libro." *Felix Ravenna* 42 (1932): 189–203.

Nauerth, Claudia. *Agnellus von Ravenna, Untersuchungen zur archäologischen Methode des ravennatischen Chronisten.* Munich, 1974.

———, ed. *Agnellus von Ravenna: Liber pontificalis: Bischofsbuch.* Freiburg, 1996.

Noble, Thomas F. X. *The Republic of St. Peter, The Birth of the Papal State, 680–825.* Philadelphia, 1984.

———. "A New Look at the *Liber Pontificalis.*" *Archivium historiae pontificiae* 23 (1985): 347–58.

Olivar, Alexandre. *Los sermones de San Pedro Crisologo, estudio critico.* Abadía de Montserrat, 1962.
Orioli, Giorgio. "I vescovi di Ravenna—Note di cronologia e di storia." *Bollettino della Badia Greca di Grottaferrata* 32 (1978): 45–75.
———. "Cronotassi dei vescovi di Ravenna." *Felix Ravenna* 127–30 (1984–85): 323–32.
Picard, Jean-Charles. "Les maîtres d'oeuvre de l'architecture ravennate au Haut Moyen Age." In *Artistes, Artisans, et Production Artistique au Moyen Age,* ed. X. Barral i Altet, 2:39–44. Paris, 1987.
———. *Le souvenir des évêques: sépultures, listes episcopales et culte des évêques en Italie du Nord des origines au Xe siècle.* Rome, 1988.
Pierpaoli, Mario. *Il libro di Agnello istorico. Le vicende di Ravenna antica fra storia e realtà.* Ravenna: 1988.
Pietri, Charles. "Bâtiments et sanctuaires annexes de la Basilique Saint-Martin de Tours, à la fin du VIe siècle." *Revue d'histoire de l'église de France* 62 (1976): 223–34.
Piper, Ferdinand. *Einleitung in die Monumentale Theologie, eine Geschichte der christlichen Kunstarchaologie und Epigraphik.* Gotha, 1867.
Pizarro, Joaquín Martínez. *A Rhetoric of the Scene: Dramatic Narrative in the Early Middle Ages.* Toronto, 1989.
———. *Writing Ravenna: The* Liber Pontificalis *of Andreas Agnellus.* Ann Arbor, 1995.
Porta, Paola. "Il centro del potere, il problema del palazzo dell'esarco." In *Storia di Ravenna,* ed. Antonio Carile, vol. 2, bk. 1, 269–83. Venice, 1991.
Rizzardi, Clementina. "Note sull'antico episcopio di Ravenna, formazione e sviluppo." In *Actes du XIe Congrès International d'Archéologie Chretienne* 1:711–31. Vatican City, 1989.
Romano, G. "A proposito di un passo di Agnello Ravennate." In *Storia dell'economia italiana,* ed. Carlo M. Cipolla, vol. 1, 23–28. Turin, 1959.
Rossi (Rubeus), Gerolamo. *Historiarium Ravennatum—Libri Decem.* 1572; 2d ed., Venice, 1959.
Sansterre, Jean-Marie. "Monaci e monasteri greci a Ravenna." In *Storia di Ravenna,* ed. Antonio Carile, vol. 2, bk. 2, 323–29. Venice, 1992.
Savigni, Raffaele. "I papi e Ravenna. Dalla Caduta dell'Esarcato alla Fine del Secolo X." In *Storia di Ravenna,* ed. Antonio Carile, vol. 2, bk. 2, 331–68. Venice, 1992.
Schmidt, W. "Das Reiterstandbild des ostgothischen Königs Theoderich in Ravenna und Aachen." *Jahrbücher für Kunstwissenschaft* 6 (1873): 1–51.
Silva, Romano. "L'imitatzione di Roma e l'attività artistica a Lucca in età carolingia: il significato di una scelta." *Arte Medievale* 1 (1989): 1–6.
Smith, Janet C. "The Side Chambers of San Giovanni Evangelista in Ravenna: Church Libraries of the Fifth Century." *Gesta* 29 (1990): 86–97.
Sot, Michel. "Historiographie épiscopale et modèle familial en Occident au IXe siècle." *Annales, Économies, Sociétés, Civilisations* 33 (1978): 433–49.
———. *Gesta episcoporum, gesta abbatum.* Typologie des sources du moyen âge occidental 31. Turnhout, 1981.
———. "Arguments hagiographiques et historiographiques dans les gesta episcoporum." In *Hagiographie, Cultures et Societes, IVe–XIIe siècles: actes du colloque organisé à Nanterre et à Paris, 2–5 mai 1979,* 95–104. Paris, 1981.

———. "Rhétorique et technique dans les préfaces des Gesta episcoporum (IX–XII s.)." *Cahiers de civilisations médiévale* 28 (1985): 181–200.
Squatriti, Paolo. "Personal Appearance and Physiognomies in Early Medieval Italy." *Journal of Medieval History* 14 (1988): 191–202.
Stein, Ernst. "Beitrage zur Geschichte von Ravenna in spätrömischer und byzantinischer Zeit." *Klio* 16 (1920): 40–71.
———. Review of *Excerpta Agnelliana*, by H. L. Gonin. *Byzantion* 8 (1933): 727–32.
Tamassia, Nino. "L'enfiteusi ecclesiastica ravennate e un racconto di Agnello." *Atti e memorie della deputazione di storia patria per le provincie di Romagna*, 4th ser., 10 (1920): 109–20.
Tamassia, Nino, and Vincenzo Ussani. "Epica e storia in alcuni capitoli di Agnello ravennate." *Nuovi studi medioevali* 1 (1923): 9–40.
Testi-Rasponi, Alessandro. "Note marginali al 'Liber pontificalis' di Agnello ravennate." Parts 1–3. *Atti e memorie della deputazione di storia patria per le provincie di Romagna*, 3d ser., 27 (1908–9): 86–104, 225–346; 4th ser., 1 (1910–11): 397–464.
———. "Note Agnelliane, la data della elezione dell'arcivescovo Giorgio." *Felix Ravenna* 12 (1913): 515–17.
———. "I documenti 'de inventione corporis beatissimi Apolenaris.'" *Felix Ravenna* 31 (1926): 1–11.
Thürlemann, Felix. "Die Bedeutung der Aachener Theoderich-Statue für Karl den Großen (801): Materialien zu einer Semiotik visueller Objekte im frühen Mittelalter." *Archiv für Kulturgeschichte* 59 (1977): 25–65.
Tjäder, Jan-Olof. "Die Bestrafung des Notars Johannicius im 'Liber Pontificalis' des Agnellus." *Italia medioevale e umanistica* 2 (1959): 431–39.
Toker, F. K. "Early Medieval Florence between History and Archaeology." In *Medieval Archaeology: Papers of the Seventeenth Annual Conference of the Center for Medieval and Early Renaissance Studies*, ed. Charles L. Redman, 261–83. Binghamton, 1989.
Vasina, Augusto. "Clero e chiese in Agnello Ravennate." *CARB* 31 (1984): 541–57.
Vassuri, Domenico. "I 'monasteria' di Ravenna: consuetudini e usi liturgici." *Rivista liturgica* 9 (1924): 210–14.
Verzone, Paolo. "La distruzione dei palazzi imperiali di Roma e Ravenna e la ristrutturazione del Palazzo Lateranese nel 9 secolo nei rapporti con quello di Constantinople." In *Roma e l'età Carolingia*, ed. Jean Hubert et al., 39–54. Rome, 1976.
Ward-Perkins, Bryan. *From Classical Antiquity to the Middle Ages: Urban Public Building in Northern and Central Italy, A.D. 300–850*. Oxford, 1984.
Weidemann, Margarete. *Kulturgeschichte der Merowingerzeit*. Mainz, 1982.
Weis, A. "Der römische Schöpfungszyklus des 5. Jh. im Triklinium Neons zu Ravenna." In *Tortulae: Studien zu altchristlichen und byzantinischen Monumenten*, ed. Walter Nikolaus Schumacher, 300–316. Römische Quartalschrift für Altertumskunde und Kirchengeschichte suppl. 30. Rome, 1966.
Wickhoff, Franz. "Die 'monasteria' bei Agnellus." *Mitteilungen des Instituts für österreichische Geschichtforschung* 9 (1887): 34–45.
———. "Das Speisezimmer des Bischofs Neon von Ravenna." *Repertorium für Kunstwissenschaft* 17 (1894): 10–17.

Zattoni, Girolamo. "La data della 'Passio S. Apollinaris' di Ravenna." In *Scritti storici e ravennati*, comp. M. Mazzotti, 113–28. Ravenna, 1975. First published in *Atti della Real Accademia delle Scienze di Torino* 39 (1904).

———. "Il valore storico della 'passio' di S. Apollinare e la fondazione dell'episcopato a Ravenna e in Romagna." In *Scritti storici e ravennati*, comp. M. Mazzotti, 185–233. Ravenna, 1975. First published in *Rivista storico-critica delle scienze teologiche* 1 (1905): 10ff., and 2 (1905): 3ff.

———. "Origine e giurisdizione della metropoli ecclesiastica di Ravenna." In *Scritti storici e ravennati*, comp. M. Mazzotti, 77–96. Ravenna, 1975. First published in 1904.

GENERAL INDEX

Aachen, 75, 77–79, 206n, 207
Abraham, 99, 155–56, 226
Aderitus, bishop of Ravenna, 27n, 52, 96, **104–5,** 307
Agapitus, bishop of Ravenna, 27n, **108–9,** 307
Agapitus, pope, 24
Agatho, pope, 5, 54n, 116n, 245–46
Agilulf, king of the Lombards, 217, 224
Agnellus, Andreas, ix–x, 4, 5n, 91–92, 102n, 103n, 104n, 105n; life, 6–13; work, 13–19, 20–65; and art and architecture, 66–90, 309–45; mentioned in the *LPR* text, 95–99, 135–35, 166, 196–97; mentioned in notes to the *LPR* text, *passim*
Agnellus, archbishop of Ravenna, 23n, 24, 54–55, 68, 157n, 176n, 183n, **198–204,** 206n, 308
Aistulf, king of the Lombards, 50–51, 70, 279–80, 318
Alboin, king of the Lombards, 41, 207–12
Alexandria, Egypt, 21n, 49, 147n, 192
altar cloth, 14n, 26, 48, 68, 182, 194, 202, 279, 310, 314–15, 318, 323, 329, 336, 339, 342, 344
Ambrose, St., bishop of Milan, 25, 59, 135
angel, 33, 103, 112, 116, 124, 131, 136, 137n, 140–42, 144, 152–56, 161, 163–64, 169–71, 179–80, 182, 184, 216, 232, 235, 287
annals, 49–50, 59–60, 118n

Apollinaris, St., bishop of Ravenna, 4, 20, 23, 31, 34, 35, 46, 48n, 77, 96n, 99, 105–6, 120, 135, 159–60, 231, 243–44, 252, 273n, 287, 289, 307, 326; Agnellus's life of, 52, **101–4,** 340; *passio* of, 23n, 30n, 31, 47n, 52, 101n, 104n, 105 archive, 54–55, 82, 89, 124n, 228, 257–58
Argentea, Italy, 12, 202–3
Arian, 52n, 55, 69, 77, 165, 168n, 186, 199–200, 323, 331
Athalaric, king of the Ostrogoths, 178
Athulf, king of the Visigoths, 150
Attila, king of the Huns, 139–44, 154, 302n
Augustine, St., bishop of Hippo, 38, 39, 136n, 195, 201n
Aurelian, bishop of Ravenna, 25n, 42, 54, 134n, **165–71,** 189, 307
autocephaly, 5, 17, 52n, 55, 56n, 227n, 234n, 246n, 334
Auxerre, 302
Avars, 207

Bacauda, 190–91
Baduarius, 163
Bagnoregio, 224
Basilius the younger, consul, 185, 187, 191–92, 199, 207
Basilius, father of Agnellus, 7–8, 271, 287n, 288
bath, 72n, 145, 182, 199, 211, 237, 250, 313, 321
Bede, 22n, 58, 225n

Belisarius, 178
Benedict II, pope, 25n
Benedict of Montecassino, St., 217
Benedict, deacon, 90, 228–29
Bologna, 11, 77, 79, 103, 148, 265
Boniface, pope, 24, 225n
Bonus, archbishop of Ravenna, 15, 23n, 25n, 27n, **225–27**, 308
Brescello, Italy, 148

Caesarea, suburb of Ravenna, 72, 136–37, 199, 207, 243, 253, 256
Caesarius, bishop of Arles, 38, 41n
Calocerus, bishop of Ravenna, 27n, 52, **106**, 192, 307
Carolingian, 4–6, 18, 21, 22n, 77, 79, 80, 200n, 202n, 284n
Cervia, Italy, 265
Cesena, Italy, 203, 265
Chalcedon, Council of, 158
Charlemagne, emperor, 4–5, 13, 41n, 69, 77–81, 83, 95, 183n, 207, 268, 285, 290–91, 296, 298, 299n
Charles the Bald, emperor, 80n, 300–304
Chrisafus, 29, 296
comet, 151, 203, 214, 224, 298n, 300
Conon, pope, 24
Constans II, emperor, 5, 55, 71, 227n, 233, 234n
Constantine I, emperor, 75
Constantine IV, emperor, 55, 233–34, 245n, 257
Constantine, anti-pope, 30, 280n
Constantine, pope, 28, 259n
Constantinople, 59n, 75–77, 78n, 123n, 128n, 130, 147n, 158, 171, 178, 185, 188–90, 203, 212, 224, 227–30, 233, 240, 244, 253–56, 259, 260–61n, 262, 272, 273n, 285, 336, 343; Chalke gate, 74–76
Constantius III, emperor, 147, 150
Cremona, 217

Damian, archbishop of Ravenna, 23n, 24, 31, 34–35, 86, 137n, 238n, **247–58**, 308
Datus, bishop of Ravenna, 27n, **108**, 307
Deodatus, king of the Ostrogoths, 178
Desiderius, king of the Lombards, 285
Deusdedit, archbishop of Ravenna, 14n
Deusdedit, cousin of Agnellus, 8, 287–89, 328
Dioscorus, bishop of Alexandria, 192

Eberhard, count of Friuli, 300
Ecclesius, bishop of Ravenna, 23n, 25n, 27n, 54, 137n, 146, 151n, **171–77**, 189, 192, 198, 307
eclipse, 300
Einhard, 77, 83, 298n
Eleucadius, bishop of Ravenna, 27n, 52, 53, **105**, 106, 192, 307
Ephesus, Council of, 53, 158n
epitaph, 23n, 54n, 84, 127n, 135, 152, 157n, 198n, 204, 218, 231, 236, 246, 258, 274, 278, 289
Ermengard, wife of Lothar, 299
Eudoxia, empress, 134, 158
Eugene II, pope, 19, 334n
Eutyches, 53
exarch, 3–46, 11n, 18, 72–73, 77, 238–40, 244–45, 256, 271, 276, 284, 321
Exuperantius, bishop of Ravenna, **135–35**, 136n, 307, 335

Faenza, 265
famine, 218, 236–37, 292
Felix IV, pope, 17, 54, 172–76, 198n, 236, 331n
Felix, archbishop of Ravenna, 5, 10n, 16, 24, 31, 34–35, 43–44, 53–55, 62, 80, 137n, 239n, **258–75**, 291n, 292n, 294, 308
Florentius, bishop of Ravenna, **117**, 307
Fontenoy, battle of, 301–2
Forli, 265

GENERAL INDEX   363

Forlimpopoli, 265
Franks, 4, 13, 18n, 203, 206–7, 217, 279, 285, 290, 294

Galla Placidia, empress, 50, 70, 71, 84, 124, 147, 148–52, 163, 331n, 337n
Gallicinus, exarch, 217
Gallinicus, exarch, 217
George, archbishop of Ravenna, 6n, 11–12, 14–19, 23n, 27n, 33, 39, 79n, 81, 96–97n, 219n, 236n, 259, 268, **298–305**, 308
George, priest of Classe, 123–24
George, son of Johannicis, 263–65, 338
Gepids, 211
gesta episcoporum, x, 20–21, 22, 24n, 30–31, 35
Gisela, countess of Friuli, 300
Goths. *See* Ostrogoths
Gratian, emperor, 158
Gratiosus, archbishop of Ravenna, 24, 44, 286n, **290–95**, 308
Gregory I (the Great), St., pope, 30, 38, 40–43, 53, 58, 61–63, 100, 167n, 213n, 214–16, 218, 251n, 334
Gregory II, pope, 22n, 24, 275n, 329n
Gregory III, pope, 15n, 24, 275n, 329n
Gregory IV, pope, 95, 298, 300
Gregory, bishop of Tours, 9–10, 32, 36n, 58–59, 87, 100n, 109n, 251n, 313n

Hadrian I, pope, 26n, 51n, 77, 299n, 317n, 334n
Hagia Sophia, 75
Heraclian, bishop of Pensauris, 113
Heraclian, father of Heraclius, 225
Heraclius, emperor, 225
Heraclius, son of Constans II, 71, 233–34
Honorius, emperor, 3, 33n, 70, 71n, 136–37, 138n, 150, 158
Hrabanus Maurus, 329
Huns, 3, 139, 146n, 151

Iconoclasm, 3, 5, 25n, 26n, 51n, 121n, 128n, 135n, 225n, 277n
Imola, 53, 54, 82, 124n, 157, 159–60, 163–65, 193, 207, 265
Isidore, bishop of Seville, 38, 88–90, 213n, 310, 313, 314n, 315n, 318n, 320n, 323, 325n, 326n, 328, 330n, 340, 341n, 343, 344

Jerome, St., 21n, 39, 54, 193, 195
Jews, 80, 201, 320, 238, 257, 268
Johannicis, 7n, 8–10, 34–35, 54, 59n, 238–40, 247, 261–63, 265–67, 270–72
John I, bishop of Ravenna, 23n, 31, 33–35, 42–44, **136–56**, 159, 167, 302n, 307, 333
John I, pope, 146, 171
John II (the Roman), archbishop of Ravenna, 23n, 25n, 47, 50, 53, 205n, **213–14**, 215, 308, 334
John III, archbishop of Ravenna, 27n, **218–21**, 308
John IV, archbishop of Ravenna, 15, 27n, 50, **221–25**, 308
John V, archbishop of Ravenna, 23n, 51n, 55, 56n, 202, 221n, **275–78**, 308
John VI, archbishop of Ravenna, 27n, 33, 126n, **286–89**, 308, 343n
John, abbot of St. John *ad Titum*, 253–56
John, bishop of Arles, 83, 297
Judith, empress, 300, 302
Julian the banker (Argentarius), 54n, 171–72, 177, 178, 190–92, 231
Justa Grata Honoria, 70, 151
Justin II, emperor, 163, 202n, 203, 205, 207, 212
Justinian I, emperor, 3, 5, 54–55, 68, 71, 75, 181, 185, 189, 195n, 198, 199n, 200, 203, 207, 212, 342
Justinian II, emperor, 257n, 259, 262, 265, 267

Lacherno, 265
Lamissio, 50, 280n
Laudicius, 192

Lauricius, 33n, 71n, 80, 136–38, 256n
Leo I, pope, 146n, 157–58, 159n
Leo II, pope, 5, 24n, 55, 230n, 246
Leo III, emperor, 3–4
Leo III, pope, 13, 26n, 28–29, 70, 74n, 116n, 207, 296–97, 317n, 325, 337n, 343
Leo the Isaurian, emperor, 206–7
Leo, archbishop of Ravenna, 5, 23n, 51n, 283n, **285**
Liber pontificalis (LP) of Rome, ix–x, 5n, 7n, 17, 19, 20–29, 30, 31, 35, 51, 54n, 68n, 82–84, 87, 89, 104n, 116n, 120n, 146n, 162n, 185n, 224–25n, 230n, 234n, 246n, 247n, 259n, 261n, 275n, 278n, 279n, 280n, 284n, 285n, 296n, 309, 310, 312n, 314, 316, 317n, 318, 322, 325, 326, 327, 329, 333, 334, 335, 337, 342
Liberius I, bishop of Ravenna, 27n, **108**
Liberius II, bishop of Ravenna, 48n, **114**
Liberius III, bishop of Ravenna, 27b, **117–18**
Liutprand, king of the Lombards, 76–77n, 275
Lombards, 3–4, 6, 41, 50, 70, 76–77n, 146n, 148n, 205, 207–12, 217, 221n, 224, 275, 278–80, 284, 285, 291, 296
Longinus, prefect, 207, 211
Lothar, emperor, 11, 15n, 19, 79, 95, 231, 299, 300–301
Louis the German, emperor, 300–302
Louis the Pious, emperor, 15, 95, 296, 297–98, 300
Lucceoli, 224
Luke, St. and gospel of, 38, 41n, 58, 100

Malasuintha, queen of the Ostrogoths, 178
Manichaeans, 193
Mantua, 217
Marcellinus, bishop of Ravenna, 27, **109**
Marcian, bishop of Ravenna, 27n, 28, 52, **106**

Marcian, emperor, 158
Marinian, archbishop of Ravenna, 23n, 27n, 43, 50, 53, **215–18**, 258n, 334
Mark, St. and gospel of, 58, 99–100
Martin, archbishop of Ravenna, 10, 15n, 18, 23n, 24, 69n, 79, 83, 285, **295–98**
Matthew, gospel of, 39–40, 43, 54
Maurice, emperor, 217, 224
Maurus, archbishop of Ravenna, 5, 10n, 16, 18, 24, 52n, 54n, 55, **227–33**, 234n, 273n, 334, 335
Maximian, archbishop of Ravenna, 5, 11, 15, 23n, 25n, 47n, 48–49, 52n, 53–54, 59, 68, 84, 105n, 134n, 144n, 146n, 150, **184–97**, 202, 213, 231, 311, 322, 328, 333–34, 338, 341n, 345
Milan, 3, 21n
Modena, 91, 110–11
Monotheletism, 245n
Montecassino, 217

Naples, 224
Narses, 178, 193, 203, 207
Nazarba, 192
Neon, bishop of Ravenna, 117n, **125–33**, 171, 316, 323, 335, 338–39, 343n
Nova, 265, 297

Odoacer, 3, 50, 71–72, 145–46, 149n
orality and oral sources, 32n, 35, 36, 45–47, 57–65, 100n, 233n
Orosius, 193
Orvieto, 224
Ostrogoths (Goths), 3, 5, 50, 77, 178, 193, 198–99, 203

Pachino, 260, 261n, 270
Palermo, 270
pallium, 4, 148, 185, 227, 231, 321, 333–34
Papia, 265
passio of Apollinaris, 23n, 30n, 31, 47n, 52, 101n, 104n, 105
Paul I, pope, 280–81, 282n, 329n, 336

GENERAL INDEX   365

Paul the Deacon, 8n, 9–10, 50, 53n, 64n, 148n, 195n, 217n, 224–25n, 251n, 275n, 280n, 319, 327, 332n, 341n
Pavia, 12, 75n, 77–78n, 178, 205, 206n, 299, 316, 342
Pepin of Aquitaine, 301
Pepin the Short, king of the Franks, 279–80
Pepin, son of Charlemagne, 296
Pepin, son of Louis the Pious, 300–301
Peter Damian, 104n
Peter Damian, 104n
Peter I (Chrysologus), St., bishop of Ravenna, 11, 23, 24, 33n, 34, 38, 40, 42, 52–54, 61–63, 82, 91, **120–24**, 139n, 152–53, 157n, 157–65, 171, 183, 184n, 202n, 274, 300, 320
Peter II, bishop of Ravenna, 25n, 91, 120n, **157–65**, 189, 319n
Peter III (the Elder), archbishop of Ravenna, 25n, 50, 124n, 134n, 163n, **204–13**
Peter, St., 4, 23, 85, 95, 100–102, 243–44
Petronax, archbishop of Ravenna, 6n, 11, 14–15, 16n, 17, 19, 79n, 83, 95–96, 194, 196, 231, 273, 298n
Philippicus, emperor, 55, 80, 268n
Phocas, emperor, 217–18, 224–25
Po, river, 97, 260–61, 263, 265, 270, 277
pope, 4–6, 17–19, 21–30, 35, 51, 83, 104n, 137n, 146n, 158–59, 190, 227, 303, 333–34
Probus I, bishop of Ravenna, 27n, **107–8**, 192
Probus II, bishop of Ravenna, 27n, 48n, 116
Proculus, bishop of Ravenna, 27n, **107**
Projectus, bishop of Imola, 53, 163
Pseudo-Ambrose, 41n, 135n, 322
pseudo-Bede, 201n, 202n

Reparatus, archbishop of Ravenna, 24, 25n, 27n, 55, 71, **233–36**, 290, 316

Rome: bishops of Ravenna and, 159–60, 171–77, 215, 218, 227, 229–30, 234, 245–47, 278, 280–82, 296–98; church of, ix, 4–5, 18–19, 21n, 28, 51, 54, 82, 135n, 159, 195, 204, 231, 233, 243–45, 334n; city, 3, 9, 12, 18–19, 26, 27n, 35, 77, 79n, 85, 95, 102, 117n, 125n, 148, 151, 178, 190, 193, 205–7, 214, 224, 251, 279, 282, 284–85, 292, 294, 298, 317, 336; Lateran palace, 74n, 75, 76n, 324, 343; Pantheon, 224, 341n; statue of Marcus Aurelius, 75, 76n; St. Peter *ad Janiculum*, 102
Rosamunda, queen, 41, 44, 50, 207–12, 309
Rotruda, daugher of Lothar, 299

Sardica, Council of, 4, 109n
Sarsina, 265
Savinian, pope, 218
Savio, 265
Sergius, archbishop of Ravenna, 5, 18, 23n, 50, 51n, 54n, 55, 79n, 83, **278–85**, 318
Sergius, deacon, 9–11, 227, 273
sermons, x, 16, 20, 36–45, 54n, 61–64, 114n, 156, 170n, 201n, 211n, 223, 258–59n, 291n, 292n, 294n, 331n; sermons of Peter Chrysologus, 34, 52–53, 62–63, 102n, 274n
Severinus, pope, 24
Severus, St., bishop of Ravenna, 4, 25n, 27n, 31, 34–35, 91, **109–14**, 213
Sicily, 89, 134, 146, 178, 228–29, 254, 260, 261n, 270
Silvester, pope, 21
Singledia, 148–49, 330
Sixtus III, pope, 159–61, 335n
Smaragdus, exarch, 214, 217, 224
Stephen II, pope, 279n, 282–84
Stephen III, pope, 30n, 51n, 55, 280n, 282–84, 285n
Symmachus, pope, 204, 317n

tax, 3, 55, 181, 233, 240, 265
Theodora, empress, 68, 71, 178, 342
Theodore, archbishop of Ravenna, 5, 15n, 17–18, 54n, 55, 177n, 234n, 236–46
Theodore, exarch, 11n, 238
Theodoric, king of the Ostrogoths, 3, 12, 50, 71–79, 145–47, 154n, 168n, 171, 186, 199–200, 205–7, 238, 256, 266n, 316, 335, 342–44
Tiberius, son of Constans II, 72, 233–34
Timothy, bishop of Alexandria, 192
Tindario, 270
Totila, king of the Ostrogoths, 178

Ursicinus, bishop of Ravenna, 23n, 25n, 27n, 47n, 151n, 172, 178–81, 189, 191
Ursus, bishop of Ravenna, 23n, 25n, 27n, 118–20, 316, 335, 341
Uviliaris, archdeacon, 10n, 283

Valentinian I, emperor, 24, 67, 117, 118n, 138, 330

Valentinian III, emperor, 70–72, 123, 124n, 147–48, 150–51, 158, 344; diploma of, 54, 56n, 147–48, 321, 333
Valerius, archbishop of Ravenna, 7n, 77, 79n, 186, 295n, 297
Vandals, 80, 200
velo di Classe, 48n
Venetians, 205, 225, 276, 278, 284
Vergil, 86, 256n, 270n, 291, 323, 326–27
Verona, 48n, 193, 211, 217
Vespasian, emperor, 102n, 104
Vetus Latina, 37, 122n, 222n, 235n, 291n
Victor, bishop of Ravenna, 23n, 35n, 137n, 151n, 172, 176n, 181–84, 185, 189
Vitalian, pope, 54n
Vulgate, 37, 86n, 87–90, 122n, 140n, 195n, 309, 313, 315, 318, 323, 327, 337, 339

Zacharias, pope, 5n, 84–85n, 116n, 146n, 279, 329n
Zeno, emperor, 78, 206–7

TOPOGRAPHICAL INDEX OF RAVENNA AND CLASSE

ad Calchi, 74n, 76, 238
ad Frigiselo, 191
ad Nimpheos, 145
amphiteatrum, 104, 252
Arian Baptristry. *See* St. Mary *in Cosmedin*

bridge of Apollinaris, 145
bridge of the millers, 119

Caesarea, 72n, 136–37, 199, 207, 243, 253, 256
cella of St. Apollinaris, 285, 332
church of the Goths, 241, 296, 330n
Classe, 3–4, 34, 59n, 66, 67, 101, 102n, 105, 107, 110, 112n, 121, 123, 136n, 146, 173, 178, 205, 221, 231n, 242–44, 253, 262, 275; area of the lepers, 275
Coriandrian field, 117, 199, 265, 277

Episcopia, Arian, 69, 77, 185–86, 199–200, 331
Episcopium, Orthodox, 74n, 119, 125–26, 133n, 134n, 162, 182, 245, 256, 270, 282–83, 286n, 289n, 319, 321, 331, 337, 343

fossa amnis, 119, 126n, 343n
fossa Lamisem, 248
fossa Sconii, 185, 193

gates: Artemetorian gate, 117, 147; Caesarean gate, 72n, 256; Golden gate, 104, 252; New gate, 118; gate of St. Laurence, 286; gate of St. Victor, 185; gate of the criminals, 248; Ovilionian gate, 163, 187, 233; Teguriensian gate, 248; Vincileonian gate, 119; Wandalarian gate, 72n, 256
golden milestone, 145, 191

Herculana region, 119, 190
Holy Apostles (now San Francesco), 117, 127–28, 171, 233n, 236, 242
Holy Cross, 70n, 71n, 148–50, 290

Lion port, 145, 265

mausoleum of Theodoric, 71, 147, 344
mint, 233, 290

Organaria, 119
Orthodox (Neonian) Baptistry, 68, 125, 270n, 316, 323–24, 325n
Ovilionian wall, 128

palace at the laurel, 11, 71, 76, 146, 148, 256
palace of Theodoric/the exarchs, 71–78, 145, 205–6, 238–39, 244, 256, 276, 297, 335, 342–43
palace, imperial, 70, 71–72, 313

367

368 TOPOGRAPHICAL INDEX

Petriana Baptistry, 161, 183, 203, 316, 323–24, 330, 331n; chapels of Sts. Matthew and James, 123, 203
Petriana church, 11, 69–70, 120–21, 123, 125, 233n, 275, 279–80, 323

region and gate *Vicus Salutaris*, 112, 205, 275
region of the apostles, 128
region of the criminals, 252
River Bedento, 103, 265
River Pantheus, 275

Sant'Apollinare in Classe, 10n, 29, 30n, 34, 41n, 52n, 67n, 69–70, 71, 86, 92, 105–6, 120, 178, 190–91, 214, 218, 221, 225, 227, 231, 233n, 234, 236, 242–46, 258, 274, 278–79, 285n, 289, 295, 296, 316, 318, 331n, 345
Sant'Apollinare Nuovo. *See* St. Martin
Santo Spirito. *See* St. Theodore
San Vitale, 33n, 54n, 67n, 68, 70, 76, 137n, 151n, 177, 184, 191, 200n, 322, 331n, 342n
Sicrestum, 73, 205
St. Agatha, 33, 152, 157n, 198, 204
St. Agnes, 134–35, 145
St. Andrew Major, 190, 196–97
St. Andrew the Apostle *(capella arcivescovile)*, 162, 289n, 319, 331, 345
St. Andrew the Apostle *Ierichomium*, 272, 330–31n
St. Andrew the Apostle, 241, 295–96, 330n
St. Apollinaris in the Arian episcopium, 199, 331
St. Apollinaris *in veclo*, 233, 290, 331n
St. Bartholemew, 10–12, 16, 179, 227–28, 258, 273, 283, 331n
St. Demetrius, 103
St. Donatus *in Monterione*, 286, 331n
St. Eleuchadius, 105–7
St. Euphemia *ad Arietem*, 69n, 103, 296
St. Euphemia by the sea, 64, 108, 213

St. Euphemia *in Sancto Calinico*, 288
St. Eusebius, 69, 185, 199
St. George, 69, 185, 199
St. John the Evangelist, 10n, 70, 124, 151, 271, 325n
St. Laurence, Caesarea, 70, 71n, 136–37, 256n
St. Martin (Sant'Apollinare Nuovo), 10n, 44, 68n, 69, 71, 72–76, 80, 92, 187–88n, 200n, 206n, 316, 323, 331n, 334–35, 341, 343n
St. Mary *ad Blachernas*, 10, 76, 96, 123, 238, 287, 296, 331n
St. Mary at the Lion port, 145, 331n
St. Mary at the Tomb of King Theodoric, 147, 331n
St. Mary *in Cosmedin* (Arian Baptistry), 199, 282, 323–24, 331n
St. Mary Major, 171, 241–42
St. Michael *in Africisco*, 190–91, 299
St. Nazarius, 70, 151, 172, 181, 184, 331n
St. Paul the Apostle, 238
St. Peter *Orphanumtrophium*, 178, 331n
St. Petronilla, 117, 331n
St. Probus, 105–9, 192, 213
St. Pulio, 118, 331n
St. Rophilius, 213, 331n
St. Sergius, 199
St. Severinus, 252, 331n
St. Severus, 111n, 112, 123, 204–5, 331n
St. Stephen, 86, 187–88, 341n, 345
St. Theodore (Santo Spirito), 199
St. Theodore deacon, 238, 331n
St. Victor, 185
St. Zacharias, 148–49, 331n
St. Zeno, 199
stadium tabulae, 117, 277, 340
Sts. John (and Stephen), 253
Sts. John (the Baptist) and Barbatian, 163
Sts. John and Paul, 303
Sts. Mark, Marcellus, and Felicula, 214, 274, 331n
Sts. Stephen, Gervase et Protase, 138

TOPOGRAPHICAL INDEX 369

Ursiana cathedral: representing the
Church of Ravenna, 10, 67, 121, 139,
149, 165; structure and decoration,
118–19, 120, 125–26, 134, 153, 157n,
181–82, 194, 202, 204n, 249, 252, 279,
285n, 298, 318, 341, 343n

Wandalaria, 123, 238, 286–87

www.ingramcontent.com/pod-product-compliance
Lightning Source LLC
Chambersburg PA
CBHW032302300426
44110CB00033B/247